THE COMPLETE WORKS OF ERRICO MALATESTA

Volume V

EDITED BY DAVIDE TURCATO

The Complete Works of Errico Malatesta

VOLUME I
"Whoever Is Poor Is a Slave":
The Internationalist Period and the South America Exile, 1871–89

VOLUME II
"Let's Go to the People":
L'Associazione and the London Years of 1889–97

VOLUME III
"A Long and Patient Work...":
The Anarchist Socialism of L'Agitazione, 1897–98

VOLUME IV
"Towards Anarchy":
Malatesta in America, 1899–1900

VOLUME V
"The Armed Strike":
The Long London Exile of 1900–13

VOLUME VI
"Is Revolution Possible?":
Volontà, the Red Week and the War, 1913–18

VOLUME VII
"United Proletarian Front":
The Red Biennium, Umanità Nova and Fascism, 1919–23

VOLUME VIII
"Achievable and Achieving Anarchism":
Pensiero e Volontà and Last Writings, 1924–32

VOLUME IX
"What Anarchists Want":
Pamphlets, Programmes, Manifestos and Other Miscellaneous Publications

VOLUME X
"Yours and for Anarchy...":
Malatesta's Correspondence

THE ARMED STRIKE
THE LONG LONDON EXILE OF 1900–13

INTRODUCTORY ESSAY BY
CARL LEVY

TRANSLATED BY ANDREA ASALI

AK PRESS

The Complete Works of Malatesta, Volume V
The Armed Strike: The Long London Exile of 1900–13

© 2023 Edited by Davide Turcato
Translation © 2023 Andrea Asali (except where noted)
Introduction © 2023 Carl Levy
This edition © 2023 AK Press (Chico, Edinburgh)

ISBN: 978-1-84935-149-2
E-ISBN: 978-1-84935-160-7
Library of Congress Control Number: 2023935631

AK Press   AK Press
370 Ryan Ave. #100   33 Tower St.
Chico, CA 95973   Edinburgh EH6 7BN
USA   Scotland
www.akpress.org   www.akuk.com
akpress@akpress.org   akuk@akpress.org

The above addresses would be delighted to provide you with the latest AK Press
distribution catalog, which features books, pamphlets, zines, and stylish apparel
published and/or distributed by AK Press. Alternatively, visit our websites for the
complete catalog, latest news, and secure ordering.

Cover design by John Yates, www.stealworks.com
Printed in the USA on acid-free paper

Contents

SECTION II
General Strike and Armed Strike

SECTION III
The Social Revolution

SECTION IV
Anarchists at Congress

SECTION V
Capitalists, Thieves, and Spies

SECTION VI
Press Clippings

Editor's Foreword

Davide Turcato

This volume, which is part of the complete works of Errico Malatesta, covers Malatesta's longest period of uninterrupted absence from Italian soil: his exile in London, which began in 1900, when Malatesta returned to Europe from North America, through 1913, the year he returned to Italy to direct *Volontà*.

The writings included in the complete works can be subdivided into four groups: (i) published writings by Malatesta himself, mostly his articles and pamphlets; (ii) unpublished writings by Malatesta himself, such as correspondence, which we will publish in a separate volume; (iii) published writings by other authors, such as, for example, interviews of Malatesta, and summaries of his speeches in newspapers; (iv) unpublished writings by other authors, such as summaries of Malatesta's speeches by spies and police officers.

This is probably the volume that contains the largest proportion of writings from the last two groups, namely writings by other authors, due to the number of interviews of Malatesta in the news reports concerning anarchists, as well as the number of police reports strewn out over such a long period of time. While we recommend the reader takes the necessary caution in trusting the documents in this last group, we decided to include a generous number of them because they help shine light on Malatesta's ideas during years in which his writings are lacking or completely missing.

As regards published writings by Malatesta himself, the longest-lasting periodical Malatesta was most extensively involved in editing during these years is *La Rivoluzione Sociale*, from 1902–3. This is the periodical for which we made the widest use of the "intellectual responsibility" attribution criterion, founded on the presupposition that unsigned writings were written or otherwise fully approved by the person directing the periodical. We excluded, as usual, brief pieces of a purely informative nature, such as the column concerning publications received. We instead included the column "Facts and Opinions," which, while taking inspiration from news reports, generally contains original comments. Rather than selecting excerpts from the column, we reproduced it in its entirety, including those sections that we would have excluded, had they appeared alone.

The same attribution criterion applied to *La Rivoluzione Sociale* was also used for the single issues of *Cause ed Effetti*, in 1900, and *Verso*

L'Emancipazione, in 1906. For other publications, we used more restrictive criteria. As regards *Lo Sciopero Generale,* a short-lived periodical that was edited collectively by several people in 1902, we included only articles that were signed by the editorial staff, or that concerned events in which Malatesta was directly involved, or that dealt with topics and themes recurrent in Malatesta's work. Occasionally the last criterion was supplemented with considerations for style. Finally, direct reports on Malatesta's contributions to specific issues of the periodical were taken into consideration. As regards the 1901 periodical *L'Internazionale,* whose circular-program Malatesta had signed, although it was directed by others, we only included the signed articles. Finally, there were no problems with the 1912 single issue *La Guerra Tripolina,* in which all articles are signed.

Articles by Malatesta are always reproduced in their entirety, while for interviews and summaries, only the parts that report Malatesta's words are reproduced. In some cases, the omitted parts were summarized, when this served to provide the context necessary to understand the reproduced text. These summaries are provided inside square brackets. As a rule, all contents within square brackets indicate interventions by the editor. Omissions have been indicated through the insertion of three spaced dots (. . .), which differ visibly from the hanging dots (...) used in the author's text.

The articles are arranged in chronological order. However, given the large number of interviews and summaries reporting current events, a double criterion was used: the publication date is used for Malatesta's articles, while for interviews and speeches the date of their occurrence is used, when known. For example, for a statement by Malatesta published on October 31, 1901 but released around September 6th of the same year, the latter date is used. This was done to facilitate reading, so that the citations of current events followed the most linear sequence possible. Finally, very brief or possibly unreliable statements attributed to Malatesta were also reproduced, for documentary purposes, but collected at the end of the volume, in the "Press Clippings" section.

Malatesta's works span a period of sixty years and were published in a broad range of publications in many countries and languages. Because of such diversity, we have not attempted to enforce uniformity of stylistic conventions. Rather, in a spirit of documentary editing, we have made an effort to reproduce those works as faithfully as possible. As a rule, unless stylistic changes were required by linguistic or cultural differences between the source language and English (such as, for example, different capitalization conventions), we have preserved typesetting styles from the original sources. Hence what might appear as inconsistencies in the present volume adhere to the original publications.

When an article has a short subtitle, this has been placed after the title proper. Otherwise, lengthier, summative subtitles have been placed at the beginning of the body of the text, in small caps. Rather than indicating in a footnote which articles have been signed, signatures have been incorporated directly into the text, just as they appeared in the original. Authors other than Malatesta are specified after the title. Unattributed articles without a signature at the foot of the text should therefore be deemed as unsigned. Footnotes by the article's author, whether Malatesta or someone else, are preceded by "[Author's Note]." All other notes are by the editor. When a text originally in a foreign language does not report the source of its English translation, this is an original translation. For all other translated parts, both in the text as well as in the notes, if the name of the translator is not indicated, it was done by the editor. Finally, as is the case for the other volumes, we excluded from the index of people and periodicals cited, other than Malatesta, the multi-issue periodicals he directed, and therefore, in this volume, *La Rivoluzione Sociale*.

I should like to offer thanks to: Ivo Giaccheri, for the transcription of texts; Tomaso Marabini, for his assiduous and expert collaboration in the research; Furio Biagini and Marisa Ines Romano, for the translations from Yiddish; Giuseppe Galzerano, for having provided me with precious materials; Natale Musarra, Franco Schirone, the Archivio-Biblioteca Enrico Travaglini of Fano and the Archivio Storico della Federazione Anarchica Italiana of Imola, for having shared their collections of periodicals; the Centro Studi Libertari / Archivio Giuseppe Pinelli of Milan, for contributing images; Franco Bertolucci and Furio Lippi, of the Biblioteca Franco Serantini of Pisa, for having granted me access to archive material; Dario Massimi, of the Fondazione Istituto Gramsci of Rome, Roberto Pagano, of the Fondazione Nevol Querci— Archivio Storico Iconografico del Socialismo of Rome, Vincenzo Romeo, of the Biblioteca Regionale Universitaria Giambattista Caruso of Catania, and Marco Tempera, of the Fondazione Lelio e Lisli Basso of Rome, for reproductions; Eric Coulaud and Gualtiero Marini, for help in finding images and periodicals, respectively; Jorge Canales and Marco Rossi, for archival research; Marianne Enckell, of the Centre International de Recherches sur l'Anarchisme of Lausanne, for her timely responses to my requests; Enrico Brandoli, Arianna Fiore, Robert Graham, and Kenyon Zimmer, for linguistic advice; Tiziano Antonelli and Amanda Floridi, for research suggestions; and Pietro Di Paola, for his ready availability to be of assistance in emergency situations.

From Bresci to Wormwood Scrubs: The "Leader" of Worldwide Anarchism in London

by Carl Levy[1]

Errico Malatesta lived in London during four periods: 1881–82, 1889–97, 1900–13 and 1914–19. The writings collected in this volume focus on the third and longest of his London exiles. By now he was an established figure in the "squalid district" of Islington.[2] In the interviews granted or stolen after the deaths of King Humbert, President McKinley, or the attempts made at the kings of Belgium and Spain, Malatesta, in his late middle to early old age (48–61), was recognized as "the leader" of world anarchism, sometimes fantasized as the wayward scion of a fabulously wealthy aristocratic Malatesta family, not the progeny of the moderately comfortable provincial Southern entrepreneurial middle classes.[3] Returning from North America in the spring of 1900,[4] he was forced to intervene in the ongoing row with his erstwhile collaborator Saverio

---

1   Carl Levy, BA (SUNY at Buffalo), MA (LSE), PhD (LSE) taught and researched at the Open University, University of Kent at Canterbury, Queen Mary, University of London, and for many years at Goldsmiths, University of London, where he was Professor of Politics. His works include eleven edited or single-authored books and eighty journal articles and edited chapters. Among his works on anarchism are *Gramsci and the Anarchists* (Berg/NYU, 1999), Carl Levy and Matthew Adams (eds), *The Palgrave Handbook of Anarchism* (Palgrave Macmillan, 2019), and Carl Levy and Saul Newman (eds), *The Anarchist Imagination: Anarchism Encounters the Humanities and the Social Sciences* (Routledge, 2019). He has written many articles and book chapters about Errico Malatesta and is writing a biography, entitled *Errico Malatesta: The Rooted Cosmopolitan.*

2   "Malatesta, Mysterious and Crafty Arch Anarchist," *The New York Press* (New York), October 13, 1901.

3   For samples see, "Malatesta has been found," *Elmira Daily Gazette* (New York), August 3, 1900; "Malatesta, through the World, Defines Anarchist Creed," *New York World*, August 5, 1900, p. 11 of the current volume; "Interview with a London Anarchist," *The Daily News* (London), September 9, 1901, p. 73 of the current volume.

4   See Errico Malatesta, *"Towards Anarchy": Malatesta in America 1899–1900,* introduction by Nunzio Pernicone (Chico, CA: AK Press, 2019), as part of *The Complete Works of Malatesta,* edited by Davide Turcato.

Merlino, who had left anarchism for *sui generis* libertarian social democracy and was calling on anarchists to vote for Malatesta as a protest candidate, so that he could return home under parliamentary immunity. Malatesta would have none of it. "I remain," he wrote in *Les Temps Nouveaux*, "an Anarchist as always, and consider as an unmerited outrage, the simple doubt that I could wish to enter the parliamentary arena."[5]

After Bresci's assassination of King Humbert in July 1900, Malatesta quickly penned a single issue manifesto, *Cause ed Effetti*, explaining why the anarchist came from America to kill the "good king."[6] Malatesta gave a series of speeches in hesitant English (to non-Italian speakers, he usually spoke in French) at the meeting of the Cosmopolitans in Tom Mann's pub located near the Covent Garden fruit and vegetable market. "Just at the period when public opinion was highly strung on Italian affairs," Mann recalled in his memoirs, "Enrico Malatesta opened a debate on anarchism which aroused so keen an interest that three evenings had to be devoted to it."[7] On September 2, 1900 Malatesta addressed a well-attended event on "Anarchism and Crime" officiated by the Radical Liberal Morrison Davison.[8] His remarks were sought after in the press, and at first he denied knowing Bresci, but then admitted he knew him from New Jersey and described him as a well-dressed family man who was deeply disturbed by the indiscriminate slaughter of the Milanese by the Royal Army in 1898, by the orders of Humbert. He also gave the *Daily Graphic* a short interview after being cornered "a few yards north of the Angel at Islington." Their correspondent described a captivating figure (in other interviews he is described as well-educated, ascetic, and laconic but polite: with piercing black or brown eyes and a Van Dyke beard), who gave the readers a chilling description of the assassin's regime of solitary confinement. "He would be far better dead," Malatesta opined, anticipating Bresci's "suicide"; rather accurately.[9] At first Malatesta did not rush to the defense of the assassin or assassinations, but his position became more ambiguous in retrospect. A year later in light of McKinley's assassination by a self-declared Polish-American anarchist, Malatesta intervened when an Italian anarchist newspaper had been too forceful in its absolute disavowal of Leon Czolgosz. After all, the dead president was merely the representative

---

5   "Réponse a Merlino," *Les Temps Nouveaux* (Paris), June 9, 1900, p. 5 of the current volume.
6   *"Cause ed Effetti,"* (London), September 1900.
7   T. Mann, *Memoirs* (London: MacGibbon & Kee, 1967), 122.
8   See reports on pp. 42–47 of the current volume.
9   "The Assassin's Punishment," *The Daily Graphic* (London), September 1, 1900, p. 38 of the current volume.

of an American plutocracy which had shot its own striking miners and slaughtered Filipinos after their putative liberation by the Americans in the recent war with Spain.[10] And in other speeches and polemics with anti-organizational anarcho-communists and individualists, at London's clubs and in various newspaper articles, although he dismissed indiscriminate terrorism and banditry as he had in the 1890s, he did declare that political assassinations could be justified and cited the cases of Bresci and Humbert and Angiolillo and Canovas (the assassinated Prime Minister of Spain). But in all his interviews on the question of assassinations and attempts, his standard response was that anarchists needed to assassinate the authoritarian and hero-worshipping spirit of the masses above all else, if they wished to advance their cause.[11]

In contrast to the frenetic 1890s, after 1900 Malatesta's life settled down into a more ordinary domestic rhythm. Since the 1890s, when in London, Malatesta had lived with the Defendi's (Giovanni and Emilia), an Italian anarchist family residing in Islington. Malatesta was, as one of the American journalists put it, on intimate terms with Emilia, and possibly at least one if not more of the Defendi's offspring had Malatesta as their biological father, with a boy, "Erricuccio," accompanying him to Ancona in 1897 and serving as messenger in the office of *L'Agitazione*. He recalled his decades-long relationship with Emilia with great tenderness, and in 1913, on departing once again from London for Ancona, he wrote to Luigi Fabbri:

> I finally left London: but what torment, my friend. A crowd of people old and young (Defendi's children and nieces and nephews) all whom I saw born and who love me and who I love, and who are in fact my family...[12]

Emilia was a strong-willed woman, who possessed a keen business sense and was the heart and soul of the family wine and grocery shop. She not only participated in the political life of Italian exiles in the London clubs (she was of the few people named in documents and by the police), but equally involved herself in several attempts to start and maintain a locally based *Università Popolare* (first on Poland Street

---

10 "Arrestiamoci sulla china," *Il Risveglio* (Geneva), September 28, 1901, p. 75 of the current volume; "Malatesta talks Anarchy," *Brooklyn Standard Union* (New York), September 13, 1901, p. 73 of the current volume.
11 This was originally argued in the 1890s during his battle against Ravacholism, see "The Duties of the Present Hour," *Liberty* (London), August 1894.
12 Malatesta to Luigi Fabbri, Harwich, July 29, 1913, in *Epistolario,* edited by R. Bertolucci (Avenza, 1984), 101.

and then Euston Road), as did Malatesta, who became depressed by its subsequent failure.[13]

By the early 1900s Malatesta's one-man electrician's workshop and business was well-established (virtually around the corner from 112 High Street at 16 Duncan Terrace and then in various locations in Soho). These years were marked by "a little electrical engineering and a little inventing,"[14] but revolutionary agitation was consistent, yet limited, at least for long stretches of time, because of disputes with fellow exiles in the Italian community. On more than one occasion work and illness prevented him from attending the London movement's ritual anniversary gatherings for the Paris Commune (which inspired him to write an interesting article commemorating the revolutionary sacrifice of the Communards but criticizing the representative democratic, rather than direct, nature of their government) or the Chicago Martyrs.[15] In any case, the anarchist exile community (except for the Jewish East End anarchists who peaked in 1913–1914) was less dynamic after the turn of the century. The French and Germans trickled back home or integrated into the host community. The Italian community, which had swelled during the nineties, was reduced to long-standing political exiles like Malatesta, Emidio Recchioni (the father of Vernon Richards, Malatesta's future biographer, Malatesta's right-hand man, and owner of the famous King Bomba Italian delicatessen and pasta: "The Sole Macaroni Factory in England" proclaimed the shop's hoarding in Soho), or Silvio Corio (the future partner of radical feminist Sylvia Pankhurst), and others who had grown deep roots in London.[16] Perhaps during this period there were twenty to fifty Italian anarchists in London with a further hundred or so sympathizers of the Italian socialist party; and as time progressed, the two groups mixed.[17]

For long periods of time Italian anarchists were undermined by ideological disputes and limited by their constant, and not unjustifiable, fear of Italian police infiltration (most famously the penetrating gaze of "Virgilio," special agent to Giolitti himself, Ennio Bellelli,

---

13   Carl Levy, "Malatesta in Exile,: *Annali della Fondazione Luigi Einaudi* (Turin) 15 (1981), 269; Pietro Di Paola, *The Knights Errant of Anarchy: London and the Italian Anarchist Diaspora, 1880–1917* (Liverpool University Press, 2013), 35, 105–7.

14   "Malatesta. Reception by Revolutionists after Release," *Daily Herald*, July 30, 1912, p. 341 of the current volume.

15   "La Comune di Parigi e gli anarchici," *La Settimana Sanguinosa*, March 18, 1903, p. 194 of the current volume.

16   For an in-depth account of Emidio Recchioni see Erika Diemoz, *A morte il tiranno. Anarchia e violenza da Crispi a Mussolini* (Turin: Einaudi 2011); a good summary of Corio's activities in 1900–1914 can be found in Di Paola, *Knights Errant of Anarchy*.

17   Di Paola, *Knights Errant of Anarchy*, 205.

a close anarchist confidante of Malatesta, more on this further down), which was so persistent and heavy handed that the British authorities expressed alarm lest a compromised and accused anarchist carry out an act to prove his bona fides, as indeed Gennaro Rubino did with his attempt on the King of the Belgians. Malatesta's position reached a low point in the winter of 1902–1903 when his handling of this case and the affair of Gaetano Scolari brought on a deep depression and alienation not only from his anti-organizationalist and individualist tormenters but organizational anarchists as well, who considered his behavior too imperious.[18] The gloomy atmosphere was deepened by the failure to establish a viable London-based newspaper to reach the global Italian diaspora (*L' Internazionale, La Rivoluzione Sociale,* and *Lo Sciopero Generale*). Malatesta also misread the longevity of the Giolittian experiment in Italy. In the period before 1905, he believed that the drumbeat of "proletarian massacres" in Apulia or Sicily were a foretaste of a return to the stormy 1890s, but in the meantime the creation of a solid network of socialist and even syndicalist trade unions, particularly among the landless laborers in the Po Valley, was creating a new, if temporary, agreement between social classes, at least in the North.[19] In any case, Malatesta refused to return to Italy in 1908 to edit an anarchist newspaper in Milan, because he did not agree with its editorial line and he was dismissive of the widespread presence of anti-organizationalist and Stirnerite anarchists in the Italian movement.[20] Many times during this decade he expressed the desire to pass the mantle of leadership on to the younger generation. But these were also years of pronounced sectarianism. Thus, after the execution of Francisco Ferrer in 1909, Malatesta was uneasy over having his legacy appropriated by more moderate Free Thinkers, Secularists, and Republicans and did not seek out alliances with them, which was rather different from his behavior in the years of Crispi and his immediate successors.[21] And even more surprising

---

18   Ibid., 135–44.

19   G. Berti, *Errico Malatesta e il movimento anarchico italiano e internazionale 1872– 1932* (Milan: Franco Angeli, 2003), 323–331. A good example of Malatesta's London journalism is "L'Assassino di Candela," *La Rivoluzione Sociale,* January 27, 1903, p. 180 of the current volume.

20   See the report of February 12, 1908 by "Virgilio" on Malatesta's reaction to a proposal from Milan's *Protesta Umana,* Casellario Politico Centrale, box 2949, Archivio Centrale dello Stato, Rome, p. 276 of the current volume. There are many articles in which Malatesta tackles the issues of anti-organisationalist and Stirnerite anarchism, but this volume (pp. 285–90) publishes a fascinating account of Malatesta engaged in a debate with an anti-organisationalist shoemaker (2 February 1909).

21   On this account, see, in this volume, Malatesta's speeches of September 17, 1909 (p. 297), October 2, 1909 (p. 299), October 30, 1909 (p. 299), November 11, 1909 (p. 300), and October 13, 1910 (p. 300).

was his openly hostile attitude toward relationships with non-anarchist anti-militarists, culminating in a series of knockdown debates with Gustave Hervé, given the fact that the antimilitarism preceding the Red Week would catapult the anarchists to the center of the unorthodox, rebel left in Italy in 1913–14.[22]

Except for several trips to Paris, most notably in 1906 to take part in an unsuccessful general strike, and once again in 1909 to visit Ferrer's widow, his most significant journey was to the International Anarchist Congress, held in Amsterdam, in 1907. Regardless of the fact that little came of this international gathering and its general correspondence committee organized by Malatesta and other Russian and Jewish anarchists in London (the correspondence committee fizzled out soon after it was established), the highlight of the congress, the famous debate with Pierre Monatte on the virtues and weaknesses of syndicalism, reflected a major preoccupation for Malatesta in this period of exile.[23]

Malatesta's stance on syndicalism was complex. In the 1890s, as Constance Bantman has shown in detail, Malatesta was the "tutor" of syndicalism or proto-syndicalism to Pouget and other French anarchists temporarily exiled in London.[24] He praised the New Unionism of the early 1890s and the epoch-making Great Dock Strike, which occurred shortly after his return from Argentina. However, the evolution of the labor movement as a whole and syndicalism in the United States, Argentina, Italy, and even France, gave him pause to reconsider his original enthusiasm. Nevertheless, Malatesta had close ties with the young direct action movement in London and the UK. Besides his longstanding friendship with Tom Mann and Sam Mainwaring (who edited *General Strike,* the English edition of *Sciopero Generale*) he also had ties with trade unionist John Turner, the eccentric "boy preacher from Clerkenwell," Guy Aldred, and many lesser known figures, who intervened in the more proletarian *Voice of Labour,* rather than the official and rather staid *Freedom,* the English-language anarchist newspaper Kropotkin founded in 1886.[25]

Malatesta participated in some labor organizing himself. In 1905 and 1906 he assisted the largely foreign community of waiters and catering staff in London. Most of the waiters were German, French, or

---

22 "Il proposto Congresso antimilitarista," *La Rivoluzione Sociale* (London), January 27, 1903, p. 178 of the current volume; "The Case of Gustave Hervé," *Freedom* (London), November 1912, p. 352 of the current volume.

23 A. Dunois (ed.), *Congrès Anarchiste tenu à Amsterdam, Août 1907* (Paris, 1908), see pp. 232–51 of the current volume.

24 Constance Bantman, *The French Anarchists in London, 1880–1914. Exile and transnationalism in the first globalisation* (Liverpool: Liverpool University Press, 2013), 98–102.

25 Levy, "Malatesta in Exile," 270–73.

Italian, and quite a few of them were socialists or anarchists. A long hard battle was fought to dismantle a particularly archaic system of in-kind payment.[26] This campaign coincided with Rudolf Rocker's battle against the sweating system in the East End, which eventually led to a massive strike of Jewish tailors. Malatesta gave a series of speeches in the East End to thousands of strikers and sympathizers, and James Tochatti (the Italo-Scottish anarchist) and Malatesta tried to get the better paid West End artisan tailors to show their solidarity.

Anticipating his interventions in Amsterdam with a series of articles, Malatesta laid down first principles concerning anarchist involvement in trade union organization. Anarchists, he explained, must lead the fight against bureaucracy by actively operating within the structure of unions, requesting frequent general meetings of the worker base to discuss general policy, and abstaining from seeking paid positions within the administrative structure (at most Malatesta conceded that an anarchist could be an official if his salary did not exceed the average wage of a worker). Corporate tendencies within the labor movement would be staved off through a line of action that educated the worker, emphasizing solidarity, by keeping dues as low as possible, and limiting the growth of mutual aid societies and cooperatives with close links to capitalist banks. Malatesta declared his opposition to closed shops, limited apprenticeships, arbitration, and labor exchanges because he felt that these policies and institutions split the working class. In the end the unemployed, the unskilled, and the immigrants formed the pool from which the employers' strike breaking societies drew recruits.[27] Thus in his contribution to *Revue*, the quadrilingual (English, French, Italian, and German) international organ of the employees of the catering union, Malatesta frankly refused to endorse the caterers' union desire for legally recognized labor exchanges. He prefaced his remarks with a short apology by telling them the truth might be especially bitter but he warned of a dangerous precedent because law meant surveillance by the police, otherwise "the employment agents, with the support of a few scabs, could establish false associations and easily continue their trade."[28] The article is remarkable in several respects but mainly because it anticipates the very same arguments British syndicalists and, at least initially, many other British trade unionists would advance

---

26   Di Paola, *Knights Errant of Anarchy*, 111–3.

27   "A proposito di scioperi," *La Rivoluzione Sociale* (London), October 18, 1902, p. 122 of the current volume; "La morte dell'unionismo classico," *La Rivoluzione Sociale*, December 29, 1902, p. 164 of the current volume; "La guerra contro i lavoranti stranieri," *La Rivoluzione Sociale*, January 27, 1903, p. 171 of the current volume.

28   "Contro una legge sugli uffici di collocamento," *Revue* (London), December 1906, p. 227 of the current volume.

when Lloyd George set up a legal system of labor exchanges throughout Britain several years later.

In two articles for *Freedom* ("Anarchism and Syndicalism," November 1907 and "Anarchists and the Situation," June 1909) Malatesta elaborated on the points raised in *Revue*.[29] The first article was republished in the French and Italian press and restated the position he advanced at the Amsterdam Congress in August 1907. Malatesta repeated his persistent fears that the bureaucratization of trade unions would also sap them of their "broad spirit of progress and human fraternity." Although French syndicalism had perhaps been a healthy countertendency, it too contained "all the elements of degeneration which have corrupted Labour movements in the past." Syndicalism, as its French proponents wished, might be a "good school of solidarity," but not inevitably so. Since trade unions, even revolutionary trade unions, were necessarily based within the competitive framework of capitalism, the laws of the marketplace would determine trade union policy. Anarchism could, therefore, provide that consciousness external to institutions which the trade union lacked. "Every institution," Malatesta noted, "has a tendency to extend its functions, to perpetuate itself." Thus, trade unions that experience success must protect their war chests, "seek the favour of public powers," get involved in "cooperation and mutual benefit schemes," in short, they must become "conservative elements in society."

But Malatesta was not calling for trade unions of convinced anarchists. A trade union solely consisting of the converted would neither reach out to the apolitical worker, the most important interlocutor, nor survive very long:

> ... since the Unions must remain open to all those who desire to win from the masters better conditions of life, whatever their opinions may be on the general constitution of society, they are naturally led to moderate their aspirations, first so that they should not frighten away those they wish to have with them, and next because, in proportion as numbers increase, those with ideas who have initiated the movement remain buried in a majority that is only occupied with the petty interests of the moment.

Anarchists, as Malatesta had so often repeated, should act as pressure groups, "they should work to develop in the Syndicates all that which can augment its educative influence and its combativeness."

In "Anarchists and the Situation" Malatesta was more optimistic,

---

29   See respectively p. 266 and p. 293 of the current volume.

praising the current French militancy at the workplace, especially among state workers. But Malatesta questioned whether the workers were capable of confronting the repressive laws of the French government. He even admitted that his reasoning "having been written for Englishmen, may strike some as fantastic." But he could not resist making a rather accurate prophecy for 1909, predicting the unprecedented labor and syndicalist unrest that gripped the nation on the eve of the First World War.

> England has not reached this point yet; but she will reach it, and sooner than is expected.
>
> To-day, even if it would, a civilised country cannot remain separated from other civilised countries; and the French and Continental movement will not be without influence on the proletariat of this side of the Channel.

Within the next few years Malatesta's close British comrades would be shaking up the trade union movement, from the "Miner's Next Step," written largely by Sam Mainwaring of the now defunct *General Strike*, a call for the libertarian organization of the South Wales coalfield miners' union, to the prominence of Tom Mann in the new rank and file movements throughout Britain, and to *The Daily Herald*, of the unorthodox socialist George Lansbury. The Industrial Syndicalist Educational League (ISEL) by Mann and Guy Bowman was precisely the sort of pressure group Malatesta had argued for in the previous article, which made propaganda for the libertarian reform of the old trade unions, not for the duplication of unions, which merely divided the working classes and did nothing to prevent the bureaucratization of trade unions of any political color.[30] Thus Malatesta was present at a 1912 New Year's dinner held by the ISEL at Fleet Street's Anderton Hotel, a syndicalist *"feu de joie,"* so reported the ISEL's new organ, the *Syndicalist*. Member of parliament George Lansbury "had magnanimously consented to become the visible representative" of parliamentarianism; and Malatesta "congratulated the League on its libertarian ideas."[31] We will return to the syndicalist revolt and worker unrest at the end of this essay when we address the dramatic events of Malatesta's life in 1911 and 1912, which caused him to become a newsworthy item in London's dailies just as he had been at the beginning of this London sojourn in the wake of Humbert's assassination. Now we turn to the overarching dialectic of Malatesta's interventions from

---

30   Levy, "Malatesta in Exile," 277–80.
31   "A Hopeful Start," *The Syndicalist* (London) 1, no. 1 (January 1912), p. 325 of the current volume.

the turn of the century to the outbreak of the Great War: the nature of imperialism and the antimilitarist response to growing international tensions throughout Europe.

Since the 1860s anarchists had pursued four strategies to reach their goal of a non-statist and non-coercive federal organization of society. The first, insurrectionalism and acts of terror had led to a dead end and forced Malatesta to consider the second road of trade unionism founded on direct action in the 1890s, but by the early 1900s this risked lapsing into routine (as the great Amsterdam debates show). A third strand of libertarian countercultural organization (anti-clerical activities, education, art, or alternative communities, press activities, and cooperatives) was important to give the anarchist movement a presence in the broader left, far beyond its own "borders." Malatesta was not totally dismissive of these efforts, but he was wary that they would lead to passivity and to reformist libertarian projects, not revolution. A fourth path, antimilitarism, had the virtue of undermining the armed forces, the chief pillar of the capitalist state, but here too Malatesta fought long and sectarian battles against middle-class pacifists and the followers of Tolstoyan anarchism.

However, it was an incident of terrorist expropriation that nearly compromised Malatesta and would come to haunt him during the final period of this sojourn. After the failure of the 1905 Russian Revolution, a new wave of Russian and Jewish revolutionaries arrived in London. Some had been actively involved in expropriation gangs in Russia and desired to continue with the old ways in their new home. But these gangs were not merely anarchists; the majority in Russia had been composed of social democrats or social revolutionaries. The first major incident, the Tottenham Outrage, did not concern Malatesta, but the second was far more spectacular. In December 1910, after robbers were disturbed at a jeweler's shop on Houndsditch, a street in the East End, by five policemen, three were shot dead and two were badly wounded by the armed gang. Two members of the armed gang of Latvians were traced to 100 Sidney Street in Whitechapel and after a gunfight that lasted much of January 3, 1911, the house caught fire and the bandits burned to death. Their mysterious leader, Peter the Painter, was never caught and soon acquired the same myth-like figure as Jack the Ripper.[32]

The response to the "Siege of Sidney Street" involved the Scots Guards led by a fully armed Winston Churchill, then the Home

---

32   For the Houndsditch affair, see, Di Paola, *Knights Errant of Anarchy*, 115–17 and in detail: Philip Ruff, *Pa stāvu liesmu debesīs* (Riga: Dienas Gramata, 2012); Donald Rumbelow, *The Houndsditch Murders and the Siege of Sidney Street* (Stroud: History Press, 2009).

Secretary. From photographs of the "Siege," one could get the impression that the entire East End had risen in rebellion. The dead Latvians had attended the Jewish anarchist Jubilee Club and had briefly made the acquaintance of Rudolf Rocker and other comrades, who were entirely innocent of the subsequent events. One of the members of the gang, Svaars, had asked to borrow some tubes of oxygen and was directed to Malatesta's workshop in Islington, where Malatesta agreed to sell him a large forty-foot cylinder of oxygen, which Malatesta did not know was to be used to burn through the jeweler's safe. Malatesta was brought to Whitechapel police station for questioning when his business card was found at the scene of the crime. He told the police that he had been paid one pound on account and later the remaining four pounds.[33] He was soon released. Malatesta denied all knowledge of the gang's activities and he later told Rudolf Rocker that the police had treated him decently and with the utmost respect.[34]

Soon after the "Siege of Sidney Street," Malatesta granted an interview to the *Evening News*, and later wrote an article printed in the London Yiddish anarchist press and then published in France.[35] Perhaps the *Evening News* reporter did let his imagination get the best of him when he claimed that Malatesta acknowledged that there was an unwritten law amongst London exiles to leave the English in peace. Malatesta always denied the existence of such agreements, for in the Italian press this rumor could be twisted to mean that the anarchists, and Malatesta in particular, were British agents. Otherwise, the articles reported Malatesta's opinions on expropriation succinctly.

"In England, if a man picks pockets, you sentence him for picking pockets," he explained, "you do not ask him if he is a Free Trader or a Tariff Reformer or a vegetarian and then raise a cry about the evils of Free Trade or Tariff reform or vegetarianism. You do not propose to suppress or expel Tariff Reformers or Free Traders or vegetarians!!!" "These men were not Anarchists," he answered the interviewer, "but burglars and murderers, and they should be called burglars and murders."[36]

The ghosts of the 1890s were put to rest: it was the interweaving of antimilitarism, anti-imperialism and a revived syndicalist movement that generated, in the global North and South, the energy that propelled

---

33   See, in this volume, Malatesta's statement made to the police (p. 305) and his testimony given during the trial for the Houndsditch murders on May 2, 1911 (p. 313).
34   Rudolf Rocker, *En la borrasca* (Buenos Aires, 1949), 296.
35   "The Brains of the Anarchist Movement," *Evening News* (London), January 6, 1911, p. 302 of the current volume. For the article see "Capitalistes et voleurs," *Les Temps Nouveaux* (Paris), February 18, 1911, p. 310 of the current volume.
36   "The Brains of the Anarchist Movement."

anarchism right to the forefront of the international Left from 1905 to
1914. Even reformist socialists like Eduard Bernstein argued for general
strikes to obtain universal suffrage or make it effective in parliaments
based on extravagant electoral laws, while the Suffragettes in Britain
did not shirk from acts of terrorism in the fight for women's voting
rights: indeed later Malatesta would recall the death of Emily Davison
at the Royal Epsom Derby in 1913.[37] One of the persistent themes of
Malatesta's writings on the British labor movement was that many of
its reforms were only possible through its use of anarchist-like methods to achieve reformist objectives. Thus, in his 1909 *Freedom* article,
Malatesta argued that the British working class would turn the very
traditions of working-class Lib-Labism, "the solid qualities of perseverance, the spirit of organisation and personal independence," against
reformism itself.[38]

For Malatesta, imperialism was the detonator for outbursts of mass
mobilization. A new era opened when a war-weakened Russia nearly suc-
cumbed to a movement of soviets founded on direct action in 1905, while
in Spain, Barcelona's 1909 Tragic Week was sparked by a call to arms to
fight the Berbers in Morocco's Rif Mountains. Industrial warfare raged
in the United States, in Great Britain, in Sweden, and Latin America.
New forms of unorthodox Marxism, from Rosa Luxemburg's to Lenin's,
theorized on the importance of the mass strike and direct action, rather
than only giving importance to the vote, the refusal of which had led to
the expulsion of anti-parliamentary socialists and the anarchists at the
Second International's London congress in 1896, and in which Malatesta
played a prominent role in the defeated opposition.[39] This new era was
discussed in a prophetic article by Malatesta in London in 1902, "Lo
sciopero armato" (The armed strike), which was a fitting title for this
volume of his complete works.[40] The incessant drumbeat of imperialist
adventures, rearmament, inflation, and mass antimilitarist action in the
form of direct action reached a crescendo in Italy with the Red Week
in June 1914, in which Malatesta was a key player in the strategic anarchist stronghold of Ancona, and which threatened the stability of Italy's

37   "Le suffragette," *Volontà* (Ancona) 1, no. 3 (June 22, 1913).

38   "Anarchists and the Situation."

39   Carl Levy, "Malatesta in London: The Era of Dynamite," in L. Sponza and
      A. Tosi (eds.), *A Century of Italian Emigration to Britain 1880–1980s five essays,*
      The Italianist (special supplement), Vol. 13 (1993): 34–36; Davide Turcato,
      "The 1896 London Congress: Epilogue or Prologue?," in *New Perspectives*
      on Anarchism, Labour and Syndicalism: The Individual, the National and the
      Transnational, ed. D. Berry and C. Bantman (Newcastle upon Tyne: Cambridge
      Scholars Publishing, 2010), 110–25.

40   "Lo sciopero armato," *Lo Sciopero Generale* (London), June 2, 1902, p. 93 of the
      current volume.

Savoyard monarchy. For a brief few days, a wide coalition of all elements of the subversive Italian left challenged with formidable efficacy the powers that were; a coalition, one must recall, far wider than the seemingly sectarian Malatesta of the early 1900s would have supported.[41]

Like Lenin, albeit with libertarian first principles intact, Malatesta linked social reformism and the rise of a privileged British skilled working class to the lures of imperial glory. At the turn of the century, the Spanish American War, the Boer War, the Dreyfus Affair, and the repression of the Boxer Rebellion in China, signaled to Malatesta that a new era of imperialism had arrived, which could serve as a road both toward radicalization as well as toward a reactionary turn. Malatesta witnessed the rabid chauvinism and inflamed nationalism induced by the Spanish American war during his sojourn in the United States and Cuba, where the American authorities of the occupation prevented him from speaking in Havana. But even more depressing for Malatesta was the apathy which the popular press and drink induced in the poorer elements of London's working class, who in the wealthiest and most modern city of the capitalist world suffered periodic unemployment crises, particularly during the long damp winters (which were a Calvary for Malatesta's weak lungs).[42] Malatesta was sympathetic to the Boers (the vast African majority is rarely mentioned), the Boxers, the rebel Filipinos, and later the Arabs, after Italy's invasion of Libya, recalling his intervention in the Urabi Pasha revolt in Egypt against the British in 1882 (he hoped that the Arabs would drive both the Italians and the Turks into the sea).[43] But like Lenin he was also sympathetic to the line taken by the British Radical Liberal anti-imperialists. As is known, Lenin's thesis on imperialism was hugely dependent on John Hobson's book on the subject. Like Lenin, Malatesta largely dismissed the politics of British Liberalism as laughable and hypocritical. "The English government," Malatesta wrote, was "the most hypocritical, and in practice the most liberticidal of governments."[44] Nevertheless, it was the very popular Radical Liberal newspaper *Star* that in 1897 demanded that the jailor Italian state release Malatesta; and it was through the equally popular and populist liberal, and pro-Boer, *Reynolds's Newspaper* (also a springboard to Tom Mann's proteiform interests and politics), that Malatesta intervened in English during his long exile of 1900–13. W. H.

---

41   The best account of the Red Week remains Luigi Lotti, *La Settimana Rossa* (Florence: Le Monnier, 1972).

42   "Società condannata," *La Rivoluzione Sociale* (London), December 29, 1902, p. 160 of the current volume.

43   See Malatesta's speech of October 20, 1911, as reported by police commissioner Frosali to the Ministry of the Interior London on October 28, 1911, p. 319 of the current volume.

44   "Scarfoglio," *Umanità Nova* (Rome) 2, no. 140 (September 23, 1921).

Thompson, the editor, invited Malatesta to write on the perennial topic of anarchism and violence, because the libertarian rather than the statist spirit was attractive to his readers even while violent anticonstitutional methods were off-putting. Thus, in an article entitled "Why Italians are anarchist," Malatesta sought to explain that unlike Great Britain, with its constitutional guarantees, Italy was not so blessed.[45] Such a distinction was readily understood by readers raised on Gladstone's denunciations of Re Bomba (and perhaps the name of Recchioni's Soho "macaroni shop" was not so obscure to many Londoners with a radical liberal background), the Bulgarian and Armenian "horrors" and the despotism of the Tsar. The real reason for political violence in Italy did not arise from the agitation of uncontrollable anarchists. Italy, he wrote, "has a great number of inhabitants who live in a perpetual state of semi-starvation," and nevertheless they "are not the stupid and resigned creatures which we find in other countries professing higher educational facilities." The spirit of revolt had been engendered through a series of cultural and historical factors. Italians overall did not "brutalize themselves with strong drink"; neither had patriotism dampened their critical facilities; and religion, even if they were superstitious, held little power over them. Furthermore, the violent legacy of the Risorgimento still made a mark on Italian politics. Post-Risorgimento Italy had been a disappointment. The dominant class had imposed itself on the people, destroying older forms of Catholic charity and dispossessing monastic corporations of their land. And for the common people, Malatesta wrote, recalling Saverio Merlino's earlier portrait of Italy after the Risorgimento, the political machinery "has been used for the enrichment of the few to the detriment of the many."[46] Ultimately, violence in Italy arose from indifference, or worse, the repression of workers' organizations by the government. The anarchist only resorted to violent self-defense as a last resort, but "only when no other means are left to him." The Italian anarchists, Malatesta concluded in a traditionally liberal mode of discourse, "only ask for freedom of propaganda, and organisation, expecting the triumph of our ideas not by a *coup de main*, not by the employment of force or violence, but by the free consent of the people."

Certain passages may seem exaggerated, such as, for example, those on the weaknesses of Catholicism or latent patriotism in the lower classes; and certainly the conclusion was overdone, pitched to a specific audience. Nevertheless, the sociological first premises connected Malatesta to the Radical Liberals rather than the Second Internationalist socialists and separated him from Lenin who used J. A. Hobson to refresh the Marxist

---

45   *Reynolds's Newspaper* (London), October 11, 1908, p. 279 of the current volume.
46   Saverio Merlino, *L'Italie telle qu'elle est* (Paris: A. Savine, 1890).

concept of surplus value. Italy after the Risorgimento was not suffering because of capitalist exploitation as such, but through the political machinery of an exploitative state in league with certain special interests. Indeed, the old regime of charity was better than the anti-feudal "modernizers" who followed them. Thus, when the Libyan War broke out in late 1911, the anti-militarism and anti-imperialism of Italian anarchist refugees found a sympathetic audience in their host community. The war opened up a chain of events, which over three years led to world war and a realignment of Left-wing politics (the Balkan Wars were ignited by Libya, which led to the 1914 July Crisis). In London Malatesta quickly realized that the war would destabilize the Giolittian system and increase opportunities for the Italian extra-parliamentary left. Unlike the early 1900s, this time Malatesta was prescient.[47]

From London Malatesta organized the publication of the Ancona-based *Volontà* until his departure for Italy in 1913. One of Malatesta's first reactions to Italy's war on the Ottoman Empire and the invasion of Libya was to publish a manifesto, addressed to his fellow Italians in London in April 1912.[48] But earlier, just after war broke out the previous autumn, Malatesta had spoken to a crowd of Italian anarchists and socialists at the Communist Club in Soho. He again expressed his radical liberal-inspired interpretation of imperialism. Did his audience perhaps believe, he asked, that England was rich because of India? England was rich because of the comparative advantage it possessed, being the first industrial nation and maintaining a near monopoly on this technology for fifty years, and because of its huge coal deposits. The Italians had enough potential back home, particularly, Malatesta the electrician continued, the "white coal" of rivers that gushed down from the mountains.[49]

The Libyan War received bad press in London's radical liberal newspapers. Much play was given to Italian atrocities and the "Little Englanders" feared (rightly, in retrospect) that Italy's rash move would undermine the equilibrium of Europe. W. T. Stead, the most notable Lib-Lab journalist of his generation, led an antiwar campaign in the *Review of Reviews*. He even attempted to arbitrate between the "Sublime Porte" and the Italian government, but with little effect; soon after he was lost in the Titanic disaster. Malatesta was contacted by British radical liberals to hold joint assemblies. But he declined the offer, explaining

---

47   See Malatesta's speech of May 7, 1913, p. 362 of the current volume: see also Berti, *Errico Malatesta e il movimento anarchico italiano e internazionale 1872–1932*, 488–502.

48   "La guerra e gli anarchici," *La Guerra Tripolina* (London), April 1912, p. 325 of the current volume.

49   See note 43 above.

that he preferred not to appear together, so as to deny the Italian press a chance of accusing him of working for British interests.[50]

It was at this point that Ennio Bellelli (a.k.a. "Virgilio"), Giolitti's secret agent and prominent Italian anarchist exile, sprang his trap. Abandoning his former beliefs, he endorsed the Italian invasion and started rumors that Malatesta's antiwar activities and those of poor Stead were encouraged by payments from the Turks.[51] This provocation was cleverly carried out, since Bellelli never circulated any written statement but forced Malatesta to rebut these charges by unwisely printing a public manifesto accusing Bellelli of being a police spy.[52] Bellelli brought a defamation lawsuit against Malatesta and the conservative magistrate, Judge Darling, was decidedly unfriendly to Malatesta. Testimony by inspectors from Scotland Yard described Malatesta as a notorious anarchist known to the police forces of a half dozen European countries and the evidence concerning Malatesta's involvement in the siege of Sidney Street was brought up. At the inquest following the Siege of Sidney Street, the criminal investigation division had testified that Malatesta lived a life beyond reproach in London. But Malatesta's trial was something of a test case for the 1905 Aliens' Act, which allowed for the deportation of undesirable aliens on the strength of, among other things, a judge's opinion. Judge Darling recommended that after his three months stay in Wormwood Scrubs prison, Malatesta be deported back to Italy. Through a neat job of anarchist counterespionage the local community exposed Bellelli as an Italian agent and he soon vanished from the scene. But we do not know, and probably will never know, if the British government or the British security services helped spring Bellelli's trap, or were involved in the wretched business once Judge Darling's order for deportation was confirmed on appeal. It now stood with the Home Secretary whether Malatesta would be deported.

It was now that Malatesta's network of friends, neighbors, colleagues, and comrades sprang into action while the rebel, orthodox socialist, and liberal press reacted with unconcealed outrage. Immediately the Freedom Group organized a Malatesta Release Committee. The *Daily Herald* led the major campaign. On May 21, 1912, it had published a detailed report of Malatesta's trial. Malatesta was well known to *Daily Herald* readers as he was a frequent speaker at the North London Herald and ISEL meetings. On May 22, the

---

50   See note 43 above.

51   For the latest summary of this affair see Di Paola, *Knights Errant of Anarchy*, 144–153.

52   See Malatesta's leaflet of April 12, 1912, "Errico Malatesta alla colonia italiana di Londra," p. 332 of the current volume.

Radical Liberal *Daily News and Leader* noted that there were several disturbing features in Malatesta's trial. Bellelli's case seemed curious to its columnist. The sentence was severe: "a sentence of three months imprisonment coupled with a recommendation for deportation is a grotesque punishment for libel." The *Daily News and Leader,* like much of London liberal opinion, was clearly disturbed by the way the opinions of Sergeant Powell had been allowed to color the outcome. The whole affair stank of a political trial.[53] In fact, on May 22, the *Daily Herald* appealed to "all free-born Englishmen," recalling how Josiah Wedgewood in his recent defense of Mann had declared in court: "Slaves cannot breathe in England any longer." In his editorial, Lansbury continued in a typically liberal vein, evoking the memory of the old exiles of the Risorgimento and the exiles of 1848, recalling how "the natural Briton thought proudly of his island and home as a haven of liberty, a refuge for the banned and persecuted patriots of the nations. The harder they hit their home tyrants the more he honored them. Tory qualms or denunciations did not affect him," and continued, "today, unless we are sadly and utterly mistaken, [England] is still on the whole in the mood to stand for that fine old ideal."[54]

In the next days the *Daily Herald* assembled a formidable array of socialists, trade unionists, and syndicalists throughout the country in defense of Malatesta. A vexed reader writing from Stockport explained that "Malatesta's only crime is that he is an international Tom Mann, and he has worked for human freedom in many countries."[55] The *Nation,* the voice of the London liberal intelligentsia, denounced the growing tendency toward restriction of public expression in an editorial on May 25: "[T]his country is, we think, getting somewhat tired of political trials." And further on, after arguing that political agitation annoyed government ministers but was not a crime, it continued: "[S]ay what we will of people like Mr Mann, or Mrs Pankhurst, or Count [*sic*] Malatesta, that is the category to which they belong, and we think it is most unfortunate that in a time of general unsettlement, but of not great violence or social peril, they should have found their way to the dock and the prison cell."[56]

The *Manchester Guardian,* another major voice of enlightened middle-class liberalism, was alarmed at Malatesta's impending deportation: "[No] reasonable person," its editorial explained, "would suggest that an alien who had lived in this country for years, should be expelled for alleging a fellow-alien was a spy." And it continued with great

---

53   "Malatesta," June 10, 1912.
54   "Malatesta," May 22, 1912.
55   "Mann and Malatesta," May 23, 1912.
56   "The Political Trials."

indignation: "[M]alatesta fled from punishment for political offences, and we give him asylum; no non-political offence is charged or proven against him during his twelve years stay; no criminal act of anarchism is brought home to him; no incitement to or complicity in a criminal act is charged against him by the police. How, then, can his anarchist propaganda and his political offences be made the ground for denying him the very asylum which so far we have given him not in spite of but because of them?"[57]

In Parliament Keir Hardie, George Lansbury, and Ramsay MacDonald passionately defended Malatesta's right to remain in Great Britain. The day before a massive demonstration in favor of Malatesta occurred, a long, passionate letter from Kropotkin appeared in *The Nation*.[58] However, on 10 June 1912, Malatesta's appeal was rejected. The demonstration was a great success: thousands gathered at Nelson's column and listened to distinguished Liberals, Socialists, and trade unionists. The north London contingent was particularly vocal in support of Malatesta. In Islington he was remembered with affection; indeed, thousands signed a petition to suspend the sentence. A member of the local Board of Guardians, and ex-anarchist now active in the local Labour Party, W. B. Parker, wrote to the *Daily Herald*, recalling how "comrade Malatesta had lived in the ward for upwards of twenty years and during this period has deservedly earned the respect of his neighbours by his uniform courteousness and upright life."[59] The residents of Islington gathered at the local common, Highbury Corner, before the long march to Trafalgar Square. Nearly every local trade union participated: the clerks' union, painters, wheelwrights, railway men, carpenters, plasters, bricklayers, municipal workers, shop assistants, along with the local ILP (Independent Labour Party) and BSP (British Socialist Party). Behind the lead banner marched Malatesta's family, followed by "the first rate band of the Edmonton Branch of the BSP." That evening Islington witnessed three local torchlight demonstrations organized by trade unionists in the streets adjoining Malatesta's home. And feelings for the Malatesta case seemed to bridge class and party lines. The protectionist newspaper, *The Islington Daily Gazette and North London Tribune*, chief opponent of the locally vibrant Labour Party, defended the anarchist's right to remain in his local abode. This was a case that concerned all "free-born Englishman" to whom "the sense of fair-play is especially clear." "Are we," the newspaper declared, "to tolerate in our country the methods of policemanism that are prevalent in the most backward Continental countries such as Russia! Are we

---

57   "The Case of Malatesta," May 25, 1912.
58   "The Case of Malatesta. To the Editor of *The Nation*," June 8, 1912.
59   "The Protests," May 30, 1912.

going to allow Judges to call upon detectives to give their opinions of a man's political views? Are we going to permit exceptional punishment to be visited upon a man because a policeman does not think as his victims thinks?"[60]

Malatesta was saved from deportation by a potent combination of direct action and the "old boys" network. Rudolf Rocker argued that the Home Secretary certainly was swayed by this massive mobilization of the London working class, just when a dock strike was reaching its climax, which was underscored by Cunninghame-Grahame's speech at Trafalgar Square, stating that this demonstration was "not merely against the iniquitous sentence on Errico Malatesta, but against the growth of officialism and the suppression of all attempts to alter our modern constitution and unjust laws."[61] In short, the protest was capable of bringing together the rebel constituencies of feminists, syndicalists, and Irish nationalists. Kropotkin, however, decided to be prudent and go directly to John Burns, the former New Unionist firebrand of the 1890s and now a member of the government. Kropotkin, his biographers Woodcock and Avakumović tell us, "reminded Burns of his own past when he led the procession of striking dockers through the London streets. Burns remarked that he had long seen the stupidity of such acts, and then Kropotkin heatedly answered that it was a good thing that there were still people willing to indulge in 'stupidities' for the good of their fellows, though by such means one could not grasp at a ministerial chair. Burns then laughed and Malatesta finally escaped deportation."[62]

Upon his release from Wormwood Scrubs, he gave an interview to the *Daily Herald* (30 July 1912). The reporter set the scene:

[V]ery few rooms in London have held so many veteran revolutionists at one time as the little back parlour in Arthur street, where Errico Malatesta held court last evening.

The *Daily Herald* representative was practically the only man in the room who could not speak at least three Latin tongues. Here was half a score of the most 'dangerous men in Europe.' Portet, the heir to the martyr Ferrer, himself on the eve of another departure to Spain; Tarrida del Marmol, whom Spain watches more vigilantly than any other of her exiles, Tcherkesoff, by title a royal prince, by choice one of Russia's most noted anarchists.

---

60   Quicquid, "Personal Impressions: Malatesta," June 12, 1912.
61   "The Cause of Freedom," *The Daily Herald* (London), June 10, 1912.
62   George Woodcock and Ivan Avakumović, *The Anarchist Prince: A Biographical Study of Peter Kropotkin* (New York: Kraus Reprint, 1970), 264.

Malatesta claimed that English prison life was far more severe than Italian. They had treated him "like a dog" and the food had been absolutely appalling.[63] The Malatesta campaign had caused a small anarchist boom. The *Daily Herald* ran several articles on anarchism and *Freedom* sales were rosy, whilst several important figures in the future shop stewards' movement started their political lives through the Malatesta Release Committee.[64] Later, Malatesta remembered the struggle with pride. He stayed in London, "despite the English government, by the will of the English people."[65] Soon Malatesta would be back in Italy for another short but eventful stay.

---

63   "Malatesta. Reception by Revolutionists," *The Daily Herald* (London), July 30, 1912. See p. 341 of the current volume.

64   John Quail, *The Slow Burning Fuse: The Lost History of the British Anarchists* (London: Granada Publishing, 1978), 272–73.

65   "L'oro straniero," *Umanità Nova* (Milan), June 19, 1920.

SECTION I
The Regicide

To the Anarchists of Italy

Translated from "Agli anarchici d'Italia," *L'Agitazione* (Ancona) 1,
new series, no. 13 (June 8, 1900)[1]

London May 30, 1900

Dear comrades,

I have learned that once again someone has proposed "anarchist" candidacies and believed it useful to put my name forth.

I do not believe I have ever deserved, either before or now, such an insult; and I am truly tired and indignant to hear myself, despite all my protests, being periodically proposed as a candidate by so-called anarchists or friends of anarchists.

I have said and repeated a thousand times my opinions on parliamentarism and on any type of candidacy to legislating bodies; and those who make use of my name are certainly aware of this. Do they believe that I speak in jest? or do they think that it is legitimate to not take into consideration the convictions of others, and to make use of someone's name for purposes he highly disapproves of?

I am against parliamentarism and the methods of parliamentary struggle, not just because I believe that these distract the people and divert them from more effective methods, inuring them to wait for freedom and well-being as a result of the work of the rulers; but also, and especially, because acceptance of this system and these methods logically implies, and psychologically produces, recognition of the principle of government, law, authority, which is the major antagonist to freedom and progress.

The ideal of the anarchists is the creation of a society as fully as possible founded on free agreement of free wills, with the exclusion of any command and any violence; and he who has these ideas would be inconsistent, immoral, and traitorous, should he usurp, solicit, or accept an office with the purpose of making laws and imposing them upon those who resist.

Motives of possible short-lived utility are worthless before the question of principle, which endures and remains.

Personally, I know well that I could, as I am told, be of much more use to the propaganda of my ideas if I were free in Italy; but would beginning to renounce one's own ideas not be a strange way of being of use to them?

---

1   The date given is the date of the second edition, from which the article, sequestered by the censors, had been removed. We accessed the article as a clipping and could not ascertain whether the date of the first edition was the same or came before.

I hope there will not be a single anarchist who allows himself to be dragged to the ballot box, either due to personal sympathies, or due to petty calculations of short-lived opportunity, or for reasons less confessable. At any rate I declare that those who would vote for me would be abusing my name and would cause me gratuitous insult.

Please publish this should you find it useful,

yours truly
ERRICO MALATESTA

Again the Merlino Supporters of Rome

Translated from "Sempre i Merliniani di Roma," *Combattiamo!* (Genoa) 2, new series, no. 21 (June 9, 1900)

Dearest comrades

I saw your note "Merlino and the Merlino supporters of Rome" in *Combattiamo!* of the 27th.[2]

Just yesterday I wrote to *L'Agitazione* of Ancona protesting how the so-called anarchists have used my name.[3]

I remain a staunch anti-parliamentarist and do not consider anyone who yields on the question of parliamentarism to be an anarchist.

Warmest regards

Errico Malatesta

London, May 30, 1900

---

2   The note dated May 27th reads: "*Il Secolo* announces a letter from attorney S. Merlino to Italian anarchists, in which he urges them to rush to the ballot box. We also learn from *Avanti* that during a meeting in Rome several anarchists (?) considered abandoning abstentionism and supporting extreme candidates, or supporting the candidacy of one of our own (speaking of Malatesta)." After having expressed disapproval, the note concluded: "As regards the candidacy of Malatesta—if it is true—we hope to soon hear our dear comrade let the whip hiss on the backs of these latest merchants of anarchy. He will certainly do so."

3   From the published versions, the date of the two letters to *L'Agitazione* and *Combattiamo!* appear to be the same.

Answer to Merlino

Freedom (London) 14, no. 150 (August 1900)

Originally published as "Réponse a Merlino," *Les Temps Nouveaux* (Paris) 6, no. 7 (June 9–15, 1900)

MY DEAR GRAVE,

The political elections are about to take place in Italy, and our old comrade, Merlino, has had the absurd idea to publish a "Letter to Anarchists," in which he invites them to enter the political (say: electoral) struggle[4] and to propose my candidature.[5]

I learn now that several French journals, when mentioning this matter, inquire whether I intend to "take the leap."

I beg you to announce that I reject all responsibility for Merlino's use of my name; I remain an Anarchist as always, and I consider as an unmerited outrage, the simple doubt that I could wish to enter the parliamentary arena.

As to the Italian anarchists, they know well at what value to appraise Merlino's attempt.

Cordially yours,
ERRICO MALATESTA.

Sorrow in London

Daily Express (London), no. 85 (July 31, 1900)

ITALIANS WITH US MOURN A "GOOD MAN."
MURDERED BY THE INTERNATIONAL LEAGUE.[6]

. . .

---

4   The original English text reads "lists." The correction is based on the French text.
5   Merlino's open letter to the anarchists originally appeared in the republican newspaper *L'Italia Nuova* of Rome on May 22nd. *Les Temps Nouveaux* published a translation by Nino Samaja, followed by his comment and Malatesta's response translated here.
6   The reference is to an alleged "International League of Anarchists." In another part of the newspaper, a report states that the September 1898 murder of Empress Elizabeth of Austria by Luigi Luccheni was decided during a meeting of this league, held in Zurich the previous July 25th, and that two Italians who intended to kill the monarchs of Romania were arrested in Budapest on September 29th of the same year, carrying a letter of instructions from the league.

Has Bressi[7] Been in London?

Was the murderer ever in London?

There was an Angelo Bressi here in June 1896, the revolutionary Italians say, and they think he is the same man.

A representative of the "Express," who inquired into the matter last night, was told that Bressi was frequently at the office of "The Torch of Anarchy," in Somers Town, and that he has been seen, not very long ago, at an anarchist restaurant in Saffron-hill.

But is he the same man?

The question was put to Malatesta, a waiter, who distinguished himself while in Italy by escaping from "domicilio-coatto."[8]

"I am not sure," replied Malatesta. "I cannot say, but I think—yes, I think he is the man. He never talked but of course he could not talk much; he did not know English. He was a man, and he will die a man, happy that like a wolf he has bitten before he has died."

. . .

Journal Man Finds Malatesta in London

New York Journal, no. 6469 (August 3, 1900)

(Copyright, 1900, by W. R. Hearst.)

LONDON, Aug. 2.—The Journal correspondent has found Count Enrico Malatesta, the mysterious leader of Anarchists, who comes into public notice when Kings are killed.

Malatesta is in London, living over a small shop in Islington, kept by Mrs. Emilie Defendi.

He came here three weeks ago from the United States on the steamship St. Paul.

He claims to have been in London every day since his arrival on this side.

"How did you find me?" was his first question.

He was told that his address had been cabled from New York by the Journal, which had received it from a sympathizer with the cause of Anarchy.

"I want no sympathy," he exclaimed, vehemently. "Let people mind their own business."

---

7   In the English-language press, particularly in the first few days after the attack, Bresci's name was mangled in several ways, including *Bressi* and *Brasci*.

8   *Domicilio coatto* means "forced residence," a preventive policy under which citizens could be forced to live in specific places, most often remote islands in the Mediterranean Sea.

Malatesta said he was working at his trade as an engineer. He has no shop, but says he goes out to work by the day.

"I am going out now," he said. "I don't want to talk. When I have something to say I will write it."

"Is it true that you are a friend of Gaetano Brasci and have expressed admiration for his work?"

"No, no! I do not know Brasci. All these statements are lies."

Brasci acknowledged after his arrest that he was a friend of Malatesta.

"I go to no Anarchist clubs now," continued Malatesta. "I have nothing to do with them. I work for my living. Let people leave me alone."

Malatesta was joined by a swarthy man with deepset eyes and pointed beard, a typical Italian.

Malatesta would not talk further. He and his friend left the house together.

At Malatesta's House.
How He Met Bresci in Paterson

Translated from "Chez Malatesta. Comment il connut Bresci a Paterson,"
Le Soir **(Paris) 33, no. 11246 (August 5, 1900)**

INTERVIEW WITH THE FAMOUS ANARCHIST —THE MONZA ATTACK —
NEITHER HIS FOLLOWER, NOR HIS ACCOMPLICE —STEP BY STEP
—IN LONDON

London, August 4.—*From our special correspondent.*—Most English newspapers insist upon making Enrico Malatesta an accomplice of King Humbert's assassin.

We went to the home of the famous Italian anarchist, who welcomed us courteously, with a smile on his lips, rather unconcerned by the rumors the newspapers are spreading about him.

— I met Bresci, in Paterson, just as I met all of the militant anarchists who live in large numbers in that city. I do not need to tell you I knew nothing about his plans. The attack surprised me, as it surprised everyone, but it did not sadden me.

Humbert owes his sad ending to the hatred that his reactionary politics accumulated: we recall the massacres in Milan and the incessant persecution of revolutionaries. Moreover, he demonstrated unprecedented cruelty towards Passanante, who made an attempt on his life twenty-two years ago. Since then, Passanante suffers in a dark cell and, despite the numerous requests for mercy made on his behalf in recent times, the king has always ruthlessly refused to restore this living cadaver to light and life.

We ask Malatesta what, in his opinion, will be the likely consequences of Bresci's act. Our interlocutor appears rather evasive; according to him, revolutions break out when they are least expected.

As regards the rumors that have been going around, attributing more or less actual complicity to Malatesta in Bresci's attack, the famous Italian revolutionary scoffs: "Police chatter and nonsense!" he tells us.

A Propagandist

We were interested in asking Malatesta for details on the life he has been living these past few months; especially since he has carried out his revolutionary activity a little bit in every country.

Returning to Italy about three years ago, Malatesta remained hidden for several months in Ancona, where, under his inspiration, *L'Agitazione* was published. He left his retreat during the hunger riots that happened a few weeks prior to the Milan massacres.[9]

Arrested, he was sent into *forced residence*, from which, two years ago, he managed to escape and reach London, where he began to work as a mechanic.

Called to America by his coreligionists to do a propaganda tour, he went and successfully gave a large number of lectures in cities of the Northeast and Florida. He finally settled down in Paterson, where his Italian comrades appointed him to direct *La Questione Sociale*. That was when he met Bresci, whom he praises.

From Paterson, Malatesta went to Cuba, where he performed propaganda activities, particularly in the provinces of Matanza, Havana, and Pinar del Rio. He left behind there, as he tells us, a powerful anarchist organization, whose mouthpiece is the Havana-based *Nuevo Ideal*.

From Cuba, he returned to London and set up, near his friend Defendi, a small workshop where he builds electric lamps, the patent for which an American inventor friend gave to him to use in England.

And that is where we found him, striking an anvil to make his living, something that does not at all slow down his activity as a propagandist.

British Royalty Immune, Anarchist Leaders Order

New York Journal, no. 6471 (August 5, 1900)

LONDON, Aug. 4—No arrests or special efforts regarding Anarchists in England apparently have been made by the police, though London is quite full of them now, as England is a safe refuge. The Journal correspondent conveyed to the officials at Scotland Yard the address of and information about Malatesta, but the

---

9   Actually, Malatesta's hiding ended on November 12, 1897, over two months before the bread riots in Ancona, which in turn preceded the Milan events by nearly four months.

detectives are not inclined to take seriously the presence of many known Anarchists.

This is because no Anarchist outrages have been perpetrated in England by common agreement among the Red societies. They know England is their only haven in Europe, and any attacks here would rouse vigorous prosecution and drive them out, leaving them no place to go to.

Inviolability for the English royal family has been strictly ordered by the older leaders of the Anarchists for many years. Sipido's attempt on the life of the Prince of Wales at Brussels is disowned by the Anarchists.[10]

The Journal correspondent saw Malatesta again to-day. He is cool and indifferent, and said the police had not bothered him. He grew angry when denouncing the stories printed about him in London, and declared he did not know Brasci or anything about the plot.

. . .

Sharp Eyes on Malatesta

The Sun (New York) 67, no. 339 (August 5, 1900)

ANARCHIST LEADER CONSTANTLY SHADOWED BY
LONDON DETECTIVES
HE PROTESTS THAT HE DOES NOT KNOW THE ASSASSIN OF KING
HUMBERT—SAYS HE IS WORKING AS A GAS ENGINEER, BUT KEEPS UNUSUAL
HOURS—LIVING IN A SUBURB OF LONDON.

Special Cable Despatch to THE SUN

LONDON, Aug. 4.—"It is supposed that Malatesta is now in London," says a cable despatch from New York published in the London newspapers this morning. As a matter of fact, Malatesta came here three weeks ago and is now living in Islington, a modern suburb, over a small grocery shop, kept by an Italian woman with whom the anarchist chief is on intimate terms. Malatesta was shadowed from the moment he landed at Southampton by Chief of the Scotland Yard Police Melville's men until he reached his lodgings. The detectives were too obtrusive in watching the Islington house, with the result that Malatesta soon discovered their presence and in consequence has behaved with the greatest circumspection. He realizes that he must be careful, for neither the British Government nor the British people are just now in a mood for stretching the

---

10   In April 1900, in a Brussels train station, fifteen-year-old Belgian Jean-Baptiste Sipido shot, without hitting, the future Edward VII, considering him responsible for the massacres of the Anglo-Boer war. At trial, Sipido was acquitted due to his young age.

law as an asylum in favor of anarchists. He says he is working at the trade of a gas engineer.

When a SUN reporter called at his lodgings to-day, it was explained by the landlady that Malatesta had left early in the morning to do some work in response to a post card. He expected to be back shortly after noon, and then be at work again until late at night. From inquiries made, that appeared to be Malatesta's usual daily programme—up early, rest during the middle of the day, absent late at night—which scarcely describes the habits of a workingman in this country. At 1 o'clock, THE SUN reporter found the man at dinner.

"I do not wish to say anything," he replied to a pointed question. "I have nothing to say, and if I had I could write it myself."

"Yes," chimed in the woman, "Malatesta is a good writer and he does not want to talk to these newspaper men."

The reporter suggested that perhaps he would like to put himself right with the British public in view of the fact that statements had been made in the London press that he knew Bresci and approved of the murder of King Humbert. The woman again took up the conversation saying:

"Malatesta has not been interviewed and does not want to be interviewed. A detective has been here and told him that if he has not made such statements, he ought to prosecute the writer. If Malatesta were my husband I would soon prosecute people who wrote that way."

Here Malatesta managed to get in a word

"I tell you what was printed was a lot of lies. I have not talked to anybody. Do you take me for a great jackass?"

"But," said the reporter, "It was categorically asserted that last Monday you were working as a waiter in a certain restaurant, and in the presence of a number of Anarchists and others, expressed knowledge and admiration of Bresci."

"It is all lies," shrieked Malatesta, "I never was in such a place. I am not a waiter. I do not know this man Bresci, and let me tell you, and others like you, and the police likewise, who are following me about, that this country is not Italy. I have done nothing against the laws of this country, and those laws will protect me as long as I behave myself here."

Malatesta is quite right. Melville's men have not the shadow of doubt that Malatesta was concerned in the murders, both of King Humbert and of the Empress of Austria, but he is extraordinarily clever and until he undertakes some crime with his own hands, he is not likely to get caught in the meshes of the law. Melville regards him as the cleverest man ever in an Anarchist conspiracy. For the present he considers himself indispensable to the movement, but sooner or later the detectives believe, he will kill somebody on his own account. Melville's men will not lose sight of him as long as he is here.

Malatesta, through the World, Defines Anarchist Creed

The World (New York) 41, no. 14229 (August 5, 1900)

ANARCHIST ARCH PLOTTER DENIES THERE WAS A CONSPIRACY TO KILL
KING HUMBERT.
TYRANTS LIKE THE GERMAN EMPEROR, LIKE CHAMBERLAIN IN ENGLAND,
HE SAYS, MAKE MEN ASSASSINS, AND WHAT WONDER
THE OPPRESSED STRIKE!

(Copyright, 1900, by the Press Publishing Company, New York World.)
(Special Cable Despatch to The World.)

LONDON, Aug. 4—Count Enrico Malatesta, the reputed friend of Bresci, and himself the arch-Anarchist and chief of the king-killers, made his first detailed statement since King Humbert was assassinated to the London correspondent of The World to-night. He said:

What is it you wish to know? I can tell you but little. It is true that our silence may cause your American police to plan repressive measures, but that is an affair of the police and does not concern us. Those who want to know our principles can easily learn them in your country. There are plenty of ways of getting at the truth.

I know nothing, nothing, about Bresci.

I do not know of any organization that planned the assassination of King Humbert.

That, if you will excuse my saying so, is a ridiculous suggestion. Rebellions against royal heads are not instigated in that manner. One society cannot essay to send a man to accomplish such a deed. It is not done in that way. We are not the instigators of individual rebellion. It is the Emperor of Germany who foments the rancor when he talks "No quarter," "no prisoners."[11] It is Chamberlain, the man of England, who is responsible when he knowingly plans the robbing of little nations of their freedom. They are the instigators. It is they who help the arm that does the deed. It is they who place the weapon in the assassin's hand.[12]

Tyrants Make Men Assassins.

Those are the men who make individual rebels, and who have made them in all ages. It has always been the same where tyranny has ruled. Men of old fought

---

11   The reference is to the speech given on July 27, 1900, by the German emperor to the troops that were departing to suppress the Boxer rebellion in China.

12   The article is accompanied by an inset entitled "Emperor William and Chamberlain responsible," where these sentences about William II and Chamberlain are repeated and highlighted.

against tyranny and strived to overthrow the tyrants. These men have sometimes been called republicans, sometimes Anarchists.

Have we not had some cause in Italy for rising? Look at our suffering. Consider the hunger that has been ours. Our women have gone to the hills to gather grass. The necessities of life are taxed until they have become to us luxuries. Even salt is made too dear for the poor. It has now become a luxury to eat salt! Think of it!

What wonder that one man strikes?

You ask us what we want. We want to expel government by revolutionary means. We want to expropriate the holders of social wealth. We would have all this world, all that it contains of good or evil, shared in equal measure by the great and the small.

Declares Revolution Will Come.

I tell you that a revolutionary attempt will come, and come surely. It may not succeed from the beginning, but we cannot help that. If to-day we fail without lowering our colors, victory will come to-morrow.[13] Triumph will be ours in the end.

Of Bresci I know nothing.

I will not say how much I know of all the plans and conspiracies concerning which the papers have said so much.

You can dismiss them all. The world will see what is coming, and must wait until then. Believe me when I say that the blows struck against kings are not planned by societies. They are not designed by conspirators. Planning and conspiring do not enter into it. They are the protests of individuals. They are the individual expressions of men striving to right a wrong.

Adieu, sir. I regret that I cannot tell you more.

Is a Fat Anarchist.

And polite and smiling Count Malatesta bowed himself into a little room behind the shop in which he had received The World correspondent.

Count Malatesta is about fifty years old. While he talked an opportunity was given to study the man. The past few years have wrought a great change in this strange character. He is of middle height, his forehead seamed with creases, eyes deep set and skin a swarthy olive. He does not bear out the characteristics of the typical Anarchist. He is fat, and bears evidence of prosperity despite the plainness of his attire.

When the secret police first knew him as an Anarchist leader several years ago he was thin and cadaverous-looking, ill-dressed and sullen. To-day he was dressed as a workman in blue serge clothes, far from new, and wore a shiny hat.

He has taken up quarters in a little shop in North London where oil, wines and fancy goods are sold. It is in a district where the Anarchist propaganda of

---

13   This quote repeats, almost word-for-word, the final sentence of the pamphlet *Anarchy.*

five nations are issued. It is for the purpose of renewing activity among the union workers of London that he has taken up headquarters here. He has been here but little more than nine months.

A beautiful signora waited on customers in the little shop while not engaged in hushing the cries of a baby at her breast or chatting with Count Malatesta. She regarded the visitor suspiciously and showed her sympathy with the Anarchist leader by demanding:

"Why does he need to be interviewed? He can write beautifully."

"And I shall not be interviewed, as I object to interviews on principle." Count Malatesta broke in pleasantly, although the next moment he belied his words as he warmed to his subject.

Malatesta on Anarchy

Daily Express (London), no. 90 (August 6, 1900)

HE TRACES THE MURDER TO THE BREAD RIOTS.

"Express" Special.

Last night, writes a representative of the "Express," I had an interview with Malatesta at his home in Islington for the space of some two hours.

Malatesta is a short, strongly-built man, of some forty-five years, with a broad, intellectual forehead, and keen, deeply-set eyes. He is dark, with just a touch of grey in his hair and Vandyke beard. The point which strikes the stranger is the grave and punctilious politeness of his manner.

He was sitting with half a dozen friends, to whom from time to time he appealed as some phrase I used puzzled him.

"I do not like the English newspapers," was his reply, when asked for an interview. "I am an engineer. I work, and I mind my own business. All that has been said about me and my friends—all is untrue."

"And this story from America that you have organized twenty-seven anarchists to wage war on the crowned heads of Europe?"[14]

"It is untrue. You, my friend, know something of the movement. You know something of the comrades. If I said to an Anarchist, 'Kill this King,' what would he say? Why, 'Kill him yourself.'

---

14   The news appeared in the *New York Herald* August 3rd and immediately traveled around the world. The article in the *Herald* began with: "Twenty-seven anarchists, dominated by a leader grown gray in plotting against social order, sailed from this port within the last few weeks, pledged, the secret service agents say, to destroy the rulers of the world. A plan so far reaching as this is said to have been evolved in Paterson, N.J., where count Nicola Malatesta has until recently made his home and directed the followers of a cult founded on social disorder." The article continued stating that the twenty-seven anarchists were heading for Paris.

Weather Forecast: FAIR.

The Entire Field of Business is covered by Sunday World Wants. If you want to buy or sell, trade or exchange, hire or work, use Sunday World Wants and reap the reward of good judgment.

"Circulation Books Open to All."

The World.

"Circulation Books Open to All."

Weather Forecast: FAIR.

The Kind of Help That Helps is the Help you get in getting Help when Sunday World Wants are used. You may have too many applicants, but you are sure to have enough.

VOL. XLI. NO. 14,629.　PRICE FIVE CENTS.　NEW YORK, SUNDAY, AUGUST 5, 1900.　Copyrighted, 1900, by The Press Publishing Company, New York World.　50 PAGES.　PRICE FIVE CENTS.

MALATESTA, THROUGH THE WORLD, DEFINES ANARCHIST CREED; TERESA BRUGNOLI SAYS "BRESCI OFFERED HIS LIFE FOR FREEDOM."

COUNT MALATESTA.

"LA BELLE TERESA" BRUGNOLI, THE FAIR ANARCHIST.

EMPEROR WILLIAM AND CHAMBERLAIN RESPONSIBLE.

MALATESTA SAYS: "It is the Emperor of Germany who foments the rancor when he talks 'No quarter,' 'No prisoners.' It is Chamberlain, the man of England, who is responsible, when he knowingly plans the robbing of little nations of their freedom. They are the instigators. It is they who help the arm that does the deed. It is they who place the weapon in the assassin's hand."

Anarchist Arch Plotter Denies There Was a Conspiracy to Kill King Humbert.

Tyrants Like the German Emperor, Like Chamberlain in England, He Says, Make Men Assassins, and What Wonder the Oppressed Strike!

BATTLE IN CHINA EXPECTED NEAR TIENTSIN TO-DAY.

30,000 Boxers, in Position of Their Own Choosing, Have Flooded Route of March and Await the Allies...

AMERICANS, BRITISH AND JAPANESE LEAD.

Russian and French Troops Are Guarding the Base of Communications with the Base of Supplies, While Others Push on to Peking.

LI HUNG CHANG A SUICIDE, SHANGHAI RUMOR SAYS.

MINISTER WU HEARS FOREIGNERS ARE ADVANCING ON PEKING.

"LA BELLA TERESA" SHIELDS BRESCI, DEFIES POLICE WILES.

Beautiful Woman Anarchist Makes Her First Public Statement to a World Correspondent in Her Cell in Milan Prison—"Bresci Offered His Life for Freedom; I Can Tell You Nothing"—Mme. Brugnoli's Life in New York.

"We Anarchists have no chief, and we have no executive committee. We are not children: we do not cast lots.[15] They say there are many Italians coming from America. Yes, there are many coming to see the Exposition.[16] But are they come to kill kings? Well, it may be; but I think they will kill more chickens than kings.[17]

Bresci Was Modest.

"Yes, I knew Bresci. He was modest and quiet, and I did not think him capable of such a deed. He came from America to see his people, and, no doubt, the miserable condition he saw them in excited him. To one coming home from America this condition would be striking. Bresci was a good comrade. He lived in Paterson, and his wife and child lived in West Hoboken. He went to see them from Saturday to Monday every week.

"I do not say I approve of this removal, but I do not shed tears, and I do not blame Bresci. Government is force, and it is right to meet force by force. But the aim of Anarchism is to educate the people, to persuade them to become free men, and to rid themselves of the kings and the bourgeoisie.

"This King who is dead—do you recollect the bread riots in Milan two years ago? The crops had failed in Italy, and all corn coming into that country must pay 8fr. per 100 kilos (about 2cwt.);[18] and then, again, before it goes into a town it pays again from 3fr. to 5fr.

"The people who were starving went and cried for cheaper bread, and the soldiers fired and killed hundreds of people—old men, women, and children, unarmed, hungry, wretches, not Anarchists. They arrested hundreds more and tried them by martial law, and those acquitted were few. You could count them on one hand.

"The bourgeoisie crowded the balconies and cried to the soldiers, 'Shoot straight and shoot strong.' You say the good King was not responsible, but General Bava Beccaris,[19] he said, 'What can I do? The King has telegraphed me his orders, and I must obey.'

"Well, a man of the people, he has come, and he has shot straight, and he has shot strong."

---

15   After Bresci's attack, a theory made the rounds in the global press that the physical perpetrator had been randomly chosen by a committee of conspirators.

16   Between April and November 1899, the Universal Exposition was held in Paris, attracting about fifty million visitors.

17   After being bounced from newspaper to newspaper and mangled in the process, this sentence landed in the *New York World*, which on August 26th entitled its version of the interview: "I would rather kill chickens than kings." In the text of the "interview" Malatesta thus develops the concept: "Chickens are good to eat. But a king, of what use is he?" It is worth recalling that these were the years of "yellow journalism," the sensationalist press represented mainly by Joseph Pulitzer's *New York World* and William Randolph Hearst's *New York Journal*, who fought a dogged circulation war with riveting news.

18   "Cwt" is an abbreviation for "hundredweight," a British unit of measurement equal to 112 pounds, or a little over 50 kilograms.

19   In the original, written as "Bana Baccasio."

Malatesta's Threat

Daily Express (London), no. 91 (August 7, 1900)

"TRY TO CRUSH US AND WE REVOLT."

"Express" Special.

Malatesta, living in peace at Islington, free to breathe all the fire and thunder he likes, so long as it is only talk, says that as soon as we try to crush the propaganda there will be revolt. "And the more persecution, the more acts of revolt."

"Recollect," he said to a representative of the "Express," "your Governments teach us one thing by words, but another by their acts. Those who denounce the Anarchists because occasionally they shed blood, what have they to say when the German Emperor cries, No quarter to the Chinese; when Salisbury says the Boers shall be finished; and when Chamberlain cries, No liberty to any but ourselves? The Chinese and the Boers fight only for what is theirs. What right has anyone to crush them?

"The papers and the police, they amuse me. You tell me of twenty-seven Anarchists coming from America to eat you. Whoever heard of them before Humbert was killed? Your papers and your police are no good. When the thing is done they know all, but never do they know anything before.

"I have a message to those who rebuke us for killing a King. Under the system we shall bring about Kings will be happier than they are now. They shall work, and they shall be honest men. And if in his desire to hasten the Social Revolution an Anarchist has taken a life, he would take his own for the same end.

"We will not be crushed. Anarchism cannot be stopped. Its progress may be slow, but it always moves. But if you wish to prevent these actions you weep over, ameliorate the conditions of the workers. Give them liberty and give them hope."

Malatesta's Contradictions

Translated from "Le contraddizioni di Malatesta," *Don Marzio* (Naples) 10, no. 219 (August 8–9, 1900)

LONDON 8—*The Daily Chronicle, Central News* and other English newspapers point out the contradictions into which Malatesta has fallen these past few days.

When news of the king's assassination first broke, he flatly denied having known Bresci.

After a few days he admitted to having met him but denied having provoked him to commit the crime. However, he also added that if he had found out in time, he would not have had the heart to discourage him, because anarchy, to reach its ideal, does not only need theoretical propaganda, but also good practical examples.

And the example of Bresci, Malatesta added, will have consequences far greater than what is generally believed.

Here we are convinced that the return of Malatesta to Islington and of many Italian anarchists from the United States is above all else due to the fact that the anarchist camp hoped that the King's assassination would be followed by a revolution. It is also probable that the anarchist leaders had planned a few revolts, which did not take place for reasons independent of their will.

Malatesta Boasts

Daily Express (London), no. 94 (August 10, 1900)

DETECTIVES CAN BE BOUGHT HE DECLARES.

"Express" Special.

Malatesta laughs at the "Tribune," and its assertion that he is the leader of the conspiracy to kill kings.

"The 'Tribune,'" he said to an "Express" representative, "is simply the organ of the police. They say just what the police tell them to say. The Italian police say they have discovered a plot, and that I am the chief of it. That is the way of the Italian police. We are all chiefs when they want us.

"Then these bourgeois ministers. They were all advocates of regicide in their youth. They owe their present position and salaries to regicides. Do you know that the acts of the revolutionists of the fifties, acts just the same as those of Bresci, are to-day celebrated and applauded all over Italy?

"Orsini, who tried to kill Napoleon, his bust is in every town. Agesilao Milano, who inflicted a wound on King Bomba, from which he died. Monti and Tognetti, who tried to blow up a barrack full of soldiers of the Pope, Oberdank, who was hanged for trying to kill the Emperor of Austria, all these men are honoured by these hypocritical bourgeoise for the very same acts for which they torture Bresci.

"Saracco is our best friend.[20] He pays his detectives so small a salary that we can buy them cheaply. A few francs, a handful of cigarettes, and you can buy an Italian detective.

"You can buy all kinds of police. It is the price only you have to think of. The Spanish police are the cheapest to buy, but they are no good when you have bought them. The Italians are the next cheapest, then the Russian, the American, the French, and the English in their order. The Germans are the dearest. That is because they are the most stupid.

---

20   Giuseppe Saracco had become prime minister on June 24th of that same year.

"With all the arrests they have not arrested any real revolutionist. They will keep the men arrested in prison a few months or a few years, and then they will release them.

"We shall shortly establish in Italy economic equality and social brother-hood. And then the whole world will follow the example of Italy."

Some of the Anarchists declare that the Italian Government have sent a number of detectives to London, to watch the Italian colony. "Before long," boasts a German known as The Master, "we shall be inviting them to dinner!"

The Truth about Anarchist Action.
A Talk with Enrico Malatesta
[by F. Banfield]

The King (London) 2, no. 33 (August 18, 1900)

112, High Str. Islington
N. London. 8 Aug. 1900

Dear Sir,

I beg to inform you that I must decline the pleasure of having an interview with you.

Yours truly
E. Malatesta

A letter from Malatesta. He first refused to be interviewed, but nevertheless saw our representative when he called. [21]

**

A good deal of nonsense is written about Anarchists in London. Some people would see Anarchists in any group of Spaniards or Italians of the poorer class. Now there is no such thing as an Anarchist quarter here. The Italians of Saffron Hill are very free from the revolutionary taint. Individual Anarchists may live anywhere. Enrico Malatesta, which is quite an Anarchist name of fame, lodges within five minutes walk of the Angel, at Islington;[22] Louise Michel, on the other hand, resides hard by the Crystal Palace. It is true, certainly, that Charlotte Street, Fitzroy Square, Tottenham Street, Goodge Street, and the whole neighbourhood, are full of foreigners.[23] But after all, the revolutionaries of the district must consti-

---

21   A facsimile edition of the letter reproduced here was published, with this cap-tion, as an illustration accompanying the interview that follows.

22   The Angel is a historical site in Islington that originally owes its name to the Angel Inn, a tavern that existed there in the sixteenth century.

23   The streets mentioned here are all located in a narrow area of London's West End including the Soho and Fitzrovia neighborhoods, which were the areas

tute but a small fraction of its foreign residents, and I doubt if much illumination on the Anarchist problem is to be found in it. At least I sought light elsewhere.

It is some six or seven years since I met Enrico Malatesta for the first time. I had been at Chiswick to visit Stepniak.[24] It was shortly after the Barcelona outrage and the bomb explosion in the French Chamber of Deputies.[25] I asked the Russian exile for information on the subject of Anarchism, and he put me very obligingly on the track of Malatesta. I wrote to 112, High Street, Islington, which was then and has been for some time past the residence of this noted Italian Anarchist, when he is in London. I remember that I was curious to know how and where he became acquainted with Stepniak. His answer was characteristic of the stormy life of the man. "In prison in Italy," said he. "What was Stepniak in prison for?" "For a revolution," said he. "Then, it did not succeed?" "No; if it had succeeded, we should not have been in prison," he replied drily. And now, after six years and more, I was to encounter Malatesta again. There were rumours that he was in America, and I feared I might not find him, and, indeed, there have been times during the last two years when one would have hunted London in vain. For since I first met him he has been again in an Italian prison, and for aught I know more than once. He told me about the last adventure, as he leaned with his back against the counter in the Islington shop. His narrative was more or less as follows: —

He was imprisoned on a charge of being concerned in the Ancona bread riots, and was kept in prison for the space of seven months. Then he was deported to a small island on the Sicilian coast, from which he would seem to have managed to escape. After this escape he went to America, and he said that he came back to London from the States four months ago.

"And what good do Anarchists suppose to have achieved by the killing of the King of Italy?" I asked.

"You should ask Bresci," said he, "not me."

Malatesta drew attention to the repression practised at Milan in connection with the riots. For that he maintained King Humbert was responsible. He spoke of the people shot down by the soldiery, of the violence offered to women and children by the police and the army; all because the people had no bread and

---

with the highest concentrations of Italians and other immigrant colonies. Islington and Crystal Palace are located further out in opposite directions from this area.

24   Sergey Kravchinsky, known as "Stepniak," was a Russian revolutionary who joined Malatesta and Carlo Cafiero in the 1877 Matese expedition. The next year he killed the head of the Russian secret police in Saint Petersburg. A few years later he moved to London, where for years he shared life in exile with Malatesta, until his early death in 1895.

25   The second reference is to the December 9, 1893, attack by Auguste Vaillant, while two attacks had taken place in Barcelona in that same year: on September 24th Paulino Pallás killed two people by throwing a bomb at a military parade, and on November 7th Santiago Salvador threw a bomb in a theater, killing twenty people.

wanted it. "Is it surprising," he asked, "if among so many people who suffered these things one man, driven to desperation, should after two years strike at the man responsible for the suffering?"

"Then," I said, "the cause of the trouble is mainly economical."

He admitted that this was so. As for himself, whether it was the republic or the monarchy it was nearly the same thing. The Government in Italy, he said, supports a system which weighs down the labourers under a great load of misery. "The labourer hasn't an earthly paradise in England," he remarked, "but he is better off than his fellow in Italy. The soldiers and police backed up the Government in maintaining this system of taxation, and so on, while it also had the strong support of about half the *bourgeoisie*, who were able to grow rich under the economic order which was maintained by force. This half of the *bourgeoisie*, as well as the Government, live on the system. It is impossible to change an economic system by argument and peaceful agitation, if you have a Government which shoots down all who wish to change that system. You can only meet violence with violence. But we do not like violence for its own sake. We wish to do away with violence altogether, with government by violence. It is a struggle. We are acting in self-defence. The capitalist has usurped the possession of the means of production, and so is able, with the support of the law, backed up by police and soldiers, to rob the workman." According to Malatesta it is not astonishing that a man here and there should "act," though Anarchists and Socialists generally do not believe in a resort to force unless there is a chance of success.

As Malatesta knows as much as any man living of the human components of Anarchism, I asked him of what class Anarchists mainly consisted. As I expected, he replied they were mainly working men, but there were a number also of *bourgeoisie* in agreement with them, and even some members of the aristocratic and wealthy classes.

"From eccentricity?" I ventured to suggest.

"From conviction," he rejoined.

He denied strenuously that there was any central or other Anarchist organisation for acts of violence such as the assassination of the King of Italy. There are groups of people holding Anarchist opinions here and there, more or less united for purposes of propaganda. Whatever organisation there is, is for purposes of propaganda—that is to say, I presume, for disseminating Anarchist writings and for indoctrinating the heads of susceptible and discontented workmen and others with the tenets of Anarchism.

Now it appears to me that one does not need to conjure up the phantom of a highly organised secret society to account for the "acts," those particular expressions of individual Anarchist opinion, which have horrified Europe. It is easily to be understood how the propaganda is enough and can accomplish all.

[*The author spends the remainder of the article elaborating the concept introduced in the previous paragraph, without making further references to Malatesta.*]

The Truth About Anarchist Action.

A Talk with Enrico Malatesta.

A GOOD deal of nonsense is written about Anarchists in London. Some people would see Anarchists in any group of Spaniards or Italians of the poorer class. Now there is no such thing as an Anarchist quarter here. The Italians of Saffron Hill are very free from the revolutionary taint. Individual Anarchists may live anywhere. Enrico Malatesta, which is quite an Anarchist name of fame, lodges within five minutes walk of the Angel, at Islington ; Louise Michel, on the other hand, resides hard by the Crystal Palace. It is true, certainly, that Charlotte Street, Fitzroy Square, Tottenham Street, Goodge Street, and the whole neighbourhood, are full of foreigners. But after all, the revolutionaries of the district must constitute but a small fraction of its foreign residents, and I doubt if much illumination on the Anarchist problem is to be found in it. At least I sought light elsewhere.

It is some six or seven years since I met Enrico Maletesta for the first time. I had been at Chiswick to visit Stepniak. It was shortly after the Barcelona outrage and the bomb explosion in the French Chamber of Deputies. I asked the Russian exile for information on the subject of Anarchism, and he put me very obligingly on the track of Malatesta. I wrote to 112, High Street, Islington, which was then and has been for some time past the residence of this noted Italian Anarchist, when he is in London. I remember that I was curious to know how and where he became acquainted with Stepniak. His answer was characteristic of the stormy life of the man. " In prison in Italy," said he. " What was Stepniak in prison for ? " " For a revolution," said he. " Then, it did not succeed ? " " No ; if it had succeeded, we should not have been in prison," he replied drily. And now, after six years and more, I was to encounter Malatesta again. There were rumours that he was in America, and I feared I might not find him, and, indeed, there have been times during the last two years when one would have hunted London in vain. For since I first met him he has been again in an Italian prison, and for aught I know more than once. He told me about the last adventure, as he leaned with his back against the counter in the Islington shop. His narrative was more or less as follows :—

He was imprisoned on a charge of being concerned in the Ancona bread riots, and was kept in prison for the space of seven months. Then he was deported to a small island on the Sicilian coast, from which he would seem to have managed to escape. After this escape he went to America, and he said that he came back to London from the States four months ago.

" And what good do Anarchists suppose to have been achieved by the killing of the King of Italy ? " I asked.

" You should ask Bresci," said he, " not me."

Malatesta drew attention to the repression practised at Milan in connection with the riots. For that he maintained King Humbert was responsible. He spoke of the people shot down by the soldiery, of the violence offered to women and children by the police and the army ; all because the people had no bread and wanted it. " Is it surprising," he asked, " if among so many people who suffered these things one man, driven to desperation, should after two years strike at the man responsible for the suffering ? "

" Then," I said, " the cause of the trouble is mainly economical." ,

He admitted that this was so. As for himself, whether it was the republic or the monarchy it was nearly the same thing. The Government in Italy, he said, support a system which weighs down the labourers under a great load of misery. " The labourer hasn't an earthly paradise in England," he remarked, " but he is better off than his fellow in Italy. The soldiers and police

backed up the Government in maintaining this system of taxation, and so on, while it also had the strong support of about half the *bourgeoisie*, who were able to grow rich under the economic order which was maintained by force. This half of the *bourgeoisie*, as well as the Government,

A LETTER FROM MALATESTA. HE FIRST REFUSED TO BE INTERVIEWED, BUT NEVERTHELESS SAW OUR REPRESENTATIVE WHEN HE CALLED.

live on the system. It is impossible to change an economic system by argument and peaceful agitation, if you have a Government which shoots down all who wish to change that system. You can only meet violence with violence. But we do not like violence for its own sake. We wish to do away with violence altogether, with government by violence. It is a struggle. We are acting in self-defence. The capitalist has usurped the possession of the means of production, and so is able, with the support of the law, backed up by police and soldiers, to rob the workman." According to Malatesta it is not astonishing that a man here and there should " act," though Anarchists and Socialists generally do not believe in a resort to force unless there is a chance of success.

As Malatesta knows as much as any man living of the human components of Anarchism, I asked him of what class Anarchists mainly consisted. As I expected, he replied they were mainly working men, but there were a number also of *bourgeoisie* in agreement with them, and even some members of the aristocratic and wealthy classes.

" From eccentricity ? " I ventured to suggest.

" From conviction," he rejoined.

He denied strenuously that there was any central or other Anarchist organisation for acts of violence such as the assassination of the King of Italy. There are groups of people holding Anarchist opinions here and there, more or less united for purposes of propaganda. Whatever organisation there is, is for purposes of propaganda—that is to say, I presume, for disseminating Anarchist writings and for indoctrinating the heads of susceptible and discontented workmen and others with the tenets of Anarchism. Now it appears to me that one does not need to conjure up the phantom of a highly organised secret society to account for the " acts," those particular expressions of individual Anarchist opinion, which have horrified Europe. It is easily to be understood how the propaganda is enough and can accomplish it all.

Let us take any propagandist who may happen to be earnest, plausible, clever, with the Socialistic and Anarchistic common-places and shibboleths at his fingers' ends. He is moving about among the men in many cities who are

full of bitter discontent with their lot of life. Some of them are young, impressionable, sensitive to tales of the sufferings of others, and here and there with the courage which for a purpose will take life in its hands, and run the heaviest risks of losing it. If your propagandist has an eye for his men, has an instinct for judging correctly the character of the people he meets in his sphere of life, of knowing a likely man for dangerous work when he sees him, he has only to concentrate his gifts of plausible presentation of facts and fancies there, and the thing may be done. Here one and there another starts off on an isolated act of aggressive " defence," or of indignant " chastisement " of one or other head of Government, " which is at war with the worker, robbing, oppressing, torturing him with poverty or with cruel repression." With such a propaganda to start with, and with a crowd of poverty-stricken youth steeped in Atheism, and cursed with just that little knowledge which is a dangerous thing, one can be surprised at nothing that may happen. It is a mistake to suppose that most of the Anarchists have anything in common with the stage ruffian or the cutthroat of melodrama. As far as my experience goes, they appear fairly harmless, quiet people, and, within limits, talk more or less to the point. But they have persuaded themselves that the world could get on without Governments and soldiers and police, that all their miseries and woes are due to the social order maintained by Governments ; and so any Anarchist who starts on a murderous errand against a chief of the State is a hero performing an individual act of war, making his contribution towards the dissolution of a social organisation which they and he hate. It strikes me that under these circumstances the frequency or non-frequency of assassinations will depend very much upon the quality of the Anarchist propagandists of the moment, for the poverty, the half-education, the infidelity of so many of the young men, especially of the Southern race, will tend to provide a field for this peculiar sort of missionary effort, where it will not expend itself unfruitfully. There is the crux of the present situation, and it is one which those whose business it is to look after matters of the sort should ponder seriously.

F. BANFIELD.

THE HOUSE IN WHICH MALATESTA RESIDES, AT 112, HIGH STREET, ISLINGTON. IT IS BEING WATCHED BY THE POLICE NIGHT AND DAY.

Everything and Anything.
A Meeting with the Leader of the
Anarchists: Enrico Malatesta

Originally published as: "Ett och annat. Hos anarkisternasgeneral: Enrico
Malatesta," *Tammerfors Nyheter* (Tampere), no. 127 (August 18, 1900)[26]

ALL MONARCHS SHALL BE ELIMINATED.

A correspondent from London sends a foreign daily paper the following article:

The anarchists in London reside in four large neighborhoods. One is Tottenham Court Road, another is Charlotte street, the third is Charles street and the
fourth, the largest, consists of the streets around Soho Square. There live Germans, French, many Belgians and now many Italians. Most of them are rather
poor workers, but there are also people who are well-to-do, owners of small commercial businesses, store managers, chemists, correspondents, typographers, and
small entrepreneurs. In these neighborhoods, they print anarchist newspapers
that will be smuggled into Russia, Italy, and Spain. Here, moreover, we find most
of the leadership, if it is possible to speak of leadership in a party whose members
do not recognize any authority and have the greatest operating freedom.

As previously mentioned, this anarchist party is comprised principally of
Italians, whose leader is the electrician Enrico Malatesta.

He is a very intelligent man, cultured, with a nonchalant way of speaking.
In the city of Ancona, on the Adriatic coast, he founded the anarchist periodical
L'Agitazione. After the terrible massacres of workers in Milan and in Sicily and
the killing of many women and children by Crispi's soldiers and cops, Malatesta
was arrested and, according to the Italian law on anarchists, sentenced to forced
residence and confined on an island in the Mediterranean. With the help of his
own comrades, he escaped and reached London, to then be called to America to
preach the Anarchist doctrine.

He lived in America for a few years preaching, writing, and making propaganda. Malatesta also founded a Hebrew anarchist periodical together with
Moritz Hertz, in addition to the Hispano-American periodical Nuova Idea
in Cuba.[27] In Paterson, a small city where Bressi lived, he organized the main

---

26   This English version is a translation of the Italian version, translated from
      Swedish by Pierangelo Sassi. We were unable to locate the original source
      of this interview which, as stated, was picked up from a foreign daily paper.
      Unfounded statements as well as atypical phrases put into Malatesta's mouth
      raise doubts concerning the reliability of this article. However, we deemed it
      worthy of publication due to its content being somewhat different from the
      other interviews of the same period.

27   Both pieces of information are unfounded. But while the latter originates from
      the fact that Malatesta was in contact with *Nuevo Ideal* and contributed an
      article to it while he was in Cuba, the report on the Hebrew anarchist periodi-
      cal is entirely incomprehensible.

headquarters of Italian anarchists in America; he subsequently returned to London.

Malatesta personally knew Bressi. When he learned of the assassination of King Humbert he declared that it was an unexpected event but at the same time it did not surprise him. *In fact, the king had been condemned to death since January 1899.*[28]

Now Malatesta has a small workshop on Greek-street in London, where he produces a new type of electric lamp for which a patent was issued to him for England. During the day he works in the workshop, while during the evening and night he is a writer, speaker, leader, and anarchist general. When he is asked about the assassination of Humbert he states:

"It is the response to the slaughter of workers in Milan and in Sicily performed by Humbert, the assassin and reactionary tyrant. Eye for an eye, tooth for a tooth.

"I met Bressi, but I did not know of his plans. We did not speak of these things. We preach hatred, and so do the people in whom this seed takes root. Everything that we anarchists do surely does not depend upon anyone's orders since we do not obey anyone. These actions are the practical demonstration of the strength of our political faith and of the depth of hatred towards the present and hope for the future.

"They say that Humbert had been a good king. Think of the thousands of starving people he had butchered by that scoundrel Crispi. They say that was the fault and responsibility of Crispi. But then what of poor Passanante?

"Passanante was the one who sought to assassinate the king upon his ascent to the throne, 22 years ago.[29] He was locked up in that horrible prison for 22 years, with his hands and feet bound. The king was asked for mercy several times. The answer was always 'no.' Is it not wicked to leave a man to rot in such a prison? What is Humbert's death as compared to the indescribable suffering Passanante has endured for 22 years?

"Now I believe—says Malatesta—that rumor has it that 27 Italian anarchists are aboard the French steamer Gascogne heading from America to Europe to assassinate all European monarchs and I heard that Bressi declared from his cell that within two months there will no longer be kings nor emperors in Europe. I repeat that I do not know if these 27 have really arrived and if they truly intend to assassinate all European monarchs, *since among us each does as he pleases. Apart from that it is an adventure story.* But if this were to happen it would not surprise me. *Because the new century shall begin in blood.* Much blood has been spilled in the struggles between the people and their oppressors since ancient times. It is time to avenge this innocent blood."

---

28   This reference is also uncertain, given that Bresci's motivation is generally traced back to the 1898 bread riots.

29   Giovanni Passannante attacked Humbert I on November 17, 1878, in Naples.

That which Enrico Malatesta, the leading spokesman of the anarchists, said here, he has also said to every foreign correspondent who was sent by his newspaper to speak with him. It seems that he believes the near future will be bloody and terrible, and the fact that he does not want to come out with it and admit that a large conspiracy is underway, of which he is in charge and upon which he is currently working, is surely attributable to his fear that this would entail his deportation from England.

A Statement by E. Malatesta

Translated from "Una dichiarazione di E. Malatesta," *Avanti!* (Rome) 4, no. 1327 (August 23, 1900)

We receive by postcard:

London, August 19, 1900.

Honorable Mr. Editor,
I would be most grateful, and it would be of use to the truth's cause, if you could warn the public to not believe anything that is being said these days about me, and anything I am presumed to have said in interviews, either completely invented, or oddly misinterpreted.

Yours faithfully ERRICO MALATESTA.
112, High Str. Islington N.

A Letter from E. Malatesta

Translated from "Una lettera di E. Malatesta," *Il Secolo* (Milan) 35, no. 12334 (August 23–24, 1900)

We receive the following letter:

London, August 19, 1900.

Honorable Mr. Editor,
Considering the crudely obvious falsehood of the news spread these days about me, I believed it was superfluous to protest.

But since this matter shows no signs of ending, and it comes to a real orgy of lies and nonsense to which the press has abandoned itself, perhaps it is not useless to warn the public to not believe anything that is being said about me, and especially anything I am presumed to have said in interviews, either completely fictional or oddly misinterpreted.

For this, I appeal to your fairness, as your good faith has certainly been overtaken.[30]

Yours faithfully ERRICO MALATESTA.

With Malatesta.
Has Italy Demanded His Expulsion

Daily Express (London), no. 109 (August 28, 1900)

There was a rumour abroad last night that Malatesta, the Anarchist, was to be expelled from England.

Three smart distinct taps at the closed door of the Defendi wine-shop in High-street, Islington, last night brought the now easily-identified face to the doorway.

Evidently somebody else was expected.

"Has any communication been made that the Italian Government demands your expulsion from England?"

"Nothing beyond a newspaper report."

"Would the fact surprise you?"

"Not in the least. A similar application was made when I took refuge in Switzerland."[31]

"And the result?"

"The Federal Tribunal maintained that it had no cause of complaint against me. I had broken no law, and it knew that the Italian police follow their own way; they do just what they please."

"And supposing the request were enforced?"

"I have no fear: I know nothing."

"But is there no system in Italy, as in Spain, to compel the unwilling to speak?"

"Not that I know of; and even then —" There was a significant shrug of the shoulders.

"Then you anticipate no trouble here?"

"None whatever. Do I not work at my trade of electrical engineer?"

. . .

---

30 *Il Secolo* had published excerpts from interviews published abroad, including the interviews from the *New York Journal* of August 3rd and *Le Soir* of August 5th.

31 This incident took place in 1891, when Malatesta, returning from a clandestine trip to Italy, was arrested and jailed in Switzerland for violating a previous expulsion order.

Malatesta Safe in England

The Omaha Daily Bee (Omaha, Nebraska), August 28, 1900[32]

HEAD CENTER OF ITALIAN ANARCHIST PROPAGANDA IS NOT LIKELY TO BE EXPELLED FROM LONDON.[33]

(Copyright, 1900, by Press Publishing Co.)

LONDON, Aug. 27.—(New York World Cablegram—Special Telegram.)—The statement which reached here from Rome that the Italian government had demanded from the British government the expulsion of Anarchist Malatesta from England receives no credence. Malatesta, when seen tonight, said: "I do not believe any such request has been made, first because the Swiss government was approached by the Italian police when I resided in Geneva, but wisely refused to do anything in the matter."

"But," I said, "suppose you are warned to leave England within twenty-four hours, where could you go?"

Malatesta replied: "I cannot suppose anything of the kind. I have committed no crime in England. I get my living as an electrical engineer. If such an order is given me by the police I should go to America."[34]

. . .

---

32 The same interview appeared simultaneously in various other US newspapers, for example in the *Seattle Daily Times* of Washington state, in the *Kansas City Star* of Missouri, in the *Grand Forks Daily Herald* of North Dakota and, the next day, in the *Los Angeles Times* of California.

33 The term "head center" originally referred to the most senior officer of the Fenian Brotherhood, the Irish separatist organization.

34 This interview is very similar to the one in the *Daily Express* from the same day, with a few differences. Although it may be a rehash of the previous interview, the possibility that Malatesta was contacted by some other London correspondent cannot be excluded.

[Untitled]

Translated from *Cause ed Effetti. 1898–1900* (London),
single issue (September 1900)[35]

Because an anarchist killed a king, the storm has been unleashed, more intensely than at other times, upon our head.

The governments manically hound us, and develop cruel, as well as vain, plans to radically suppress anarchists and their idea. The bribed or spontaneously servile press slanders us as people, and slanders our ideals in the most grotesque manner. And not just the monarchist and bourgeois press; but also the republican press, which even has the habit, when there is no longer any danger, of paying tribute to the "avenging sword that slaughters the despots"; and also a good part of the socialist press, which, in a cowardly impetus of foolish fear, makes acrobatic efforts to deny any relationship with us, any moral and intellectual link between Socialism and Anarchism, which are just two aspects of the same problem, of the same ideal of human redemption. And some of our own comrades—overly upset by the displays of public opinion artificially constructed by the thousand voices available to privilege and sustained by the condemnation that rains down upon he who dares to express a thought less-than-faithful to the monarchy—find themselves uncertain, almost fearing that the gunshot that claimed Humbert of Savoy as its victim, had gone on to wound the heart of the ideal for which the assailant intended to sacrifice his life.

Facing such a situation, those who publish this paper intend to reaffirm their ideals, claim the share of moral responsibility that may pertain to them in the daily struggle between oppressed and oppressors and in its sad episodes, and show that they remain at their battle positions, more than ever full of trust in the definitive triumph of justice over inequality, of freedom over tyranny, of peace and love over the war and hatred that now tear apart the human race.

---

35   This single issue, whose masthead was followed by the words "Published by an Anarchist-Socialist group," intended to provide an anarchist perspective on Bresci's killing of Humbert I, which occurred in Monza on July 29, 1900. The key to understanding the title ("Causes and effects") is provided by the date range that follows it. 1898 was the year when bread riots were bloodily repressed by General Bava Beccaris under the orders of Humbert I. Hundreds of workers were killed in Milan, and a few weeks later, King Humbert decorated the general for his services rendered "to institutions and civilization." This was the "cause." Bresci's bullets, which were intended to avenge the Milan bloodshed and took the king's life in 1900, were the "effect."

What Is Anarchy

Translated from "Che cosa é l'anarchia," *Cause ed Effetti. 1898–1900* (London),
single issue (September 1900)

Three adverse powers always battle against any new doctrine that disturbs the intellectual laziness of the majority and attacks and threatens a privilege: ignorance, slander, and persecution.

This has happened throughout the entire course of human evolution, and it is natural that this also happens for anarchism, which so deeply subverts all traditional ideas and inspires so much fear among those who live and intend to continue living by exploiting and oppressing others. Indeed, a little more truth and a little more honesty were to be expected from those who, although not being anarchists, profess ideas of freedom and justice: but narrow-minded party spirit (which recommends taking advantage, even in an unfair manner, of the difficulties an opposing party goes through), dogmatic blindness into which every authoritarian school falls, and livid fear abundantly explain the sad agreement which, with regards to us, the Italian socialist and republican press find themselves in today with the lowest organs of the police.

"Anarchy is violence," they shout from all sides; when instead it is commonly known that Anarchy is the negation of violence, that it is an ideal of a society in which there is no sort of imposition of one man over another—neither of the few over the many, nor of the many over the few.

Many and various are the trends that divide anarchists. As Anarchy is a doctrine of freedom and critique that does not recognize dogmas and authority, its followers take up different thoughts and actions, according to each one's moral and intellectual dispositions and the external circumstances under which each one acts.

There are communist, collectivist, and individualist anarchists; there are nonreligious anarchists and religious anarchists; there are those who believe the concept of organization is an integral part of the anarchist idea, and there are those who believe organization is in material and logical contradiction with Anarchy; and a hundred different, and often contradictory, criteria divide them on questions of strategy. They debate, quarrel, bicker; but in the midst of all the divisions, a shared idea characterizes them all, and gives all the right to lay claim to the title of anarchist. And this idea is the negation of physical force used by man upon man, as a factor of order and social evolution.

This is the fundamental idea, the truly new idea that anarchism brought about: an idea that must revolutionize everything about how men live and open a new way to humanity. Not government, not legislative power, not armed force; no right nor possibility of a few men to force others to let themselves be exploited and controlled. And if any concept in contradiction with this idea can be found in the writings and in the acts of any anarchist, then it is but a leftover from the authoritarian education received and not completely undone, it is but an environmental influence, which not all are able to resist, or not always.

Is this an unattainable utopia? Or is it not, rather, an acknowledgement of the fact that humanity has succeeded in living and evolving inasmuch as the principle of freedom has been able to resist the principle of authority, of obligation?

We believe that, once violence is eliminated, men will organize in a way that best suits everyone. They will be prompted to do so both by the necessities of life and the interest of each, and by the spirit of fraternity and solidarity that will expand to the extent that the possibility of dominating, for the ones, and the need to resist domination, for the others, will decrease. This is what already happens and has always happened in those fields of activity where privilege does not enter, and among those people who, having an interest in staying together and doing a given thing, cannot use force to impose themselves over others.

Our adversaries, those who want to defend their privileges with force, and those who believe in the possibility and expediency of doing good for others by force and in their own way, have the right to confute us if they can; but they do not have the right, if they wish to be considered honest and fair men, to misinterpret our ideas and make us appear to be the opposite of what we are.

*
**

War against violence: here is the guiding reason for all anarchist work.

Unfortunately, very often there is no other way but violence to defend oneself against violence. But even then, the violent actor is not he who defends himself, but he who forces others to need to defend themselves: the violent actor is not he who uses the homicidal weapon against he who attacks his life, his liberty, his bread, with weapons in hand; but the assassin who puts others in the terrible necessity of killing or being killed.

It is the right of defense, which achieves the standing of sacrifice, heroism, sublime holocaust to the principle of human solidarity, when someone does not defend himself, but defends others to his own detriment, calmly facing slavery, torture, death.

Everyone recognizes, and practices as he can, the right of defense; all pay tribute to or have paid tribute to someone who opposed force with force in defense of one cause or another.

Will it be a crime to do so, only when one does so in defense of the poor? Will it be a crime only in the person of the anarchist, who sometimes is individually violent, and if he aspires to violent revolution, he does so not in the spirit of hate or revenge, but because he is convinced of the necessity of force in destroying a homicidal regime which sustains itself by force, and is inspired by the desire to do good, not for a class or for a party, but for all men?

The Monza Tragedy

Translated from "La tragedia di Monza," *Cause ed Effetti, 1898–1900* (London), single issue (September 1900)

Another act of bloodshed has come along to sadden sensitive souls... and to remind the mighty that placing oneself above the people and trampling over the great precept of equality and human solidarity is not without its dangers.

Gaetano Bresci, worker and anarchist, has killed Humbert the king. Two men: one prematurely dead, the other condemned to a life of torments a thousand times worse than death! Two families plunged into grief!

Where does the blame lie?

Whenever we criticize present institutions and mention the unspeakable pain and countless deaths they cause, we never fail to caution that such institutions are harmful, not just to the great proletarian masses whom they thrust into poverty, ignorance, and all the other woes that spring from poverty and ignorance, but also to the very privileged minority who suffer, physically and morally, from the tainted environment that they create, and live in constant fear that the people's rage will make them pay dearly for their privileges.

Whenever we look forward to the redemptive revolution, we always speak of benefits for all men without distinction; and we mean that, regardless of the competing interests and party rivalries that divide them today, they should all set aside hatred and resentments, and become brothers in the shared work for the well-being of all.

And every time that capitalists and governments perpetrate an extraordinarily wicked act, every time that innocents are tortured, every time the savagery of the powerful erupts into bloodshed, we deplore that event, not merely for the pain it directly generates and for the trespass against our sense of fairness and mercy, but also for the remnants of hatred it leaves in its wake, for the seed of vengeance it plants in the minds of the oppressed.

But our warnings go unheeded; on the contrary, they are used as a pretext for persecution.

CAUSE ED EFFETTI.

1898-1900.

Pubblicato a cura di un gruppo Socialista-Anarchico.

Perchè un anarchico ha ucciso un re, la tempesta si è scatenata, e più intensamente che altre volte, sul nostro capo.

I governi ci perseguitano all'impazzata, e maturano feroci, quanto vani, progetti di sopprimere radicalmente gli anarchici e la loro idea. La stampa prezzolata, o spontaneamente servile, ci calunnia come persone, e calunnia nel più grottesco modo i nostri ideali. E non solo la stampa monarchica e borghese; ma anche la stampa repubblicana, che pur suole, quando non v'è più pericolo, inneggiare al "fiero vendicatore che trucida i tiranni", ed anche buona parte della stampa socialista, la quale, in un accesso vile di sciocca paura, fa sforzi acrobatici per negare qualsiasi rapporto con noi, qualsiasi nesso morale ed intellettuale tra il Socialismo e l'Anarchismo, che pur sono due i due aspetti d'uno stesso problema, di uno stesso ideale di redenzione umana. Ed alcuni dei nostri stessi compagni, troppo impressionati dalle manifestazioni di un'opinione pubblica fatta artificiosamente dalle mille voci che il privilegio tiene a sua disposizione, e sorretta dalle condanne che piovono addosso a chi osa esprimere un pensiero men che ligio alla monarchia, si stan dubbiosi, quasi temendo che il colpo di cui è restato vittima Umberto di Savoia, sia andato a ferire al cuore l'ideale pel quale il ferisore intese far sacrifizio della vita.

Innanzi a tale situazione, coloro che pubblicano questo foglio intendono riaffermare i loro ideali, rivendicare la parte di responsabilità morale che può spettar loro nella lotta odierna tra oppressi ed oppressori e nei tristi suoi episodii, e mostrare che essi restano al loro posto di combattimento, più che mai pieni di fiducia nel trionfo definitivo della giustizia contro l'iniquità, della pace e dell'amore contro la tirannia, della pace e dell'amore contro la guerra e l'odio che ora straziano il genere umano.

CHE COSA E' L'ANARCHIA.

Contro ogni nuova dottrina che disturba la pigrizia intellettuale dei più ed attacca e minaccia un privilegio, lottano sempre tre potenze nefaste: l'ignoranza, la calunnia e la persecuzione.

Così è avvenuto durante tutto il corso dell'evoluzione umana, ed è naturale che così avvenisse anche per l'anarchismo che tanto profondamente sconvolge tutte le idee tradizionali e tanta spinta inspira a coloro che vivono e si propongono di continuare a vivere sfruttando ed opprimendo gli altri. C'era invero da aspettarsi un po' più di verità ed un poco più di onestà da coloro che, pur non essendo anarchici, professano idee di libertà e di giustizia: ma il gretto spirito di partito (che consiglia di profittare anche in modo sleale delle difficoltà in cui versa un partito avversario), la cecità dommatica in cui cade ogni scuola autoritaria, e la livida paura, spiegano il triste accordo in cui, a riguardo nostro, la stampa repubblicana e socialista d'Italia si trova oggi coi più bassi organi di polizia.

"L'Anarchia è la violenza", si grida da ogni parte; quando invece è risaputo che l'Anarchia è la negazione della violenza, che essa è un ideale di società in cui non vi sia nessuna specie d'imposizione dell'uomo sull'uomo—nè dei pochi sui molti, nè dei molti sui pochi.

Molte e varie sono le tendenze che dividono gli anarchici. Essendo l'Anarchia una dottrina di libertà e di critica che non riconosce dommi ed autorità, il pensiero e l'azione dei suoi seguaci si atteggiano diversamente, a seconda delle disposizioni intellettuali e morali di ciascuno e delle circostanze esteriori in mezzo a cui ciascuno si agita.

E vi sono anarchici comunisti, collettivisti e individualisti; vi sono anarchici irreligiosi e anarchici religiosi; ve ne sono che credono il concetto dell'organizzazione essere parte integrante dell'idea anarchica, e ve ne sono che credono l'organizzazione in contradizione logica e materiale coll'Anarchia; e cento criterii diversi, e spesso contradittorii, li dividono nelle questioni di tattica. Essi discutono, polemizzano, si bisticciano; ma in mezzo a tutte le divisioni, un'idea comune li caratterizza tutti, e da il diritto a tutti di rivendicare la qualifica di anarchico. E quest'idea è la negazione della forza fisica impiegata dall'uomo sull'uomo, quale fattore d'ordine e di evoluzione sociale.

Questa è l'idea fondamentale, l'idea veramente nuova che ha apportato l'anarchismo: un'idea che deve rivoluzionare tutto il modo di vivere degli uomini ed aprire una via novella all'umanità. Non governo, non potere legislativo, non forza armata; non diritto nè possibilità in alcuni uomini di costringere gli altri a lasciarsi sfruttare e comandare. E se alcun concetto in contradizione con questa idea si può trovare negli scritti e negli atti di qualche anarchico, esso non è che un avanzo dell'educazione autoritaria ricevuta e non completamente disfatta, non è che un'influenza d'ambiente, cui non tutti e non sempre riescono a resistere.

E' questo un'utopia irrealizzabile? O non è piuttosto un riconoscimento del fatto che l'umanità in tanto è riuscita a vivere ed a svilupparsi in quanto il principio di libertà ha potuto resistere al principio di autorità, di imposizione?

Noi crediamo che, eliminata la violenza, gli uomini sia per le necessità della vita e per l'interesse di ciascuno, sia per lo spirito di fratellanza e di solidarietà che si allarga a misura che diminuisce negli uni la possibilità di imporsi e negli altri la necessità di resistere all'imposizione, si organizzeranno nel modo che meglio conviene a tutti; come avviene fin da oggi, come è sempre avvenuto, in quei campi di attività dove non entra il privilegio, e fra quelle persone che, avendo interesse a stare insieme ed a fare una data cosa, non possono imporsi colla forza l'una all'altra.

I nostri avversari, coloro che colla forza vogliono difendere i loro privilegi, e coloro che credono nella possibilità e nella convenienza di fare il bene degli altri per forza e a modo proprio, hanno il diritto di confutarci e lo possono; ma non hanno il diritto, se vogliono essere considerati come uomini onesti e leali, di travisare le nostre idee e farci apparire il contrario di quel che siamo.

Guerra alla violenza: ecco il movente informatore di tutta l'opera anarchica.

Disgraziatamente, molto spesso contro la violenza non vi è altro modo di difendersi che la violenza. Ma anche allora il violento non è chi si difende, ma chi costringe altri a doversi difendere: non è violento colui che usa l'arme omicida contro chi con l'armi alla mano attenta alla sua vita, alla sua libertà, al suo pane, ma l'assassino che mette altri nella terribile necessità di uccidere o farsi uccidere.

E il diritto della difesa, il quale assurge a dignità di sacrifizio, di eroismo, di sublime olocausto al principio di solidarietà umana, quando uno non difende sè stesso, ma difende gli altri con discapito proprio, affrontando serenamente la schiavitù, la tortura, la morte.

Tutti riconoscono, ed esercitano come possono, il diritto di difesa; tutti inneggiano od hanno inneggiato a chi ha opposto la forza alla forza in difesa di una o di un'altra causa.

Sarà un crimine il farlo, solo quando si sia in difesa dei poveri? Sarà un crimine solo in persona degli anarchici, che se qualche volta sono realmente violenti e sè ad una rivoluzione violenta aspirano, lo fanno non per ispirito di odio e di vendetta, ma perchè convinti della necessità della forza per distruggere un regime omicida che colla forza si sostiene, ed inspirati dal desiderio del bene, nou di una classe o di un partito, ma degli uomini tutti?

LA TRAGEDIA DI MONZA.

Un altro fatto di sangue è venuto ad addolorare gli animi sensibili.... ed a ricordare ai potenti che non è senza pericoli il mettersi al disopra del popolo e calpestare il grande precetto dell'eguaglianza e della solidarietà umana.

Gaetano Bresci, operaio ed anarchico, ha ucciso Umberto re. Due uomini: uno morto immaturamente, l'altro condannato ad una vita di tormenti che è mille volte peggiore della morte! Due famiglie immerse nel dolore!

Di chi è la colpa?

Quando noi facciamo la critica delle istituzioni vigenti e ricordiamo i dolori ineffabili e le morti innumeri che esse producono, noi non machiamo mai di avvertire che esse istituzioni sono dannose non solo alla grande massa proletaria che per causa loro è immersa nella miseria, nell'ignoranza ed in tutti i mali che dalla miseria e dall'ignoranza derivano, ma anche alla stessa minoranza privilegiata che soffre, fisicamente e moralmente, dell'ambiente viziato che essa crea, e sta in continua causa dell'ira popolare che le faccia pagar caro i suoi privilegi.

Quando noi auguriamo la rivoluzione redentrice, noi parliamo sempre del bene di tutti quanti gli uomini senza distinzione; ed inten-

And then, when the pent-up anger from protracted torments bursts into a storm, when a man driven to despair, or a generous soul moved by the suffering of his brothers and impatiently waiting for sluggish justice to arrive, raises an avenging arm and strikes at what he reckons is the cause of the woe, then the guilty parties, the ones responsible... are us.

It is always the lamb that gets the blame!

Absurd conspiracies are concocted and we are held up as a social menace; they pretend to believe—and perhaps some actually do believe—that we are bloodthirsty monsters, criminals whose only options should be the penitentiary and the criminal asylum...

After all, it is only natural that things should be so. In a land where the likes of Crispi, Rudinì, Pelloux, and all those who have slaughtered and starved the people can live free, are powerful and are feted, there can be no room for us, who rebel against massacres and starvation!

But let us set aside the incorrigible police folk; let us set aside the interested parties who lie knowing that they are lying; let us set aside the cowards who hurl themselves at us to ward off any blows that might land also upon them—and let us reason for a moment with people of good faith and common sense.

*
**

First of all, let us bring things back into proportion.

A king has been killed; and since a king is still a man, that fact is to be deplored. A queen has been widowed; and since a queen is also a woman, we sympathize with her sorrow.

But why all the hubbub over the death of one man and over the tears of one woman when it is accepted, as a natural fact, that every day so many men fall dead, and so many women weep, because of wars, accidents at work, revolts crushed by gunshot, and thousands of crimes spawned by poverty, by the spirit of revenge, by fanaticism, and by alcoholism?

Why such an outpouring of sentimentality over one misfortune, when thousands and millions of human beings die of starvation and malaria, amongst the indifference of those who might have the means to remedy this?

Perhaps it is because this time the victims are not vulgar workers, not some ordinarily good man and good woman, but a king and a queen?... Actually, we take a greater interest in the case, and our grief is more poignant, livelier, more authentic, when we are dealing with a miner crushed by a landslide while working, and a widow left behind to perish of hunger with her little children!

Nevertheless, even the sufferings of royals are human suffering and are to be deplored. But lamentations are pointless if one does not investigate the root causes and seek to eliminate them.

*
**

Who is it that provokes the violence? Who is it that makes it necessary, inevitable?

The entire present social order is founded upon brute force at the service of a tiny minority which exploits and oppresses the vast majority; all the education delivered to children boils down to a continuous glorification of brute force; the whole atmosphere in which we live is an unbroken example of violence, a continual incitement to violence.

The soldier, that is to say professional murderer, is revered. And most revered of all is the king, whose most distinguishing feature, historically, has been that he commands soldiers.

Through brute force, the laborer is obliged to suffer the theft of the product of his labors; through brute force, weaker nations are robbed of their independence.

The kaiser of Germany urges his troops to give the Chinese no quarter; the British government treats the Boers who refuse to bow down to the foreign bully as rebels, and burns their farms, hunts down housewives and even pursues non-combatants and re-enacts Spain's ghastly feats in Cuba; the Sultan has the Armenians slaughtered by the hundreds of thousands; and the American government massacres the Filipinos, having first cravenly betrayed them.

Capitalists send workers to their deaths in the mines, on the railways, in the paddy fields by refusing to make the necessary expenditures for safety at work. They call for soldiers to intimidate and, if need be, gun down workers asking for better conditions.

Again, we ask, from whom, therefore, comes the incitement, the provocation to violence? Who is it that makes violence appear to be the only way out of the existing state of affairs, the only means whereby one may not be eternally subjected to the violence of others?

And in Italy things are worse than elsewhere. The people are perennially hungry; our lordlings tyrannize worse than they did during the Middle Ages; the government competes with the property owners in bleeding the workers, to line the pockets of its own and squander the rest on dynastic ventures; the police are the judge over citizens' freedom, and every cry of protest, every lament, though subdued, is strangled by jailers, and smothered in blood by soldiers.

The list of massacres here is a lengthy one: from Pietrarsa to Conselice, Calatabiano, Sicily, etc.

Just two years ago the royal troops massacred the defenseless people; just a few days ago the royal troops afforded the landowners of Molinella the support of their bayonets and their conscript labor, against famished, desperate workers.

Who is to blame for the rebellion, who is to blame for the revenge that erupts from time to time: the provocateur, the offender, or he who denounces the offense and seeks to banish its cause?

But, they say, the king is not responsible!

We certainly do not take seriously the farce of constitutional pretenses. The "liberal" newspapers, which now argue that the king is not accountable, were well aware, when it came to themselves, that above parliament and ministers, there was a powerful influence, a "high sphere," that the king's prosecutors would not permit being alluded to too bluntly. And the conservatives, who now look forward to a vigorous "new age" from the new king, indicate that they know that, at least in Italy, the king is not the puppet they would have us believe, when it comes to identifying responsibility. And besides, even if he does not do the harm directly, any man who fails to prevent it, though is able to do so, is still responsible for it—and the king is the leader of the soldiers and can always, at the least, stop his soldiers from opening fire on defenseless populations. And he is even responsible if, unable to prevent evil from being done, he allows it to be done in his name, rather than renounce the benefits of his office.

True, if factors such as heredity, education, environment are considered, the personal responsibility of the mighty is greatly attenuated and perhaps disappears altogether. But then, if the king is not answerable for his actions and his omissions, if despite the oppression, deprivation, the people massacred in his name, he should have remained in the highest office in the land, why on earth should Bresci be held responsible? Why on earth should Bresci atone with a lifetime of unspeakable suffering for one act which, no matter how wrong-headed one might like to think it, no one can deny was prompted by altruistic intentions?

But this matter of tracing responsibility is of mediocre interest to us.

We do not believe in the right to punish; we repudiate the idea of revenge as a barbaric sentiment: we do not mean to be either executioners or avengers. The mission of liberators and peacemakers strikes us as a holier, nobler, more productive calling.

We would gladly reach out our hand to kings, oppressors, and exploiters just as soon as they decide to again be men like any others, equals among equals. But if they insist upon relishing in the existing order of affairs and defending it using force, thereby leading to martyrdom, brutalization, and death by hardship for millions of human creatures, we need and are obliged to meet force with force.

*
**

Meet force with force!

Does that mean that we revel in melodramatic conspiracies and are always in the throes of or bent on stabbing some oppressor?

Not at all. As a matter of sentiment and principle, we abhor violence and always do whatever possible to avoid it: only the necessity of resisting evil through suitable and effective means could induce us to resort to violence.

We know that these singular acts of violence, without sufficient preparation among the people, remain futile and often, triggering backlashes against which one is unable to resist, they produce incalculable suffering and harm the very cause they were intended to serve.

We know that the essential, indisputably purposeful act lies, not in the physical killing of a king, but in killing all kings—those of courts, parliaments, and factories—in the hearts and minds of people; meaning the eradication of belief in the principle of authority worshipped by so many of the people.

We know that the less ripe revolution is, the bloodier and more uncertain it proves to be.

We know that violence being the source of authority, indeed at its core one and the same with the principle of authority, the more violent the revolution turns out to be, the greater the risk is that it may spawn fresh forms of authority.

And so, before using the ultimate justifications of the oppressed, we strive to acquire that moral and material strength required to reduce to a minimum the violence necessary for bringing down the regime of violence to which humanity is subjected today.

Will we be left in peace to do our work of propaganda, organization, and preparation for revolution?

In Italy they prevent us from speaking, writing, and associating. They ban workers from joining together and struggling peaceably, not just for emancipation, but also for the slightest improvement to their uncivilized and inhumane living conditions. Prisons, forced residence, and bloody repressions are the means deployed not just against us anarchists, but against anyone who dares to contemplate a more civilized state of affairs.

Is it any wonder if, having lost all hope of fighting successfully for their own cause, ardent spirits let themselves be swept away by acts of vengeful justice?

*
**

The police measures, which always victimize the least dangerous people; the frantic searches for nonexistent instigators, which look grotesque to anyone who has some familiarity with the spirit that prevails among anarchists; and the thousands of farcical extermination schemes advanced by dilettantes in police work, all of these serve only to highlight the savagery lurking inside the minds of the ruling classes.

If a bloody revolt by the victims is to be utterly ruled out, there is no other course of action except the abolition of oppression, by means of social justice.

If such revolt is to be reduced and its outbursts attenuated, there is no other way than to allow everybody freedom of propaganda and organization, to leave the disinherited, the oppressed, and the discontented the option of civilized struggle, and to give them the hope that, albeit gradually, they might secure their own emancipation by bloodless methods.

The government of Italy will have none of this; it will carry on with its repression... and it will carry on reaping what it sows.

As for us, while we deplore the short-sightedness of rulers who make the struggle unnecessarily harsh, we shall continue fighting for a society without any violence, in which all will have bread, freedom, and science, and where love is the supreme law of life.

Errico Malatesta.

[Untitled]

Translated from *Cause ed Effetti. 1898–1900* (London),
single issue (September 1900)

There are those who pay homage to Orsini, Agesilao Milano, Monti and Tognetti, Oberdank... and vituperate Bresci;[36] who praise conspiracies, attacks, insurrections against Austria, the Bourbons, the Pope... and call the anarchists delinquents.

It is the moral criterion of Baker's savage: "when I kidnap the neighbor's wife it is good; when the neighbor kidnaps my wife it is bad."

For the bourgeois, violence used to benefit bourgeois ideals and interests is worthy of odes and statues; used to defend the victims of the bourgeois regime, it deserves pitchforks and prisons.

This is savage morality, but it is intelligible and logical.

But what to make of those who sing the praises of Angiolillo, Caserio, Vaillant and repudiate Bresci?[37]

Simply this: that they have not understood that when one cannot absolutely say what he thinks, it is better to keep quiet than say something he does not think.

---

36   For information on these figures of the *Risorgimento*, see the article "Malatesta Boasts" on p. 17 of the current volume.

37   Angiolillo, Caserio, and Vaillant carried out anarchist attacks between 1893 and 1897.

The Paris Congress

Translated from "Il Congresso di Parigi," *Cause ed Effetti. 1898–1900* (London), single issue (September 1900)

In the coming days a congress of anarchists will meet in Paris.

Without the pretension of imposing their judgments upon anyone, the comrades meeting in Paris will study the problems that greatly interest our movement, and will propose solutions which, whether they are accepted or not, will still be the subject of study and fertile discussions.

We hope the aforementioned Congress succeeds in further tightening the bonds of solidarity and cooperation that exist among anarchists, so that all united, they can continue the struggle with greater efficacy against the common enemy: Capitalism and the State.[38]

An Initiative

Translated from "Un'iniziativa," *Cause ed Effetti. 1898–1900* (London), single issue (September 1900)

Seeing how at this time it is almost impossible to keep an anarchist press alive in Italy, and that those organs of the party which succeed in sustaining themselves against persecution are compelled to castrate their own thought, a group of comrades residing in London would like to attempt publication of an Italian-language organ in this city.

However, to succeed, there is a need for cooperation from comrades in other emigration centers, and therefore it is necessary to know if said cooperation can be relied upon.

Ergo we request that comrades who intend to help with this initiative, make their intention known, so that the group of initiators can reckon which forces it can depend upon and whether these are sufficient for the endeavor.

---

38   The congress, which would have taken place on September 19–22, was prohibited by the police.

The Assassin's Punishment

The Daily Graphic (London) 43, no. 3337 (September 1, 1900)

MALATESTA SPEAKS FROM EXPERIENCE.
"HE WOULD BE FAR BETTER DEAD."

On Thursday night, a few yards to the north of the Angel at Islington, says a correspondent, I met a dim, self-absorbed figure rapidly pushing through the throng. It was Enrico Malatesta, of whom we have heard so much lately in connection with the alleged Anarchist conspiracy. Seeing me he stopped, and we had a few minutes' conversation with regard to Bresci's probable life in prison.

"He would be far better dead," was Malatesta's reply to the first question. "It would be far more merciful to hang him. These Italian prisons—well, I have spent years in them, and I know the truly fearful life the prisoners lead. I dream sometimes that I am back again, and start awake, trembling at the very thought.

"For Bresci, he will spend seven years in solitary confinement. He will live in a dimly-lighted cell, that the sun will never visit. During all those years he will hear no voice, he will see no face. Once a day a warder will push his food through a trap-door, but he will not see him, and he will not speak to him. Only one man, perhaps, may during those seven years see Bresci. That is the Director of Prisons, and, believe me, it will not be a happy day for Bresci when the Director pays him a visit. It will be to torture him that this visit will be paid. Yes, literally to torture him, so as to force him to implicate some one else; to say that some one was in his confidence, so that this man may, in his turn, be arrested and tortured. The priest? Yes, the priest would see ordinary prisoners at very long intervals, but not Bresci. He is an atheist. Besides, the priest in an Italian prison is only an additional warder.

"His food? Ah, you English, you will never make revolutionists. You think always of eating and drinking. Well, he will not eat much. Every day he will get about a pound and a half of bread and some vegetable soup. On Sunday he will get a small, a very small morsel of meat. Do you know what he will do with this food? He will eat it in half-mouthfuls to try and make the time pass quicker, to have something to do. For all that seven years he will have nothing to do, nothing to read, no one to see, no one to look at. And the seven years will seem like an eternity.

"You will put, you say, what I tell you in the DAILY GRAPHIC. Well, I ask you to put this in. Say that it is not only Bresci who has killed a king who lives thus. Say that this is how all prisoners are treated in Italy, and say that some of these prisoners have done nothing that would be a crime in England. Against some of them, moreover, no charge has ever been made. They are kept in prison without a trial. If you say this in the DAILY GRAPHIC those who read it will understand why there are Anarchists in Italy.

"How will Bresci be treated after the seven years are over? Come, my friend, what do you think men are fit for after seven years in rigorous solitary confinement? If they do not die they go mad. It is always one or the other. But if Bresci does not die? Well, he will then work in the prison like the other prisoners. He will be fed better. Yes, he will get some more to eat. But above all he will get some work. He will have something to do; and he will be paid for his work. All the Italian prisoners get about a farthing a day if they work hard.[39] They do not get this all at once, but half is kept back until they leave prison. But as Bresci will never leave his prison he will get all his wages. What will he do with it? I do not know. Most prisoners spend their earnings in snuff.

"No, I have heard nothing of the application of the Italian Government to have me expelled from England. I saw it in the paper, but I myself have heard nothing, nor do I expect to hear anything. I have committed no crime. The English refused to give up Orsini, why should they give me up? The Italian police made the same request to the Swiss Government, and it was refused, and I have no fear that England will be less just than Switzerland. No, I am not afraid," and smilingly raising his cap Malatesta pushed onwards to his home in Islington High Street.

Malatesta Laughs

The Evening News (London) 20, no. 5900 (September 1, 1900)

FAMOUS ANARCHIST DECLARES THE ITALIAN POLICE
MANUFACTURE EVIDENCE.

Malatesta shrugged his shoulders and laughed outright when a representative of THE EVENING NEWS called at his lodgings in Islington and told him that the Italian Government had demanded his extradition from Britain on the ground that he was a common criminal.

Then, speaking slowly and quietly in perfect English, the famous Italian anarchist said: "They made the same demand in 1891 of the Swiss Government. But they did not get me, and I am perfectly confident that they will be equally unsuccessful this time also."

"Why should the demand be made at all?"

"Well, you know (with a smile) the Italian police must make it appear that they are doing something, or where would their next supply of secret service money come from?"

"They allege they have discovered letters written in cipher to Bresci which show that you were implicated in the plot," remarked our representative.

---

39   In the British monetary system, a farthing was worth one quarter of a penny.

"The old, old story," said Malatesta. "When the Italian police cannot find evidence they make it and dish it up to suit themselves and those who pay them. They have a very capable assistant in such things in the person of a

FORGER NAMED BARTALONI,

a one-time banker, who is now serving a long term of imprisonment at Palermo.

"I shouldn't be at all surprised to learn that this man had had a hand in 'getting up' those letters. He has obliged the police several times before in this particular way, especially where my comrades have been concerned. Poor wretch, the police are always promising him his liberty if he helps them well, but he never gets it.

"How do I regard this attempt to associate me with Bresci in the death of Humbert? Just as I regard all the other accusations that have been brought against me by the Italian authorities, and that is with indifference.

"For the last seventeen years nothing has happened in Italy, but they have charged me with having been at the bottom of it. Here is an instance. Just before March 18, 1883, some young men posted a number of manifestoes in praise of the Paris Commune on some boardings in Rome. I was in Egypt at the time working as an engineer. When I came back to Italy I was arrested and thrown into prison, charged with having instigated the whole affair.

"After a year's imprisonment I was brought to trial and condemned along with Merlino on

MANUFACTURED EVIDENCE."

Malatesta, who from time to time has spent years in prison, then went on: "I was blamed for the 1st of May riots that took place at Rome in 1891. Next year, while in Spain—on the very night I was lecturing in Madrid—some peasants far away to the south in Xeres made an attack on the local gaol. 'Malatesta,' said the police, 'you have done this thing.'

"During the riots in Sicily in 1893–4 I was in London, but that didn't prevent the Italian police accusing me of being the prime mover in the whole affair and manufacturing evidence to establish my complicity.

"In 1897 there was trouble in Ancona—bread riots they were called—I should have termed them 'No Bread Riots,' for the peasants were famishing with hunger. 'More of Malatesta's work,' said the police, and I was clapped into prison straightaway and condemned.

"While I was behind the bars, the riots in Milan broke out. Again Malatesta was blamed, and again the police strained every nerve to drag me into it.

"Don't think, however, that my case is by any means a solitary one," Malatesta added, "the same thing has happened to many and many another."

MALATESTA, THE STORMY PETREL OF REVOLUTIONISTS.

Source: *Daily Express* (London), August 13, 1900

[Speech Given in London on September 2, 1900]

REPORTS [BY T. C.][40]
Freedom (London) 14, no. 151 (September–October 1900)

On Sunday, September 2, by invitation of The Cosmopolitans, at the Enterprise,[41] 96 Long Acre, comrade Malatesta gave an address on "Anarchism and Crime." The room was crowded some time before the chairman, Morrison Davidson, opened the proceedings. Malatesta gave us a brief statement of the general condition of the Italian workers: unable to buy bread, it being 5d. a loaf and wages 7d. a day; and the multi-millionaire, Saint Humbert, lately deceased,—who protected and countenanced the bank thief Crispi, while sending troops to dragoon into submission the workers who wanted a little more pay. Humbert did not mind the workers killing each other; but when some Italian comrades formed an association for the discussion of social questions, the members of which were pledged not to carry knives or other deadly weapons generally carried by Italians in Italy, the government dissolved it as imperilling the maintenance of order, etc. The police, too, were allowed a wide indiscretion; they tolerated no liberty of press or public meeting, they would even arrest a man who *looked* sympathetic, and it was not wonderful under these circumstances that Humbert—in whose name this was done—came in for a little attention occasionally. Malatesta then gave a summary of Anarchist principles; and after numerous questions, more or less relevant, an interesting discussion followed which by general request was resumed on Sept. 9th, the opener being Mr. John Lane. He "wanted to know" a great deal for about 1½ hours, and some of us endeavored to inform him.[42] Malatesta's speech in the discussion was received with applause, which culminated in a remarkable burst of enthusiasm. The discussion is to be continued on the 16th as a sort of quadrilateral debate—Martin Judge, Malatesta, Amstel and Needes being the speakers in rotation.[43]

---

40   The report's author is probably Thomas Cantwell, typographer at *Freedom*.
41   The Enterprise was a pub managed by Tom Mann, a well-known figure in the British labor movement.
42   Joseph Lane was a historical figure in English socialism. Three years older than Malatesta, he had also participated in the 1881 London congress. According to the summary in *Reynolds's Newspaper* of September 16th, Lane stated in his speech that "while he remained a Social Democrat he was somewhat carried towards Anarchy by the powerful discourse of Malatesta on the previous Sunday." On the September 9th lecture, see also "Malatesta Declares War," on p. 47 of the current volume.
43   According to the aforementioned summary in *Reynolds's Newspaper* the evening's theme was going to be "Anarchism versus Social Democracy," with Malatesta and Needes explaining the reasons for anarchism and the other two speakers the reasons for social democracy.

Malatesta has certainly made a good impression, and overcame the difficulties of the English language to a degree surpassing our expectations. A good number of his audience took some Anarchism home with them to be studied at leisure.

THE GOSPEL OF ANARCHY

The Daily News (London), no. 16987 (September 3, 1900)[44]

EXPOUNDED BY MALATESTA.

At a very largely attended meeting, last evening, of the Cosmopolitan Club, Endell-street, Signor Enrico Malatesta, the well-known Italian Anarchist, lectured on "Anarchy versus Crime."

After apologising for his imperfect English, the lecturer said that all Europe had been thrown into a turmoil because a man of the people killed King Humbert; but it should be remembered that for years Italian soldiers had been killing off Italians by order of the Government, and chiefly at the time of the so-called bread riots. With regard to the relation between Anarchy and crime, the question arose what was crime? It was a purely social conception, formed according to incorrect ideas put forward by churchmen, by capitalists, and professional politicians. Now, the objects aimed at by Anarchists were love, justice, liberty, brotherhood, and equality; and their conception of crime was that it was an act committed against these ideals. The true theory of Anarchy was that no violence should be used; but all other bodies were parties of violence. Anarchists differed much among themselves. There were Communistic, Individualistic, Spiritualistic, and Materialistic Anarchists, but all agreed in objective to the use of violence. There was, however, one illogical body of Anarchists, who were Non-Resistants. They were perfectly wrong, for every man should resist violence. Many Anarchists had done violent actions, but these were done, not as Anarchists, but as men of like passions and sentiments with others. The whole history of the world was a story of violence, and the basis of present society was violence. The charge was made against Anarchists that they incited to murder; but the incitement did not come from Anarchists, but from the pressure of every-day events. Surely a little while ago the German Emperor had incited to crime in his "no quarter speech," and Chamberlain and his supporters when urging the crushing of the Boers were indulging in a propaganda of violence. If violence were used to support oppression and to legalise robbery, was it strange if a workman thought he might use violent remedies for his wrongs. Englishmen hardly grasped the position, owing to the different circumstances of the British and Continental proletariat. Here reforms

---

44   The same report also appeared in the *Echo* of London on the same day, under the title "Anarchism versus Crime."

were effected by freedom of speech, there violence must be used against oppression and violence. In Italy speeches such as those delivered that night would be punished with 5 years' imprisonment. Bread was 2d. a lb, yet in many districts the net wage was 5d. a day. Yet if the people struck, soldiers were sent either to kill the strikers or to do their work. King Humbert was responsible for all that was done by the military against the people, and permitted the systematic massacre of Italian working men. Anarchists and Socialists once formed a league to stop this, but the Government dissolved the League and imprisoned the leaders. If the death of a King would end oppression and better the condition of the people, he would gladly kill any crowned head in Europe. Italians only resorted to violence to meet violent acts of oppression. With them political assassination played the same part as was played in this country by freedom of speech, propaganda, and organization.

AN ITALIAN ANARCHIST
The Standard (London), September 3, 1900

Signor Enrico Malatesta, for whose extradition the Italian Government has applied, last evening delivered a lecture on "Anarchy and Crime," at the Cosmopolitan Club, Endell-street. Although he speaks imperfect English, he made himself well understood. The theory of Anarchism, he maintained, was that of non-violence. It was a theory of self-defence. It was true that Anarchists disagreed amongst themselves upon almost everything. Why? Because the vast majority reprobated violence. But the oppression of either a majority or a minority could not be passively suffered. It was only logical that a man who did not wish to use violence should not permit violence in others. The violence of Anarchists was not because they desired violence but because of their environments. It was said that Anarchists incited to murder, but the incitement to murder came from things which were happening every day. The Italian people were anxious to accomplish the emancipation of Society without violence; but violence was the mother of violence; but when men were shot down for the simple crime of organisation, then they were bound to fight the oppressor. Bressi's act was committed for the good of the people. In Italy the people were crushed not only by economical power but by political power. A speech like that he was delivering would in Italy gain for him five years' imprisonment. The social condition of the people in Italy was the most miserable in the whole world. Men, women, and children were in a state of systematic starvation, and King Humbert he made responsible for much of the suffering. That men were more violent in Italy arose not from the fact that they were Anarchists, but because they were downtrodden and oppressed. No English Anarchist would have thought of killing King Humbert. English Anarchists held the same principles, but they did not suffer as Italian Anarchists did. Italian Anarchists did not claim the right to impose their opinions on others; but they did and would claim the right to propagate and experiment their ideas. They were obliged to defend themselves. Naturally they did not wish to be always the people that were killed. If the killing of King Humbert signified the emancipation of a people, then he would frankly say he would be satisfied with the killing of all Kings, for the dispatch of one King might spare the deaths of thousands of honest working-men. Unfortunately, the killing of Kings was not sufficient. They wanted to kill the principle of Monarchy and authority. Because a man with a good intention had killed a King, they now wanted to kill all Anarchists.

MALATESTA ON ANARCHY

Daily Express (London), no. 114 (September 3, 1900)

A FIERY DEFENCE OF BRESCI.

At Tom Mann's public-house at the corner of Endell-street and Long Acre, last night Enrico Malatesta, the Anarchist, fulminated against Society, in the presence of an enthusiastic and cosmopolitan crowd.

The Italian is evidently determined to have his say before, if ever, he is deported. His lecture was announced as "Anarchism versus Crime."

Going upstairs, writes an "Express" representative, I found the room simply packed. Every seat was occupied, people were standing in the gangway and half-way down the stairs.

Among the audience Tom Mann, John Morrison Davidson, Higgins Malanesi, Cantwell, D'Ebendi Milne, and other well-known representatives of the forward school were noticeable.[45]

In introducing the lecturer Mr. Davidson said that all Governments were bad, and that the best Governments were the worst.

"For myself," he said, "I would rather stand to-day in Bresci's shoes than change places with Chamberlain or Rhodes or Kitchener, aye, or Bobs."[46]

Characteristic.

Malatesta had sat self-absorbed and inscrutable during the chairman's address, but on being called upon he sprang up to the table with that fierce abandon that characterises the man in moments of excitement.

There was no doubt about his reception. He was greeted with a perfect storm of cheers which were renewed again and again during his address.

---

45 "Higgins Malanesi" and "D'Ebendi Milne" might be incorrect spellings of other names.

46 Chamberlain, Rhodes, and Kitchener were leading figures, respectively, in the political, economic, and military spheres of the British empire. "Bobs" was the nickname of Frederick Roberts, the commander in chief of the British forces in the Anglo-Boer war.

The applause, however, was under perfect control, and when there appeared any chance of it interfering with the orator "Hush! hush!" and a silence like death fell upon the crowded room.

The influence the man has could be perhaps understood by anyone who witnessed last night's meeting.

The room was truly cosmopolitan, Englishmen, Germans, French, Italians, Russians, all nationalities were present, and all speedily fell under the sway of the fiery Italian.

He protested against Anarchists being considered criminals. Because a man had killed a king who a few months before had killed hundreds of people—unarmed men, women, and children—the papers declared Anarchists were criminals. They were not.

They disbelieved in violence. They thought government of man by man was oppression, and for him, he thought it right to meet violence by violence.

Mr. Davidson was a Christian Anarchist, who believed in non-resistance. Christian-Anarchists were illogical. If violence was wrong, then it was right to resist violence. Christian-Anarchists were Anarchists who lived in England. If they lived in Italy or Spain they would become less Christian and more Anarchistic.

Indicting the Dead.

To say that King Humbert was not responsible, how absurd it was! He had 15,000,000 francs a year. His was the hand the workers felt. In England Queen Victoria was of no consequence, and no Anarchist in England would dream of hurting her.

The people of importance here were Chamberlain and Rothschild and the capitalists. It was they who oppressed the workers in England.

But in Italy, the people could not afford to eat bread. They could not afford salt. If they asked for better conditions they were shot or thrust into prison. He had known women sent to prison for months because they had fetched water from the sea to use for salt. All this was by order of the King.

The late King had backed up the reactionaries. He had always been the enemy of progress. He was mainly responsible for the expedition to Africa. The people of Italy were against the expedition. The Parliament was against it. King Humbert, the father of his people, he shut up the Parliament, and only allowed it to meet to vote the Budget.

And once when the Parliament would not vote the Budget, he voted it himself by Royal warrant. "I think," cried the orator, "that you have killed a King in England for this!"

And as he sat down a fierce, deep cry from his excited audience fitly rounded off his fiery peroration.

ANARCHIST PROPAGANDA

Daily Chronicle (London), no. 12014 (September 3, 1900)

MALATESTA'S VIEW OF THE MONZA CRIME.

Signor Malatesta, the Italian Anarchist whose name has been so much in evidence since the murder of King Humbert, delivered a lecture in Long acre last night on "Anarchy versus Crime." In the course of his speech—for it was de facto a speech and not a lecture—he referred to the act of Bresci as simply an "incident" in the struggle between the oppressors and the oppressed. The former meant the Government, the latter the people. The oppressors were responsible for the act—not Bresci. Such acts were impossible in England, where the right of public meeting and the freedom of the Press obtained. King Humbert, he contended, accepted the sweets of his position, but shrank from its responsibilities. Every effort made by the people for emancipation in Italy was met by the soldiery.

Signor Malatesta's main argument was in a nutshell this:—There must be no Government of any kind. All Governments were autocratic, whether Monarchical or Democratic. He referred to France and the United States, and triumphantly asked a by no means altogether sympathetic audience—composed mainly of Social Democrats—whether in either of these countries the people ruled? The "lecture" was followed by a series of questions from the members of the audience, to which Signor Malatesta responded with readiness, displaying a considerable capacity for repartee. Briefly, the intelligent Italian who is now enjoying our hospitality denounced the institutions, political, social, and economic, of England.[47]

Malatesta Declares War

Daily Express (London), no. 120 (September 10, 1900)

At Tom Mann's public-house last night the Cosmopolitans again mustered in full force.

When Mr. Lane, a Social Democrat, had addressed those present, Malatesta said that he had heard Socialists to-night say they wanted no Government. If they were sincere they were Anarchists.

---

47   A comment on another page of the newspaper concluded by observing that Malatesta's two arguments—that "there must be no government of any kind" and that "the crime of Bresci must be regarded as an 'incident' in a struggle between oppressors and oppressed"—"are hostile to the cause of good government in this country or elsewhere, and people have been imprisoned with indignity in Ireland for saying things which by comparison were harmless."

"In history one fate has always dogged the steps of the tyrant. That fate is assassination. For the tyrant to complain of assassination only proves that the tyrant is a fool.

"They who say Bresci's act was an act of revenge speak falsely. It was an act of war. He and I, and all our Anarchist comrades, have declared war on this corrupt Government—war to the knife.

"The Anarchist went to prison; the Socialist went into Parliament."

SECTION II
General Strike and Armed Strike

"L'Internazionale": Socialist-Anarchist Periodical[48]

Translated from "'L'Internazionale': Periodico socialista-anarchico,"
London, Cosmopolitan Printers, [November 1900][49]

COMRADES.

Since anarchism emerged in the social agon to declare war to the death to the principle of authority, the need for anarchist action and propaganda has certainly always been great and urgent, as the material and moral suffering inflicted by authority upon the people has always been great and the need for remedy has always been urgent.

However, there are historical moments in which the need to fight against oppression is greater than ever, as the duty to act is greater than ever among those who believe they know the way by which humanity must reach its redemption.

And such is without a doubt the present moment.

A reactionary wind blows everywhere. In Italy the so-called basic freedoms, which were won by our forefathers with so many sacrifices and so much blood, and that after all have never been a very serious thing, are flagrantly violated and continually threatened by complete suppression.

In France, a large mass of people, disillusioned by the hopes they had put into the republic, disgusted by the show of weakness, corruption and betrayal performed by the men who were in power during the republican period, throw themselves into the arms of the clerical-military reaction, the worst kind.

In England, save for a few honorable exceptions, the people, literally dazed by the lowest kind of national arrogance, forget the struggle for freedom that made them glorious and civil, forget the defense of their economic interests, tread on every ideal of justice, law, civilization, and abandon themselves en masse to indecent revelry over the joy of knowing that a people who heroically fight for their independence are oppressed, ten against one, exclusively on account of greedy capitalists. And the same happens in the United States of America, where democracy is transforming into Empire, and the inauspicious military spirit,

---

48   This circular-program was published as a leaflet. Above the title appears the wording "Publication forthcoming," and above that, the wording "Circular." Malatesta contributed to this periodical, but was not its editor.

49   The date is inferred by two facts: a piece of correspondence dated November 14th from London appeared in *Risveglio* of Geneva on November 24th, announcing that the circular-program would be distributed shortly; and on December 8th, *La Questione Sociale* of Paterson already published a summary.

unknown or scorned until a few years ago, is taking possession of the popular soul.

We are going backwards. It would seem that all past struggles have been useless, and that humanity is constrained to continually wrestle to emancipate itself from the same prejudices, to win the same illusory reforms, which, after a period of triumph and more or less happy experimentation, disappear, to drive the people back to the previous conditions.

Situations from the past recur. Is it therefore necessary to return, in substance and in form, to the struggles of the past?

This is what various non-anarchist socialist parties seem to believe. Faced with the threatening reaction, they put aside class struggle, unite with the liberal bourgeois parties, postpone the fight for socialism until "liberty" is assured; hence they practically stop being socialists and transform into simple political parties of the opposition. If this method prevails, what would be the consequence?

Our forefathers won a certain amount of freedom and hoped that this would be enough to generate gradual, progressive, safe development of civilization. And after years of sterile existence, these freedoms are threatened, they are close to disappearing.

The dominion of the priests had been destroyed, and the most enlightened and energetic part of the people, the part that makes history, after getting rid of religious convictions, at least the most vulgar ones, considered clericalism the enemy of progress, the enemy of the people: and today clericalism rises again, threatening and powerful.

The military spirit seemed to be suffocated by science, by industry, by commerce, as well as by the spread of ideals of justice and the feeling of human solidarity; and this atavistic tendency to brutal violence, to ferocious joy of conquest and oppression reappears today in all its unsightliness in the most civilized nations of the world, France, England, the United States.

If we return to fight, as our forefathers did, for formal liberties, for doctrinal anti-clericalism, for abstract humanitarianism, even assuming that victory is achieved, will we not again return to the current position and restart once again the same struggles for the same illusory outcome?

With the persistence of the same causes of suffering, and use of the same remedies to fight them, will not the same consequences be produced?

The great merit of socialism is precisely the discovery of the vacuity of political liberties, the meager solidity of moral progress, when said liberties and progress are not accompanied by substantial economic transformations. What is happening today was already predicted by the socialists: and instead of serving as a reason or pretext for abandoning pure socialist doctrine, it should be valued as experimental proof of the doctrine itself and serve as encouragement to persevere on the path of socialism.

Have we not said thousands of times, we socialists of all schools, that political liberties, conquered with the people's blood, but on behalf of and in the interest of the bourgeois, would be respected only where and as long as workers show they intend to make use of them for their emancipation?

Have we not said that clericalism would not be definitively annihilated and would rise up continually from its ashes as long as priests find populations with no hope for happiness on this earth to deceive, consoling them with the unsubstantiated promises of religion?

Have we not said that a society founded on the struggle between man and man, between people and people, for the conquest of bread, would have to end up glorifying soldiers?

And now that all of this occurs like the necessary result of a mathematical calculation, should the socialists repudiate principles and become simple republicans, simple liberals, in the service of that fraction of the bourgeoisie which, after not receiving a satisfying part of the spoils of the workers, declares itself liberal, republican, and perhaps revolutionary!!

This would mean renouncing all progress of modern thought in the field of sociology and returning to pre-1848 conditions when workers were the instruments of the bourgeois and confused their cause with the cause of the bourgeois.

It is what the democratic socialists are doing now.

Socialist-anarchists are alone today in uncompromisingly defending socialism; they represent the workers' interests in conflict with all parasitic classes; they fight for the radical disappearance of the bourgeoisie as a class and for the transformation of all men into useful workers; they consider all those who wish to conserve even the minimum trace of exploitation and oppression to be enemies: therefore it is up to them to take on the task of holding high the flag, which the so-called democratic socialists have folded before the bourgeois in exchange for a few electoral and parliamentary results. It is up to the anarchists, remaining firmly and closely loyal to their program, to save the future of socialism, which is the hope and the salvation of civilization.

To do this it is not necessary to withdraw from real life and remain inert in contemplation of the ideal. Much to the contrary.

Humanity gradually walks, by evolution, even when it is moved by the most intense revolutionary storms: and we must foster all moral and material progresses.

Infinite and various are the factors which determine social life and we cannot lose interest in any of them; any lightening of political and economic oppression, even if transitory, is a benefit; liberties can serve as useful tools for greater achievements, facilitate propaganda and the preparation for the future; and it is certainly a good strategy to take advantage of internal strife existing in the opposing camp and resort to the less dangerous or less immediate enemy to have enough force to tear down the worse enemy.

But all this must be done by anarchist and socialist criteria, without ever forgetting one's own goals, without ever assuming someone found fighting at our side is a friend, without ever recognizing the institutions that need to be destroyed and without ever becoming part of them.

For evolution would be delayed and diverted, and the so-called parties of progress would simply play the game of reaction, if the fact that evolution is necessarily gradual and that every even minimal action produces proportionally good or bad effects, should ever serve as a pretext for pusillanimous devotions and transform for example socialists into republicans and induce the republicans to shed hypocritical tears on a king's tomb, as has recently happened in Italy.

We must always fight for complete emancipation and the fulfillment of our program as a whole; and thus fighting, we must benefit from all partial victories and from whatever amount of freedom and well-being we succeed in tearing away from the enemy. This is indeed a step toward a larger victory, but only if it is torn away by direct action of the people; if it is taken as a spoil of war, without gratitude toward he who under force yielded a part of what he had usurped; and if we keep demanding more.

Only when the people themselves have won something and remain vigilant custodians of their conquests, only when they know that if they are not satisfied they must themselves demand and take what they lack, only then will they stop trusting this or that bourgeois party, in search of that well-being they will never receive from their oppressors of any color; only then will the means, that today confuse and reverse the socialists who are not socialist enough, become impossible; only then will workers warned by experience that all reforms end in nothing, instead of turning back, will decide to destroy the fundamental cause that produces social suffering and sterilizes all progress: individual property and the State.

In this manner, and not by joining parliaments and ministries, one prepares for the future; and also, in this manner, if it is true that they are worth something, those partial concessions can be obtained, concessions which so many are deceived in hoping for, and which governments and owners only grant in fear of being obligated to give more.

∗
∗∗

Forced to live far from our country of origin, which is where we would perform our work with greater efficacy, we do not want to remain inactive, and we propose, now that intense propaganda of anarchist methods and ideals is so necessary, to publish a new periodical.

When there are anarchists who heroically sacrifice their lives for the ideal, we would be ashamed to not bring at least a modest contribution to the cause; and the contribution we can now make is to explain to the people the reason behind these magnanimous sacrifices and make it so that martyrdom does not remain in vain and that the word, the hope of the martyr is realized as soon as possible.

Certainly, other Italian-language periodicals exist that worthily represent the anarchist idea, and perhaps it would be better to concentrate forces to support them. However, the fact, deplorable but well established, is that one does not make the sacrifices for a faraway organ that one does for a nearby one, and that the existence of many periodicals, even if they struggle to survive, creates more propaganda, and provokes more activity and more initiatives than what one or a few can do, even if under prosperous conditions.

Therefore, we devote ourselves to the attempt, and we appeal to the financial, literary, and moral involvement of comrades so that this may succeed.

For the editorial group:

ARCELLI; ANTONIO BASILICO; BRUTO
BERTIBONI; ARTURO CAMPAGNOLI; PIETRO
CAPPELLI; CARLO CAZZANIGRA; SANTE
CENCI; GUGLIELMO CUCCIOLI; GIOVANNI
DEFENDI; ENRICO DEFENDI; FELICE FELICI;
FRANCESCO FERRARI; A. GALASSINI; GIORGIO
GIORGI; PIETRO GUALDUCCI; LANFRANCHI
GIUSEPPE; CARLO MAGNONI; VINCENZO
MAIOLIO; ERRICO MALATESTA; FERRUCCIO
MARIANI; LUIGI MUSSO; ATTILIO PANIZZA;
GENNARO PIETRAROJA; G. POZZO; G. ROMUSSI;
CARLO ROSSETTI; CARLO ROSSI, GIULIO
ROSSI; ENRICO RUBINI;[50] GAETANO SCOLARI;
A. TONZI.

[*The periodical's address follows.*]

---

50   Enrico is the brother of Gennaro Rubini, mentioned in the article on p. 149 of the current volume.

[Speech Given in London on January 5, 1901][51]

Translated from a report by "Bornibus" to the French police,
London, January 6, 1901[52]

. . .

Malatesta gave a long speech on libertarian philosophy and explained how he saw things from the standpoint of propaganda. He also went over the events that took place in Milan 2 or 3 years ago, but only briefly mentioned Bresci's act and individual propaganda. It was observed that he exercised a lot of caution in his speech, which was delivered in Italian.

. . .

The Anglo-Boer War

Translated from "La guerra anglo-boera," *L'Internazionale* (London) 1,
no. 1 (Jan 12, 1901)

The war, which they initially said would be nothing but a military stroll towards Pretoria, and the end of which they then announced several times, continues and is expanding.

No one can predict with certainty when and how it will end; but it already begins to appear probable that, with the help of possible international complications, the little Boer people will be the David who will take down the British Goliath.

However the war ends, the Boers have won the world's admiration with miracles of courage, ability, moral strength; they have shown themselves to be human and civilized as much as courageous, and they have given one of the most splendid examples in history of how much people are capable of when they are truly determined to resist oppression.

The English, pushed to war by the greed of a group of politicos and capitalists, have shown, with ineptitude and brutality in the theater of war, and with the thoughtlessness of the masses in the homeland, the

---

51 The speech was given at Athenæum Hall, during a libertarian celebration to support the prospective periodical *L'Internazionale*. Other speakers included Louise Michel, the Georgian Varlaam Cherkezov and the Spaniard Fernando Tárrida del Mármol. It was followed by a performance of Pietro Gori's play *Primo Maggio* (May First).

52 Manuscript, Archives de la Préfecture de Police, Paris, box BA1510, folder "350.000-18-A, Anarchistes en Angleterre, 1897 à 1911."

morass of mud and blood into which a large civilization can sink when it is founded upon struggle and competition between men.

It seems therefore obvious that any man of heart would vote for the victory of the Boers; and this is certainly the case for the majority of freedom's sincere friends, even among the English. But there is no lack of other equally sincere men, especially among the Marxist socialists, who state that it is in the interest of the proletariat and of general civilization that the English be not defeated. And it is with them that we wish to discuss.

They start from the "scientific" preconception that the proletariat cannot emancipate itself and that a society of free and equal people cannot come about until after the modern capitalistic bourgeoisie has subjugated everything to itself and only two clearly separated large classes are left in the world, each armed against the other, the grand bourgeoisie and the proletariat.

England, they say, is the European nation where the bourgeoisie is most advanced, most free; and therefore, while deploring capitalistic and militaristic excesses, we wish for England to win. Its defeat, slowing down the development of the bourgeoisie, would slow down the triumph of the proletariat.

This preconception is far from being justified by constant and universal facts, necessary for a hypothesis to be accepted as scientific. Many facts render the other hypothesis at least equally probable, that capitalistic centralization and development cannot go much further than where they have already gone, and that they find a natural limit in the conditions that capitalism for the most part produces.

For example: the sloth and madness of grandeur cause the degeneration of those who come into money and therefore the incapacity and squandering that unmake large fortunes and make the accumulation process start over again.

The expansion of technical culture, the advantages, for capitalists, of low wages and market proximity, and the awakening of backward peoples as they come into contact with more advanced civilizations tend to equalize the industrial possibilities of various countries and to let every country produce by itself what it needs, thus almost determining the disappearance of that global market whose dominion has created the power of the English bourgeoisie, when they alone possessed the powerful new means of production.

The system of joint stock companies has enabled the participation of small capital in the benefits of large industry and holds back incorporation of small businesses.

New inventions, already indicated by the transport of electrical energy into homes, could make small industry rise again.

And thus, the occurrence of that state of affairs, which some Marxists continue to consider as necessary for the triumph of socialism, becomes more than uncertain.

But even supposing that all social wealth is accumulated in a small number of hands, and that facing a few billionaires there is all the proletariat without the middle classes, it is not certain that the social revolution come out. Due to the dehumanization of the masses, a state of affairs comparable to Asian slavery could also triumph.

Everything depends on the degree of consciousness of the proletariat: on the will of men.

Now, formulas aside, who is most capable of understanding socialism, who is nearest to socialism: the man who resists invasion and defends the independence of his race and his country, or he who, demeaned by alcohol, applauds the massacres his masters' mercenaries perform in a faraway country, upon people who he does not know and against whom he has no reason for hatred? Who is nearest to socialism: the man who under healthy conditions of life has conserved the beautiful virility that the Boers show, or the slaves of industrial prisons, and those demoralized by the thousand forms of alms by which the English capitalists keep alive the masses of the unemployed, who serve as their reserve of labor domestically and as cannon fodder abroad?

It is not the victory but the defeat of England that will be of use to the English people, that will prepare them for socialism.

They say, "woe to the defeated"; but for a people that goes to oppress another, for anyone who performs work of violence and injustice, it is truer to say, "woe to the victors."

An English victory would be the victory of militarism and would prepare the ground for the suppression of English freedoms.

It would reinforce that idiotic national pride, which makes the most miserable English person believe he has the right to dominate the world, and which is such a big obstacle to the advance of emancipatory ideas.

On the other hand, as long as the English proletarians live on the products of export and therefore benefit from the subjugation of other people, they will scorn and hate foreigners and will feel supportive of the capitalists of their country; this condition of fact and spirit, is certainly unfavorable to the advent of socialism.

And that which is true for England, is true for all countries that possess colonies. Colonization is a school of corruption, of robbery, of savagery; it is harmful to the colonizers as well as the colonized, and only benefits those who live off the sweat and pain of others. And true socialism consists of hoping for and provoking, when possible, the subjected people to drive away the invaders, whoever they are.

Therefore, may the Boers live and win.

The regime they will probably establish will certainly not have our sympathies; their social, political, religious ideas are the antipodes of our own. But they have affirmed the right of each man and each human aggregate to have a will, and have it respected; and this is what matters most.

ERRICO MALATESTA.

Precautions against Anarchists

The New Zealand Herald (Auckland) 38, no. 11608 (March 23, 1901)[53]

A DECLARATION BY MALATESTA. A DESPATCH FROM LONDON, SENT JUST BEFORE THE QUEEN'S FUNERAL, SAYS: —

Scotland Yard, fearing the influence of the presence of so many crowned heads at the late Queen's funeral, is taking drastic precautions to frustrate a possible attack by regicidal Anarchists next Saturday, when King Edward, with Emperor William, King Leopold, and other visiting monarchs, will drive or ride through the streets of London. Every known Anarchist in England will be located and hounded. Some of the most dangerous of them will be arrested on trumped-up charges the night before the funeral, and will be detained until it is over.

Protective measures for the present are confined to shadowing the home of Enrico Malatesta, the famous Italian Anarchist leader, who lives in London in exile. Four of Inspector Melville's detectives watch the little Milanesian night and day, and scrutinize his callers in his Islington lodgings. Recently Malatesta, his black eyes flashing, said in an interview: —

"Scotland Yard is unduly alarmed. Kings and Queens are with us always, and we need no sudden assemblage of them to stimulate our intention of over-throwing monarchy. We know that this cannot be accomplished by murder. The Sovereigns who die would only be succeeded by other Sovereigns. We must kill kings in the hearts of the people; we must assassinate toleration of kings in the public conscience; we must shoot loyalty and stab allegiance to tyranny of whatever form wherever it exists. These are the things of which we desire to rid the world, and not the mere accidents of birth who happen to sit on the high places.

---

53   The despatch shown here was immediately published, in the United States, by the *New York Herald* and *New York Evening Journal* on January 29, 1901. However, these two versions differ in a few ways. We chose the *New Zealand Herald* version, though it came much later, because it is the most complete one, encompassing and reconciling the differences between the two aforementioned versions. Queen Victoria had died on January 22nd and her funeral, to which the article refers, took place on February 2nd.

"Organised Anarchy has never sanctioned the murder of the head of any State. President Garfield, President Carnot, and King Humbert were the victims of men suffering from fancied private wrongs. Our grievance is rather against the political systems which maintain these capitalistic puppets.[54]

"We shall strike our blow at a time when we know that our heads are not endangered. That time has not yet arrived."[55]

Malatesta added that Anarchists view the accession of King Edward "with indifference." He continued:—

"Cecil Rhodes will be king of England more than Edward VII, who is a gambler and something worse.[56] The British empire will continue to be ruled by capitalists."

Funeral Is Rehearsed

The Washington Post, no. 8999 (January 30, 1901)

PRELIMINARY MARCH OF CORTEGE OVER LONDON ROUTE.
GUARDING ROYALTY FROM HARM
EVERY RESOURCE OF THE LONDON POLICE AUTHORITIES EMPLOYED TO
PROTECT HIGH PERSONAGES FROM ANARCHISTS AND CRANKS —EMPEROR
WILLIAM'S SAFETY A MATTER OF ESPECIAL CONCERN —PLANS TO PREVENT A
CRUSH AT FUNERAL ON SATURDAY.

. . .

Malatesta and other anarchists residing in London assert that there is not the slightest probability of violence, because England is "an asylum for the persecuted of the continent."[57]

. . .

---

54   The US president James A. Garfield was killed by his former supporter Charles J. Guiteau in 1881; the French president Sadi Carnot was killed by the Italian anarchist Sante Caserio in 1894.

55   Instead of "we shall strike our blow at a time," the *New York Evening Journal* wrote "we shall strike one blow at a time," thus putting into Malatesta's mouth words that corroborated conspiracy theories spreading at the time.

56   Cecil Rhodes was a magnate of the mining industry in South Africa and a powerful advocate of British colonialism in that region.

57   In the October 7, 1902, issue of *Fanfulla* of Rome, correspondent C. Gonnelli describes an anarchist meeting to discuss the approach to be taken during Edward VII's coronation: "One of the most intransigent—whose name has regretfully escaped me—suggested killing him too; but Malatesta, who presided over the gathering, immediately interrupted him, and told him: —*Take the train and go kill your King, you will be doing holy work, because he is a tyrant! This country has remained the only free and safe refuge for us, and you want to have us lose it by making an attempt on the life of its Sovereign?*" On Gonnelli, see "Idiot Pen Pusher," on p. 127 of the current volume.

Spain Rises Again!
To the Readers of *Heraldo de Paris*

Translated from "¡España resucita! A los lectores del Heraldo de Paris," *Heraldo de Paris* 2, no. 18 (February 16, 1901)[58]

Proletarian Spain erases the disgraces inflicted upon the Spanish name by the governing classes.

Onwards, always onwards towards emancipation, towards the creation of a world of liberty and peace!

Salvation must come from the proletariat. Spanish workers, who hold such a luminous position in the history of the old International, play a leading role in the new International, which must bring us to Victory.

They know better than anyone else—because more than anyone else they have experienced it—the power of the general strike, the powerful weapon of our days. The strike, spreading, will bring about social revolution in Spain.

But may our Spanish comrades keep one thing well in mind.

The dominant class, its privileges threatened, will defend itself at any cost. It has rifles at its disposal. As a last resort, the issue will have to be resolved by gunshot.

May our comrades in Spain organize, therefore, the general strike; but may they also prepare the material means to which recourse will surely be made before the struggle is over.

Enrico MALATESTA.

---

58   *Heraldo de Paris* was a strongly progressive periodical printed in the Spanish language in Paris by Luis Bonafoux, Malatesta's friend and a supporter of the anarchist cause. The very first page of this issue contains, in addition to Malatesta's article, an admiring portrait of Malatesta by Bonafoux. Malatesta's article was then republished in the December 22, 1903 issue.

Giovedì 14 Marzo 1901, ore 8 p.m.

Festa Libertaria

A FAVORE DEL GIORNALE SOCIALISTA-ANARCHICO "L'INTERNAZIONALE."

ATHENÆUM HALL—73, TOTTENHAM COURT ROAD

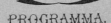

PROGRAMMA.

Apertura ... ... *(Piano)* ... ... Prof. L. SALOMONE.

ROMANZE { Signor G. GROSSI *tenore*.
{ „ A. COLLO *baritono*.

Il Canto del Galeotto *(monologo)* Sig. G. FERRARONE.

SENZA PATRIA

Bozzetto Sociale in due atti di Pietro Gori.

PERSONAGGI.

Giorgio, *agricoltore, ex garibaldino*, Sig. G. BARBERI—Annita *sua figlia*, Sig.na A. SCOLARI—Arturo, *giovane bracciante*, Sig. MAGNONI—Giovanna *madre di Giorgio*, Sig.a CESIRA—Tonio *vecchio marinaio*, A. CAMPAGNOLI —Don Andrea, *parroco del paese*, Sig. G. PIFFERI—Beppino, *carrettiere*, Sig. G. SCOLARI.

CONFERENZE DI L. MICHEL, TARRIDA DEL MARMOL, E. MALATESTA
Mr. KELLY.

Romanza inglese, Miss JENNY ATKINSON | L' INFAME, *(poesia)* Bruna Magnoni.

LES "NOMIS" DANS LES ŒUVRES DES POETES MONTMARTROIS.

MAIS QUELQU' UN TROUBLA LA FETE.

Action en vers de Louis Marsolleau, interdite par la censure a Paris le Juin 1900, jouée par un groupe libre de langue francaise.

PERSONNAGES : Le paysan, l' ouvrier, l' inconnu *M.* JACQUES BONHOMME— Le financier, *M.* VAN-DERBIELT—Le politicien, *M.* JEVA-ES—Le général, *M.* GAL-IFFAIT—Le juge, *M.* PUYS BARREAU—L'évêque, *M.* DE PARISSE— La duchesse, *madame* DE LAMBALLE—La courtisane, *madame* PAULETTE.

M. RAYMOND *dans son répertoire*. — M. MILLARD *monologue*.

Mad.'Frédé *Diction*. — Sig. Gemignani *Pezzi d'opera*. — Les Frédés *Duettistes*.

CORO RIVOLUZIONARIO SPAGNUOLO.

Mad. Krueger *Romance Allemande* | M. Frédé-Rick *dans son répertoire*.

CORO ITALIANO.

Prezzo di ammissione 6d. e 1s.

Source: International Institute of Social History, Amsterdam

[Speech Given in London on March 14, 1901]

SOCIAL MOVEMENT. FROM ABROAD. ENGLAND
[BY G. LANFRANCHI]

Translated from "Movimento sociale. Dall'Estero. Inghilterra," *La Questione Sociale* (Paterson, New Jersey) 7, new series, no. 82 (April 6, 1901)

London, March 16, 1901.

On the evening of March 14th, a libertarian event was held at *Atheneum Hall* to benefit the newspaper *L'Internazionale*. The outcome of this evening, the second in a series begun by our anarchist socialist group *l'Internazionale*, was in every respect, whether artistic or moral or financial, far greater than every expectation.

. . .

The second lecture, given by E. Malatesta, roused a true delirium of applause from the entire audience.[59]

Comrade Malatesta first gave the audience a very clear explanation of the sketch *Senza Patria* before it was staged, and briefly discussed our ideas concerning our great and true homeland, which in a not-distant future will be that of all workers, meaning: redeemed and free humanity, united in a single and large family of happy and free producers. Then he spoke with regards to the sad fact, unfortunately noted by all with pain, that many Italians enlist in mercenary English armies, decimated by the heroic Boer people who fight for their own independence.

. . .

The *event*, spontaneously transformed into a political meeting, unanimously and to clamorous applause approved a resounding protest *agenda*, formulated by the comrades, stigmatizing the sell-outs from Italy, the mercenaries of English capitalist greed, who drag the name of Italy through the mud, offending human dignity, ignominiously treading upon the purest human sentiments.

This evening will certainly leave an indelible impression in the hearts and minds of all participants.

---

59 Louise Michel had spoken prior to Malatesta. During the evening two social sketches had also been presented, *Senza Patria* by Pietro Gori, and another one in French.

LONDON NEWS [BY CRASTINUS][60]
Translated from "Cronaca londinese," *L'Agitazione* (Ancona) 2, new series, no. 52 (March 28, 1901)

Thursday evening in the hall of the Athenaeum there was a very successful event to benefit L'Internazionale, held among the gathered French, Spanish, Italian comrades.

Aside from the entertainment, attention was paid to propaganda. Speakers included Michel, who keeps the youthful faith intact in her old age, and Enrico Malatesta, who had words of intense protest against those Italian wretches, who, forced by hunger, agree to enlist as mercenaries in the service of England, to go slaughter the courageous Boer people.

The following agenda was approved:

"The 300 people present at the political assembly to support the anarchist newspaper *L'Internazionale,* learning about the shameful behavior of some Italians who allow themselves to be recruited by the English tyrant to fight against the generous and heroic Boer people, denounce these reckless sell-outs and invite the people, the press, and those who love freedom and justice to protest against this other Italian shame and strive to mend it."

. . .

FROM ENGLAND [BY CRASTINUS]
Translated from "Dall'Inghilterra," *L'Avvenire Sociale* (Messina) 6, no. 13 (March 27, 1901)

. . .

There were speeches by Louise Michel, who in spite of her late age keeps her youthful faith intact, and Errico Malatesta, who demonstrated what homeland and patriotism are and affirmed the right of the homelandless to win a homeland: that is, he incited all Italians to appropriate the Italian soil now taken from the people by a few landowners.

Malatesta ended by pointing out, as a sign of the degradation into which the government has thrown the Italian people, the fact that Italians enlisted as mercenaries to go and fight the generous Boers under the English flag.

How shameful the present hour is, he exclaimed indignantly amid a deluge of applause. Once there was no battlefield where freedom was disputed that was not scattered with the bones of Italians, always ready to defend the oppressed; there was no place of political confinement that did not resound with the accents of Italian martyrs always ready to give life and possessions for freedom: and now?

---

60 "Crastinus" was the pseudonym of Silvio Corio.

However, he concluded, the Italians gathered here will know how to redeem the Italian name of the present shame, washing infamy in the blood of tyrants.

. . .

TRANSLATION OF A REPORT BY "BORNIBUS" TO THE FRENCH POLICE, LONDON, MARCH 15, 1901[61]

. . .

Malatesta spoke longer[62] about the homeland. He spoke about the poverty that exists in Italy and forces the proletarians to emigrate to faraway countries to find the means for subsistence that are lacking in their birth country, despite the soil's fertility and richness. He showed that property owners are internationalists, that capital has no borders and concluded saying he did not understand how men who emigrated to earn a living in North and South America can be so stupid as to form patriotic associations there. Such an aberration of the human spirit cannot be excused as ignorance either; it is a matter of pure madness, etc.

. . .

The Situation in Italy

Translated from "La situazione in Italia," *L'Internazionale* (London) 1, no. 3 (March 15, 1901)

The big, and unfortunately not new, news that arrives from Italy is: hunger. Terrible in Apulia and in Basilicata, a little less spectacular elsewhere, it prevails throughout the expanse of the blessed Savoy kingdom, and shapes and demoralizes all of Italian life.

But the ministry has changed. Giolitti—the one of the Banca Romana affair—and Zanardelli, the one of the Penal Code, are in power in fraternal union with Prinetti, the one of the states of siege, and with the king's direct agents Morin and Ponza San Martino.[63]

---

61   Manuscript, Archives de la Préfecture de Police, Paris, box BA1510, folder "350.000-18-A, Anarchistes en Angleterre, 1897 à 1911."

62   As compared to Louise Michel, who had spoken earlier.

63   Giuseppe Zanardelli's government had succeeded the Saracco government on February 15, 1901, achieving the Chamber's confidence with a favorable vote from the socialists. In 1890, under Zanardelli's initiative, then minister of justice, the new penal code was introduced, in which article 248, on association of malefactors, represented a sword of Damocles on the head of the anarchists. The Banca Romana scandal had erupted in 1892. The bank had issued a quantity of banknotes surpassing the legal limit, including false banknotes issued in a double series. A good part of the excess circulation was used for loans to

The liberals rejoice, and the "socialists" take on an attitude of benevolent expectation.

We could say every possible evil thing about the new ministers without danger of slandering them. We could demonstrate that between these champions of bourgeois monarchist liberalism and Crispi, Rudinì, and Pelloux, the only difference is that, if these are more prone to resort to brute soldierly violence, those in exchange are better equipped for quibbling Jesuitism.

But it is useless to take an interest in the men, since the situation in Italy is such that, given the continuation of the monarchist and bourgeois system, the individual tendencies of governing authorities can be of very little importance.

The fundamental evil of Italy as a nation is poverty, and this poverty is the fatal consequence of the capitalist system.

In a system of production and exchange founded on competition, Italy, having arrived late in the agon of the international market, without colonies to exploit, without the coal that plays such a role in modern production, with scarce capital and even more scarce technical preparation, had to be defeated and so it was.

Then given the class divide and the political system, it was natural that the most significant part of the lean national wealth would be absorbed by the property-owners and politicos and that the workers were left just enough to not die of starvation.

A bad harvest, the refusal abroad of a major Italian product, a rather prolonged commercial crisis, and behold famine, acute hunger.

The only remedy is to change the regulatory principle of the public economy: instead of producing to trade, produce to consume. But this remedy presumes the destruction of the class regime, the abolition of the capitalistic system.

What can be done by the ministers, whose mission is to defend the very institutions that need to be abolished?

Reduce military expenses, say the radicals and the socialists.

We do not believe much in the economic value of reducing and perhaps abolishing the army, even if we would welcome it with joy for political and moral reasons. On the contrary it seems to us that, with the continuation of the current system, taking laid-off soldiers and all those workers who are now employed in the arsenals and military supplies and throwing them into the labor market, would only make the crisis more acute.

---

deputies and ministers, including Giovanni Giolitti, now minister of the interior. Although the Zanardelli government had a liberal influence, minister of foreign affairs Giulio Prinetti came from the ranks of the conservatives, while the minister of the navy Enrico Morin and the minister of war Coriolano Ponza di San Martino were respectively an admiral and a general.

But, whatever the possible economic consequences of a reduction in the army, what is certain is that it will not happen, both because it would be too dangerous an experience for the bourgeoisie, and because, as the radical, republican, and socialist newspapers say, THE KING DOES NOT WANT IT.

We will point out, in parentheses, that if someone should lose patience and get angry at the king, then these same newspapers will say that the king has nothing to do with it and that it is a crazy thing—an anarchist's thing—to attribute any responsibility to him.

Therefore, if the stopgap that even the most optimistic deem indispensable in order to emerge from the current sad state cannot be applied, how to explain the jubilation of the liberals and the benevolent expectation of the socialists?

Poor Italy, if it only has these kinds of liberals and socialists to save it!

Fortunately, the workers of Genoa and the farmers of the Mantua area are clearly saying that the people of Italy are not yet dead.

ERRICO MALATESTA.

For Freedom

Translated from "Per la libertà," *L'Internazionale* (London) 1, no. 3 (March 15, 1901)

Another municipal council in France, that of Courtenay (Loiret), has prohibited priests from wearing cassocks within the precinct of the town, under penalty of arrest and fine.

And thus we have another stretch of land in which gendarmes, police, and rural guards see, added to their natural mission of persecuting men of progress who preach a better future and the poor devils who do not adjust to dying of hunger while thanking god and master, that truly unexpected mission of revolutionary agents, propagators of free thought... by means of handcuffs and "passages à tabac"![64] Perhaps this will bewilder them; but they will not for that be less ready to be as brutal with priests as with anarchists and the starving. Catch dogs trained to hunt man under a master's orders, blind instruments of those who pay them, beasts accustomed to relish the suffering inflicted upon others, they gladly obey the orders of Mr. Mayor:—black and very plump game is added to the red and tattered game; the hunt will only be more abundant.

---

64   "Passages à tabac" is an idiomatic French expression for "beating."

And Mr. Mayor of Courtenay will indeed be very happy, he who, in step with those who preceded him in this puerile as much as hateful struggle against the cassock, will believe himself a revolutionary, perhaps a socialist, and will have the illusion of having given who knows what mortal blow to clericalism. Instead he will have simply supplied the government and the priests with an argument to justify much more serious blows, which the true revolutionaries will be victims of.

In fact, if the legal majority in a town has the right to prohibit the wearing of cassocks in public, why would another majority in another or in the same town not have the right to prohibit the display of the red flag? If it is lawful to prohibit clerical propaganda, why would it not be lawful to prohibit anarchist propaganda, or any other kind that displeases the more or less contrived and more or less fickle majority of any parliament?

But the priests preach lies.

Agreed: but is Mr. Mayor of Courtenay entirely sure he knows and preaches the truth? By making the people believe that police and handcuffs can be instruments of struggle against the reaction and obscurantism, for us he comes out to be as harmful as the priests themselves:— will he grant us the right to tell him to go away and to prohibit him from wearing the union scarf?

There are many of us, including priests, who say and believe we are right, although professing completely opposite ideas. Will the town council members be the new pontiffs who shall decide, by majority of half plus one, what truth is... in the precinct of their town?

All this would be absurd if it was not odious; if it did not reveal the persistent tendency of the bourgeoisie, so-called radical and anticlerical, and of the segment of the people who follow it, to want to fight the reaction by means of authority, which by its nature can only be reactionary.

The priest is certainly a vile beast: he is the policeman of the spirit and as such he is the most valid support of privilege and tyranny. There is no friend of freedom and human solidarity who does not want to fight him to death.

But how to fight him?

Freedom is not established by the instruments of tyranny: it is not possible to discover and disseminate the truth with the means by which one concocts and asserts falsehood. At most, one could succeed in abolishing a type of priest, only to replace it with a new type, with or without a cassock, which would all the same preach subjugation to masters, it does not matter if in the name of a god, or in the name of presumed knowledge, just as false and deceitful as gods. Usually persecution only succeeds in rendering likable even the worst crooks: priests, for example.

Oh when will those who call themselves friends of freedom, decide to desire truly freedom for all!

Those who claim to destroy the evils that a hateful past has transmitted to us, first among these evils the dominion of the priests, and establish a better society through police actions, can very well believe themselves to be revolutionaries, but in reality they are as revolutionary as a vice-superintendent of public safety can be.

Only anarchism, by establishing equality, destroys the priest's raison d'être as a social power; only anarchism, with its vast understanding of freedom, can get rid of clericalism.

The Jacobins, who dream of transforming the world by dint of decrees, can only wander in a circle of violence: violence of red priests alternating with the violence of black priests.

E. MALATESTA.

Social Movement. From Abroad. England.

Translated from "Movimiento Social. Exterior. Inglaterra,"
La Protesta Humana (Buenos Aires) 5, no. 129 (June 29, 1901)

Tarrida and Malatesta gave a lecture in London on the movement and development that a general strike will evoke. The two were in agreement on its consequences. Only, according to Malatesta, it is necessary to clearly tell workers that if the general strike happens, the army will come out with rapid-fire weapons, and facing such aggression, it is necessary that workers also respond with force, given that force is held back by force. And thus the strikers must prepare themselves henceforth.

l'Internazionale

ONE PENNY. PERIODICO SOCIALISTA-ANARCHICO 10 CENTESIMI.

ANNO I. LONDRA, 15 MARZO, 1901 No. 3.

Cambiamento di Indirizzo.

Per tutto ciò che riguarda il giornale spedire a:

"L'INTERNAZIONALE"
418-420, EUSTON ROAD, N. W. - LONDON.

Ai compagni d' Italia, che ci invieranno anticipate le spese postali (una lira italiana per ogni 40 copie, ed in proporzione) noi manderemo "l'Internazionale" gratis.

La situazione in Italia.

La grande, e purtroppo non nuova, notizia che giunge dall' Italia è: la fame. Terribile in Puglia ed in Basilicata, un po' meno spettacolosa altrove, essa domina in tutta l'estensione del beato regno sabaudo, ed informa e deprime tutta la vita italiana.

Ma il ministero è cambiato. Giolitti, quello della Banca Romana, e Zanardelli, quello del Codice Penale, sono al potere in fraterno connubio con Prinetti, quello degli stati d'assedio, e con Morin e Ponza San Martino agenti diretti del re.

I liberali esultano, ed i socialisti stanno in un atteggiamento di benevole aspettativa.

Noi potremmo dire dei nuovi ministri tutto il male possibile senza pericolo di calunniarli. Potremmo dimostrare che tra questi campioni del liberalismo monarchico borghese ed i Crispi, i Rudinì, i Pelloux, la sola differenza è che se questi sono più proni a ricorrere alla bruta violenza soldatesca, quelli in compenso sono meglio dotati di gesuitismo curialesco.

Ma è inutile occuparsi degli uomini, poichè la situazione in Italia è tale che, data la continuazione del sistema borghese e monarchico, ben minima importanza possono avere le tendenze individuali dei governanti.

Il male fondamentale dell' Italia come nazione è la sua povertà, e questa povertà è la conseguenza fatale del sistema capitalistico.

In un sistema di produzione e di scambio fondato sulla concorrenza, l' Italia, arrivata tardi nell'agone del mercato internazionale; senza colonie da sfruttare, senza il carbone che à tanta parte nella produzione moderna, con scarsi capitali ed ancora più scarsa preparazione tecnica, doveva esser vinta e lo fu.

Data poi la divisione di classe ed il sistema politico, era naturale che la più grossa parte della magra ricchezza nazionale fosse assorbita dai proprietari e dai politicanti e che ai lavoratori restasse appena da non morire di fame.

Una cattiva raccolta, il rifiuto all'estero di un prodotto italiano importante, una crisi commerciale alquanto estesa, ed ecco la carestia, la fame acuta.

Solo rimedio il cambiare il principio regolatore dell'economia pubblica: invece di produrre per commerciare, produrre per consumare. Ma questo rimedio suppone la distruzione del regime di classe, l'abolizione del sistema capitalistico.

Che cosa vi possono fare dei ministri, i quali ànno la missione di difendere le istituzioni che urge abolire?

Diminuire le spese militari, dicono i radicali ed i socialisti.

Noi non crediamo troppo nel valore economico della diminuzione e magari dell'abolizione dell'esercito, che pur saluteremmo con gioia per ragioni morali e politiche. Ci pare anzi che, durando il sistema attuale, il gettare sul mercato del lavoro i soldati licenziati e tutti quegli operai che sono ora occupati negli arsenali e nelle forniture militari, non farebbe che rendere più acuta la crisi.

Ma, checchè ne sia delle possibili conseguenze economiche di una diminuzione dell'esercito, il certo si è che essa non si farà, tra perchè sarebbe per la borghesia una esperienza troppo pericolosa, e perchè, come lo dicono i giornali socialisti, repubblicani e radicali, IL RE NON LA VUOLE.

Osserveremo, in parentesi, che se qualcuno perderà la pazienza e se la piglierà col re, allora quegli stessi giornali diranno che il re non c'entra e che è cosa da matto—cosa da anarchico—il far risalire a lui una qualsiasi responsabilità.

Dunque, se l'espediente che anche ai più ottimisti sembra indispensabile per uscire dal triste stato attuale, non si può applicare; come spiegarsi l'esultanza dei liberali e la benevole aspettativa dei socialisti?

Povera Italia, se non avesse per salvarla che questa specie di liberali e di socialisti!

Fortunatamente, gli operai di Genova ed i contadini del Mantovano dicono chiaro che il popolo d'Italia non è ancor morto.

ERRICO MALATESTA.

Lo sfruttamento dello Stato.

Quale è la rivendicazione fondamentale del Socialismo? L'abolizione dello sfruttamento, sia esso compiuto da un uomo, dalla società, da non importa chi.

Possono chiamarsi socialisti coloro che vogliono conservare lo stato, mentre che il popolo è appunto dallo stato che è più gravemente sfruttato?

Si, è lo stato che rovina i popoli, che sviluppa il parassitismo sociale, che divide, abbruttisce ed opprime l'umanità.

Eccone le prove:

Le sei grandi potenze, prelevano "colla forza" ai loro sudditi, 16 miliardi all'anno. Se aggiungiamo alla enorme cifra di questo furto legalizzato le spese provinciali e comunali obbligatorie, imposte esse pure colla forza, noi arriviamo ad una somma di 20 miliardi (20.000.000.000) strappati violentemente ai 300 milioni di abitanti di queste potenze.

Sapete voi, o compagni, a quanto questa somma corrisponde per ogni singolo produttore?

Secondo la statistica, solamente un ottava parte dell'umanità è ritenuta quale produttrice.

Per conseguenza noi vediamo che solo 38 milioni di produttori pagano i 20 miliardi: ogni operaio, ogni contadino è derubato dallo stato ogni anno per una somma di 520 franchi.

In altre parole ogni produttore dovrebbe privarsi ad esclusivo beneficio del parassitismo militare burocratico, clericale e poliziesco di quasi metà del suo salario annuo!

E si predica lo stato dichiarandosi socialisti, legalizzando ancora una volta, questo enorme sfruttamento!

L'idea erronea di uno stato socialista—lo stato servitore—fu formulata da Louis Blanc or son cinquant'anni.

Di poi essa si estese per opera specialmente dei socialisti parlamentari, che vogliono conservare anche nella società futura la funzione dello stato.

Ebbene: le sei grandi potenze tiravano la forza al popolo in imposte, nel

1810	... ...	2.954 milioni
1850	... ...	4.945 "
1890	... ...	16.000 "

Vale a dire che durante i primi quarant'anni, quando tutti gli amici del progresso si opponevano all'oppressione ed allo sfruttamento dello stato, il bilancio annuo non giungeva a raddoppiarsi.

Invece, durante gli ultimi quarant'anni, quando in nome del socialismo e della rivoluzione si cantarono le lodi dello stato, vediamo che il bilancio del 1900 supera di tre volte quello del 1850, sei volte quello del 1810 con una progressione che può esprimersi con le cifre 3, 6, 16.

Mai lo sfruttamento da parte dei capitalisti può raggiungere una cifra sì formidabile. E poi il capitalismo, senza la magistratura ed il militarismo, senza la polizia e la burocrazia non può resistere a lungo, sopra tutto se i produttori sono organizzati sul terreno economico e non elettorale; sopra tutto se essi sono preparati per una lotta rivoluzionaria e non per le parate elettorali.

Si, il capitalismo e lo sfruttamento individuale non potranno resistere ai produttori, solidali ed autonomi, se lo sfruttamento formidabile dello stato è abbattuto con una lotta energica da parte dei socialisti.

Ecco per quale ragione ogni socialista deve combattere lo stato—e forse attaccarlo prima d'ogni altra cosa—oserei aggiungere.

W. TCHERKESOFF.

I calunniati d'ogni tempo.

Or fa quasi un mese, a Montceau-les-Mines, durante lo sciopero, in una dimostrazione, alcuni anarchici ànno inalzato una bandiera nera, con l'ardita divisa: Nè dio, nè padrone, ed echeggiò il risonante grido di: viva l'anarchia!

Sulla piazza comunale dovevan parlar agli scioperanti gli oratori dell'Unione socialista, i propugnatori del Proletariato organizzato, e della lotta di classe, per affermare il diritto negli operai di difendere la loro libertà di cittadini e di discutere liberamente il prezzo del loro lavoro. Invece, cangiando tema, si fu contro il nero stendardo degli anarchici che essi parlarono. In nome del loro socialismo essi rinegarono i proletari affamati dalla coalizzazione capitalista.

Stolida codardia o vile ipocrisia politica?

Ignoro: ma questo affermo: che il doloroso nero stendardo libertario, che su tante sconfitte operaie si è ripiegato e contro cui tante basse calunnie si sono avventate, o ben in alto lo isseremo, in un prossimo giorno: le filippiche socialiste non avranno distolto il popolo dalla via della emancipazione. Ma ciò che giova intanto notare si è che il linguaggio dei parlamentaristi operai, pretesi socialisti, è ben strano in bocca a gente che si vuol dire antesignana di progresso, e come esso sia simile a quello dei reazionari di ogni tempo.

E per citar della sola Francia, sotto Luigi Filippo i liberali dicevano: Noi desiriamo il miglioramento della costituzione, ma siamo avversi ai repubblicani, poichè sono quelli che impediscono quelle concessioni che il re sarebbe disposto fare.

Più tardi sotto Napoleone III, i soliti lusingatori del popolo dicevano: Siamo repubblicani, ma non vogliamo aver alcun punto di contatto con i socialisti, poichè son essi che danneggiano il paese.

Nel 1880, i difensori, a parole, dell'operaio, gli amici del progresso, gridarono su tutti i toni: Siamo radicali-socialisti, ma respingiamo vivamente l'utopia socialista, poichè è essa che causa le giuste apprensione degli agricoltori e dei bottegai.

Ora si grida a squarciagola: Noi siamo collettivisti, ma abbasso l'anarchia, poichè essa ritarda il progresso che il governo e il parlamento ci promettono.

Così in ogni epoca si denunziano e si calunniano gli arditi combattenti di avanguardia. Ma quando poi è vinto, grazie alla loro persistente abnegazione, alla loro audacia, l'ostacolo davanti al quale ci si perdeva in chiacchere, o allora essi vengono glorificati ed innalzati così esageratamente che dianzi erano vilipesi. Allora tutti diranno a gara, prendendo una posa eroica: anch'io, o anch'io ci fui! Ma nuovamente, come sorgano nuovi ostacoli, essi ricomincieranno a gridar contro gli audaci novelli... che comprometteranno le libertà conquistate e che ritarderanno l'avvenire! (1).

(1) Questa frase ci fa pensare che non abbia del tutto torto l'amico Ciccioli quando dice che la discordanza fra socialisti e anarchici non sia, in fondo che una questione di meno o più paura, o se la frase spiace, di meno o più coraggio.

Nota del redattore.

ATTORNO A UN REGICIDIO

III.

Oltre il sentimentalismo di cui ò parlato nell'articolo precedente i "sovversivi" che disapprovarono il Bresci, altre ragioni aggiunsero per giustificare il loro contegno.

"L'uccisione di Umberto I, dissero alcuni, piuttosto che indebolire la monarchia in Italia, l'à rafforzata" — "il revolver del Bresci, affermarono altri, anarchici, più che uccidere il re à ucciso il nostro partito."

Io credo che se gli uni e gli altri avevano torto di invocare contro il regicida un sentimentalismo ipocrita, altrettanto ne avessero invocando l'interesse di partito.

Ciò che faceva credere ai primi che la monarchia sabauda si fosse rafforzata con la tragedia di Monza, erano le acclamazioni a cui furono fatti segno il nuovo re e altri membri della famiglia reale nelle varie città della penisola. Ora l' ignorare come tali manifestazioni "spontanee" si organizzino nel nostro mondo, non è permesso neppure agli abitanti del pianeta Marte, e chi volesse ostinarsi a crederle l'espressione sincera dei sentimenti del popolo correrebbe rischio di divenire il ridicolo della gente.

Io convengo volentieri che a quella specie di dimostrazioni si mescoli talvolta parte della massa che non vi sarebbe obbligata nè per ragione di mestiere, nè per esser stata pagata a tal uopo; ma prima di affermare che essa vi sia spinta da un sentimento di affetto verso il personaggio che vi si acclama, devesi considerare come a certi popoli, specialmente nella parte giovane, sia sommo godimento il correr per le vie e far del chiasso, togliendosi in tal modo, per qualche momento, alla monotonia di una vita sempre uguale. Molti si privano di quel godimento effimero quando può esservi pericolo, ma quando lo si può gustare impunemente vi si abbandonano con tutta libertà: ed ecco perché le dimostrazioni volute dai governanti sono spesse volte più rumorose e più affollate di quelle contro loro dirette.

Ma a questo punto io mi domando se debbo spendere ancora parole per dimo-

Source: International Institute of Social History, Amsterdam

From London

Translated from "Da Londra," *L'Avvenire* (Buenos Aires) 7, no. 149 (July 4, 1901)

June 9, 1901.

By initiative of the French Libertarian Group a large *meeting* took place in *Athenoeum Hall* to support the victims of Spanish oppression, the Montjuich martyrs, and anarchist prisoners and propaganda in Italy.[65]

The *meeting* took on colossal proportions and the space was too small to contain the immense stream of people who rushed to hear the words of our best comrades.

Present with their respective families were the Spaniards who were victims of the reaction in the horrific castle and of whom a good number still reside in London,[66] and although ill, comrade Kropotkin also participated, and others who will gradually be named.

Malatesta immediately took the floor, and with his usual vigor declared that the worker has the right to go on a general strike, in the struggle he sustains with capital, and to obtain any improvement.

Authority, he said, has no right to intervene in this dispute, nor to interfere without committing an attack against public order. Otherwise, the worker, not just in the spirit of preservation, but to repress the disorder caused by the intervention of authority, must use force against force.

It is necessary, urgent, that the people cease to act like a flock of sheep being led to the slaughterhouse.

With brief, energetic, stinging sentences, he told the story of the latest successes in Barcelona and in Corunna,[67] recalling meanwhile the loathsome Montjuich Castle and evoking the shadows of Canovas and Angiolillo.

He finished amidst applause, with a vigorous call to the Spanish people and to the proletariat in general so that they have the foresight to arm themselves in time to be able, if provoked, to resist violence with violence.[68]

. . .

---

65   The meeting took place on Saturday, June 8th.

66   After a June 1896 attack on the Corpus Domini procession in Barcelona, a terrible repression against anarchists was unleashed in Spain. Many of them were locked up and tortured in the Montjuïc Castle. The atrocities committed by the Spanish government provoked a widespread international protest campaign. Many anarchist victims of the repression subsequently emigrated to Great Britain.

67   In early May, a strike in the Barcelona tramway sector had pushed the government to proclaim a state of war throughout the province. In La Coruña a striker was killed on May 30th. During the night a general strike was declared, while a state of war was proclaimed throughout this entire province, too. On May 31st there were clashes in the streets in which seven people, workers or mere bystanders, were killed.

68   Cherkezov, Louise Michel, and Tárrida del Mármol spoke after Malatesta.

Social Movement. France.
Labor Movement [by P. Delesalle]

Translated from "Mouvement Social. France. Mouvement ouvrier,"
Les Temps Nouveaux (Paris) 7, no. 9 (June 29–July 5, 1901)

[*The report by Delesalle, a prominent representative of revolutionary syndicalism, concerns the London visit made by a French trade union delegation in the latter half of June 1901, in order to participate in the peace demonstration organized by the English Trades Unions. The excerpt provided here is part of the long report's final section.*]

Besides the "Against the war" demonstration, the "International Worker Group" had organized, on Tuesday,[69] a friendly meeting to which the French delegates present in London were invited. About thirty had responded to the group's invitation.

Our comrade, Yvetot, explained how, as anarchists, we understand trade union propaganda; how we counter electoral political action with the economic action of the working class, and how trade unions are at the same time a training school where workers, defending their immediate interests, also prepare themselves to take over the instruments of labor that allow their owners to perpetuate our exploitation.

In addition, Albert Henri explained our understanding of the "General Strike" and how we intend to make use of this revolutionary weapon, which led to a virulent retort from Malatesta, who explained why and how, at the time of the Milan riots, the Italian revolutionaries were defeated and their heroic act drowned in blood.

. . .

Anarchy Celebrates

The Evening Times (Washington), October 31, 1901[70]

A day or two after the dastardly shooting of President McKinley, the anarchist chief, Malatesta, said, in London, that it would be ridiculous for anyone to hold

---

69   June 18th.
70   This article, of which we are reprinting the opening lines, reports about the alleged displays of joy among anarchists over the cocky attitude of Leon Czolgosz, who assassinated the US president McKinley, in facing death. Although Czolgosz's execution took place on October 29, 1901, and this article is dated October 31st, its inclusion in the chronological sequence of writings takes into consideration the date of Malatesta's statement, issued, according to what is claimed here, not long after the attack, which took place on September 6th. McKinley died from his injuries on September 14th.

the society[71] responsible for the crime, which it would have been contrary to its interests at the present time to countenance. Anarchists everywhere, and in the United States especially, have rung the changes on this theme, declaring that nothing could be further from their thoughts than to plot the murder of an American President, whatever their feelings or wishes might be.

Interview with a London Anarchist

The Daily News (London), no. 17308 (September 12, 1901)[72]

A representative of the Press has interviewed a well-known "comrade" who has during the last few days been in the company of the more enlightened Anarchists, from whom he gathered some idea of their views of the attempt on Mr. McKinley's life. "My own opinion," he said, "is that the culprit is no more than a vain-glorious fellow, who understands little, if anything, of the nature or effects of his action. I have been speaking with several influential Anarchists about it. Prince Krapotkin declared that it was simply a common murder, and that it would be so dealt with. When asked whether the act had not some political significance, he refused to offer any opinion. Enrico Malatesta, the well known Italian refugee, said to me that 'there was no reason for it in a country like America,' and that more trouble fell upon the innocent than the guilty, as was the case in Spain and Italy immediately after the Anarchist outrages there a few years ago."

Malatesta Talks Anarchy

Brooklyn Standard Union (New York), September 13, 1901

LONDON, Sept. 13. —Malatesta, the Italian Anarchist, when interviewed today regarding the attack on President McKinley, said:

"Why should Anarchists condemn Czolgosz when the American Government is the real teacher of violence? Anarchy wishes to abolish violence, but the Americans slaughter weaker peoples in the Philippines and Cuba, and England slaughters the Boers. Why should there be a cry of 'good' when the Government, and 'bad' when the individual resorts to force?

"The people call Czolgosz a traitor for holding one hand toward the President while he held a pistol in the other. Let the Americans remember how

---

71   In their conspiratorial vision of the anarchist movement, the US press sometimes referred to it as "the society." Malatesta indisputably never used that term.

72   This dispatch from the Press Association was published on the same date by several British and US newspapers.

Aguinaldo was captured. We cannot condemn Czolgosz, nor can we condone Funston.[73] Anarchists do not advocate such acts, which, frankly, are those of a revolutionist. But revolutionism is not individual; we must have the people with us in an organized body.

"The Anarchist plotters the papers talk about are a silly myth. We are not disturbed by the talk of repression. In a month's time, if the President recovers, we will hear no more of it. The people are too busy making money. Also, history shows the futility of repression. If it is tried it will only make the tracing of the Anarchists the harder."

When asked if there was any special reason for Czolgosz's act, Malatesta tapped his forehead significantly and said:

"Probably here."

"Then the Anarchists do not sympathize with McKinley" was asked.

"Why?" Malatesta replied. "He tasted the fruits. The seed of violence was sown by Government Anarchists."

London Anarchist and the Outrage

Nottingham Daily Guardian, no. 14212 (September 14, 1901)

Enrico Malatesta, the well-known Italian refugee and Anarchist, interviewed in London by a correspondent regarding the attempted assassination of Mr. McKinley, said he thought rather of the suffering Cubans and Filipinos than of the President. Mr. McKinley was an Imperialist, and had brought America to the level of a European Power. He was an oppressor, and had allowed the trusts to grow in America until the workman had to work for what the rich would pay him, not for what he was worth.[74] There was in America to-day a despotic Monarchy which ruled by Gold. Anarchists, continued Malatesta, did not love blood; their gospel being one of peace, not war. He himself would never kill, but there were some among them who felt they could not see oppression around them without doing something for the cause. He ridiculed the suggestion that Americans were

---

73   Emilio Aguinaldo, head of the Filipino guerrillas fighting against the occupying US troops, was tricked into his own capture on March 23, 1901, by General Frederick Funston. Having learned from a Filipino deserter close to Aguinaldo that the guerrillas were expecting reinforcements, Funston sent him a column of Filipino mercenaries, disguised as guerrillas and commanded by Funston himself who, together with other US soldiers, was in turn disguised as a prisoner of war. He was able to thus penetrate Aguinaldo's general quarters undisturbed and catch him completely by surprise.

74   The issue of trusts dominated the 1900 presidential campaign, during which the democrats presented the republican McKinley as a defender of monopolistic capital.

going to stamp out Anarchism in the United States."It is so like the Americans," he remarked, "they will take stern measures for perhaps a month, and then they will go back to money making. There is no Government in the world which can stifle us to-day. They may try, but worse will come. We profess ourselves openly now. If they make it impossible for us to do these things in daylight, we shall do them at night."

Let's Halt down the Slope:
As Regards the Buffalo Attack

Translated from "Arrestiamoci sulla china: A proposito dell'attentato di Buffalo," *Il Risveglio Socialista-Anarchico* (Geneva) 2, no. 20 (September 28, 1901)

Mac Kinley, the head of North American oligarchy, the instrument and defender of the great capitalists, the traitor of the Cubans and the Filipinos, the man who authorized the massacre of the Hazleton strikers, the tortures of Idaho miners and the thousand disgraces being committed every day against workers in the "model republic," he who incarnated the militaristic, conquering, and imperialist policies on which the fat American bourgeoisie has embarked, has fallen victim of an anarchist's revolver.[75]

What do you want us to anguish over, if not for the fate awaiting the selfless person who, conveniently or importunely, with good or bad strategy, gave himself in holocaust to the cause of equality and freedom?

We repeat on this occasion, as in all similar occasions: we are in a society of wolves, in which violence surrounds us and bombards us from all sides; so, while we continue to calmly fight to bring an end to this horrible necessity of having to respond to violence with violence, and while we hope that the day soon comes when the antagonisms of interests and passions among men can be resolved by human and civil means, we save our tears and our flowers for other victims than these men, who, putting themselves at the head of exploiting and oppressing classes, assume the responsibility and face the risks of their position.

Yet anarchists have been found who deemed it useful and good to offend the oppressed who rebels, without having a word of reproach for the oppressor who paid the price for the crimes he committed or allowed to be committed!

Is it an aberration, is it an immoral desire to seek the approval of one's enemies? Or is it misguided *shrewdness* that seeks to conquer the freedom to propagate one's own ideas while voluntarily renouncing the

---

75   The correct spelling of the names of the two protagonists in this event are, respectively, "McKinley" and "Czolgosz." In the latter, "cz" is pronounced as "ch" in "checkers" and "sz" as "sh" in "shoe."

right to express the soul's true and deep sentiment, nay, falsifying this sentiment by pretending to be other than what one is?

I do so regretfully, but cannot help from showing the sorrow and indignation caused to me and many comrades I have had the chance to see in these days, by the rash words that *L'Agitazione* dedicated to the Buffalo attack.[76]

Czolgosh is a fool! But do they know him? *His act is a common crime, that has none of the indispensable characteristics to be considered political!*

I believe that no prosecutor, royal or republican, would dare to go this far. In fact, is there any reason to judge Ciolgosh as driven by personal grudges or interests? Is it not clear that he acted for reasons of public order, and he meant, with or without reason, but certainly with sincerity and abnegation, to sacrifice himself for a cause? And are these not the elements that lend the event the most pronounced character of a political-social attack?

Of course, it is inappropriate to speak of crime in similar cases. The code does it, but the code is built against us, against the oppressed, and cannot be used as a criterion for our judgment.

These events are acts of war; and if war is a crime, it is for those who are on the side of injustice and oppression. The English invading Transwaal can be, they are, criminals; the Boers are not, when they defend their liberty, even if the defense has no hope of succeeding.

Czolgosh's act (*L'Agitazione* might respond) *did not at all advance the cause of the proletariat and of the revolution: Mac Kinley is succeeded by his peer Roosevelt and everything remains as it was before, except the situation has become a little more difficult for the anarchists.* And perhaps

---

76 The reference is to the article "*L'attentato di Buffalo,*" published in *L'Agitazione* of Rome on September 13, 1901 and unsigned, but written by Luigi Fabbri. In republishing Malatesta's article in *Studi Sociali* of June 10, 1932, Fabbri recalls: "Malatesta immediately sent his protest article to *L'Agitazione*; but there, to my great chagrin, his text was sequestered by the judicial authority of Rome, and came out... blank. However, it was immediately republished in *Il Risveglio* of Geneva and in *La Questione Sociale* of Paterson." However, in the two issues of *L'Agitazione* following September 13th (September 20th and 27th) neither any blank space nor Malatesta's article appeared. Therefore, Pier Carlo Masini is also mistaken when he writes that Malatesta's article appeared in *L'Agitazione* of September 22nd, then was sequestered and released again in a second "whitewashed" edition (*Storia degli anarchici italiani nell'epoca degli attentati* [Milan, 1981], 180). Malatesta's article was in fact only published in the October 4th issue—after already appearing in *Risveglio*—and this is the issue that was sequestered. As confirmation, in the summary of the trial against Malatesta and Ettore Sottovia, manager of *L'Agitazione*, that followed publication of the article, the April 11, 1902, issue of *L'Agitazione* notes that "the incriminating article was taken from a foreign newspaper to which Malatesta had sent it—*Il Risveglio* of Geneva." In brief, the *Risveglio* edition is to be considered in every respect to be the first.

L'Agitazione would be right: indeed, in the American environment, from what I know, it seems to me probable that this is the case.

This means that in war there are successful moves and wrong moves; there are wary combatants and those who, allowing themselves to be carried away by enthusiasm, offer themselves as an easy target for the enemy and may even compromise the position of their comrades; this means that each one must advise and defend and practice the strategy which he thinks most suitable to achieve victory in the shortest time and with the least sacrifice possible. But it cannot alter the fundamental, obvious fact that he who struggles, well or poorly, against our enemy and with our same objectives, is our friend and has a right, certainly not to our unconditional approval, but to our warm sympathy.

Whether the fighting unit is a collective or a single individual cannot change any part of the moral aspect of the issue. An armed insurrection carried out inopportunely can produce real or apparent harm to the social war we are fighting, just like an individual attack that irritates popular sentiment; but if the insurrection was started to conquer freedom, no anarchist would deny it his sympathy, no one especially would dare deny the social-political combatant nature of the defeated insurgents. Why should it be different if the insurgent is a single individual?

L'Agitazione has said that strikers are always right against the masters, and it has said so rightly, though obviously not all strikes are advisable, since an unsuccessful strike can, under given circumstances, produce discouragement and scattering of the labor forces. How, then, what is true in the economic fight against masters should not be true in the political fight against the governing authorities, who want to subjugate us to them and the capitalists by means of the soldier's rifle and the policeman's handcuffs?

This is not about discussing tactics. If it were, I would say that in general I prefer collective action to individual action, also because collective action, which requires average qualities that are fairly common, can be more or less relied upon, while one cannot count on the exceptional heroism, by its nature sporadic, that calls for individual sacrifice. This is an issue of a higher order; it is about the revolutionary spirit, it is about that almost instinctive feeling of hatred of oppression, without which the dead letters of programs do not matter, however libertarian the claimed intentions are; it is about that combative spirit, without which even anarchists become domesticated and end up, by one road or another, in the morass of legalitarianism...

Frankly, I cannot believe that the article in *L'Agitazione* corresponds to the true feelings of that newspaper's editors, and I know them well enough to be sure that no cowardly thought of personal security has inspired them. For this it is enough to be silent. They must have believed to save the relative (oh! how relative) freedom of propaganda that in this moment is left to them, they must have believed they were acting in the interests of our party, of our organizations, of our newspapers: all things that I believe excellent, but that do not compensate for the damage produced by lying about own's own convictions.

It is foolish to save life by destroying the reasons for living. What use are revolutionary organizations if they let the revolutionary spirit die? What use is freedom of propaganda if one no longer propagates what one thinks?

And the worst is that the anti-organizationist anarchists, those who are against participation in the labor struggle, establishment of a party, etc., will not fail to say and believe that this extinguishing of the revolutionary spirit is a consequence of the method they disapprove of. They will not be right, but they will seem to be right, and this will cause more damage to our work than all possible persecutions.

In my opinion, the secret of our success lies in knowing how to reconcile revolutionary action and spirit with everyday practical action; in knowing how to participate in small struggles without losing sight of the great and definitive struggle. And to me the matter does not seem difficult.

I hope the friends at *L'Agitazione* will be able to forget a moment of bad inspiration, and maintain the newspaper's frankly revolutionary character, which corresponds to anarchist principles.

Errico MALATESTA

The Reign of Anarchy

Yorkshire Telegraph and Star (Sheffield), October 7, 1901

CZOLGOSZ LAUDED IN LONDON.
REMARKABLE UTTERANCES.

A fairly numerous gathering of the most thorough-going of the anarchists now in London assembled yesterday at the Athenæum Hall, Tottenham Court Road, to hear a lecture on the late President McKinley from the anarchist standpoint. The majority of the audience were foreigners. A few women were present, and also, it was stated, one or two members of the American Secret Service, and an official from Scotland Yard. The anarchists applauded all references by the lecturer, who hails from New York, to their newest "Saint." Czolgosz.[77] Among the speakers was the notorious Malatesta. The lecturer deplored the giving of a martyr's crown to the dead President through the "meritorious act" of Czolgosz. Malatesta declared

---

77   Harry Kelly was the speaker.

that the assassin had "performed a deed of heroism." Killing was no crime if exercised by the oppressed against the oppressor. Every British soldier who shot a Boer was a murderer, but every Boer who slew a Briton was a hero, because he was upholding his right to freedom . . .

Most Sneers at Marooning

The Evening News (Washington), December 10, 1901

SAYS THE HOAR PLAN IS NONSENSE.
MALATESTA'S VIEWS ARE SIMILAR.
"IF IDEA WOULD WORK AT ALL," SAYS, HERR JOHN, "IT WOULD REDOUND TO ANARCHY'S GLORY"—CLAIMS HE ORIGINATED THE PLAN.[78]

. . .

What Malatesta Thinks.
LONDON, Dec. 10.—Malatesta, the Italian anarchist, when interviewed by your correspondent regarding United States Senator Hoar's scheme for the marooning of anarchists, said that such action would be worse than useless. From his point of view, Malatesta said, repression in any form only increases the followers of the cause which it is sought to repress.

"Under such conditions," Malatesta said, "anarchy, instead of being an open organization, would become a clandestine one. Anarchists would call themselves by some other name. They would not appear on the public platforms, but the agitation would continue. You could only lay hands upon a score of leaders, while the great body of anarchists would not be touched.

Would Become Heroes.
"The marooned leaders," the Italian anarchist continued, "would become martyrs and heroes. You remember that the vitality of the Dreyfus case was the power of his unusual punishment upon the popular imagination and sympathy. The public soon forgot him when he was no longer a lone prisoner on Devils Island.[79] History is full of similar instances.

---

78   After McKinley's assassination, US senator George F. Hoar proposed that all countries worldwide come to an agreement to designate an island to which anarchists could be deported and left to their own devices. German anarchist Johann Most had been living in the United States since 1882 and was therefore a well-known figure in the national press. According to the statements attributed to him in the first part of the article, he had proposed ten years prior that the world powers reserve an area for anarchists in which they could put their ideas into practice without interference.

79   This is an islet off the coast of French Guiana.

"In a month the Americans will have some new scheme for money making and will forget Hoar's silly resolution."

Pell-Mell. They're Better Off in Bombay

Translated from "Pêle-mêle. Mejor están en Bombay," *Heraldo de Paris* 3, no. 47 (March 22 1902)[80]

London, March 5.

Dear Bonafoux:

I see from the HERALDO that my article did not reach its destination. I sent it to your private residence.[81]

Send me a safe address, as it appears that the police are stealing your correspondence.

Your friend,
E. MALATESTA.

[*This is followed by a comment from Bonafoux on the methods of the police in Latin countries.*]

[Speech Given in London on March 8, 1902]

Translated from a report by police commissioner Prina to the Ministry of the Interior, London, March 12, 1902[82]

Subject: Malatesta Errico[83]

. . .

---

80   "Pêle-mêle" was a regular column in the newspaper directed by Bonafoux. He later republished the letter reproduced here in his book *Bilis* (Paris: Sociedad de Ediciones Literarias y Artísticas, 1908, ix).

81   In the March 1, 1902 issue of *Heraldo de Paris*, the front page displayed, under the title "Malatesta" and signed by "B.," a short article with the following content: "The article that Malatesta sent me, according to a message from him, concerning the events in Spain, arrived neither at our newsroom nor at my private residence..." For Malatesta's point of view on the matter in question, see "After the Defeat" on p. 86 of the current volume.

82   Manuscript, Archivio Centrale dello Stato, Rome, Casellario Politico Centrale, box 2949.

83   Note in text margin.

He[84] (questioned some days ago by several of the most influential in a private house in Manor Park, regarding what he thought about matters in Italy and whether he found it opportune for someone to go on-site to *channel the current,* especially after the riots in Calabria)[85] self-consistently responded more or less as such: "The time has not yet come, although I do not believe it is very far off, to act and show ourselves. If however someone wants to make an attempt, they are quite free to do so, but I will not take a step away from London, for now. The uprisings in Calabria, which we did not foresee, and those that perhaps could break out elsewhere in Italy, are destined to be promptly crushed; this however must not discourage us, since they will bear fruit. Right now they signal that the revolutionary tendency is consolidating among the people, and this, in addition to being most useful in the moment of action, will hasten the catastrophe pushing the Government to reaction. In sum, what I recommend you do is be ready and not do anything rash."

He presented the same ideas on the evening of the eighth inst. in a public debate with Petraroja Gennaro, held in the usual room of the International Anarchist Group on the subject: *The duty of anarchists in the present era.* Malatesta sought to demonstrate that in order for the revolution to be a success, the following would above all be necessary: a firm will among the masses to carry it out, a solid proletarian consciousness and a good organization of workers so as to render possible the issuing of precise orders and the achievement of preordained objectives, and a certain pecuniary potentiality.

Now, says Malatesta, while there may be a firm will, especially in Italy, consciousness, organization and means are lacking, therefore our duty is to strive with all of our force to bridge these gaps, otherwise the events will replicate what happened in Barcelona and in Turin, what is about to happen in Calabria, and what could happen soon in other parts of Italy.[86] However, we must not hamper or denounce such vain attempts, because by bringing about repression as a

---

84   The subject in question is Malatesta.

85   Between late February and early March there were uprisings in Cassano allo Ionio and several other places in Calabria, triggered particularly by unkept promises concerning the construction of rail lines, in a region that had been progressively impoverished without any glimpse of possible redemption. Municipal councils resigned en masse and various municipal buildings were invaded by farmers and set on fire.

86   In Barcelona, a strike of metal workers fighting for the nine-hour workday transformed, on February 17th, into a general strike that paralyzed the city. Participation was estimated between eighty and one hundred thousand workers. A state of war was declared and the army's intervention was followed by clashes in the streets throughout the next week. The number of victims varies depending on the source but is definitely at least several dozen. In Turin, a strike begun on February 3rd by the gasmen's union quickly widened becoming, on February 21st, the city's first general strike. After days of tension and conflict with police, on February 24th the Labor Chamber signed an agreement that, although rejected by most of the workers, put an end to the strike.

consequence, they provoke the reaction that is entirely to our advantage. There-fore let's hope that other and more serious events will happen to hasten the un-folding of events with a change of Cabinet, even though, in my opinion, there is no or very little difference between the current Government and a Sonnino–Rudinì Ministry. But if a Sonnino Rudinì Cabinet came to power it would obvi-ously have to change direction in a reactionary way—though more in appearance than in substance—and this, in my opinion, would hasten the outbreak, which is not far away. Let us penetrate socialist organizations, so that, besides men, at the opportune moment we will also be able to have money at our disposal, and mean-while let us not desist from continuous propaganda, by any means, in any place; let us always keep in touch with the masses and, even if so far we have suffered defeats and perhaps we shall have to lament a few more, let us not lose our spirit, that soon victory shall smile upon us.

. . .

To Begin

Translated from "Per incominciare," *Lo Sciopero Generale* (London) 1, no. 1 (March 18, 1902)[87]

With the skepticism brought about by many years of experience, but with an unshaken faith in our principles, today we undertake the publication of a new anarchist propaganda paper.

At the present time, under such complex circumstances, vigorous acts of protest and resistance to the spread of oppression are needed more than "PRINTED PAPER."

However, not everyone is in a position to carry out what the arm and the mind, desirous, would want.

Awaiting the luminous day of a battle in which—every veil of com-promise or hypocrisy lifted—we can give substance, even if in a fleeting moment, to our radiant dream of rebellion, awaiting that day we strive to propagate it through modest propaganda work.

It is our intention to make a monthly paper that, while abstaining from all lazy theoretical questions that too often divide us, attempts to

---

87   This periodical consisted of two parts, each two pages long: *Lo Sciopero Generale*, in Italian, and *La Grève Générale*, in French, each with a different editorial group and content. In the first issue, the Italian portion displayed the following quote from Malatesta next to its masthead: "Popular insurrection is the necessary means to abolish tyranny." In addition to the articles pub-lished here, this issue contained another article by Malatesta, "Agli uomini di progresso" (To the men of progress). This was an excerpt from the pamphlet *Against the Monarchy*, which we published in its entirety in the volume of these *Complete Works* covering the years 1899–1900.

diffuse the principle of the union of all proletarian forces in unanimous revolutionary effort.

A few years of personal experience in proletarian movements and a crumb of knowledge learned from the history of prior revolutions have taught us that the propaganda of theoretical principles must always keep up with practical action, or else the consciousness already raised will dissipate.

Every social environment has its saturation limit for the infiltration of new ideas, which cannot be surpassed, unless revolutionary action—in the common sense of the word—by creating a new state of affairs and a different orientation of interests, prepares a new favorable environment.

Capitalistic exploitation has a tangible, real foundation in the handcuffs of the cops, in the bayonets of the soldiers.

The best dialectic argument, even if crafted by expert thought, will never be enough to significantly affect the resistance of capitalistic interests, materialized by rifles and bayonets.

However, it will help to prepare that hostile army, which opposing force to force, body to body, weapon to weapon, may decide the outcome.

The reforms—transitory and temporary—with which now a part of socialism tinkers, are often nothing more than new conditions of adaptation to unaltered exploitation.

Capital, due to its adaptable and malleable essence, concedes to labor politics as much greater political liberty as it can get back in turn through more intense economic exploitation.

The general strike, namely the entire army of producers ceasing work, would lead to the social revolution if the only people facing us were the rich, the exploiters, the parasites.

But behind them—in front of them, we mean—is an entire formidable army of people paid or brutalized or forced, ready at the first signal from the bourgeoisie to shoot, arrest, deport, destroy the proletarian forces.

The revolt of folded arms is only the first step in a revolutionary attitude that finds its natural fulfillment in the popular insurrection. Only the latter, aimed at tearing down the government using the same arms by which it defends its privileges, and coupled with abstention from work by all working classes, can result in a true revolutionary period.

This is what we mean by general strike, from which our new paper has taken its title.

Our French-speaking comrades, who today begin an identical effort with us, have ensured us their mutual support.

THE EDITORS.

ANNO I   LONDRA, 18 MARZO 1902.   N. 1

LO SCIOPERO
✿ ✿ ✿ GENERALE

L'insurrezione popolare è il mezzo necessario per abolire la tirannia.

E. MALATESTA.

Per incominciare

Con quello scetticismo che arreca l'esperienza di molti anni, ma con inalterata fede ne' nostri principj, noi imprendiamo oggi la pubblicazione di un nuovo foglio di propaganda anarchica.

L'ora presente, d'avvenimenti sì complessa, più che "CARTA STAMPATA," vorrebbe virili atti di protesta e di resistenza al generalizzarsi dell'oppressione.

Non a tutti però è dato attuare quanto il braccio e la mente, desiosi, vorrebbero.

Aspettando il luminoso giorno d'una battaglia in cui — deposto ogni velo di transigenza o d'ipocrisia — ci sia dato incarnare, sia pure nell'attimo fuggente, il radioso nostro sogno di ribellione, aspettando quel dì noi ci sforziamo di propagarlo con l'opera modesta di propaganda.

E' nostro proposito fare un foglio mensile il quale astenendosi da tutte quelle ozioso questioni teoriche che troppo sovente ci dividono, tenti diffondere il principio dell'unione di tutte le forze proletarie in concorde sforzo rivoluzionario.

Qualche nimo di personale esperienza ne' movimenti proletari; un briciolo di sapere appreso dalla storia delle rivoluzioni precedenti, ci hanno insegnato che i principj de' partiti teorici deve tenere sempre dietro l'azione pratica, pena il disperdersi delle coscienze già fatte.

Ogni ambiente sociale ha, per l'infiltrazione d'una nuova idea, il suo limite di saturazione, oltre questo non è possibile andare, se una nâtura rivoluzionaria — nel senso comune della parola — creando un nuovo stato di cose, una diversa orientazione d'interessi, non prepari un novello ambiente favorevole.

Lo sfruttamento capitalistico ha una lacerabile, reale, nelle masnade degli sbirri, nelle bajonette de' soldati.

Il migliore argomento dialettico anche se foggiato da pensiero maestro non varrà mai a smuovere in modo sensibile la resistenza degli interessi capitalistici, materiata di fucili e di bajonette.

Ma varrà a preparare quell'esercito ostile, che opponendo forza a forza, corpo a corpo, scuota ed arma derisa dell'odio.

Le riforme — transitorio e passeggero — in cui esso si trastulla una parte del socialismo sovente non sono altro che nuove mediazioni di adottamento di un inalterato sfruttamento.

Il capitale, per sua connessa inalienabile ed adattabile, concede alla politica operaja quel tanto di maggiori libertà po itiche che può in equivalenza riavere con un più intenso sfruttamento economico.

Lo sciopero generale, ossia il cessare dal lavoro di tutta l'armata de' produttori condurrebbe alla rivoluzione sociale se noi ci trovassimo di fronte le sole persone de' ricchi, degli sfruttatori, de' parassiti.

Ma dietro ad essi — avanti ad essi volevamo dire — sta tutto un formidabile esercito di gente pagata ed abbrutita e costretta, pronta al primo cenno della borghesia a sparare contro, arrestare, deportare, distruggere le forze proletarie.

La rivolta delle braccia sorrette non è che il primo passo d'un atteggiamento rivoluzionario che trova il suo naturale consiglio nell'insurrezione popolare. Questa, diretta ad abbattere il governo con le stesse armi con cui esso difende i suoi privilegi uniti all'astensione del lavoro di tutte le classi operaje potrà sola determinare un vero periodo rivoluzionario.

Così intendiamo noi lo sciopero generale, da cui il nostro nuovo foglio ha tratto il titolo.

I compagni di lingua francese che in questo giorno iniziano con noi un identico tentativo, ci hanno assicurato il loro modesto appoggio.

LA REDAZIONE.

Dopo la sconfitta

Delle giornate di febbraio dimani dirà la Storia tutto l'eroismo sviegato dagli operai Catalani, tutte le cose atroci che la borghesia spagnuola ha commesso soffocando nel sangue le loro aspirazioni.

I nepoti di Loyola non hanno punto esitato a sparare sulla "canaglia," che nelle strade era andata a gridare tutto l'immenso suo dolore, a urlare gli strazi della sua fame secolare.

Anche —deposta ogni parvenza di legale procedura — le autorità militari hanno fucilato, nei primi giorni del movimento, nel maledetto castello di Montjuich i nostri compagni arrestati.

Ciò facendo, le forze reazionarie della Spagna, non si sono scostate di una linea da ciò che la più elementare logica loro consigliava.

Di fronte al popolo che pareva deciso a finirla una

buona volta con la propria schiavitù, che pareva stanco di promesse fallite e di riforme vane e che si poteva stimar pronto ad adoperare l'ultimo argomento — il solo valido e decisivo — quello della forza opposta alla violenza, quello dell'impossessamento delle ricchezze per tanti anni prodotte altrui ; di fronte a tali cose la borghesia spagnola non aveva altra uscita che questa : fucilare, fucilare, fucilare.

E' la logica delle cose che inesorabilmente si impone.

E' stolido gridare ora la sua ferocia, la sua crudeltà ditali repressioni. Sarebbe un riconoscere la tragicità solenne della vita : sarebbe dimostrare d'avere ben poco intendimento di quanto terribili debbono essere gli urti di due opposte classi sociali, per la formazione di uno stato novello di cose.

Quando centinaja nostre di compagni, nelle carceri spagnuole a. tendono una oscura sorte, forse la morte, forse una lunga carcerazione ; quando ancora le strade di Barcellona sono rosse di sangue, stonerebbe detta da noi che nulla abbiamo fatto, una semplice parola che suonasse rimprovero dell'insuccesso.

Ma poichè è forte una corrente d'idee — diffusa da alcuni socialisti e da parecchi anarchici — che lo sciopero generale possa di per se condurre alla rivoluzione generale o almeno al conseguimento di alcune conquiste sul terreno stesso della lotta, per la formazione di un vero stato, per la rivoluzione che noi vogliamo, noi dobbiamo tacerci al proposito.

Coloro che hanno fatto credere al popolo che semplicemente astenendosi dal lavoro costringendo la borghesia a cedere, sono i direttamente responsabili del sangue catalano ora sparso.

Non così leggermente si assumono la responsabilità delle lotte sociali.

"Allo sciopero generale deve esser contemporanea una preparazione per una " politica , ed armata resistenza ,,

Il popolo deve esser avvertito — speriamo che gli avvenimenti finiscano per insegnarglielo — che la borghesia di fronte allo sciopero generale non sa, non può opporre altro che la reazione dei suoi fucili.

Durante uno sciopero generale il popolo non dovrebbe scendere nelle vie senza essere pronto a sparare sui soldati che la borghesia gli opporrà.

Sono nostri fratelli, dicono i predicatori del placide evoluzioni, ed il popolo non deve mai dimenticarlo. Sia.

Ma anche noi siamo i fratelli loro.

Quando la fratellanza è così rotta, il popolo non è più oltre obbligato a nutrire falsi sentimenti di umanità.

Del pari, i giorni di attesa, dopo che lo sciopero è dichiarato, scorsi in una pacifica aspettativa, sono la disfatta preparata, anticipata.

Lo sciopero generale è diretto ad affamare la borghesia non ad affamarci : il lavoratore per conservarsi combattente valido deve mangiare, e poichè non ne ha, non può comperarlo — e non dovrebbe - deve prender il cibo suo, il suo bisognevole nei magazzini che egli ha precedentemente empito nei giorni di lavoro.

La sconfitta del proletariato catalano per quanto dolorosa non è definitiva : ammaestrato dalla dura esperienza, traendo forza dalle estese federazioni operaje e non dimenticando di preparare quella organizzazione che meglio lo possa fornire di mezzi d'offesa materiale — armi ed esplosivi — noi ci auguriamo che gli possa scrivere un'altra pagina gloriosa.

La causa della rivoluzione molto attende dalla generosa Barcellona !

Noi non vogliamo "emancipare" il popolo ma vogliamo che il popolo si emancipi.

AGLI UOMINI DI PROGRESSO

I ferrovieri vengono militarizzati.
La classe '78 è chiamata sotto le armi.
Decreti regj.

Oramai ogni illusione di progresso pacifico è diventata impossibile.

Non è egli tempo che tutti coloro i quali non sono complici e beneficiari della tirannia e non vogliono rasserenarsi al presente orribile stato di cose, esaminino quale è la linea di condotta che impongono le circostanze ed avvisino al da farsi ?

Egli certo ormai che la monarchia italiana non conta più che sulla sciabola, ed alla sciabola affiderà in definitivo la difesa di se stessa e della classe che con essa è solidarizzata,

Si tratta di opporre la forza alla forza e l'insurrezione popolare si presenta di nuovo come mezzo necessario per abbattere la tirannia.

Ma non basta insorgere, bisogna vincere.

Bisogna dunque se si vuol vincere e non affrontare inutilmente periodici massacri, prepararsi in modo adeguato alla forza controo cui si deve combattere.

Ma qui si tratta di una questione materiale, che si subordina con tutta la brutalità della forza ai problemi economici e morali da cui è tormentato il paese

Il governo ha soldati, cannoni, mezzi rapidi di comunicazione e di trasporto ; esso ha tutta una possente organizzazione pronta all'opera di repressione ; ed ha mostrato quanto sia capace e voglioso di adoperarla.

Per metter fine ad un'agitazione, la quale si riduce poi a dimostrazioni inermi ed a piccoli tumulti, (che l'abolizione del dazio e qualque altra anodina concessione avrebbero facilmente calmati), il governo non ha mai esitato a massacrare cittadini e operaj a centinaja. Che cosa non sarebbero capaci di fare le belve gallonate che stanno al servizio del re quando un pericolo serio li minacciasse ?

Una città che volesse dare la speranza che altre risponderanno al suo esempio, sarebbe probabilmente ridotta in rovine prima che la notizia arrivasse altrove. Una popolazione che volesse manifestare il pro prio malcontento con energia, ma senza armi adeguate, sarebbe soffocata nel sangue prima che il movimento avesse potuto prendere sviluppo.

Bisogna dunque colpire di consenso, con forza e decisione. Bisogna che, prima che le autorità sieno rinvenute della sorpresa, il popolo, o per parlare più propriamente, i gruppi precedentemente organizzati per l'azione, abbiano messo la mano sul più gran numero possibile dei capi dell'esercito e del governo ; bisogna che ciascun gruppo insorto, ciascuna folla tumultuante, senta che non è sola, e incoraggiata dalla speranza della vittoria, persista nella lotta e la spinga all'estremo ; bisogna che i soldati si accorgano che sono di fronte ad una vera rivoluzione e sieno tentati a disertare e fraternizzare col popolo, prima che l'ebbrezza del

LA GRÈVE

GÉNÉRALE

> Il est un droit qui prime
> tous les autres : le droit à
> l'insurrection.
> Émile HENRY.

Pour toutes communications et correspondances s'adresser à

LA GREVE GENERALE

33, GRESSE STREET, RATHBONNE PLACE, LONDON, W.

LA GREVE GENERALE

Camarade lecteur, nous te présentons le premier numéro de notre journal. A l'heure où les gouvernants de tous les pays préparent de nouvelles lois contre la Pensée libre, il est de bonne tactique de répondre par l'affirmation de notre action révolutionnaire.

La "Grève Générale" est aujourd'hui une des armes nécessaires pour édifier une société plus juste et plus équitable.

De tout temps la résistance à l'oppression s'est manifestée par des révoltes plus ou moins bien réprimées et dans le régime capitaliste, ces révoltes, ont pris le caractère particulier de cessation complète de travail. Cette nouvelle tactique c'est la "grève" qui caractérise le conflit permanent du capital et du travail, et qui doit être pour le producteur le moyen de conquérir son indépendance.

Partout, en France, en Espagne, en Italie, aux Etats Unis, les travailleurs se préparent à l'action libératrice. Un vent de liberté souffle sur le monde entier, et c'est l'heure où les parias et les maudits vont revendiquer leur droit à l'existence.

Notre journal "La Grève Générale" attaquant l'armée, cette école de meurtre et d'assassinat, fera comprendre aux jeunes prolétaires, le crime qu'ils commettent en prenant les armes qui serviront à tuer leurs frères de misère. Sous la livrée militaire, l'homme se transforme en chien de garde, défendant la société bourgeoise c'est à-dire les coffre-forts de la haute finance.

Que ceux à qui plaît ce triste rôle, se resignent. Quand aux autres, aux fiers, aux jeunes hommes d'avant-garde, la ligne de conduite est toute tracé, et "la Grève des soldats" surgit nécessairement.

Dans ce journal, nous démontrerons les iniquités de l'heure présente; les crimes qui se commettent journellement sous les masques de Religion, Honneur, Patrie, etc.

Impitoyablement, nous flagellerons les heureux et les puissants, tous ceux dont la fortune s'est édifiée sur la misère des travailleurs.

Nous ferons comprendre qu'il est temp que les ouvriers se libèrent de leur esclavage et qu'ils ne doivent compter pour cela que sur eux-mêmes. Ce ne seront pas de nouveaux gouvernants qui pourront améliorer notre situation. Tous les gouvernements se valent: l'Empire avec les massacres de la Ricamarie, la République avec Constans avec Fourmies, ou celle de Millerand avec Châlon.

Il n'y a pas de bons maîtres, il n'y a que des maîtres.

Nous démontrerons que l'agitation électorale avec laquelle on détourne les masses de la voie révolutionnaire, n'est qu'une fourberie de plus, servant aux décrocheurs de mandat, en mal de socialisme, de tremplin politique.

Ce que nous voulons, c'est que se libèrent à jamais les cerveaux enténébrés de préjugés, et que les travailleurs comprennent bien qu'ils ne doivent compter que sur eux pour ameliorer leur situation.

C'est pourquoi ils commenceront "la grève des électeurs", prélude de la grève générale economique.

Car qu'on le sache bien cette grève générale "c'est la Révolution Sociale" révolution violente fatalement, amenant sans retard l'expropriation capitaliste, et balayant dans sa tourmente salvatrice, l'ignoble société dans laquelle nous végétons misérablement.

La Grève Générale, ce sera la diane des grands jours de bataille, et, au sen des ténèbres qui enveloppent l'humanité ignorante, c'est la lueur qui perce l'obscurité et oriente les foules vers des horizons de clarté

Par delà les frontières, présageant magnifiquement des révoltes implacables, la "Grève Générale" s'annonce pleine de terreur pour les maitres, les riches, et les tyrans, emplie d'espoir pour les parias et les maudits.

Demain peut être le jour libérateur, où du choc des haines meurtrières, surgira la Révolution libératrice. Il import d'être prêts et de savoir où orienter ses efforts.

C'est le but que nous nous proposons, et que nous atteindrons, quand les forçats des mines et des ateliers auront compris que l'heure de la justice sociale a enfin sonné.

LA GREVE GENERALE.

ENCOURAGEMENTS

A propos de la "Grève Générale" le camarade Matha nous écrit ces lignes :

" ...Bravo! l'idée est bonne! il faut multiplier nos organes de propagande le plus possible. Les bourgeois en ont des milliers, hacun d'une puissance formidable, et nous n'en avons que quelques uns et encore bien chétifs.

Faisons que notre énergie supplée à l'outillage. Vive les Jeunes! "

L'ACTION

Aux groupements libertaires du monde entier s'adresse cet appel, ainsi qu'aux camarades isolés.

Le moment est venu de ne plus se contenter de rêves pour la Société future : l'idéal avec lequel on hypnotise les simplistes, doit faire place, à la lutte au jour le jour, lutte implacable et de tous les instants.

En France, le mouvement de la Grève Générale prend une orientation de plus en plus anarchiste, et nombreux sont les groupements qui contribuent à en propager l'idée. A Paris, fonctione le Comité de "Propagande" de la Grève Générale, et à Lyon, Marseille, Saint-Etienne, le Havre, Montpellier, Albi,

Bourges, Dijon, Elbœuf, Vierzan, Agen, etc. d'autre comités spéciaux issus des congrès corporatifs de ces deux années, activent cette propagande. C'est un résultat qui ne doit pas rester cantonné en France.

La Grève Générale doit être propagée internationalement ; il faut donc sans retard, se fondent dans tous les pays, des groupements s'occupant spécialement de cette tactique, révolutionnaire et ayant entre eux de continuelles relations. La grandeur d'une telle action d'ensemble incombe aux camarades anarchistes, car il ne faut pas que la cancre politique s'infiltre dans cette grève générale et cela arrivera, si nous ne prenons pas les devants.

Ici à Londres nous faisons paraitre le même organe, en française et en italien, qui sera repandu dans les contrées où se parlent ces deux langues, en plus de Londres, même.

Nous prions donc les camarades, de

LA BATAILLE, de Namur ;
LE REVEIL DES TRAVAILLEURS, de Liège ;
L'ÉMANCIPATION, de Bruxelles ;
FREEDOM, de Londres ;
LE REVEIL-IL RISVEGLIO, de Genève ;
NEUES-LEBEN, de Berlin ;
TIERRA y LIBERTAD, de Madrid ;
L'AGITAZIONE, de Rome ;
LA QUESTIONE SOCIALE, de Paterson ;
GERMINAL, de Paterson, etc., etc.

en un mot, les compagnons de tous les pays, à mettre cette idée à exécution. C'est un travail serieux et efficace, aux énergies de s'y consacrer.

Nous enregistrons avec plaisir toutes les objections qui nous parviendront, et nous prions nos amis de tous les pays de reproduire cet appel dans leurs organes libertaires, pour que notre action aie toute l'ampleur que nous en attendons.

LA REDACTION.

N. B. Prière au "Libertaire" et aux "Temps Nouveaux" de reproduire intégralement.

Germinal !

> Que vienne le soir de Germinal où,
> parmi les blés neufs, marcheront, libres
> de servitude, exempts de crainte et
> contiants de leurs droits les peuples
> rénovés.   L. TAILHADE.

Ils se sont levés les fiers gars de l'usine, forçats de toutes catégories, et en cette Barcelone, foyer d'insurrection, ils ont fait entendre leurs revendications. Une fois de plus, la sauvagerie bourgeoise a écrasé cette tentative révolutionnaire, la plus belle que nous ayons à enregistrer depuis la Commune de Paris.

Mais l'exemple ne sera pas perdu. Ce premier essai de grève générale a démontré la puissance de cette tactique, et s'il faut voir que si les travailleurs des autres villes d'Espagne avaient marché de l'avant, l'insurrection aurait triomphé.

Malheureusement, là encore, et particulièrement à Bilbao et Saragosse, les pires ennemis de toute action ne furent pas les détenteurs de l'autorité, mais les socialistes, qui comme à Saragosse dénoncèrent à la police, deux des camarades anarchistes qui avaient commencé l'agitation gréviste.

A Bilbao, ils éditèrent un manifeste dans le seul but de protester contre les violences des anarchistes, et leurs organes "El Socialista" et "La lutte de classe" ont flagellé lachement, les libertaires détenus prisons.

L'attitude du laquais de Sagasta, qu'est Pablo Iglesias est assez connu sans qu'il soit utile d'insister.

Aux prochains jours de l'insurrection, qui ne tar-

After the Defeat

Translated from "Dopo la sconfitta," *Lo Sciopero Generale* (London) 1, no. 1 (March 18, 1902)

These days of February will go down in History for all the heroism exhibited by the Catalonian workers and all the atrocious acts that the Spanish bourgeoisie committed, smothering their aspirations in blood.

Loyola's descendants did not hesitate one minute to shoot the "scoundrels" who had taken to the streets to shout out all their immense pain and all the torments of their secular hunger.

Setting also aside any semblance of a legal procedure, in the first days of the movement the military authorities gunned down our arrested comrades in the cursed Montjuich castle.

In so doing, the reactionary forces of Spain did not budge a millimeter from what the most elementary logic advised them.

Faced with a people who seemed determined to be done with their slavery once and for all, who seemed tired of failed promises and vain reforms, and who could be considered ready to use the last argument—the only valid and decisive one—that of force against violence, that of seizing wealth produced for others for so many years; faced with all this the Spanish bourgeoisie had no other exit but this one: to shoot, shoot, shoot.

The logic of affairs inexorably comes to the fore.

It is inane now to cry out about the ferocity, the cruelty of these repressions. It would just mean acknowledging the solemn tragedy of life: it would demonstrate having very little understanding of how terrible the collision of two opposing social classes must be, for the formation of a new state of affairs.

When hundreds of our comrades in Spanish prisons await an obscure fate, perhaps death, perhaps a long incarceration; when the streets of Barcelona are still red with blood, any word that sounded like a reproach of the failure would be out of place if uttered by us, who have done nothing.

But since there is a strong current of ideas—diffused by some socialists and many anarchists—that the general strike can, in and of itself, lead to the general revolution, or at least deliver some conquests, we cannot be silent on this subject.

Those who made the people believe that by simply abstaining from work the bourgeoisie would be forced to yield, are directly responsible for the Catalonian blood now shed.

One does not assume the responsibilities of social struggles so lightly.

"Preparation for a 'political' and armed resistance must take place simultaneously with the general strike."

The people must be warned—let us hope that events end up teaching them this—that the bourgeoisie, faced with a general strike, cannot put forward anything but the reaction of its rifles.

During a general strike, the people should not go out into the streets without being ready to shoot at the soldiers the bourgeoisie will put against them.

They are our brothers, say the preachers of calm evolutions, and the people must never forget it. So be it.

But we are also their brothers.

So why are they the first to raise weapons against us?

When fraternity is thus broken, the people are no longer obligated to nurture false sentiments of humanity.

Likewise, once the strike has been declared, the days spent waiting, in peaceful anticipation, simply amount to a prearranged, expected defeat.

The general strike is aimed at starving the bourgeoisie, not starving us: to maintain himself as an effective fighter the worker must eat, and since he has no food and cannot buy it—nor should he—he must take what he needs from the warehouses he previously filled up during work days.

The defeat of the Catalonian proletariat, as painful as it is, is not definitive: trained by harsh experience, drawing strength from extensive labor federations and not forgetting to prepare that organization that can best provide means of material offense—weapons and explosives—we hope that they can write another glorious page.

The cause of the revolution expects much from generous Barcelona!

From London: Trade Unions Meeting [by Luis Bonafoux]

Translated from "De Londres: Mitin de Trade Unions,"
Heraldo de Madrid 13, no. 4151 (March 29, 1902)

It is absolutely necessary to record the essential points of the mass meeting that took place yesterday[88] evening in Trafalgar Square, following the latest events in Barcelona, which are:

1. The participation of the Trade Unions in an event concerning Spain.

2. Malatesta's statement concerning the true character that should be attributed to the Barcelona movement.

---

88   The meeting took place on Sunday March 23rd. See the corresponding flyer, shown on p. 89 of the current volume.

[*A summary follows of speeches by Spanish and British speakers, who spoke before Malatesta.*]

Down in the street, there was a swirl of curiosity among the audience; and the anemic light of day, serene and melancholy, illuminated Malatesta's earthy face, with a sinister and vengeful expression, so lean within his muscular armor. He spoke in Italian; with his body hunched forward, his hands buried, immobile, in the pockets of his pants, preferably seeking the gaze of the Italian part of the audience, a group of figures who also had the color of dirt and bile, separated from the speaker by a line of police helmets.

And he said:

—Since other speakers made an effort to present the events of Barcelona as exclusively unionistic and not anarchist, I want to reclaim the anarchist character of these events, as a glory of anarchism. (Sensation.) Given that the government intervened by sending troops against the workers, the latter had to defend themselves against the government, not because it was specifically the Spanish government, but because it was the authority established in the defense of capitalism.

In fact, as bad as the Spanish government is—and it is extremely so—as far as the social question is concerned, neither the French Republic is better, as it shoots the workers of Chalon and Martinique;[89] nor the Italian Monarchy, which guns down the strikers in Milan and militarizes the railroad workers to prevent them from going on strike; nor is it possible to defend the acts of the American Federation in Pittsburgh; nor those of the English democracy in Ireland, in India, and in the Transvaal (big applause); nor those of the so-called civilized nations in the Celestial Empire. Therefore, it is not against a specific government, but rather against *government* in general, that those who called the general strike in Barcelona had to defend themselves, and because of that I consider this movement to be anarchist.

It is the dawn of other movements of the same nature, which very soon will arise in various regions of Europe, and I must defend my coreligionists, the anarchists, because, if they are never seen mixed up in electoral contests, nor in political schemes that can procure them personal benefits, they are always found in the place of danger at the time of the battle (bravo, bravo), being in reality those who maintain order, given that those tasked to enforce the law are the first to violate it and suspend it.

. . .

---

89   In early February 1900, in Fort de France, on the island of Martinique, French soldiers shot at striking miners, killing nine; on June 2nd of the same year, the police killed three strikers in Chalon-sur-Saône.

A
MASS MEETING

will be held in

Trafalgar Square

at 3.30 on
SUNDAY, MARCH 23, *1902*

to call the attention of
TRADES' UNIONISTS and the PUBLIC generally to
THE BARCELONA STRIKE

and to express sympathy with the victims of military oppression. Hundreds of innocent people have been killed, wounded and imprisoned for daring to ask for a **Nine-hours Day** for 10,000 metal workers.

Chairman : Mr. J. E. GREGORY,
(Chairman L. T. C.),

Supported by Mr. J. KEIR HARDIE, M. P.,

and the following Trades Unionists and speakers :

J. Abbott (Secretary, Bus and Tram Union), **C. F. Davis** (L.T.C.), **H. Brill** (President, Coal Porters), **H. Quelch** (Editor of *Justice*), **A. E. Holmes** (Organising Secretary, London Society of Compositors), **G. C. Jones** (Warehousemen), **J. Michaels** (Cabmen's Union), **S. Guthrie** (L T.C.), **C. Todd** (French Polishers), **P. Vogel** (Waiters), **W. H. Hillier** and **C. Holleyman** (Farriers), **G. Vernall** (L.T.C.), **W. Pizey** (L. T. C.), **C. Watts** (L. T. C.), **Tom Chambers** (International Transport Federation), **T. del Marmol, Errico Malatesta, H. Kelly, Baldomero Oller** (Barcelona Metal Workers), **G. Cullen** (Operative Painters), **Stan Gale** (L.S.C.). **G Cole** (London Secretary Operative Plasterers), **Lothrop Withington, S Mainwaring** (A.S.E.) **W. B. Parker** (L. T. C), **G. Copsey** (L. S. C.) **Councillor Garrity** (Railway Workers).

BRITISH WORKERS! COME IN YOUR THOUSANDS!

Freedom printery (T. U.), 127 Ossulston Street, N. W.

Deceived People

Translated from "Popolo ingannato," *Lo Sciopero Generale* (London) 1, no. 2 (April 15, 1902)

The telegrams announce serious turmoil in Belgium—serious to the point of appearing to be the prelude to an imminent general insurrection.[90]

As this concerns a movement inspired by the socialists, in a country that counts on a powerful socialist party, and where the army, already weak due to the kingdom's special conditions, is profoundly undermined by antimilitarist propaganda, one could reasonably hope that we are going to witness the outbreak of a social revolution, from which would result, if not the triumph of socialism, at least a more or less radical transformation that would actually improve the material conditions of the people and would open new and easier ways to future progress.

But unfortunately, for those who are knowledgeable of previous events and know the inauspicious strategy of democratic socialists, it is not difficult to predict that everything will end with a little blood uselessly shed and yet another joke played upon the foolish people.

It suffices to say that the movement was started in order to demand... universal suffrage, which is the right for all to cast a vote in choosing rulers and therefore cease hating them and fighting them as public oppressors.

The Belgian people have already at other times gone out into the streets and faced gunshot to win this demanded right, which an already long experience could show even the most thickheaded person, is nothing but a shameful mystification.[91] Democratic socialists, who insist on believing that human society can only be saved if they come to power, then as now pushed the people to put pressure on the government through threatening the general strike and revolution, so that a path to the yearned-for parliamentary seats would open up for them; but when they saw that things became serious and that the movement showed signs of surpassing the narrow limits within which they had meant to contain it, they made haste to accept the scant concessions the government was disposed to make, and extinguish the fire they had lit.

This time the same thing, more or less, will happen.

---

90   Under the pressure of growing popular discontent and demonstrations in the street, on April 13th the Belgian Workers' Party declared a general strike to win universal suffrage.

91   A general strike to win universal suffrage had already been declared in 1893. At that time Malatesta had gone from London to Belgium to see the situation firsthand.

The movement has no future, since it is made in the name of a demand that does no damage to capitalistic and monarchist institutions and that actually, instead, strengthens them. When the government no longer feels the strength to resist, it always has the means to stop everything, giving itself the appearance of yielding and making concessions, and sending the people home happy and gulled. And the elected socialists, or those aspiring to be so, are there to help it with the work.

Certainly, the method implemented in Belgium to obtain universal suffrage is based on a true principle, which is that the dominators never renounce any of their privileges, unless constrained by force or pushed by fear. And for having recognized that, at least incidentally, the Belgian democratic socialists show themselves superior to their comrades in other countries. Yet the authoritarian biases inherent to their program, and the necessity to prevent the people from doing it themselves and realizing therefore the uselessness and harmfulness of parliaments, prevent them from drawing from this method all of the advantages it entails. And this sets them up to renounce the coveted universal suffrage rather than see the revolution triggered.

Anyhow, it is certain that with the method adopted, sooner or later, the Belgian workers will win the right to vote. And then? A larger number of hacks in politics will find it convenient to disguise themselves as friends of the people to jump on the gravy train and replace the current parasites and oppressors; many sincere socialists will succeed in getting elected to then be paralyzed and corrupted by the parliamentary environment; and the people, if they want to emancipate themselves, will again be constrained to be victorious by force, against the so-called socialist and democratic rulers exactly the same way as against the overtly reactionary and bourgeois ones.

Is it not painful to see the people's blood shed and energy wasted in this manner? And the democratic socialists who cry out against the anarchists when the latter push the people to fight directly to capture real gains, they who say it is madness or crime to expose oneself and others to ferocious bourgeois repression when victory is not certain, and condemn revolts like those in Barcelona when in reality they are the first attempts at training for the great social revolution, do they not feel remorse to have spilt blood to rise to power upon the cadavers of naive workers, to whom they promise things that can only be obtained when the workers want to and are able to win them on their own?

Finally, what purpose would this universal suffrage serve?

In the best case scenario it would be used to elect deputies, who once they are in a sufficient number would vote for reforms. But since it is understood that the bourgeoisie only yields under force, and it is necessary to tear away by force what in practice is only a hope of future reforms, why not demand by the same means the immediate concession of the desired reforms?

For example, the socialists promise to establish, when they are in power, the eight-hour work day. It is a small thing, but in the end it is something, so let's go for it, if the people do not yet know how to desire better things: but the eight-hour day would already have been a reality for some time, if the Belgian workers had asked for it with the same energy by which they ask for universal suffrage.

Instead they won nothing, and when they will have suffrage... they will be in the same conditions as workers are in countries where suffrage exists, namely, in the same conditions as before.

But, it is argued, if it is true that universal suffrage does nothing, how is it that governments do not voluntarily grant it, and it needs to be torn away from them by force?

The reason is simple: universal suffrage, or any reform in the electoral mechanism, does not benefit the people, it does not harm the bourgeoisie as a class nor the government as an institution, but it produces a change in the ruling personnel and those who are in power wish to stay there more than anything else. Which is further proof that it is not true that governments are only the representatives and defenders of bourgeois interests: they are above all else, the defenders of the interests of the rulers.

And the socialists, who want to come to power, should they arrive there, would be defenders of themselves, rather than representatives and defenders of the poor.

The events in Belgium are further proof that revolutionary energies are alive in the people, and that the democratic socialists already serve no other purpose than to anesthetize these energies, or to divert them from the path that leads to emancipation.

May the anarchists be able to benefit from the lesson.[92]

---

92   On April 18th a socialist proposal for constitutional reform was rejected by parliament. The Belgian Workers' Party declared resolutely for the continuation of the general strike. That evening, police shot at a procession of demonstrators in Leuven, killing six and wounding fourteen. Following these events, the Belgian Workers' Party voted to end the strike. A new general strike for universal suffrage would be proclaimed in 1913.

The Calcagno Candidacy

Translated from "La candidatura Calcagno," *Lo Sciopero Generale* (London) 1, no. 2 (April 15, 1902)

The republicans and some socialists in Milan suggest electing Pietro Calcagno to protest his being sent into forced residence.[93]

It seems to us that it time to stop this... even as we graciously thank our benevolent "kindred."

For us, being a deputy is not only useless and dangerous for popular emancipation but is also immoral in itself; for it is immoral, and therefore dishonorable, to hold a position that carries the responsibility to make laws, that is, to impose one's own will upon others by force.

For us, wanting to elect someone as a deputy to get them out of prison or forced residence is as if, with the same objective, one wanted to elect them to be a police officer: it would be an insult. In fact, it is difficult to understand why the police officer who enforces the law would be more hideous than the deputy who creates it.

Let republicans and authoritarian socialists prostitute themselves as long as they want in parliaments and with parliaments: but leave us to fight our battle.

The Armed Strike

Translated from "Lo sciopero armato," *Lo Sciopero Generale* (London) 1, no. 3 (June 2, 1902)

The likely appearance of a new Spanish-language anarchist newspaper, entitled *The armed strike*, has been announced.

Its title defines its program.

Whether or not the planned publication is realized, we hope that the title will be taken up and become the motto of a new approach in revolutionary tactics. Words, slogans, are of great importance in popular movements; and the expression *armed strike* may prove very useful, because it is the happiest encapsulation of a pressing need at the present time. And it is good that it has come from Spain, where there is already a mass of organized and conscious workers, who have already shown what

---

93   The story of anarchist Pietro Calcagno was particularly sad. For him, the past decade had been a sequence of arrests, prison, forced residence, exile, and returns to Italy. When, sick with tuberculosis, he returned to his homeland in late 1901, to then be again arrested and sent into forced residence, an intense campaign for his liberation was promoted.

they are worth and who are better placed than anyone else to provide a practical example of the new tactics.

Propaganda for the general strike has done and is still doing an immense amount of good.

By showing workers an effective means by which they can emancipate themselves, it destroys the blind and harmful faith in parliamentary and legislative methods; it banishes from the labor movement the ambitious types who use it as a springboard to power; it provides revolutionaries with the means of involving the great toiling masses in the struggle, and puts that struggle in such terms that a radical transformation of social relations must naturally, in an almost automatic manner, ensue.

But the major advantages of this propaganda and the success it has had, have given rise to a serious threat to the cause itself, the triumph of which it is directed toward.

An illusion has been forming, that the revolution can be made almost peaceably, by folding one's arms and reducing the masters to discretion by simply refusing to work for them. And by dint of insisting on the great importance of the economic struggle, it has been all but overlooked that the master who starves us is flanked and defended by the government who starves and kills us.

In Barcelona, in Trieste, in Belgium, the price of this illusion has already been paid in the blood of the people.[94] The strike has been mounted with almost no weapons and without any definite intention of employing the few that were available;—and with a few shots the governments restored everything to order.

When thought of as merely a lawful, peaceful strike, the general strike is an absurd idea.

To begin with, given the proletariat's circumstances and given the specific nature of farm production, it can be *general* only in a manner of speaking: in actuality, it will merely be the handiwork of a more forward-looking minority, a forceful minority, capable of determining the course of events with its moral and material energies, but it will always be a numerically tiny minority, that could only slightly impact the equilibrium of production and consumption. But even if we supposed the strike to be authentically general, things would be even more absurd... provided, we say again, that it be thought of as a lawful, peaceable movement.

---

94   In Trieste a strike of stokers from the Lloyd Austriaco shipping company, proclaimed on February 13, 1902, transformed into a citywide general strike. On February 15th, a procession of demonstrators was attacked by police, leaving fourteen dead and about fifty injured. On Barcelona and Belgium see, respectively, note 86 above and the article "Deceived People," on p. 90 of the current volume.

What would there be to eat? What would be used to purchase life's necessities?

Workers would starve to death well before the bourgeois would be forced to give up any morsel of their surplus.

So, if one wants to mount a general strike, one has to be ready to seize possession of the means of existence, despite any of the alleged rights of private ownership. But then along come the troops, and one must flee or fight.

So, if we know that the strike will necessarily lead to a clash with armed forces and turn into a revolution, why not say so and make our preparations?

Must this inept farce of periodical clashes carry on for all eternity, in which for hundreds of proletarian deaths, scarcely a soldier or policeman is struck by a stone?

Let us go on strike but let us do so under circumstances in which we can defend ourselves. Since the police and the troops show up wherever a clash between masters and workers occurs, let us ensure that we are in a position to command their respect.

Revolutionaries should arm themselves so that they are ready to start the revolution whenever the opportunity arises. Non-revolutionary workers should arm themselves, if only to avoid being beaten like so many sheep.

With their savings, proletarians will never be able to amass the capital needed to fight the masters' capital; but with a modicum of good will, they may well get their hands on a revolver. And a mass of strikers armed with revolvers or any other weapons commands a lot more respect than one blessed with a strike fund, no matter how hefty.

Long live the general strike, but let it be an ARMED STRIKE.

Ideas and Persons: An Explanation

Translated from "Idee e persone: Una spiegazione,"
Lo Sciopero Generale (London) 1, no. 3 (June 2, 1902)

It is the habit of democratic socialists (and in London, we recently had an example of it) to go and look for weaknesses, inconsequences, or vices of this or that anarchist and make use of them as an argument against our ideas. Sometimes one of them resorts to slander and thus places himself underneath any honest debate; but even when the accusations are true, this method of arguing is foolish and reprehensible, since it does not prove anything, it aggravates the spirit and immensely damages the calm search for the truth, which should be the common goal of all.

The socialists say we do the same when we attack, for example, Turati, Millerand, Iglesias, and the like. For this reason, it would not be useless to say a few words on the essential difference between the questions of persons that we raise and those that they raise.

We have never allowed ourselves to reproach the socialists for the bad actions of the many whom they have expelled or otherwise distanced from their party; and if Turati and the others, disavowing in practice the ideas they claimed to profess, had been renounced by their comrades, we certainly would not want to reproach the sincere socialists for the conduct of leaders who had betrayed them. At most, if the instances were numerous, we would make use of them to argue that the practice or desire for power exerts a corrupting action on men, and note the risk that one runs by bowing down to leaders.

But these gentlemen are still followed as commanders and masters by the majority of socialists and treated with respect, even by the meager minority resistant to their maneuvers. Therefore we have the right to consider those who approve their conduct to be in agreement with them, and we can logically seek in the party's ideas and general trend an explanation for this humiliating reality, of a mass of people who claim to be conscious but sheepishly follow a leader, accepting without protest all of the changes in tactic and all of the practical and theoretical contradictions, which the interest, vanity, or hysteria of the leader imposes upon them.

Nothing similar happens with the personal issues that the democratic socialists try to hold against us.

We do not recognize leaders; and when an anarchist contradicts anarchist principles, we cease considering him to be a comrade, and we cannot have any responsibility for conduct that we condemn.

Today, for example, they are in the habit of throwing Calcagno's name in our face, both as an accusation of moral weakness and as proof of anarchism's presumed evolution toward parliamentarism.

Now, that Calcagno has not stood up against the insult lobbed at him by Milanese republicans, and that instead he has appeared to be over the moon with happiness, like a vain wimp, at the idea of being made deputy, is certainly a painful thing—painful especially because it shows how much debilitating influence illness and suffering can have on the human psyche. But it takes an entirely socialist logic to go on to reproach us for conduct that has outraged us.

May the socialists learn to think with their heads, and then they will not find it so difficult to understand that there are men such as anarchists who do not demand and do not accept responsibility for anything but their own acts and their own words.

On Guard

Translated from "In guardia," *Lo Sciopero Generale* (London) 1,
no. 3 (June 2, 1902)

The police world, especially at the Italian consulate, is buzzing with activity.

We know that attempts have been made to lure honest people to the vocation of spy and that they responded by spitting in the face of those who made them the obscene proposal—and we also know of some cowards who accepted the hateful role. We know of imaginary reports, of attempted conspiracies intended to be denounced to the police, etc.

We cannot yet give all the names and details; we will do it as soon as we have collected sufficient elements of proof. For now we limit ourselves to pointing comrades toward the person named Gennaro Rubini, so-called socialist and anarchist, but for that matter always on the sidelines, who—by his own written confession—acted in the service of the infamous vice-inspector Prina, collecting 3 and a half sterling pounds weekly as compensation for his information.

Both Rubini and Prina are still in London. Comrades are warned to remain cautious.

Popular Action and Electoral Action

Translated from "Azione popolare e azione elettorale," *Non Votate* (Faenza),
single issue (July 12, 1902)

As we asked him for an article, Errico Malatesta writes us the following letter, which we gladly publish, dedicating it to those comrades who wish to draw a distinction between administrative elections and political elections.[95]

Dear comrades,

You ask me for an article on the advantages of direct, popular action, as compared to parliamentary, electoral action.

This issue is of the highest importance, since one's way of thinking and acting on this subject constitutes, in my opinion, a sort of touchstone, by which one can distinguish a true anarchist and a true socialist from the politico, whether he is delusional or a trickster.

---

95   The single issue in which this article appears was published on the eve of the administrative elections in the Romagna town of Faenza.

However, this issue is old, and takes up so much space in our publications that I do not feel the desire now to repeat what has already been said and said again a thousand times.

So I will limit myself, at least this time, to calling your attention to some recent events that have confirmed our reasoning and our predictions with experiential evidence.

Look at what the democratic socialists are becoming. When we said that by waging a parliamentary and electoral battle, they would end up forgetting the cardinal principles of socialism, they treated us as ignoramuses, as fanatics, as slanderers. And now they have surpassed our most pessimistic predictions and put their influence at the service of Giolitti and Zanardelli.[96] Today, ignoramuses, fanatics, slanderers are those few comrades among them who still remain loyal to socialist principles... but, for that matter (consider this other prediction) they will do like the others, if they continue believing in parliamentary and electoral action.

On the other hand, look at what is happening among the anarchists.

Rarely, but still from time to time, there are some anarchists who start to say "we need to make use of all means," that the cause can also be served by elections, that protest elections are an exceptional thing, that so-called administrative elections are different than parliamentary elections, etc.

Well, **all** those anarchists who said they want to make parliamentarism serve the interest of anarchy, after a few weeks, or a few months, abandon every anarchist ambition and fully repudiate the principles they professed. Perhaps they were sincere when they said they would remain anarchist while becoming parliamentarists: but logic is stronger than desires, and logic won.

Therefore continue, you who are true anarchists, to fight with the people while staying among the people, and consider as an enemy anyone who invites you to compromise with this great enemy of popular emancipation that is called parliamentarism.

I remain Your comrade

ERRICO MALATESTA.

June 1902.

---

96   See note 63 above.

SECTION III
The Social Revolution

To the Italian-Language Anarchists

Translated from "Agli anarchici di lingua italiana," London, September 1902[97]

Comrades,

Confident that the reasons which caused us to fail in previous, similar attempts have been eliminated, we call for your involvement in the publication of a socialist-anarchist organ that shall take the title:

"LA RIVOLUZIONE SOCIALE."

Following is a brief account of the reasons that move us and that we propose to fully develop in the aforementioned periodical.

There was a time when anarchists, scornful of the small struggles which comprised daily life, did not think about much except the grand days of the longed-for revolution. And they prepared for it, morally developing their own ideal, materially collecting those means for fighting that they were capable of procuring. Unable to deal with the practical necessities of propaganda in the midst of a hostile environment, and poorly perceiving, out of excessive boldness, the enormous disparity between the extreme poverty of their means and the grandiosity of the pursued objective, they remained far from the masses that did not understand them; and, despite audacious attempts and major sacrifices, their action failed to effectively impact social events, and they wound up following people for whom socialism was merely a means to obtain power.

Then they realized their error and sought to correct it.

Having seen the powerlessness of simple theoretical propaganda and small, more or less secret bands; clearly understanding that the revolution, and especially a revolution with anarchist leanings, is not made without the sympathy of the masses to be liberated, they threw themselves into public life, taking an active part, and not seldom a prevalent part, in the labor movement, and gather from this new activity abundant fruit in terms of propaganda and positive influence.

But unfortunately, what usually happens in all reactions against a mistake has come to pass: they fell into the opposite mistake.

They acknowledged the damage of isolation, but there was too much fraternization with people who, due to their interests or ideas, are naturally enemies.

---

97   We reproduce this circular-announcement from its original release as a leaflet. It was then republished, entirely or in part, in various Italian-language anarchist newspapers, including *Il Risveglio Socialista-Anarchico* (Geneva) of September 13th, *Il Grido della Folla* (Milan) of September 18th, *L'Agitazione* (Rome) of September 26th, *La Questione Sociale* (Paterson) of September 27th and *L'Avvenire* (Buenos Aires) of October 25th.

They acknowledged the utility and importance of our active participation in the labor movement but it ended with the belief among many that, should this movement indefinitely evolve, it could by itself resolve the issue.

They acknowledged that continually calling for the revolution often prevented us from being able to say why this revolution was invoked, and that making public propaganda in spite of the police required the ability to attenuate our own language and make ourselves understood in oblique ways. But by no longer saying always and everywhere, clearly and explicitly what they wanted to say, they often ended up forgetting the existence of that which was left unsaid, and believing—or at least acting as if they believed—that the entire anarchist program is that which can be presented before the royal prosecutors without excessive danger.

They acknowledged that, using stones and a few old shotguns, one cannot successfully take on the perfected weapons of modern armies. This resulted in disregarding all expectations of material struggle, and acting as if the soldiers no longer had rifles, and did not have them specifically to shoot at us and the people.

Hence, a widening of the movement was pursued, but at the cost of overlooking the danger of losing in intensity what was gained in extension.

Meanwhile, the events follow their course.

The general restlessness of the working classes shows that the people are increasingly becoming intolerant of the yoke, and that we are perhaps on the eve of one of those violent crises that leave their mark in the history of social evolution. And the recent events that have shaken and stained with blood various cities in Europe have proven yet again that the rulers are mightily armed, and no scruple restrains them from using weapons to drown in blood any heave of rebellion. Hence, if we are not organized and prepared to meet the government's material force with adequate force, the brutal repression shall triumph over the force of the idea for a long time still.

Are the anarchists capable of handling the situation? They who, more than anyone else, demonstrate they have the consciousness of this harsh necessity of the armed insurrection, are they prepared, or are they preparing, to be able to act so that the insurrection triumphs?

Moreover, it is not enough that an insurrection triumphs for the people to become truly free. Depending on the ideas that prevail among the masses, depending on the direction in which competing and opposite efforts of men and parties succeed in driving the movement, the coming social revolution could open to humanity the main road to full emancipation, or simply serve to elevate a new layer of the privileged above the masses, leaving unscathed the principle of authority and privilege.

Are anarchists conducting themselves, in associations and in public unrest, so as to then be able to debunk the illusions of the naive, who expect good from the action of new rulers, and to fight the wicked arts of politicos who, under the mantle of friends of the people, remain ready to exploit people's selfless efforts to their own advantage?

And if the anarchists can neither resist the material force of the governments, nor paralyze the action of those who seek to replace the current masters, is this a result of causes they can do nothing about, or is there something in their strategy that prevents them from accomplishing their chosen mission?

We believe that an important cause of the anarchists' powerlessness in confronting the necessities of the situation is found in the mistakes we mentioned, and that the remedy lies in bringing together new and old tactics, which both have some good to them.

We believe that it is necessary to make an effort to be practical, and not lose the sense of the real and the possible while contemplating the ideal. But, at the same time, it is necessary to vigilantly be on alert so that practical concerns do not come to diminish the ideal.

We believe that it is necessary to take an active part in the labor movement but without allowing ourselves to be absorbed, without compromising with the reactionary and conservative parts of it, and always remembering that, in the end, it can only be another means of making propaganda and gathering forces for the revolution.

We believe in the great, immense necessity of propaganda, but we believe it is necessary, at the same time, to materially and psychologically prepare ourselves for action, either to initiate it, or to take advantage of the increasingly more frequent opportunities.

So, we want to create a newspaper to defend this direction, also because, given the country in which we reside, we can say things that comrades in Italy are prohibited from saying but people still need to know.

Let the comrades who agree with the proposed aims help the prospective newspaper to be born and live.

PIETRO CAPPELLI—ENRICO CARRARA—
SANTE CENCI—SILVIO CORIO—GUGLIELMO
CUCCIOLI—P. CURETTI—GIOV. DEFENDI—ENRICO
DEFENDI—FELICE FELICI—CARLO FRIGERIO—
ANTONIO FOLLI—A. GALASSINI—G. GOLDONI—
CARLO MAGNONI—ERRICO MALATESTA
—F. MARIANI—ATTILIO PANIZZA—ALFREDO
PIERCONTI—G. QUARANTINI—CARLO ROSSI—
GIULIO ROSSI.[98]

---

98   Administrative and editorial addresses follow, as well as the following note:

We and Our "Kindred"

Translated from "Noi ed i nostri 'affini,'" *La Rivoluzione Sociale* (London), no. 1
(October 4, 1902)[99]

Do we have kindred, meaning collaborators and possible allies in the battle that we fight against the current political and economic order of society?

If you look at the theoretical programs expressed by various parties, the issue does not seem ambiguous. All those who do not want to fully preserve the present or return to an even worse past, have something to fight alongside us, some common enemy to destroy, as we are the adversaries of all current institutions. The democratic socialists, as authoritarian and anarchist-eating as they are, want to destroy the capitalist organization of production and the master's exploitation of the work done by others: they therefore would be our natural allies in the fight against capitalism. And since the government is, in fact and by law, the defender of established interests, they should agree with us in fighting the government.

The republicans must, by definition, want to create a republic. We are naturally less enthusiastic over a transformation that would leave intact the sources which give rise to the social suffering we want to destroy. But since it is necessary to start with overthrowing the monarchy, which is the current, immediate obstacle to any radical change, as much for creating a republic as for realizing our ideal of freedom and solidarity, the republicans, the socialists and us could all cooperate in the charge against the monarchy.

And given that every major transformation, every revolution is preceded by a number of small moral and material changes, which prepare for the event and make triumph possible, there would be ample work of education and preparation that could in part be done together.

Therefore, since we are sharing a long stretch on the road to the future, it would seem logical and convenient to walk it together. To unite when we are in agreement and have something to gain that interests all of us; to act each on their own behalf when the agreement ends and the goals we wish to reach are different: this would seem to be a clever and prudent tactic which would benefit general progress without

---

LA RIVOLUZIONE SOCIALE shall be published every fifteen days starting this coming October 2nd.

Those subscribed to *Lo Sciopero Generale,* an organ released under special circumstances, that has now merged with la RIVOLUZIONE SOCIALE, shall be considered subscribers of the new newspaper.

99   The newspaper's subtitle is "Anarchist-Socialist Periodical."

undermining or damaging the particular aspirations of the different factions.

Instead, in practice, cooperation between us and democratic socialists and republicans has proven to be either impossible or damaging.

At various times the anarchists have tried to drag the other anti-constitutional parties into common action, and whether the matter was a direct, armed attack against the monarchy, or simply an agitation against forced residence, a strike, a protest, we always ended up scorned. When there were no insults or slander, and they deigned to put on a good face, it always ended with an invitation for us to send them to parliament, or to go there ourselves.

Meanwhile, in addition to wasting our time, we risked letting go of part of that intransigence which is the strength and protection of a party that wants to keep intact its own ideal.

At this point it would be foolish to continue deluding ourselves.

With these people corrupted by parliamentarism, who have prostituted themselves to power and have become the most dangerous corruptors and anesthetizers of the people, there is nothing to do. If they could still do something good and useful, they would do it under external pressure, coming from the war that we will wage against them, or coming from a desire to keep the prestige which induces the government to caress them, and indeed not out of a sincere, heartfelt desire to do good. People (we are especially talking about socialists) who—having professed and still claiming to profess ideas of emancipation, of justice, of freedom—have descended down, down to the point of excusing and nearly justifying those directly responsible for the murders in Berra and Candela, these are lost people, prostituted people.[100]

At this point in Italy, other than the still semi-conscious masses, only we, the anarchists, are the true adversaries of the government and the bourgeoisie. Let us try to measure up to the requirements of the situation we find ourselves in, due to the sloth and corruption of the parties which should have cooperated with us in the fight for freedom.

Alone against everyone, let us fight with flag unfurled for our full ideal, against any expression of the authoritarian principle, against any exploitation and any subjugation of one man by another. This will still be the only means by which, awaiting the final triumph, those improvements that are attainable prior to the revolution can be delivered.

---

100   In Berra, in the province of Ferrara, on June 27, 1901, during a dispute involving day laborers, police and soldiers opened fire on the demonstrators, killing two. In Candela, in the province of Foggia, on September 8, 1902, the police shot at striking farmers who attempted to block the arrival of scabs. Eight were killed.

***

When we deplore the direction that the republican and socialist parties have taken, and we propose to break all "kindred" relations, we do not mean to doubt the good faith and the good will of the masses of socialists and republicans. The proletarians of both parties, those who work and suffer, certainly truly want freedom and justice for all. They are deceived, fooled, exploited in the name of socialism or the republic by a swarm of misfit petit bourgeois, thirsty for power, just as other proletarians are tricked, fooled, exploited in the name of God and homeland, by priests and monarchist politicos.

We consider all those who suffer to be brothers and potential comrades in arms, all the more so if, like the socialists and republicans, they already are conscious of the suffering that victimizes them and aspire to free themselves from it.

Let us fight their errors, let us draw their attention to the betrayals of their leaders, let us seek to awaken in them the desire to act as conscious men and not as disciplined sheep; and let us wait for them amongst us, desired and valued comrades in arms.

After a Congress

Translated from "Dopo un Congresso," *La Rivoluzione Sociale* (London), no. 1 (October 4, 1902)

Since Filippo Turati let slip the phrase: "there is little doctrine in the Italian socialist party"—we, who have a more austere understanding of socialism, can add: "there is also little consciousness."

And we truly cannot accustom ourselves to calling "socialist," in the well-defined sense of the word, that assembly of journalists, petty lawyers and windbags that, artfully gathered and with duplicity, called itself "representative of the Italian working people."

In the political field, any deviation, any sleight-of-hand is possible, but this is one of the biggest. Today, damaged and adulterated goods are openly and easily trafficked: hence it is that a socialist party which spends only 1808 lire on propaganda throughout Italy seems to have acclaim and luck, while it spends as much and more to bring together the "Leadership"; which squanders five out of eight of its great sessions in a gossipy duel of sophistic oratory, while it barely mentions the extremely impoverished conditions of unemployed farmers, and does so when a large number of congress participants have already left. It is so unconcerned with respecting the free expression of thought as to shout over

Saverio Merlino's voice, and with each passing day it further subjugates and tames the people of the factories and the fields, diluting their most upright aspirations.[101]

The fortune that the new formula of "resignation"—called: "conquest of public powers"—seems to find among the working masses and the consequent pride and noise made by the socialist party are a phenomenon of reverse selection, achieved by the influence of the long-lasting coercion the Italian people underwent and undergoes.

The valid, selfless elements, "the healthy blood cells," were expelled, incarcerated, dispersed; the sound voices of anti-authoritarian socialism were suppressed and one formula of socialism was allowed, legalized, welcomed, sometimes coddled: the innocuous one, the parliamentary one.

It would not astonish us if even the prefect could attend the congress with a complimentary ticket.

Within the true, healthy movement "of the emancipation of the workers done by the workers," according to Marx's formula, a solidarity of bourgeois interests has been created, so as to muzzle the voice of the great worker demands, overpowered by the noisy shouting "by the bourgeois, by the ambitious and by those who seek a small secretary's salary in the party... and by directors of "Il Tempo"... since by now there is little to risk, and the possibility of making a career in the socialist party" to use the words of Treves, Dugoni, and Rigola.

Thus, in Italy's anemic public life, after socialist leanings have deviated from the straight revolutionary path and from proletarian aspirations and discontent, and after the bourgeois trend in socialism has taken control, little by little Italian socialism is becoming "ministerialist."

To vote for a government that handcuffs, shoots, and sends soldiers to replace strikers means, for Turati, "to win reforms, to put a proletarian influence on the reform."

For us, that means taking advantage of the good faith and the ignorance of the people.

For us, that means giving public schooling for political immorality.

And such was the education resulting from the sessions of the seventh socialist congress.

The only person there who took the liberty to recall that "socialism is only possible through the rupture of the fundamental relationships which permit the exploitation of work" was treated as a loner, and seen as a tad heretic.

---

101   The seventh national congress of the Italian socialist party took place in Imola on September 6–9, 1902. At the congress, a dispute arose between Filippo Turati's reformist faction and Enrico Ferri's revolutionary faction. This is the "duel of sophistic oratory" to which Malatesta refers. Francesco Saverio Merlino's speech at the congress had been loudly contested.

We dare doubt, with Rigola, that working people were truly very interested in the doctrinaire question that divided Ferri and Turati.

But even supposing that the workers, and not just the bourgeois part of the party, would have actively participated in the congress debate of the party "reformist because revolutionary and revolutionary because reformist," let us take a look at the enormous deceit being hid from the people under these mystical words.[102]

When a political party is forced to yield, grant, or propose alliances with adversaries, whether in elections, or in parliament, it is either weak or on the path to weakness.

But then when a socialist party, which a few years ago claimed to be leaning toward democratic nationalization of the means of production, today has sunk so low as to leverage or help governmental work to obtain social laws and reforms, we think that such a party has dug its own grave and is waging a farcical fight.

It would be as if two opposing and enemy armies lent each other mutual support to cross a difficult mountain pass, with the promise to fight tomorrow.

Wait, donkey, for the grass to grow!

This is the meaning of the vote issued during the Congress on the subject of the two schools of thought.

That vote was certainly performed with the government's benign agreeableness, which delayed the news of the Candela massacre by 24 hours.

Such a precious warning to the meek and innocent socialist souls!

But already during the congress, the Apulian Tucci had the bad taste to say that in Southern Italy it "is close to rioting in the streets. Already there are a few signs. The unemployed and those employed at 25 cents for 16 hours of work already run from town to town looking for crumbs of bread."

What a shame! We were so delighted with the intact, invulnerable "Unity of the Party"!

However our objection does not concern the greater or lesser opportunity to vote for one government rather than another.

We object for a reason that is much more important: fundamental.

We consider socialism's acceptance of the parliamentary tactic to be erroneous, fatal.

If we did not think this way, we would be forced, for sake of logic,

---

102   The phrase quoted is the conciliatory formula found in the final resolution, proposed by reformist Ivanoe Bonomi and approved by the socialist congress in Imola.

to acknowledge that Turati is right, because he is able to accept, to its extreme consequences, the false premise of the conquest of public powers and participation in the government's legislative work.

Parliamentary action—the function of a capitalist government—gradually includes the most advanced parties within an order of trends and actions increasingly suitable for the governmental function—therefore more and more conservative.

It is a phenomenon of political gravitation, corresponding to the law of physics that causes meteors passing through the earth's sphere of influence to fall on it.

And the government's sphere of influence is that entire tangle of laws and reforms in which any aspiration of the workers will get lost, whenever they fail to assert their rebellion against the central principle: that of authority, an immediate derivative from the principle of property.

Italian socialism, which here and there has indicated that it would have men and strength to sprout seeds of new strength in Italian life, is however a galley slave who pathetically drags behind him the chain of an error, of a false premise: parliamentarism.

Effectively implementing any social law, such as, for example, labor laws for women and children, is just as feasible as lending an anarchist structure to society.

To implement a social law means to modify, but not improve worker conditions—since such a law leaves unchanged the reasons for suffering: capitalist production.

Such a law would always tend to support the rebirth—to the benefit of its own existence and interest—of those errors, of those evils that the law was supposed to cure.

And since the bourgeoisie, which embodies this form of production, will still be the strongest at this point—which is demonstrated by the need for the law—it will oppose the law's practical working.

It will be said: we have such and such a law to defends us; but the evil will always persist, plus the deceit, from which the leaders of the alleged socialist movement will benefit for general, equally ironic, or personal objectives.

History is there to teach us. Furthermore, it is not true that reforms—whatever they may be—mere modifications to political form—are truly helpful in developing a socialist party that grows stronger every day, a revolutionary faction that grows bolder every day.

The benefit of reforms, whenever a benefit is actually felt—and by just one class of workers, anyway—is ephemeral and temporary.

To believe in the opposite is to ignore the complexity of modern social economic life; it is to live in the clouds, or in a party where there is little doctrine, as Turati rightly said.

A decreased duty on wheat—for example—can all of a sudden become meaningless for workers, due to a consequent and almost necessary depression in the wages of farmers.

To confute some of the childish economic theories of the alleged scientific socialism, sometimes the proletariat benefits not from the depression of the bourgeoisie, but rather from following its luck in parallel, so that they are less poor when the bourgeoisie is richer, and therefore stronger.

Furthermore, any economic improvement or reform must be defended by the actual force of the proletariat, organized or not, but conscious: hence the upward progress of a movement cannot last longer than a generation—rarely two.

Every generation fights its own battles, in the form and for the needs that are its own.

If it does not win, all the work needs to be redone, to be restarted, we would dare say.

The idea of indefinite progress is one of those ideological suppositions, which the socialists have not yet been able to free themselves from.

Socialism is bound to win, if it uses all of its strength to pursue its goal: destroy the bourgeoisie's power and establish the regime of free production, free trade, and free consumption.

Otherwise it will consume its strength in illusory battles and will be sometimes a scam, sometimes a mirage of an unreachable promised land.

Anarchists in Labor Unions

Translated from "Gli anarchici nelle società operaje," *La Rivoluzione Sociale* (London), no. 1 (October 4, 1902)

We will soon address, as thoroughly as possible, a subject of vital importance to us, the strategy of anarchists within and before labor organizations.

Meanwhile, since there is much discussion about the matter among comrades at this time, we want to express our opinion about whether anarchists can, without contradicting their principles, accept positions in resistance societies, labor chambers, and similar institutions—and if it is useful for them to do so.

The matter of principle is clear: anarchists cannot, without ceasing to be anarchists, accept any role of authority and must instead, whenever they encounter it, call for its abolition, demonstrating how an association of free men can and should exist without authority. Accepting a position, which entails the power of imposing one's will over others, with the intention of using it to do good for the association and correct its shortcomings, means yielding to the error, eminently anti-anarchist, of wanting to destroy authority by means of authority; it means justifying socialists who have themselves appointed council members and deputies and manage, or aspire, to be nominated ministers; in sum, it means no longer being anarchists.

Instead, when it is a matter of non-authoritarian positions, that is, doing work for a collective that assigns a task, according to the will and under the control of the collective itself, nothing prevents an anarchist from accepting the task. On the contrary, refusing would often amount to enjoying social advantages without taking on one's due share of work and trouble.

Therefore, from the perspective of consistency with principles, anarchists could accept positions in freely organized associations, in which the appointees are merely executors of the collective will, and they should refuse positions where there is the slightest trace of authoritarianism.

But the issue is much more complex when it comes to practical cases, and one considers the good or bad effect that solicitation and acceptance of social positions by anarchists can have on propaganda.

First of all, it is almost impossible in the current environment that a labor organization, which cannot survive on ideals and must welcome men of all opinions and undergo the necessities of life and struggle, can organize itself in a truly libertarian manner. The mission of anarchists is to fight against any trace of authoritarianism, and their position would become absurd if they participated in the authority that they want to destroy.

Similarly, as a labor union cannot be exclusively comprised of anarchists—rather the large majority are always non-anarchists, and anarchists and non-anarchists use different criteria to judge things and situations—an anarchist in charge, who should act on behalf of and according to the will of his principals, would continually be forced to either do things his own way, and thus betray the mandate—as representatives usually do—or respect the will of others and betray his own convictions.

On the other hand, seeing the orgy of vanity and ambitions flaunted by the parties we fight against, seeing the people's mistrust, which we have an interest in feeding, of those who derive material and moral personal advantage from propaganda and political agitation, and seeing that in the simple worker's state of social inferiority, positions and appointments that carry a title before the public constitute a true privilege, it is wise for anarchists to rigorously abstain from anything that could have even the appearance of these weaknesses that they fight in others.

The masses, upon whom we want to act, are very primitive and do not clearly see the difference between delegation of power and delegation of work, and if they see us take positions and accept titles, they will think that we are like the others. And the masses might not be wrong! We have ideas that, naturally, since we profess them, we believe to be superior to others; but we would be wrong to believe ourselves, as human beings, to be better than the average of our contemporaries, and it would be prudent to avoid opportunities to err, which little by little have led into an abyss of corruption so many men who began modestly, and generally with good intentions, to "take upon themselves the sacrifice" of a position that raised them above their comrades.

But—one could object—if you want labor organization, you must also want the means necessary for it to survive.

Very well, we respond; but if, due to the environment and especially the degree of consciousness among members, an association cannot act anarchically, it is the business of the non-anarchists to adopt and implement non-anarchist conduct. Instead it is up to the anarchists to provide the revolutionary, propulsive force, which with critique and by example seeks to put as much anarchy as possible into the ideas and conduct of the members, that is: as much freedom and equality as possible in relations between members; solidarity in relations with all the working class; and rebellion, energy, and intransigence in the fight against masters and the government.

But what if no one wants to accept positions anymore? Oh! then the time would have already come, and long since, to be done with all of the dealings and palliatives in which unfortunately the masses still believe.

When there is no longer anybody who wants to preach calm and negotiate with the masters and authority to settle strikes and avoid "rash rebellions," the fatal hour will have rung for masters and governments. The coming of this radiant day must be the purpose of our activity.

The Partial Strike

Translated from "Lo sciopero parziale," *La Rivoluzione Sociale* (London), no. 1 (October 4, 1902)

Some argue that it is wrong to squander the labor forces on useless and petty partial strikes, and that instead it would be worthwhile to consolidate trade organizations, federate them, and go on a general strike.

There is certainly a lot right in this observation; but on the other hand, it would be very harmful if, waiting for the final big battle, we grew accustomed to remaining calm, and gave up practicing the fight.

It is good that workers organize themselves into strong associations building up strength and class consciousness, in order to fight until the capitalist regime is overthrown. However, it seems to me an almost comical illusion, as the idea completely abandons the laws of history and evolution, that during this work of organization, workers should abstain from any individual or collective insurrection against the masters' greed and abuse, which they are continually the targets of, to not provoke petty strikes or cause harm to existing organizations, until they are ready to give the signal for the general strike to the proletarian world.

It may be true that the improvements won from a partial strike are illusory on the economic side, since that which the bourgeois is forced to yield to workers in wages, they will take back by increasing the price of everyday merchandise or rent on homes—as the bourgeois hold all of the social wealth and are the forgers of all laws that sanction the usurpation of private property. Nevertheless, the advantages morally won by the workers in these everyday skirmishes are important, since they gradually acquire class consciousness, they train for battle, they learn to understand their strength, and they grow accustomed to seizing on their own, whether from a master or the government, that which they believe they have the right to own, without the intervention of medaled guardians.[103]

From these skirmishes, workers will learn that to win even in just a partial strike, against the cowardly ferocity the bourgeois use to keep the workers enslaved to their capital, it will in turn be necessary to put forward resolute action. Without much sentimentality, they must hit the master at least, if nothing else, in his vulnerable part, property, if necessary destroying, by fire or any other means, the factory, the workshop, or other things that belong to the enemy.

The efficacy of this means was demonstrated by 750 Italian workers who went on strike in Croton, at the New York drinking water supply facility,[104] and by the striking farmers of a Tuscan town,[105] whose victo-

---

103   "Medalled guardians" refers to members of parliament, who were given small gold medals as insignias, indicating the legislature and the name of the deputy or senator.

104   [Author's note] In Croton, 750 Italian workers who worked at the New York drinking water supply facility went on strike to win improvements. Before making their demands, the workers had mined the edges of the water supply facilities, and to their demands they added the threat that, in the case their demands were denied, they would blow up the edges of the water storage facilities, thus flooding the great capital of New York below.

The American government, like the governments of all countries in similar cases, sent a large contingent of soldiers to the strike location, but the strikers, expecting them, repeated the threat of flooding at the first shot from the militiamen's rifle.

The unofficial newspapers shrieked at the violence, but powerless against the strikers' determination, the business owners had to yield.

105   [Author's note] The farmers from there went on strike, following the denial of improvements they had asked for. The master, a count who was happily living

ries should be a lesson for that part of the proletariat that truly intends to fight to emancipate themselves from the bourgeois yoke.

In a word, action is necessary more than anything else to keep the struggle going, so that the masses evolve in a revolutionary manner, and so that the worker does not let himself be led up the garden path into the legislative maze by politicos.

Continued action (Kropotkin says) incessantly repeated by the minorities, makes the transformation.

In fact not everyone can be persuaded by theoretical propaganda alone, because most of the time we have seen that only a partial strike can awake a certain interest in class struggle among workers who until then had been indifferent to theoretical propaganda.

Only by action can the spirit of revolt, sedated by paper struggles and platonic demonstrations, be restored in the workers' souls. This certainly does not happen through passive regimentation, while waiting for the majority to be convinced by dint of words that a revolution is needed.

I say revolution, because the general strike understood as a means for overthrowing the capitalist regime cannot be anything but the social revolution under a different name. And since history teaches us that all revolutions were preceded by a series of revolts—as illustrated by Taine's claim that more than three hundred revolts took place in France before the storming of the Bastille—so, even the coming one shall certainly not be exempt from the laws traced by evolution in human history.[106]

Man's nature and character do not change all of a sudden. Therefore, if it were true that repressing proletarian revolts had the power to weaken and discourage him, as Gavilli believes, no revolution of any kind would ever have happened, as we can see.[107]

---

in the capital of Tuscany enjoying the income from his exploited workers, sent word that he would not deign to negotiate with the farmers.

So the farmers began to burn shacks, threatening much worse. This happened without the persons responsible for the fires being discovered.

Alarmed by so much courage, the arrogant and haughty count hurried to yield to the strikers' demands.

106   The historian, philosopher, and literary critic Hippolyte Taine wrote *Les origines de la France contemporaine*, in 6 volumes, the first of which was released in 1876 and the last, posthumous, in 1894. On Malatesta's point of view on revolt and revolution, see also "A Revolt Is No Revolution" in the volume of these *Complete Works* covering the years 1889–97.

107   Giovanni Gavilli, a well-known figure in Italian anarchism, was at that time the editor of *Il Grido della Folla* in Milan.

Facts and Opinions

Translated from "Fatti ed Opinioni," *La Rivoluzione Sociale* (London), no. 1 (October 4, 1902)

In the Republic

From a protest manifesto by the Argentinian Workers' Federation, we take the following account of one of the many events that every day, in every country, whether monarchies or republics, demonstrate that so-called constitutional guarantees have no value. Argentina is a republic, whose constitution is among the most liberal, and this is what is happening there:

"On Friday September 8 at 4 in the afternoon, in the space occupied by the secretarial offices of the Federation and of 18 worker societies, comrades Oliveri, Calvo, Ghio and another two, watched in astonishment as a group of about thirty police officers came running in with their pistols drawn, led by two individuals who later were known to be judge Navarro and commissioner Costa.

"Recovering from the surprise, the aforementioned comrades went out into the courtyard to inquire about the motive for this aggression, and in response saw the pistols pointed at their chests.

"Then the assailants asked who the president was, and since the comrades responded that the role of president did not exist there, they sent for an ax and began to break open the offices' doors. Seeing this, the custodian, comrade Oliveri, said that he had the keys to open the doors. Those opened, the police officers asked for the keys to the desks and cupboards. As the response was that these keys were in the possession of the respective secretaries, with the ax and an iron chisel, which certainly they had brought for this purpose, they set about breaking desks, cupboards, and everything that came under their hand. Then they collected the accounting books and all the papers, member lists, blank ledgers, circulars with and without addresses, regulations, manifestos, seals, blank paper and even postage stamps and filled the wagons that were waiting at the door. Anything that could not be loaded was destroyed or rendered unusable.

"And after this, judge Navarro, showing the comrades a medal bearing a scale, symbol of justice (!), told them: "I am judge doctor Navarro; I appoint Oliveri to remain here and guard this place and I declare all present are under arrest."

"During the night and the next day the people arrested were released... and good night."

Fantasies of republican judges!

Revolutionary Consciousness

There is a state of siege in Catalonia.[108] The workers of Barcelona, invited to request the reestablishment of the ordinary laws, responded that they do not know what to do with the law's protection, since they know that, whatever the laws are, they will only have as much freedom and respect as they are able to demand.

Proof lies in the fact that the Catalonian workers, precisely because they have greater consciousness and are able to count on their own strength, despite the state of siege, are in reality more free and better paid than those in other Spanish towns, where constitutional guarantees are in force.

Capitalistic Economy

We take the following from "Reynolds": "When fishermen have an abundant catch they are not at all happy. They know that when they bring their fish to the wharf, the merchant will not want to buy it. He does not want to clutter the market and can therefore lower the price. The fishermen must sell the fish to farmers, who use it to fertilize the ground, and must obviously sell it at the price of fertilizer.

"The poor of London would be happy to be able to buy fish at a good price; but those who monopolize the fish trade do not permit it. In the Billingsgate market (the London fish market) they throw away about seventy tons of fish, because the merchants do not want to sell it at a low price."

---

108   During this time, the state of war declared during the general strike of February 1902 (see note 86 above) was still in force.

No. 1   PREZZO : 10 CENTESIMI.   4 OTTOBRE 1902.

LA RIVOLUZIONE SOCIALE

PERIODICO SOCIALISTA-ANARCHICO

Int. Instituut
Soc. Geschiedenis
Amsterdam

REDAZIONE
C. FRICERIO, 33 Cross St., Rathbone Place, W.
AMMINISTRAZIONE
A. GALASSINI, 106, Victoria Dwellings,
Clerkenwell Road, E. C.

Esce ogni quindici giorni

ABBONAMENTI
ANNO 4/-
SEMESTRE 2/-
TRIMESTRE 1/-

AVVISO

Come annunciammo a suo tempo nella nostra circolare, il nuovo periodico di cui imprendiamo la pubblicazione verrà inviato a quanti ricevevano lo SCIOPERO GENERALE.

I compagni che approvano l'indirizzo del giornale e che possono aiutarci mandandoci scritti, indirizzi, oblazioni, sono pregati di farlo sollecitamente.

IL GRUPPO EDITORE.

Noi ed i nostri "affini."

Abbiamo noi degli affini, cioè dei cooperatori e dei possibili alleati nella lotta che combattiamo contro il presente ordinamento politico ed economico della società?

Se si bada ai programmi teorici affermati dai vari partiti, la cosa non sembra dubbia. Tutti coloro che non vogliono conservare integralmente il presente o ritornare ad un passato anche peggiore, hanno con noi, che siamo gli avversari di tutte le istituzioni vigenti, qualche cosa da combattere insieme, qualche comune nemico da abbattere. I socialisti democratici, per quanto autoritari e mangia-anarchici sieno, vogliono distruggere l'organizzazione capitalistica della produzione e lo sfruttamento padronale del lavoro altrui : essi dunque sarebbero i nostri alleati naturali nella lotta contro il capitalismo. E poichè il governo è, di fatto e di diritto, difensore degli interessi costituiti, essi dovrebbero trovarsi d'accordo con noi nel combattere il governo.

I repubblicani debbono, per definizione, voler fare la repubblica. Noi siamo naturalmente poco entusiasti di un cangiamento che lascerebbe intatte le fonti da cui traggono origine i mali sociali che vogliamo distruggere ; ma poichè, senza per fare la repubblica quanto per realizzare il nostro ideale di libertà e di solidarietà, bisogna pur cominciare col buttar giù la monarchia, che è l'ostacolo attuale, immediato ad ogni cambiamento radicale, i repubblicani, i socialisti e noi potremmo cooperare tutti nell'attacco contro la monarchia.

E siccome ogni grande trasformazione, ogni rivoluzione è preceduta da una quantità di piccoli cambiamenti morali e materiali che ne preparano l'avvenimento e ne rendono possibile il trionfo, vi sarebbe un vasto lavoro di educazione e di preparazione che potrebbe in parte essere fatto d'accordo.

Insomma, poichè nella strada verso l'avvenire v'è molta strada comune da fare, parrebbe logico e conveniente si facesse in comune. Unirsi quando siamo d'accordo ed abbiamo qualche cosa da conquistare che c'interessa tutti ; agire ognuno per proprio conto quando l'accordo cessa e gli scopi che si vogliono raggiungere sono diversi : sembrebbe tattica abile e prudente che, mentre avvantaggerebbe il progresso generale, non pregiudicherebbe nè danneggerebbe le aspirazioni speciali alle diverse frazioni.

Invece, in pratica la cooperazione tra noi ed i socialisti democratici ed i repubblicani si è palesata o impossibile o dannosa.

A varie riprese gli anarchici han tentato di trascinare gli altri partiti anti-costituzionali ad un' azione comune, e sia che si trattasse di un attacco diretto, armato, contro la monarchia, sia che fosse solo questione di un' agitazione contro il domicilio coatto, di uno sciopero, di una protesta, si sono sempre trovati burlati. Quando non ci hanno derisi o calunniati, e si son degnati di farci buon viso, è stato sempre per finire coll'invitarci a mandarli in parlamento, o ad entrarci noi stessi.

Ed intanto noi, oltre che perdervi il tempo, abbiamo rischiato di lasciarvi parte di quell'intransigenza che è forza e salvaguardia per un partito che vuole serbare intatto il proprio ideale.

Oramai sarebbe sciocco farsi ancora delle illusioni.

Con questi corrotti del parlamentarismo, che si sono prostituiti al potere e sono diventati i più pericolosi corruttori ed addormentatori del popolo, non v'è nulla da fare. Se qualche cosa di buono e di utile potranno fare ancora, lo faranno per la pressione che viene dal di fuori, per la guerra che noi faremo loro, per conservare quel prestigio che induce il governo a carezzarli, e non già per sincero, sentito desiderio del bene. Della gente (parliamo specialmente dei socialisti) che avendo professato e dicendo tuttora di professare idee di emancipazione, di giustizia, di libertà, è scesa giù giù fino a mendicare scuse e quasi giustificazioni per i responsabili diretti degli assassini di Berra e di Candela, è gente perduta, gente prostituita.

Oramai in Italia, di avversari veri del governo e della borghesia, oltre che la massa ancora semi-cosciente, non vi siamo che noi, gli anarchici. Cerchiamo di mettersi all'altezza della situazione in cui ci ha collocati l'ignavia e la corruzione dei partiti che avrebbero dovuto cooperare con noi nella lotta per la libertà.

Soli contro tutti, combattiamo a bandiera spiegata per il nostro ideale tutto intero, contro ogni manifestazione del principio autoritario, contro ogni sfruttamento ed ogni soprafazione dell'uomo sull'uomo. E sarà ancora il solo mezzo col quale, aspettando il trionfo finale, si potranno conseguire quei miglioramenti che sono conseguibili prima della rivoluzione.

• • •

Quando deploriamo l'indirizzo che han preso il partito socialista ed il repubblicano e facciamo proposito di rompere ogni relazione di "affinità," non intendiamo metter in dubbio la buona fede e la buona volontà dei proletari dell'uno e dell'altro partito, quelli che lavorano e soffrono vogliono certamente per davvero la libertà e la giustizia per tutti. Essi sono ingannati, mistificati, sfruttati in nome del socialismo o della repubblica, come sono stati sino ad ora sotto uno sciame di borghesucci spostati, assetati di potere, come altri proletari sono ingannati, mistificati, sfruttati, in nome di Dio e della patria, dai preti e dai politicanti monarchici.

Noi consideriamo come fratelli e come possibili compagni d'armi tutti quelli che soffrono, tanto più se, come i socialisti ed i repubblicani, hanno già la coscienza dei mali di cui sono vittime ed aspirano a liberarsene.

Combattiamo i loro errori, attiriamo la loro attenzione sui tradimenti dei loro capi, cerchiamo di svegliare in loro la volontà di agire da uomini coscienti e non da pecore disciplinate ; ed aspettiamoli in mezzo a noi, commilitoni desiderati ed apprezzati.

Dopo un Congresso

Poi che Filippo Turati si è lasciata sfuggire la frase : " nel partito socialista italiano di dottrina ce n'è poca "—noi che del socialismo abbiamo una conoscenza più severa, possiamo aggiungere : " coscienza eziandio ve n'è poca."

E davvero non possiamo assuefarci a chiamare "socialista " nel saldo senso della parola, quella assise di giornalisti, avvocatucci e spostati che ad arte radunate e con infingimento, si stesso dissi "rappresentante del popolo lavoratore italiano."

Sul terreno politico, ogni travisamento, ogni finzione è possibile, ma quanto sta in via maggiori. Oggi la merce avariata ed adulterata trova spaccio facile ed aperto : ond'è che pare aver plauso e fortuna un partito socialista il quale spende in tutta Italia soltanto lire 1808 per la propaganda, mentre altrettante o più ne spende per riunire la " Direzione " ; che sciupa cinque su otto delle sue magne sedute in un pettegolo duello di sofistica oratoria, mentre appena accenna, e quando gran parte già di congressisti è ita, alle condizioni miserrime dei contadini disoccupati ; che è tanto incurante del rispetto alla libera manifestazione del pensiero da coprire con urla la voce di Saverio Merlino, e che ogni dì più assoggetta, addomestica, emascula delle sue più sane aspirazioni il popolo delle officine e dei campi.

La fortuna che fra le masse lavoratrici pare incontrare la nuova formula di "rassegnazione" chiamata : "conquista dei pubblici poteri " ed il conseguente vanto e rumore che fa il partito socialista è un fenomeno di selezione a rovescio compiuto per l'influsso della lunga costrizione sotto cui il popolo italiano stiede e sta.

Gli elementi validi, generosi, "i globuli sanguigni della salute," furono espulsi, incarcerati, dispersi, le voci sane del socialismo anti-autoritario soppresse od una formula di socialismo permessa, legalizzata, accolta, talvolta accarezzata : la innocua, la parlamentare.

V'è punto da stupirsi se anche il prefetto avrebbe potuto con biglietto di favore assistere al congresso.

Entro al movimento vero, sano, "dell'emancipazione dei lavoratori fatta dai lavoratori " secondo la formula Marxiana, si è creata una solidarietà d'interessi borghesoidi, ond'è che la voce delle grandi rivendicazioni operaje è messa al bavaglio, sopraffatta dal vociono gridare " dai borghesi, dagli ambiziosi e da quelli che nel partito cercano uno stipendiuccio di segretari... e da direttori dei "Tempo"... poichè omai c'è poco da arrischiare a possibilità di far carriera nel partito socialista" per usare le parole di Treves, Dugoni e Bissola.

Così, fra l'anemica vita pubblica italiana, deviata sulla tendenza del socialismo dalla retta via rivoluzionaria e del malcontento o dalle aspirazioni proletarie, avendo assunto governo e dominio la tendenza borghesoide del socialismo, piano, piano, il socialismo italiano sta diventando "ministerialista."

Votare per il ministero che ammazzetta, fucila, manda i soldati a prendere il posto degli scioperanti vuol dire per Turati "conquistare le riforme," dare impronta proletaria alla riforma."

Per vuol dire giocare sulla buona fede, sulla ignoranza del popolo.

Per noi vuol dire dare pubblica scuola d'immoralità politica.

E tale fu l'insegnamento scaturito dalle sedute del settimo congresso socialista.

Quegli solo che là si permise ricordare che "il socialismo è possibile solo con la rottura di quei rapporti fondamentali che permettono lo sfruttamento del lavoro" s'è visto trattato da solitario, e da eretico un tantino.

Che davvero il popolo lavoratore s'interessasse assai della quistione dottrinaria che divideva Ferri e Turati noi ci permettiamo dubitarlo con Rigola.

Ma supposto pure che i lavoratori e non la sola parte borghesoide del partito prendesse parte vitale al dibattito nel Congresso del partito "riformista perchè rivoluzionario e rivoluzionario perchè riformista," vediamo un po' quale immenso inganno si nasconda pel popolo sotto queste cabalistiche parole.

Quando un partito politico è costretto a cedere, concedere o proporre alleanze con gli avversari, sia sul terreno elettorale, sia sul parlamentare, vero è che egli è o debole o sulla via delle debolezze.

Ma quando poi un partito socialista che pochi anni or sono diceva voler tendere alla socializzazione democratica dei mezzi di produzione, sia oggi sceso a tanto da giovarsi, od aiutare l'opera governativa per ottenere leggi sociali e riforme, a noi pare che tale partito s'abbia scavata la propria fossa e faccia della lotta da burletta.

Sarebbe come se due opposti eserciti ed avversari si accordassero mutuo appoggio a superare un valico difficile, con la promessa di battersi la dimane.

Aspetta asino che l'erba cresca!

Questo il significato del voto emesso nel Congresso sull'argomento delle due tendenze.

Il qual voto fu certo avuto con la benigna compiacevolezza del governo che ritardò di 24 ore la notizia dell'eccidio di Candela.

Prezioso monito questo alle mansuete e candide anime socialiste!

Ma già nel congresso stesso il pugliese Tucci aveva avuto il cattivo gusto di dire che nel mezzodì d'Italia "si è vicini alla rivolta di piazza. Già se ne ha qualche sintomo. Disoccupati e occupati a 25 centesimi per 16 ore di lavoro corrono già di paese in paese in cerca delle bricciole di pane."

Che peccato! Eravamo sì lieti noi con l'"Unità del Partito" intatta, invulnerabile!

* * *

Non è però sulla maggiore o minore opportunità di votare per un ministero piuttosto di un altro che noi dissentiamo.

La dissenzione è ben più importante: fondamentale.

Noi stimiamo erroneo, fatale al socialismo l'accettazione della tattica parlamentare.

Se non la pensassimo così saremmo costretti per amor della logica riconoscere che Turati ha ragione, in quanto che sa accettare fino alle estreme conseguenze la falsa premessa della conquista dei pubblici potere e della partecipazione nell'opera legislativa del governo.

L'azione parlamentare — funzione di governo capitalista — fa rientrare man mano i partiti più avanzati entro un ordine di tendenze e di azioni più e più consone alla funzione governativa — più e più quindi conservative.

E' un fenomeno di gravitazione politica corrispondente alla legge fisica che determina la caduta alla terra di quei bolidi che vengono a passare nella di lei sfera di influenza.

E la sfera d'influenza governativa, è tutto l'intrico di leggi e riforme nelle quali qualsivoglia aspirazione operaja verrà a imprigionarsi ogni qualvolta non riesca ad affermare la sua ribellione al principio centrale: quello di autorità, derivato immediato di quello di proprietà.

Il socialismo italiano, che pure quà e là ha indicato che avrebbe uomini e forza da gettar germi di nuova forza nella vita italiana è però un galeotto che si trascina dietro penosamente la catena d'un errore, di una falsa premessa: il parlamentarismo.

E' altrettanto possibile applicare con efficacia una legge sociale qualsiasi, quella ad esempio sul lavoro dei fanciulli e delle donne che dare assetto anarchico alla società.

Applicare una legge sociale vuol dire variare, ma non migliorare le condizioni operaje — poichè tale legge lascia immutate le ragioni dei mali: la produzione capitalistica.

Essa tenderà ognora a far rinascere — a benefizio della propria vita e del proprio interesse quegli errori, quei mali che la legge tendeva curare.

E poichè la borghesia che impersona questa forma di produzione sarà ancora a questo punto la più forte — il che è dimostrato dal bisogno della legge — essa si opporrà al suo pratico funzionamento.

Si dirà: abbiamo la tale e tale legge che ci difende; ma il male perdurerà sempre, più l'inganno, di cui trarranno benefizio i capi del preteso movimento socialista per scopi generali, egualmente ironici, o personali.

La storia è là ad ammaestrarci. Di più non è vero che le riforme — quali essi siano — le modificazioni alla forma politica sola — siano di vero ajuto per la formazione di un partito socialista ogni dì più forte, d'una corrente rivoluzionaria ogni dì più audace.

Il loro benefizio quando alcuno veramente — e per una classe soltanto di lavoratori — si faccia sentire, è effimero e passeggero.

Credere il contrario è ignorare la complessità della vita economica sociale moderna; è vivere nelle nuvole, od in un partito ove dottrina ce n'è poca come diceva bene Turati.

La diminuzione del dazio sul grano — ad esempio — può essere di punto in bianco ridotta a non avere alcun valore per l'operajo per un conseguente e quasi necessario avvilimento della mercede dei contadini.

A confutare qualcuna delle infantili concezioni economiche del socialismo preteso scientifico, talvolta il proletario si avvantaggia non della depressione della borghesia, ma pare anzi che ne segua parallelamente la fortuna, così da essere meno povero colà ove la borghesia è più ricca, più forte in conseguenza.

Inoltre ogni riforma o miglioramento economico deve essere difeso dalla forza viva del proletario organizzato o no, ma cosciente: onde il progresso ascendente d'un movimento non può durar più di una generazione — raro due.

Ogni generazione dà le proprie battaglie, nella forma e pei bisogni che ella sente.

S'ella non vince, tutto il lavoro è a rifare, oseremo dire da ri-incominciare.

L'idea di un progresso indefinito è una di quelle supposizioni ideologiche di cui i socialisti non hanno saputo ancora liberarsi.

Il socialismo è destinato a vincere se tenderà al fine con tutte le sue forze: distruggere il potere della borghesia e stabilire il regime della libera produzione, del libero scambio e del libero consumo.

O egli consumerà sue forze in illusorie battaglie e sarà talvolta un inganno, talvolta il miraggio d'una irraggiungibile terra promessa.

Il movimento rivoluzionario

IN RUSSIA

In meno di due anni, due ministri uccisi, due governatori feriti, un generale, direttore delle ferrovie dello Stato, ed un capo di polizia uccisi; attentati contro la vita di due altri capi di polizia.

Ma, si dirà, deve esservi in Russia una grande propaganda terrorista? Niente affatto.

In questi ultimi dieci anni, da dopo che l'antico partito rivoluzionario-terrorista col suo famoso Comitato esecutivo fu distrutto dagli sforzi di tutto il mostruoso impero dello zar, nessuna pubblicazione terrorista ha avuto circolazione degna di menzione. Al contrario, in nome del socialismo "scientifico" marxista, i socialisti democratici russi menarono una campagna accanita contro i terroristi, tanto nella stampa legale quanto in quella pubblicata all'estero, o clandestinamente in Russia.

Da dove trae origine dunque questa esplosione così energica del terrorismo? Non dalla propaganda di un partito. Essa è provocata dallo stato generale del paese, dall'oppressione barbara dell'assolutismo di una burocrazia onnipotente, dalla rovina completa dei contadini che costituiscono l'80 per cento della popolazione, dalle sofferenze e dalla disperazione generali.

"Il mio complice più attivo," diceva ai giudici il giovane ed eroico Balmacheff, "era il governo dispotico ed oppressore." Ed egli diceva la verità, tutta la verità. E' il governo che ha rovinato il paese (1); è esso che soffocò la scienza, l'istruzione popolare e ogni idea umanitaria; ed uccise con mezzi vari tutti gli uomini indipendenti delle ultime due generazioni: è esso che paralizzò tutta la vita sociale locale (2), e soppresse la più elementare giustizia (3).

Visto questo stato di cose, che meraviglia se una grande nazione, stanca di tanta miseria, di tanta atrocità ed ingiustizia comincia a ribellarsi? V'è piuttosto da meravigliarsi che dei milioni d'esseri umani abbiano potuto per tanto tempo sottomettersi docilmente ad una simile degradazione.

E' vero che una minoranza eroica della gioventù universitaria ed operaia si è continuamente ribellata contro il despotismo. Dal 1861-63 fino ai giorni d'oggi la propaganda socialista e rivoluzionaria si è andata sempre più sviluppando; qualche volta, come nel periodo 1873-78, il movimento è divenuto più attivo e pieno di spirito di sacrificio, di abnegazione; o, come nel 1879-84, la lotta prendeva un carattere titanico con le mine esplose nel palazzo imperiale, le bombe lanciate in pieno giorno, i capi di polizia pugnalati, lo zar giustiziato nel bel mezzo della capitale... Ma tutto ciò era l'opera di poche centinaja di bravi, sostenuti da poche migliaja di correligionari. La grande massa, il vero popolo, e la stessa classe istruita restavano inerti, e non solamente non si movevano, ma nascondevano scrupolosamente le loro opinioni e le loro simpatie. Cospirare — cospirare non solo per agire, ma anche per nascondere le proprie convinzioni è diventato pei russi una seconda natura. In tutto quest'immenso impero, fra questi 130 milioni d'abitanti, nessuno, eccetto i rivoluzionari, e questi solamente innanzi ai tribunali, osa dire in pubblico quello cha pensa.

Ed ecco che ora tutti dicono ad alta voce che non si puo vivere in condizioni così umilianti, sotto un assolutismo che rovina il paese. Individualmente ed in massa durante le manifestazioni tanto numerose, e spesso sanguinose, che han luogo in tutte le grandi città e fino nei centri industriali più isolati, gli uomini e le donne gridano ad alta voce: "viva la libertà! abbasso il despotismo!"

Il governo voleva intimidire i primi manifestanti colla repressione sanguinosa; sopratutto nelle due capitali e nelle città universitarie la repressione fu atroce. Ma questa volta il colpo non è riuscito; — le manifestationi aumentavano, l'entusiasmo spingeva i più coraggiosi a vendicare la società sui capi dell'oppressione. I due ministri hanno espiato la loro atrocità; i loro subalterni, i governatori, pagano colle loro persone.

Noi tutti salutiamo questo risveglio dello spirito di ribellione. La nostra più sacra aspirazione formulata fin dal 1868 si realizza: il popolo esce in istrada, si raccoglie sulle piazze per acclamare la rivoluzione.

E' vero che non è una rivoluzione sociale quella che si acclama. Nullameno i nostri cuori sono pieni di gioja, poichè questa volta è il popolo che entra in iscena. E sapete voi quel che significa l'insurrezione dei contadini russi? Ebbene, questi contadini "ignoranti," che vivono in comune agricola, sono persuasi che la terra tutta intera deve appartenere al comune dei produttori, e che i beni dei signori e dei capitalisti debbono essere divisi fra i membri di questa comunanza di produttori. I contadini ribelli delle provincie di Pottava e di Kharkoff han dimostrato coi fatti questa concezione di eguaglianza comunalista rivoluzionaria.

W. TCHERKESOFF.

(1) Da dopo l'abolizione della servitù la cultura del frumento è diminuita del 42 per cento; il numero dei cavalli è diminuito del 30 a 40 per cento; gli arretrati d'imposte sono saliti del 65,80 ed in qualche provincia fin del 200 per cento... Ed il bilancio dello Stato, che al tempo dell'abolizione (1861) era meno di 400 milioni di rubli, sale oggi a 2 miliardi per anno. Da ciò la carestia cronica, la rovina del popolo, la bancarotta dell'impero.

(2) I consigli elettivi provinciali ottenuti al tempo di Alessandro II sono stati quasi aboliti da Alessandro III e dallo zar attuale; in egual modo sono stati annientati i municipii e le corporazioni di mestiere.

(3) Ad eccezione delle grandi città, invece dei giudici di pace elettivi, che esistevano prima, sono i capi della polizia rurale che fan da giudici. Nella stessa Turchia la giustizia è già separata dalla polizia e dall'amministrazione.

GLI ANARCHICI NELLE SOCIETA' OPERAJE

Tratteremo prossimamente e nel modo più completo che ci sarà possibile questo argomento, d'importanza vitale per noi, della tattica degli anarchici dentro e di fronte alle organizzazioni operaje.

Intanto, poichè la cosa in questo momento si discute molto fra i compagni, vogliamo dire la nostra opinione sulla questione se gli anarcnici possono senza mettersi in contradizione coi loro principî, accettare cariche nelle leghe di resistenze, camere di lavoro e simili istituzioni — e se conviene che lo facciano.

La questione di principio è chiara: gli anarchici non possono, senza cessare di essere anarchici, accettare nessuna funzione autoritaria e debbono invece, sempre che ne incontrano, reclamarne l'abolizione, dimostrando come un'associazione di uomini liberi possa e debba sussistere senza autorità. Accettare una carica, che comporta il potere di imporre agli altri la propria volontà, colla intenzione di servirsene per fare il bene dell'associazione e correggerne i difetti, significa cadere nell'errore, eminentemente anti-anarchico, di voler distruggere l'autorità per mezzo dell'autorità; significa giustificare i socialisti che si fan nominare consiglieri e deputati e riescono, od aspirano, a farsi nominare ministri, significa insomma non essere più anarchici.

Invece quando si tratta di funzioni non autoritarie, quando si tratta cioè di fare dei lavori per una collettività che ne dà l'incarico, secondo la volontà e sotto il controllo della collettività stessa, niente impedisce ad un anarchico di accettare l'incarico, anzi spesso il rifiutarvisi sarebbe un voler godere dei vantaggi sociali senza prender la giusta parte di lavoro e di noje.

Quindi, dal punto di vista della coerenza coi principî, gli anarchici potrebbero accettare le cariche in quelle associazioni organizzate libertariamente, in cui gl'incaricati non fossero che semplici esecutori della volontà collettiva, e dovrebbero rifiutarvisi là dove vi fosse la menoma traccia d'autoritarismo.

Ma la questione è ben più complessa quando si viene ai casi pratici, e si considera l'effetto buono o cattivo che la sollecitazione e l'accettazione delle cariche sociali da parte degli anarchici può fare sulla propaganda.

Prima di tutto è quasi impossibile nell'ambiente attuale che un'organizzazione operaja, la quale non può vivere d'ideali e deve accogliere degli uomini di tutte le opinioni e subire le necessità della vita e della lotta, possa organizzarsi in modo veramente libertario. La missione degli anarchici è quella di combattere ogni traccia di autoritarismo, e la loro posizione diverrebbe assurda se essi stessi partecipassero a quell'autorità che vogliono distruggere.

Similmente, non potendo una società operaja essere composta esclusivamente di anarchici, anzi la grande maggioranza essendo sempre dei non anarchici, ed essendo diversi i criteri con cui gli anarchici ed i non anarchici giudicano le cose e le situazioni, un anarchico in carica, che dovrebbe agire in nome e secondo la volontà dei suoi mandanti, si troverebbe tutti i momenti nella necessità o di fare a modo suo, e così tradire il mandato secondo la pratica comune di tutti i mandatari, o rispettare la volontà degli altri e venir meno alle proprie convinzioni.

D'altra parte, vista l'orgia di vanità e di ambizioni di cui danno spettacolo i partiti che noi combattiamo, vista la diffidenza che il popolo ha, e che noi abbiamo interesse ad alimentare, contro coloro che dalla propaganda e dalle agitazioni politiche ritraggono un vantaggio personale morale e materiale, e visto che nello stato di inferiorità sociale in cui si trova il semplice lavoratore le cariche e le rappresentanze che danno un titolo innanzi al pubblico costituiscono un vero privilegio, è bene che gli anarchici si astengano rigorosamente da tutto ciò che potrebbe avere anche la sola apparenza di quelle debolezze che combattono negli altri.

La massa, su cui vogliamo agire, è molto primitiva e non vede chiaro nella differenza fra delegazione di potere e delegazione di lavoro, e se ci vede occupar cariche ed accettar titoli penserà che noi siamo come gli altri. E non è provato che la massa avrebbe torto! Noi abbiamo idee che, naturalmente, poichè le professiamo, crediamo superiori alle altre; ma avremmo torto di crederci, come uomini, migliori della media dei nostri contemporanei, e sarebbe prudenza l'evitare quelle occasioni di peccare, che poco a poco han condotto in un abisso di corruzione tanti uomini che cominciarono modestamente, ed in generale con buone intenzioni, a "sobbarcarsi al sacrifizio" di una qualsiasi carica che li metteva al di sopra dei loro compagni.

Ma — si potrebbe obbiettare — se si vuole l'organizzazione operaja bisogna pur volere i mezzi necessari a farla vivere.

Sta benissimo, rispondiamo; ma se, a causa dell'ambiente e sopratutto del grado di coscienza dei soci, un'associazione non può agire anarchicamente, è affare dei non anarchici l'adottare e l'attuare una condotta non anarchica; agli anarchici spetta invece la parte di forza propulsiva, rivoluzionaria, che con la critica e coll'esempio cerca di mettere nelle idee e nella condotta degli associati quanto più di anarchia è possibile, vale a dire quanto più è possibile di libertà e d'uguaglianza nelle relazioni fra i soci, di solidarietà nelle relazioni con tutta la classe operaja, di ribellione, di energia d'intransigenza nella lotta contro i padroni e contro il governo.

Ma se nessuno più volesse accettar cariche? Oh! allora sarebbe già venuto, e da molto, il tempo di farla finita con tutte le transazioni ed i palliativi a cui disgraziatamente la massa crede ancora.

Quando non vi sarà più nessuno che vorrà predicare la calma ed andare a trattare con i padroni, l'autorità per comporre gli scioperi ed evitare "le ribellioni inconsulte," sarà sonata l'ora fatale pei padroni e pei governi.

La venuta di quel giorno radioso deve essere lo scopo della nostra attività.

Lo sciopero parziale.

V'è chi sostiene che è male sciupare le forze operaje con scioperi parziali, meschini ed impotenti, e che converebbe invece consolidare le organizzazioni di mestiere, federarle insieme e fare lo sciopero generale.

V'è certamemte molto di giusto in questa osservazione; ma sarebbe d'altra parte un gran male se, in attesa della gran lotta finale, ci si abituasse a star tranquilli e si rinunziasse all'esercizio della lotta.

Che gli operai si organizzino in forti associazioni per forza e coscienza di classe acciò combattere sino al rovesciamento del regime capitalista sta bene; ma che attraverso questo lavoro d'organizzazione gli operai debbano astenersi d'ogni insurrezione sia individuale che collettiva contro l'esosità e le prepotenze dei padroni da cui sono continuamente fatti segno, per non provocar scioperi meschini o recar danno alle organizzazioni esistenti sinchè non siano pronte per dar il segnale al mondo proletario dello sciopero generale, mi sembra un'illusione direi quasi amena, poichè questa idea esce completamente dalle leggi della storia e dell'evoluzione.

Se è vero che i miglioramenti conquistati in uno sciopero parziale sono apparenti dal lato economico, giacchè quello che i borghesi sono costretti a concedere in salari agli operai se lo riprendono col rincaro dei generi di prima necessità o sù gli affitti delle case — essendo essi borghesi i detentori di tutta la ricchezza sociale ed i fucinatori di tutte le leggi che sanzionano l'usurpazioni della proprietà privata — ciò nondimeno sono importanti i vantaggi che conquistano moralmente gli operai in queste scaramucce di tutti i giorni, inquantochè vi acquistano gradatamente la coscienza di classe, si addestrano alla lotta, imparano a conoscere la loro forza, e s'abituano a strappare da loro stessi quello che si credono in diritto di avere, sia dal padrone che dal governo, senza l'intervento di tutori medagliettati.

Da queste scaramucce gli operai apprenderanno che per vincere, sia pur in uno sciopero parziale, alla vigliacca ferocia di cui si valgono i borghesi per tenerli schiavi del loro capitale, sarà necessario oppongano a loro volta la risolutezza d'azione, colpendo senza tanti sentimentalismi il padrone, se non foss'altro almeno nella sua parte vulnerabile: la proprietà, all'occorrenza distruggendo, coll'incendio o con qualche altro mezzo, l'officina, il laboratorio od altro appartenente all'avversario.

L'efficacia di questo mezzo l'hanno dimostrato i 750 operai italiani che scioperarono a Croton, al deposito dell'acqua potabile di New-York (1), ed i contadini scioperanti di un paese toscano le cui vittorie dovrebbero essere d'insegnamento a quella parte di proletariato che intende realmente combattere per emanciparsi dal giogo borghese.

In una parola, più d'ogni altro è necessario l'azione per tener accesa la lotta, perchè le masse evolvino in senso rivoluzionario e perchè l'operaio non si lasci trascinare pel naso dai politicanti nei meandri legislativi.

L'azione (dice Kropotkin) continua, ripetuta incessantemente delle minoranze opera la trasformazione.

Difatti non sempre colla sola propaganda teorica si convince tutti, perchè il più delle volte si è veduto col solo sciopero parziale destare un certo interessamento alla lotta di classe in quegli operai che fino allora erano rimasti refrattari alla propaganda teorica.

Solo coll'azione lo spirito di rivolta narcotizzato dalle lotte cartacee e dalle dimostrazioni platoniche potrà ritemprarsi nell'animo degli operai e non certo coll'irreggimentarsi passivamente in attesa che la maggioranza si convinca a forza di parole che bisogna far la rivoluzione.

Dico rivoluzione, perchè lo sciopero generale inteso come mezzo per abbattere il regime capitalista non potrà esser altro che la rivoluzione sociale cambiata di nome. E siccome la storia c'insegna che tutte le rivoluzioni furono precedute da una serie di sommosse, tanto da far dire a Taine che più di trecento sommosse si verificarono in Francia prima della presa della Bastiglia, così anche questa prossima che si annunzia non potrà certamente esimersi dal subire le leggi tracciate dall'evoluzione nella storia dell'umanità.

La natura e il carattere dell'uomo non si cambiano ad un tratto. Se dunque fosse vero che le repressioni delle sommosse proletarie avessero la potenza di sfibrarlo e sfiduciarlo, come crede il Gavilli, non sarebbero, come si vede, mai avvenute rivoluzioni di sorta.

(1) A Croton, 750 operai italiani che lavoravano al deposito dell'acqua potabile di New-York si misero in isciopero per ottenere dei miglioramenti. Prima di far delle domande, gli operai avevano minato i margini dei depositi d'acqua, ed alle domande aggiunsero la minaccia che, in caso di risposta negativa, avrebbero fatto saltare in aria i margini dei depositi d'acqua, innondando in tal modo la sottostante gran capitale di New-York.

Il governo americano, come quello di tutti i paesi in simili casi, inviò un buon nerbo di soldati sul luogo dello sciopero, ma i scioperanti che li aspettavano ripeterono anche a questi la minaccia d'allagamento al primo colpo di fucile da parte dei militi.

I giornali ufficiosi strillarono alla violenza, ma impotenti contro la risolutezza degli scioperanti, gl'impresari dovettero cedere.

(2) I contadini di laggiù scioperavano in seguito al rifiuto di migliorie che avevano chiesto. Il padrone, un conte che se ne stava beatamente nella capitale della Toscana a godersi le rendite dei suoi sfruttati, fece dire che non si degnava trattare coi contadini.

Allora questi cominciarono ad incendiare dei cascinotti, minacciando molto di peggio. Ciò avvenne senza che se ne scoprisse l'autore.

Allarmato da tanto ardire, l'altero e sdegnoso conte si affrettò a cedere alle domande degli scioperanti.

Fatti ed Opinioni

In repubblica

Da un manifesto di protesta della Federazione Operaja Argentina, togliamo la seguente narrazione di uno dei tanti fatti che ogni giorno, in tutti i paesi, monarchie o repubbliche che siano, vengono a dimostrare il niun valore delle cosiddette garanzie costituzionali. L'Argentina è una repubblica, con una costituzione tra le più liberali, ed ecco che cosa vi avviene:

"Il venerdì 8 settembre alle 4 del dopopranzo, trovandosi nel locale che occupano la secreteria della Federazione e quelle di 18 società operaje, i compagni Oliveri, Calvo, Ghio ed altri due, videro con meraviglia entrar di corsa un gruppo di una trentina di poliziotti con le rivoltelle in mano, capitanati da due individui che poi si seppe essere il giudice Navarro ed il commissario Costa.

"Rinvenuti dalla sorpresa, i detti compagni uscirono nel cortile per domandare il motivo di quella aggressione, e per tutta risposta si videro presentare le rivoltelle al petto.

"Poi gli assalitori domandarono chi era il presidente, e siccome i compagni risposero che là non esisteva la carica di presidente, mandarono a prendere una scure e cominciarono a scassinare le porte delle secreterie. Vedendo ciò, il portiere, compagno Oliveri, disse che egli teneva le chiavi per aprire le porte. Aperte queste, i poliziotti domandarono le chiavi delle scrivanie e degli armadi ed essendo loro risposto che esse si trovavano in possesso dei rispettivi secretari, con la scure ed uno scalpello di ferro, che certamente avevano portato apposta, si misero a rompere scrivanie, armadi e tutto quello che venne loro sotto mano. Poi raccolsero i libri di contabilità e tutte quante le carte, liste di soci, bollettari in bianco, circolari con e senza indirizzi, regolamenti, manifesti, timbri, carta bianca e perfino i francobolli postali e ne caricarono le vetture che tenevano alla porta. Tutto ciò che non poteva esser caricato fu distrutto o reso inservibile.

"E dopo ciò, il giudice Navarro, mostrando ai compagni una medaglia con sopra una bilancia, simbolo di giustizia (!), disse loro: 'Io sono il giudice dottor Navarro; incarico Oliveri di restare a guardia del locale e dichiaro in arresto tutti i presenti.'

"Nella notte e nel giorno dopo gli arrestati furono rilasciati... e buona notte."

Fantasie di giudici repubblicani!

Coscienza rivoluzionaria.

In Catalogna v'è lo stato d'assedio. Gli operai di Barcellona, invitati a domandare il ristabilimento delle leggi ordinarie, han risposto che essi non sanno che farsi della protezione della legge, poichè sanno che, qualunque che siano le leggi, avranno solo quel tanto di libertà e di rispetto che sapranno esigere.

In prova sta il fatto che gli operai catalani, appunto perchè hanno maggiore coscienza e sanno contare sulle proprie forze, malgrado lo stato d'assedio, sono in realtà più liberi e meglio pagati che quelli degli altri paesi di Spagna, dove sono in vigore le garanzie costituzionali.

Economia capitalistica.

Togliamo dal "Reynolds'": "Quando dei pescatori fanno una pesca abbondante non sono punto contenti. Essi sanno che quando porteranno il loro pesce sulla banchina il mercante non vorrà comprarlo. Questi non vuole ingombrare il mercato e può così ribassare i prezzi. I pescatori debbono vendere il pesce agli agricoltori, che se ne servono per ingrassare la terra, e venderlo naturalmente a prezzo di concime.

"I poveri di Londra sarebbero felici di poter comprare del pesce buon mercato; ma coloro che monopolizzano il commercio del pesce non lo permettono. Al mercato di Billingsgate (il mercato del pesce di Londra) si butta via circa settanta tonnellate di pesce, perchè i mercanti non vogliono venderlo a prezzo basso."

Fra le Pubblicazioni

Da Napoli riceviamo l' *Armonia*, rivista di scienze, lettere ed arti, diretta da Raffaele Valenti. Indirizzo: Via Sopramuro al Carmine, 36, Napoli.

* * *

Il compagno Luigi Molinari ci manda una circolare per la pubblicazione in Italia del libro *La Conquista del Pane* di Kropotkin, per cui gli abbisognano L. 1000. Egli propone ai compagni l' acquisto di azioni da L. 50 ciascuna che danno diritto all' invio di 100 esemplari ad opera compiuta. Noi non possiamo che compiacerci di quest' utile iniziativa e la raccomandiamo all' interesse di tutti i compagni.

Indirizzarsi all' Avv. Luigi Molinari, Via Tito Speri 13, Mantova.

VERSO L'ANARCHIA

Da un recente libro di Kropotkin: "Memorie di un Rivoluzionario" — opera magistrale di cui l' ottima rivista l' "Università Popolare" pubblica nelle sue colonne la traduzione che speriamo di veder presto stampata in volume — stralciamo un brano in cui l' autore, narrando del suo secondo soggiorno fra gli operori lavoratori del Giura, dice degli sforzi fatti da lui e dai suoi amici operai per formulare i principi del socialismo anarchico dai punti di vista teorico e pratico.

Noi scorgevamo nelle nazioni civilizzate il germe di una nuova forma sociale destinata a soppiantare la vecchia: il germe di una società composta d'individui fra loro eguali, non più costretti a vendere le loro braccia ed il loro cervello a chi li fa lavorare secondo il proprio capriccio, ma che potranno essi stessi adoperare le loro cognizioni e capacità per la produzione — in un organamento proprio a combinare gli sforzi di tutti — onde procurare a tutti la maggior somma possibile di benessere, sempre lasciando libertà piena ed intera all' iniziativa individuale. Questa società si comporrà d' innumerevoli associazioni unite fra di loro per tutto quanto richieda uno sforzo comune: federazioni di produttori per ogni genere di produzione, agricola, industriale, intellettuale, artistica; comuni per il consumo, incaricate di provvedere a quanto concerne l' alloggio, l' illuminazione, il riscaldamento, il vitto, le istituzioni sanitarie, ecc.; federazioni dei comuni fra di loro e federazione dei comuni coi gruppi di produzione; infine, dei gruppi ancor più estesi, conglobanti tutto un paese od al caso più paesi, e composti di persone che lavoreranno in comune a soddisfare quei bisogni economici, intellettuali ed artistici che non si limitano ad un territorio determinato. Gli sforzi di tutti questi gruppi si combineranno liberamente mediante una intesa reciproca, come già lo praticano attualmente le compagnie ferroviarie e le amministrazione postali dei vari paesi che non hanno una direzione centrale ferroviaria o postale, sebbene le prime non cerchino che il loro egoistico interesse e le ultime appartengano a stati differenti e nemici; o meglio ancora, come i meteorologi, i clubs alpini, le stazioni di salvataggio in Inghilterra, i ciclisti, i maestri, ecc., che uniscono i loro sforzi per il compimento d' opere d' ogni sorta, siano esse d' ordine intellettuale o di semplice divertimento. La completa libertà presiederà allo sviluppo delle forme nuove di produzione, d'invenzione e d' organizzazione; verrà incoraggiata l' iniziativa individuale e combattuta ogni tendenza all' uniformità ed all' accentramento.

Inoltre, questa società non sarà plasmata in forme determinate ed immutabili; ma si modificherà senza posa, come organismo vivo, costantemente in istato di evoluzione. Il bisogno di un governo non sarà sentito, perchè l' accordo e l' associazione liberamente consentiti avranno sostituito tutte le funzioni che oggigiorno i governi considerano come proprie e perchè i conflitti divenendo sempre meno frequenti essi saranno, ove ancora se ne producessero, regolati dall'arbitrato.

Non uno di noi si dissimulava quanto importante e profondo fosse il cambiamento propostoci. Noi capivamo che le opinioni in voga — secondo le quali la proprietà privata della terra, delle officine, delle miniere, delle case, ecc. sarebbe necessaria per assicurare il progresso industriale ed il salariato sarebbe indispensabile per costringere gli uomini al lavoro — non sbarazzerebbero tanto presto il cammino alle concezioni più elevate della proprietà e della produzione socializzate. Noi sapevamo di dover attraversare un lungo periodo di propaganda ininterrotta e di lotte continue, di ribellioni isolate e collettive contro le vigenti forme della proprietà, di sacrifici individuali, di parziali tentativi di riorganizzazione e di parziali rivoluzioni, prima di riescire a modificare le idee correnti circa la proprietà privata.

Ed anche capivamo che l'umanità non rinuncerebbe e non poteva rinunciare d'un tratto alle idee attuali rispetto alla necessità dell' autorità in mezzo alle quali siamo tutti cresciuti. Lunghi anni di propaganda ed una lunga seria di rivolte parziali contro l'autorità, ed inoltre una revisione completa delle dottrine attualmente dedotte dalla Storia, saranno necessarie prima che gli uomini arrivino a capire d'essersi sbagliati attribuendo ai loro governanti ed alle loro leggi quanto in realtà non costituiva che la risultante delle loro proprie abitudini e sentimenti sociali. Noi sapevamo tutto ciò. Ma sapevamo altresì che propugnando una trasformazione in quelle due direzioni, noi ci saremmo trovati sospinti dalla corrente dell' umanità incamminata verso il progresso.

Man mano ch' io faceva più intima conoscenza con la classe operaia e con gli uomini delle classi colte che con quella simpatizzavano, venivo accorgendomi che essi si preoccupavano assai più della loro libertà personale che del loro benessere. Cinquanta anni fa gli operai eran pronti a vendere la loro libertà individuale ad ogni genere di padroni, persino ad un Cesare, in cambio di promesse di benessere materiale. Ma le cose eransi cambiate. Ed io vedeva la fiducia cieca nei capi eletti, anche quando questi eran scelti fra gli uomini migliori del movimento proletario, sparire d' infra gli operai di razza latina. "Innanzi tutto ci occorre di sapere quel che ci abbisogna ed allora sapremo farlo da noi stessi meglio che chichessia" ecco l' idea da cui li trovai ovunque penetrati, assai più che non si soglia crederlo. Il principio posto dagli statuti dell' Associazione Internazionale dei lavoratori: "L' emancipazione dei lavoratori dev' esser opera dei lavoratori stessi" era stato ben accetto a tutti ed aveva gettato profonde radici negli spiriti. La triste esperienza della Comune di Parigi non aveva che confermato questo principio.

Allo scoppio di quest' insurrezione un numero considerevole d' uomini appartenenti alle stesse classi medie eran pronti a fare, o per lo meno ad accettare, una trasformazione sociale... "Quando sortivo di casa con mio fratello per discendere in istrada — mi diceva un giorno Eliseo Reclus — ci vedevamo assaliti e tempestati di questioni da gente appartenente alle classi agiate. "Diteci che dobbiamo fare! Noi siamo pronti a lanciarci verso l' avvenire" ci si diceva da tutte le parti; ma noi... noi non eravamo preparati ad una risposta!" Mai sin allora un governo aveva rappresentato in modo sì completo tutti i partiti avanzati quanto il Consiglio della Comune di Parigi, eletto il 25 marzo 1871. Tutte le sfumature dell' opinione rivoluzionaria — Blanquisti, Giacobini, Internazionalisti — erano rappresentate nelle loro giuste proporzioni. Ma siccome gli operai stessi non avevano idee nette di riforma sociale da suggerire ai loro rappresentanti, il governo della Comune nulla fece in tale senso. Il fatto solo di essersi segregati dalle masse rimanendo rinchiusi entro il recinto del Palazzo municipale paralizzò ogni loro sforzo. Bisognava dunque, per assicurare il successo del socialismo, propugnare le idee di soppressione di ogni governo, d' indipendenza, di libera iniziativa individuale — in una parola le idee dell' anarchismo — accanto alle idee di socializzazione della proprietà e dei mezzi di produzione.

P. Kropotkine.

Continua.

UN' INIZIATIVA.

Qui a Londra un gruppo di compagni delle diverse nazionalità si sono tempo fa costuiti in Società Internazionale per l' edizione di opere sociologiche in tutte le lingue, iniziativa di non poca utilità per la diffusione delle idee anarchiche. A tal effetto si è proceduto all' impianto di una tipografia propria che ora funziona regolarmente. I benefici che questa potrà trarre dai lavori commerciali sarà devoluto alla pubblicazione di scritti di educazione rivoluzionaria e di volgarizzazione scientifica. E' progettata pure una Libreria sociologica e la creazione di una Università Popolare Internazionale.

A render attuabili questi propositi, il comitato della Società ha emesso una serie d' azioni da 5 scellini (£. it. 6. 25) rimborsabili dopo un anno e che danno diritto all' invio delle pubblicazioni èdite dalla Società.

La tipografia della Società s' incaricherà di stampare opuscoli di qualsiasi lingua, per gruppi o compagni isolati, ai prezzi più vantaggiosi ed ove gli scritti appajano di efficace ed utile propaganda, una tiratura supplementare gratuita ne sarà fatta. Inviare comunicazioni od altro al segretario Gaston Lance, 33 Gresse Street, Rathbone Place, Londra W.

SOTTOSCRIZIONE

PER LA "RIVOLUZIONE SOCIALE."

Da Parigi, a mezzo B....	£	0	12	0
G. Lanfranchi, Westcliff-on-Sea...		0	2	0
G. Daporto		0	2	0
Rossi, mosaicista		0	1	0
Ilario		0	1	0
Bertoni		0	1	0
Bomben		0	1	0
Isaja Pacini		0	5	0
C. Bandi		0	5	0

Collettore per le quote fisse dei compagni del Gruppo è il compagno E. Defendi.

Preghiamo i giornali amici a volerci favorire il cambio all' indirizzo della Redazione.

Published by A. Galassini, on behalf of the Group "La Rivoluzione Sociale," 106, Victoria Dwellings, Clerkenwell Road, E. C.

Printed for the Publishers by the International Printery, 33, Gresse Street, W.

Giarratana

Translated from "Giarratana," *La Rivoluzione Sociale* (London),
no. 2 (October 18, 1902)

Another name is added to the long list commemorating the massacres of workers, perpetrated by the monarchy's bandits to defend the privileges of the bourgeoisie.[109]

Fits of outrage, fiery words remain choked in our throats. The thing, "the incident," continues to happen often enough and has become such a banal characteristic of Italian life—whether the conservatives or the "liberals" dear to the "socialists" govern—that we no longer know how to express our ire without falling into broken-winded and wordy rhetoric.

Facing such events, we find it foolish and criminal to bring out questions of methods and principles. Workers cannot make a move without finding themselves facing assassins armed to the teeth, who ruthlessly kill because they know that the government will pay them for the blood shed with praise, promotions, and money. And when one finds himself in the presence of the assassins resolved to seize any pretext to kill, he must above all else, before all else, think of defending himself.

May the workers know that when they encounter police and soldiers, they must quickly prepare themselves to defend... or to attack, which often is the best means of defense. And if they do not have the weapons, or the desire, or the courage to face armed force, may they get even with the property owners and their things, once armed force is absent. Soldiers and police cannot be everywhere!

The only means, and urgent means, to slow down this homicidal mania of the privileged classes is for the workers to show themselves determined to demand a tooth for a tooth, in fact ten teeth for just one tooth.

So be it.

---

109   In Giarratana, in the province of Ragusa, unionized farmers were striking to win a wage increase. On October 13, 1902, there were clashes with the police, during which an innocent child and a day laborer were killed, while one of the police who had fired at the crowd was followed and beaten to death.

On Strikes

Translated from "A proposito di scioperi," *La Rivoluzione Sociale* (London), no. 2 (October 18, 1902)

The United States, France, and Spain are the scenes of important and more or less violent strikes. Because of a strike, in the past fortnight Geneva has seen civic life brought to a standstill, republican troops combing the street, sabering the population, and the government arresting, expelling, persecuting.

The intervals between issues of our newspaper and the distance from where it is headed prevent us from chronicling events, which comrades should be monitoring attentively through the daily newspapers. All we can do is draw attention to the lessons emerging from these events.

The ever-growing frequency of strikes and the size that they are taking on, to the point of deeply disrupting social life and rattling the very foundations of the State, clearly show that the simultaneous suspension of work, as determined and implemented by the workers for whatever reason, has now become a great training ground, and will very likely be the occasion from which the final insurrection will spring, ending Society's current, nonsensical, and murderous make-up.

It is therefore of the utmost importance for us anarchists, who want to spark that insurrection, to be able to exercise decisive action upon the direction of these strikes and the organization of labor, from which the strikes originate. And so the greatest and most pressing problem presently claiming our attention and consideration is the purpose and tactics that we should follow as we participate in labor organizations and strikes.

We will discuss labor organizations another time; today we shall say a few things about strikes.

If economic forces were all that was involved in disputes between capitalists and proletarians, the strike would be doomed to inevitable defeat. In the battle between millions and pennies, between the property owners gambling with a part of their profits, their surplus, and the workers who have no bread for tomorrow and are racked by the screams of their famished children, the latter are usually overpowered by the former. And even when due to some exceptionally favorable circumstance, a strike proves victorious, its outcome, in terms of the wages that the worker gets and the purchasing power of those wages, proves to be an illusion. After having spent a more or less long time without wages and having braved often harrowing suffering, the victorious striker sees his meager earning increased by a few pennies... but promptly realizes that the masters recoup their losses from consumers, that the cost of things increases as wages increase and that, ultimately, even with more money, he cannot afford any more than he used to buy and is, consequently, as badly off as before.

But there are moral and political forces at work, which change the terms of the problem and lead, or may lead, to different outcomes.

Besides being an economic conflict, a strike is a moral revolt. The worker who goes on strike and risks starvation for himself and his loved ones in order to win some improvement in his situation, is no longer the docile and compliant slave who endures oppression, albeit grumbling, as if it were some inescapable fate. He asserts his rights, or at least some of his rights; and demonstrates he has realized that for the acknowledgment of such rights he should neither wait for the grace of god, nor the generosity of the mighty, but must look to his own strength in association with the strength of those in his same position. And this means that he gets better treatment, because when all is said and done, collectively speaking, the masters can only treat folk as badly as folk will allow. And meanwhile the worker becomes accustomed to desiring a better standard of living, and acquires a clear consciousness of the antagonism there is between his interests and those of the masters and of the need to do away with the ruling class so that labor can emancipate itself.

Essentially this is the only good that can come from strikes, and so anarchists should take an interest in them from an economic point of view and try to steer them to victory, not through passive resistance sustained as long as possible with the help of resistance funds and subscriptions, but by adopting an aggressive attitude and using all worthwhile means to show that the workers are serious about wanting what they want and will not tolerate it being withheld from them with impunity.

Two phenomena, certainly not new, but which are becoming increasingly serious and widespread, can be observed in the present-day strikes.

One is the meddling of the State, in the form of police and soldiers, in clashes between capital and labor. Whether we are talking about feudal, monarchist Spain, or about France, Switzerland, or America, republican and democratic countries, always and everywhere the government massacres strikers.

Must we give up on every demand and submit unconditionally to the good will of the capitalists, or allow ourselves to be slaughtered eternally?

Let us leave the preaching of patience and calm to those who view the slaughter of the people as an opportunity for them to go fishing for a parliamentary seat... and issue an interpellation to the minister. We, who know the worth of deputies and their interpellations and who seek ultimately to revolutionize the world by means of agitation and revolts, should be pointing out to the workers how, these days, every strike is exposed to military repression, and persuade them to prepare themselves just as they would for an insurrection.

These days, resistance funds are no longer the issue. With the colossal strikes mounted these days and the coalitions the masters have learned to form, it would be extremely ridiculous for the workers to try to fight by dint of money. The workers are starting to understand this and are showing a tendency to turn to different means. Governments are fully aware of the dangers of this trend and are placing their rifles and cannons at the disposal of the masters. The point is to counter those rifles and cannons with suitable weaponry: that is all.

The other phenomenon is that the *scabs,* or *"yellows"* as they are called in France these days, are beginning to stand up brazenly to the organized workers, and even to pit organization against organization. This is a very serious development because it triggers conflict between one worker and another, which is wholly to the benefit of the masters, and generates hostility, resentment, and hatred, which later may prove a tremendous obstacle to the triumph of the proletarian revolution.

While "strikebreaking"—meaning the existence of workers who feel and practice no solidarity with their fellow comrades and are on the side of the masters and work for cut-rate wages and take the jobs of the strikers—is sadly a necessary feature of a society that is unable to provide work for all its members and reduces so many men to the condition of starving beasts who care for nothing and can care for nothing except for the pursuit of a crust of bread, it is nevertheless largely the fault of the organized workers themselves, who purport to be conscious of their class interests. Wishing to fight against the capitalists within the confines of the law, they sought to restrict the availability of jobs as much as possible, and so, whilst on the one hand they insist that the masters not hire non-union labor, on the other, as soon as their unions felt strong enough, they placed obstacles to the entry of new members within their midst, reduced the numbers of apprentices, and waged war against foreign labor... and have thereby been a mighty help to the growth of strikebreaking. Heedless of the needs of the jobless and unskilled, have they any real right to complain if the latter do not feel bound to them by ties of solidarity, and steal their jobs out from under them when the opportunity presents itself?

In the ranks of the enemy, there are certainly some who are slaves at heart; and they are poor wretches, who might attain human consciousness and dignity only by means of material comfort and fraternal treatment. But there are also those who feel repugnance at what they are doing, and do it only out of harsh necessity. We can still remember what one American scab told a reporter a few years back. "I know that I play a thuggish and odious part," he said, "but there you have it! I have not been able to find regular employment for years. I cannot get into the factories because I am not a member of the union and they will not have me in the union because I am out of work and cannot pay the entrance fee. The strike has opened up my chances of working. I know that once the strike is over there will be no more job for me, but then I knew there would be none even had I stood four-square by the strikers. My kids were starving to death and I had to send them out and go myself to pick through the garbage cans for leftovers; and my wife blamed me for our wretchedness. A chance to eat came along and I grabbed it. Did I do wrong? I do not know; in the meantime I eat and I can see smiles on the faces of my kids who knew only how to cry! Now the strikers are threatening me and might attack me at any moment. I go armed and may well kill somebody. It is ghastly! ... but I cannot let myself be killed without fighting back. Like it or not, my sense of duty toward my kids stops me from doing so."

Who would dare to condemn that man in the name of labor solidarity, of which he has borne all the brunt without ever having any of the benefits?

Yet it is only natural, it is human for strikers to feel angry at those who turn up to take their jobs, but we who are guided by higher principles must temper that anger with a little logic and a little justice. Why attack scabs, who are our brothers, albeit a little more ignorant and a lot more unfortunate than us, rather than the masters who are the source of our shared misfortunes? In any event, whether ones or the others come under attack, the police step in and we have to toe the line or fight back. Better then to attack the real enemy.

If the current trend toward big, more or less general strikes is to deliver the beneficial revolutionary benefits with which it is laden, rather than petering out gradually due to weariness and discouragement, giving way to long years of monotonous calm, the workers have to get it into their heads that the strike should not be an end in itself, but a tool for social transformations. And the task of getting this across to them falls to the anarchists.

Let us take the example of the coalminers' strike in America.[110]

This tragicomedy has been going on for years now. The workers ask for improvements and the masters, who have large stocks of coal to fall back on, deny them. The workers go on strike, and suffer, and leave the

---

110   The 1902 coalminers' strike was declared by the United Mine Workers of America in the anthracite mines of Pennsylvania and began on May 12th. The miners asked for the recognition of their union, a 20 percent wage increase and a reduction in working hours from ten to eight hours.

public, the poor part of the public who has no coal, to suffer. Meanwhile the masters sell off their stocks at higher prices. Once those stocks are approaching the point of exhaustion, negotiations and compromises begin, and the workers are granted some of what they were asking for. Then, gradually, as the stocks are rebuilt, the masters snatch back the concessions they made until the workers put forth new demands... and it starts all over again.

Likewise, this time around. At the time of writing, the dispute will probably have been settled. The miners' long months of suffering and the wretchedness, distress, and countless deaths caused among the poorer classes of Americans by lack of coal will have served only as yet another act in the usual farce.[111]

Instead, what great consequences could have ensued from the situation, if only the strikers' mentality and that of their leaders had been different!

The miners' strike is useless unless the railway men simultaneously refuse to carry the coal that the masters are holding in reserve. In America, the railway men are organized just like the miners and are federated with them; and if there was no rail strike, this was because the leaders did not know where that road would end up and were afraid of seeing their economic and political position compromised.

The poor population of the big American cities, to whom coal shortage matters as much as bread shortage does to us, were irritated and threatening. If the miners and railway men had by common consent set about working the mines and shipping the coal themselves on the people's behalf, organizing distribution free of charge along the route and receiving whatever folk might have been willing to give them in return, the population would have vigorously backed the strikers' bold initiative.

The government would certainly have stepped in... come of that what might. But the world's great revolutions were made from more paltry causes and means and much more modest principles!

The objection will be made that this is all more easily said than done and we readily agree with that. We will be told that the people are not prepared, not ready for such things, and we agree. If the people were prepared and ready, they would have done so without waiting for our advice.

But everything has to start somewhere. Today, and right from the

---

111   The strike ended on October 23, 1902, when president Theodore Roosevelt created a commission that the parties accepted as an arbitrator. This was the first example of the federal government's intervention in a union dispute. The miners got a 10 percent wage increase and a nine-hour work day, while the owners obtained a higher sale price for coal. The union remained unrecognized.

outset, the American labor movement seems to be made more for the benefit of its leaders than that of its workers. Starting with the president, who takes a ministerial salary and wields considerable political influence, and going right down to the least important branch secretary, there is a whole hierarchy of employees who live off the movement and, having lost the habit of working and developed a taste for being regarded as important characters, fear nothing so much as having to return to the mines and toil like simple workers. This is the main reason why the entire movement boils down to a monotonous round inside a vicious circle. They deal with the government, threaten, make concessions, enter into compromises... but ultimately they take care that everything is done according to the law, quietly, and ends in blessed peace. This way they can keep the friendship or at least the tolerance of the government and the masters, their sway over the workers, and their salaries.

If the workers could be persuaded to free themselves from all these parasites, and to look after their own affairs themselves, strikes would soon take on a different character. And with relentless active propaganda, propaganda of words and examples, what may look today like a utopia, might soon become a fact.

The road may be long or may be short, depending on the circumstances; what counts above all else is the direction in which one walks.

Idiot Pen Pusher

Translated from "Pennajolo imbecille," *La Rivoluzione Sociale* (London), no. 2 (October 18, 1902)

At this moment in London there is a poor penniless devil, a certain C. Gonnelli, who cannot do anything better, to miserably get by in life, than make himself a champion of all the filth of this society, despite its being so ungenerous to him. And he sends to *Fanfulla* of Rome bandit stories about the anarchists of London, which other newspapers, including the (socialist?) *Tempo* of Milan, make haste to copy.[112]

He tells tales of bombs and daggers, of plots, of the ins and outs of regicides, of death sentences written in blood, of meetings presided over by Malatesta, in which he allegedly gave another anarchist the tragicomic injunction to leave one king in peace and to go kill another... In brief, the usual garbage, a thousand times repeated, that we would not bother to notice if it were not for the pleasure of remarking the stupidity of some of our enemies.

---

112   See note 57 above.

May Gonnelli continue inventing tall tales, as long as he finds someone to pay for them. We would laugh gleefully at them… if it did not
sadden us to see what low jobs poverty can make a man stoop to!

Organization. Freedom Is Not the Issue

Translated from "L'organizzazione. La libertà è fuori questione,"
La Rivoluzione Sociale (London), no. 2 (October 18, 1902)

In all discussions of thorny issues, undecided people (who, we agree,
could also be the wisest) often muddle through, making appeals to freedom and tolerance.

This recently happened during one of the many polemics, more or
less deplorable, on the eternal subject of organization.

Now, it seems to us that freedom should be beyond question in any
discussion among anarchists. Each person defends and propagates the
ideas he believes to be best and seeks to persuade others, but nobody, if
he is an anarchist, has or can have the intention to force others to think
and act like him.

And this with regards to any and every topic.

We, for example, are adversaries, enemies of *all* religions in general
and of the Christian religion in particular; but must it be said that, while
making every effort to persuade them of their error, we leave the believers
free to practice their religion, and that persecution against religion would
disgust us even more, if such a thing is possible, than the religion itself?

We are communists; but it is evident that we want a free, voluntary
communism, since forced communism and anarchy would be the most
absurd contradiction imaginable.

And thus it is, and must necessarily be, for organization and the
issues related to it.

Freedom, we repeat, is not the issue: and when freedom is respected,
tolerance is a necessity. When one cannot and does not want to impose
his own will upon those with whom he lives and works, it is truly necessary to tolerate and get along in the best way possible. Tolerance in life,
in daily practice: which does not at all implicate a lesser right to defend
one's own ideas and strive, through discussion and through examples,
to make them prevail. To be intolerant in life would mean having little
respect for the freedom of others: to be tolerant and compromising in
thought would mean having little respect for oneself and for what one
believes to be true.

As for organization, we have been persuaded, by dint of hearing all
sorts of arguments, that it all comes down to a colossal misunderstanding,

which unfortunately has been embittered, and often intentionally generated, by mistrust, resentment, and personal rivalries. In fact "organizationists" and "anti-organizationists" have always done the same identical
thing: when they wanted to do something, they came to an understanding, an agreement, they "organized," we say, with those who shared the
same purpose in order to be able to do it. Where is the difference? In the
method, in the people, in the circumstances of time and place; but not in
the very principle of organization.

Aside from this, it is a question of definition. According to us *organizing* means *adapting to the desired objective,* seeking, creating the means,
the *organs* necessary for the objective. One can differ on the objective,
or, even agreeing on the objective, one can consider a means more or less
appropriate for that objective; but there can be no doubt, it seems to us,
on the utility, on the necessity of adaptation…

But we will let it go, otherwise we will start a new polemic; the more
certain issues are discussed, under certain circumstances, the more they
become unclear and aggravating. If instead they are not talked about
they dissipate and die; and then, later, with a calm mind, one struggles to
understand why on earth such an uproar was made over nothing, over a
question of words.

Labor Movement

Translated from "Movimento operajo," *La Rivoluzione Sociale* (London),
no. 2 (October 18, 1902)

FRANCE.—The congress of French labor unions, which recently met in
Montpellier, answered our hopes. It showed that the organized workers of
France are quite resolved to no longer allow themselves to be led up the
garden path by politicos and to handle their affairs by themselves.

The principle of the *General strike* was praised almost unanimously.

Many anarchists were present.

Comrade Niel summarized the objective proposed by the anarchists
actively participating in the labor movement as follows.

"What we want," he said, "is to return to the initial idea of the
founders of the great Workers' International, freeing it, from the start,
from the authoritarian poison that killed it.

"The task is arduous, we know; but we have faith: the workers, for
too long deceived and scorned, are finally opening their eyes.

"Brought together outside of any extraneous influence, they will go
forward and forward up to the abolition of masters and wage-earning,
the last form of slavery."

*
**

ENGLAND.—The habit has spread among the miners of the country of Wales to stop work from time to time, in order to reduce production and thus prevent wages from decreasing.

This year as well, given the enormous abundance of coal, the Federation of miners of England advised its members to abstain from work for a few days.

This is not how the capitalists of the *Colliery Owners Association* understood it, as they see their interests significantly damaged by this practical and sensible measure of the workers. They sued the Federation of miners in the courts for compensation for damages, rising to 100 thousand sterling pounds (2 million 500 thousand francs). And the verdict the judge issued on this case has raised the deepest apprehension in all English labor organizations. In fact the judge acquitted the Federation with the justification of presumed good faith, in that the association had understood its suggestion would protect the interests of its members as well as those of the Company shareholders. This means that in the future, as the mitigating factor of good faith decreases, labor unions will be made materially responsible towards companies for damages that the companies bear due to the resistance of organized workers.

This episode, which seriously endangers the heritage of the powerful *Trade Unions*, and the attitude to take towards this danger were amply discussed during the last congress held weeks ago in London. It was decided that a labor party would be created which, duly subsidized, shall send a good number of representatives to the Chamber of Commons, to defend the interests of the working class and support the implementation of social laws.[113]

We must strongly deplore this move by the English workers, who now naively deem to advance their demands by dragging themselves into parliamentary politics, which has proven to be so fatal everywhere it has had the upper hand over direct and revolutionary resistance by workers.

However we note with pleasure that another current, wiser and more revolutionary, is appearing. In fact, an address aimed at the workers by a

---

113   As early as 1900 a *Labour Representation Committee* had been formed, with the purpose of coordinating efforts to support labor representation in parliament. The urgency of having influence over legislation was particularly felt after the historic verdict on the 1901 Taff Vale case, according to which a union could be held responsible for damages caused to the company by a strike (on the verdict, see the article "The Death of Classic Unionism" on p. 164 of the current volume). At the September 1902 Trade Unions congress, the priority need for a centralized organization that guaranteed strong political representation was thus expressed.

group of *unionists*, criticizes parliamentary means and concludes that the *general strike* is an effective means of defense.

Here is the response which, according to the manifesto's authors, labor associations should give capitalists:

"You say that you will crush our unions: and the judges you pay have already received your orders to this end. Well, go right ahead. We dare you. Touch a cent from the unions' funds, and we will stop all the industry in the country. When the great national holiday, the general strike, will spread from city to city and countryside to countryside, when Babylon will be in flames, and the Antichrist, that you call Empire, Wealth and Power, will be struck in the heart, then the new Jerusalem shall be inaugurated, and the kingdom of the People shall dawn on earth."

The style is biblical and has a strange effect on those who are not English: but the idea is good and will make its way.

American Competition

Translated from "La concorrenza americana," *La Rivoluzione Sociale* (London), no. 2 (October 18, 1902)

The newspapers, especially the German ones, are once again concerned with what they call the "American danger," and speak of an economic league among European states to create a dyke against the competition that American products make to domestic products in European markets.

Naturally they will do nothing about it; the interests of the capitalists of Europe conflict amongst themselves just as much as they do with those of the capitalists of America, and they will never succeed in reaching an agreement. They will continue to live by expedients, seeking to make the workers shoulder the damage that America can do to them, and, if they see they can profit, they will bring their capital to America (as many have already done), in spite of the patriotism they invoke when it is useful to cheat and entertain the people.

We are concerned with the phenomenon, which has no remedy in a capitalistic and individualistic regime, only because it most clearly demonstrates the absurdity of the present social organization.

The American danger! But what the hell might these blessed Americans ever send to Europe? An inhabitant of the moon might wonder, if the sound of the laments being raised from this side of the Atlantic should reach him. Poison? Lethal weapons? Pathogenic microbes?

Not at all: they send wheat, meat, fruit, timber, fabric, tools, machines... in other words all things used to satisfy the needs of men and make life more pleasant.

So? Why do they complain, if America brings them abundance?

There is a small inconvenience, and it is that the Americans do not give away those things for free: they sell them, meaning they want money in exchange, with which they can buy European products. If Europe, ultimately, did not have merchandise of an equivalent value to give in exchange to the Americans, they would not send anything anymore.

Very well, the inhabitant of the Moon would still say... supposing that on the moon one reasoned with common sense. This means that the Europeans will receive merchandise that costs less labor to produce in America, and vice versa will give what it can produce more easily. If this was not the case, there would not be mutual benefit, and trade would stop.

On this earth however, in spite of common sense, reason, and logic, things happen otherwise. Here abundance often produces poverty; often a good harvest is a disaster for the farmers; a machine that saves human labor and increases production brings unemployment and hunger precisely to the category of workers whose suffering it would seem to lighten; the things brought from outside increases scarcity in the country that receives them.

All this because those who manage production and trade are not those who work, and because production is not organized with the objective of satisfying as best as possible the needs of people, but is governed by the interests, well or poorly understood, of those who own the means of production and only think about their profit.

If a given item is furnished in abundance, and therefore at a good price, to a country, the domestic producers of that or similar items, who cannot produce at the same price, are ruined, because the buyers consider nothing but their own advantage. And here is why the invasion of American products threatens the profits of many categories of capitalists and, more interestingly, the employment, meaning the bread, of so many workers.

Certainly, when all is said and done, since products are paid for with products, equilibrium ends up reestablishing itself—the sad equilibrium between the loafers who revel and the workers who barely earn enough to feed themselves. How much destruction, though! how much poverty! how many deaths before emigration and the new industries replacing those that cannot withstand competition have reestablished that equilibrium... which will soon enough be broken again.

It is the acute evil that comes to continually aggravate the chronic evil from which the proletarians ordinarily suffer.

And capitalistic society has no worthy remedy. Customs tariffs, which are the only way imaginable without getting out of the system, can benefit a given category of people and harm another, but they do not solve anything. If one taxes the entry of a product, it benefits the capitalists and perhaps even a little the domestic workers employed in that branch of production, but it forces the public to pay dearly for what could have been better and cheaper. If entry is left free, the consumers win, but the producers are reduced to poverty. And given that normally each person is both a producer and a consumer, in this way, on average, what one wins on one side one loses on the other.

The true, unique remedy needs to be sought in the abolition of capitalism and competition, and in the solidarity of workers in possession of the means of production.

Then every country will produce what it is best adapted to produce, and maximum abundance will be achieved with the minimum effort possible, to the advantage of everyone.

Unproductive Expenses

Translated from "Le spese improduttive," *La Rivoluzione Sociale* (London),
no. 3 (November 1, 1902)

Italy is in a state of depression and poverty. Socialists, republicans, and radicals concur in seeing a remedy in the elimination—no, not even that—in the reduction of "unproductive expenses," meaning expenses for the army and for the navy.

They attach so much importance to this reduction, they put so much hope in it, that someone like Barbato,[114] who seemed at another time to have a wider understanding of socialism (and perhaps he merely had a little more courage than his comrades) but then ended up like the others in the parliamentary morass, seeing the army only as a means of armed repression against the proletariat's demands, came to say that the bourgeoisie needs to be reassured so that it does not "fear that, without a large army at its disposal, we would immediately decree the transformation of the current society into a collectivist society."

Now, this reduction, in hopes of which the socialists renounce their ideal, relegating it to the distant future, and apologize for old revolutionary desires, and humiliate themselves obscenely before the bourgeoisie, is a thing that cannot be done in today's society—and if it were done, it would resolve nothing, instead it would aggravate the country's economic unease. To direct the people's hopes toward this impossible

---

114   Nicola Barbato had been one of the most important figures in the Sicilian Fasci movement of 1893.

and useless reform and abandon the fight to expropriate property owners and radically transform the social order, means betraying not only the cause of full emancipation for the workers, but also their immediate interests.

The main reason why today reducing standing armies, and even more so general disarmament, is an unachievable utopia, is not that the governments and the bourgeoisie need to control the people. Certainly, since there are soldiers, they are used to defend those who command them and they are trained and kept ready for massacres; but we are convinced that the dominators would find better value in having themselves defended by a smaller but safer army of police, of Praetorians—, as they were once called—career killers who have completely left the people with no prospects of returning, rather than a vast and forcibly recruited army that could very well show itself to be a double-edged sword one day.

The main reason for the persistence and continual increase of modern armies are the immense interests that concern not just the capitalists, but also the workers.

The most powerful part of the bourgeoisie earns a lot from the war and navy budget, and certainly will not give that up for the socialists' beautiful eyes. They will allow, should it be useful to throw dust into the workers' eyes, a mountain of laws and bylaws, which the socialists will decorate with the name of "social legislation," but they will not permit anyone to touch their real interest: their purse.

And the workers… they need first and foremost to work, in one way or another, doing whatever, just to manage to feed themselves. Do we not see every day that the very people who shout against military expenses then get worked up to prevent an arsenal from being removed from their city, or so that a weapons factory is set up there, or a regiment is stationed there?

Today, in every country, the army and the navy, with everything connected to them, have become a large industry, the largest national industry—and people want to preserve the industry upon which they live, no matter how immoral, useless, detrimental it is: for them it always has the supreme utility of allowing them to live.

Let us imagine that tomorrow soldiers who are on duty return to the labor market and increase the already very large number of the unemployed, and that arsenals, weapons factories, and military production of every type shut down! what a frightening crisis! what a sudden increase in poverty! Perhaps the situation would become so serious that the revolution would erupt; but this is merely another reason to not hope that the governments ever decide on such a move.

But the government, they say, could use the money now squandered in arming and maintaining the army for useful works; and the capitalists would redirect to other businesses the capital that now generates profit in the army industry. That is not true.

Due to the crisis the State's income would decrease; and the capitalists would not be able to use in new ventures the means accumulated for business of a different nature. And the surplus that would remain in the budget would go toward compensation, however disguised, to friends who were ruined, and in increased expenses for "public security."

The useful works that they promise us remain undone because of the social system and the dominators' frame of mind, which is both the cause and the effect of that system: not because the means are lacking.

In fact, are there not unemployed workers who want to work? is there not uncultivated or poorly cultivated land that asks to be fertilized by human sweat? Are there not inactive machines which rust lying idle, while so many people would need the products that could be made with them?

Why are all of these forces not put to work? Because, some respond, we do not have the capital necessary to feed the workers while waiting for what they produce. But these workers, today unemployed, still live, very poorly, immensely poorly, but they live. How could they not find a way to live, when they would be gladdened by anticipation of what they produce?

Certainly, it seems absurd that there should be economic utility in keeping young and strong men like soldiers idle and using others to manufacture lethal weapons. Yet in a society in which we see famished farmers and deserted land, barefoot people and idle shoemakers, etc., even digging holes to be immediately filled up and dug again is useful work, if this work of fools would earn a salary for those doing it. In a society like this, one understands that the army, detrimental from a moral point of view, can be useful from an economic point of view: and this is the reason that it remains and will remain until the social system changes.

The socialists understood and said these things when they were truly socialists. Now they are too busy courting the assassins of Berra, Candela and Giarratana to remember those things.

It is up to the anarchists to make workers understand them, so that they stop chasing after delusions and palliatives that are not even palliatives, and get to the heart of the matter.

Anarchists in Labor Unions

Translated from "Gli Anarchici nelle Società Operaje," *La Rivoluzione Sociale*
(London), no. 3 (November 1, 1902)

In response to what we said on this subject in our first issue, we received
the following observations from our comrade CATILINA, in Rome:[115]

> I agree with what you said in issue 1 of *R. S.* about anarchists tak-
> ing positions in labor organizations, when this concerns the case you
> envisaged and discussed, that is, when such organizations are mostly
> comprised of non-anarchists and workers in general who do not agree
> with us on the direction the labor movement must take. Then anarchists
> must remain only members of the associations, and simply serve as pro-
> pellers, as propagandists of an idea and a method.
>
> But there is the case in which the vast majority of workers are either
> anarchists or accept our anti-authoritarian criteria for managing labor
> associations; this happens, I believe, in Spain, France, Holland, South
> America and a few other places. So what harm is there in anarchists taking
> positions to manage labor unions? Do you not think that, instead of es-
> tablishing absolute non-participation in positions, we could recommend
> that anarchists accept these positions only in those associations in which
> the higher workers' consciousness, or prior agreements, or the sharing of
> libertarian ideas by associates make it possible for comrades to take up a
> given position without creating such contradictions with the idea?
>
> CATILINA.

Rome, October 20, 1902

So, our friend CATILINA, in agreement with us that anarchists should
not, in general, accept positions in labor associations, would like to make
an exception for cases where these associations are largely comprised of
anarchists or supporters of anarchist methods and ideas.

But do labor unions exist (meaning, resistance societies against capitalists) in which anarchists are the large majority?

And is it desirable that they exist?

A labor union comprised of anarchists would be a duplicate of the
anarchist circle and would not meet the specific purposes of an organization for economic resistance.

Naturally, if one imagines a country in which the entire labor population is anarchist, everything that would be done in that country would

---

115   "Catilina" was one of Luigi Fabbri's pseudonyms. The article mentioned is
published on p. 110 of the current volume.

be done by anarchists... and so one could do better and more than what unions of resistance do and can do. But this is not the case.

In reality, the majority of workers everywhere are an inert mass, broken by suffering and slavery; and those among them who have risen to human consciousness and have formed or are forming an ideal of social life different from the current one, are divided by political, religious, and economic ideas. The only thing that unites all workers is their common condition of being exploited, and the desire, which everyone has, independent from any broad view, to fare better than they do.

The resistance society—which unites workers as workers to force capitalists, through collective endeavor, to make concessions they would not make out of their own initiative and good will—is the terrain in which agreement can be found among conscious workers of different opinions, and is the appropriate means for attracting the resigned mass and shaking them from their lethargy.

The "Chambers of Labor," the "unions," must be *neutral*, the anarchists say, in opposition to the democratic socialists who would want, using the excuse of socialism, to transform them into electoral agencies at the service of their ambitions. And this neutrality means that they must remain open to all workers, whatever their religious and political belief.

On the other hand, it is evident that the resistance society as such, the resistance society that remains extraneous to politics and religion, is not enough to lead to emancipation.

As long as workers believe in the lies of priests and politicos, and until they destroy the State, the government that keeps finances, schools, police, soldiers, judges, jailers at the service of the capitalists, the workers will not be able to free themselves from either economic or political oppression. And the anarchists in labor unions, like everywhere, remembering always and before all else that they are anarchists, must combat religion, authority, and private property, must demonstrate to workers that these are the three rings of the chain that binds them, and push them to dismiss the priest, destroy the government, and expropriate the property owners.

But how can anarchists reconcile the "neutrality" of labor organizations with the confessed intention to make use of them as a field for propaganda and as a means of engaging the masses in the revolutionary movement?

Precisely by not accepting positions and by remaining simple members, active, vigilant, always ready to seize the occasion to sow an idea of emancipation, to provoke an act of rebellion.

An anarchist who has a position in a union is compelled, at least in his official role, to hide his flag. If he acted as an anarchist he would officially give an anarchist character to the union, and thus on one hand he would drive away the non-anarchists, and on the other he would authorize the socialists, the republicans, the monarchists, and the clericalists, when they are in charge, to give the union a character corresponding to their own ideas.

Instead, as simple members, who act in their own name and under their own responsibility, anarchists can say and do what they want without obligating the union.

Thus, without insisting on making it an absolute rule and a question of principle, and without wanting to jeopardize the very special cases that can arise during the struggle, we remain firm in the idea that anarchists should not accept positions in labor organizations.

Anarchists or Anarchist-Socialists?

Translated from "Anarchici o Socialisti-Anarchici?" *La Rivoluzione Sociale* (London), no. 3 (November 1, 1902)

A comrade, who does not wish to be named, writes us, in polite terms but with the evident desire to argue, asking why our periodical is called "anarchist-socialist" and not simply "anarchist."

He seems to believe that the adjective "socialist" is there to attenuate the concept expressed by the word "anarchist," while in our opinion and, we believe, in the opinion of all who bear our same denomination, it is an integration.

After all our comrade, with all of his repugnance for the word "socialist," is a socialist himself. Only he believes that the idea of socialization of wealth is included in the anarchist idea, since freedom is not possible without the means to be free—and he is right, in the same sense that the anarchists are right when they say that true socialism is necessarily anarchist, since it is not possible to abolish economic privilege without destroying authority. At any rate, in our case this is but a pleonasm. In fact, most of the time, for the love of brevity, we just call ourselves anarchists, as we would not hesitate to say simply socialists (as we used to do in Italy before Costa's about-face) if there were no danger of being confused with the democrats and other so-called socialists.

Words are a convention, and often a very vague convention; and therefore they lend themselves to all types of quarrelsome games.

For our part, while remaining loyal to the terminology that seems to us most logical and most clear, we are determined to do everything possible to understand the significance that others give to words and get to the bottom of their thought, to be able to discuss ideas and not just bicker over words.

If the comrade who writes us disagrees with us, either about our way of understanding the ideal or about the methods of struggle we prefer, may he present his criticism and we will welcome and discuss it. But if this merely concerns preferring some words over others, let him do as he wishes and let us do likewise: propaganda will not lose anything; quite the contrary!

That anarchist-socialists may have said or done things we do not like, is not a sufficient reason to make us renounce the title that, in our opinion, best represents the whole of our ideas. Or is our interlocutor prepared to accept without reservations anything that can be said or done by someone who calls himself anarchist?

And it would be humanly [im]possible to take on any name, if this entailed responsibility for the words and deeds of all those who, rightly or wrongly, took the same name.[116]

Facts and Opinions

Translated from "Fatti ed Opinioni," *La Rivoluzione Sociale* (London), no. 3 (November 1, 1902)

EXPERIMENTAL POLITICS (?!).—A socialist newspaper that follows, or at least has followed, until now, the Turati school of thought, *Il Secolo nuovo* of Venice, is upset that starving farmers continue to be slaughtered and says that it is time the socialist deputies move to the opposition. According to the newspaper, the socialists have done well to support the government to probe its liberalism; but it thinks the experiment has already been completed and has failed; that neither freedom nor reforms have arrived, that one can hope for nothing from this government and therefore it needs to be abandoned.

And this is well: the bloodshed in Candela and in Giarratana will have at least served to open the eyes of some socialists.

But, we ask, if the socialists begin to practice this type of experimentalism, what will ever distinguish them from monarchist and bourgeois parties?

What did the recent experiment prove? That Zanardelli and Giolitti are scoundrels and if anything distinguishes them from other government men of the Italian monarchy, it is only a greater dose of hypocrisy?

---

116   The meaning of the original sentence remains obscure, probably because of a typo. We have tentatively rectified the sentence through the interpolation in square brackets.

This did not amaze us and one did not really need to be excessively well-versed in psychology and modern history to understand and predict it. But if the socialists believed in Zanardelli and Giolitti's promises, with a naivety that exceeds the plausible, they will all the more believe—or at least grant the benefit of doubt—to the new men the king will call to his service. And then they will be ministerial again. Therefore the grandiose socialist movement, which was pregnant with an entire civilization, will have ended up in a parliamentary party that is alternatively in the majority or the opposition of His Majesty!

To know is to predict: if the socialists do not understand that the poverty, injustice, and tyranny of which the masses suffer fully depend upon a combination of things and people that a government could not disturb, even if it wanted; if they do not know that in order to change the people's conditions it is necessary to change the present social system—political and economic—and not the people in charge of directing and defending the system, then by what right do they call themselves socialists, and moreover scientific socialists?

MILITARY SERVICE.—There is currently much discussion among French comrades about whether an anarchist should meet the draft obligation, evade the draft, or desert.

Some say that the anarchist, who naturally abhors militarism and continuously makes propaganda against it, must at any cost refuse to wear the abhorrent uniform and take up fratricidal arms, in homage to our principles and to set a good example.

Others say that refusing service forces one to go abroad, where, for economic reasons and because of differences in language and customs, he is incapable of making propaganda, whereas it is useful and necessary to bring the spirit of rebellion and the yeast of anarchist ideas within the very ranks of the army.

We believe that the matter does not have a single solution, applicable to all individuals, under all circumstances.

Aside from considerations of personal advantage, which we shall not get into, it is certain that, depending on each person's particular talents and the dose and type of courage he possesses, some can be more useful by entering the army, making propaganda among soldiers and setting an example, when the case arises, of refusing obedience and open rebellion, while others better succeed by deserting and facing the vagabond life of a man in an illegal position.

The essential thing is that, within or outside of the army, one always keeps aflame his hatred against the institution, always keeps alive the spirit of propaganda and sacrifice.

∗
∗∗

ASININITIES.—A friend would like us to respond to some nonsense, not always in good faith, that *Goliardo,* from *L'Asino* and *Avanti,* has been writing on anarchy and the anarchists.[117]

We are not up for it. Sometimes Goliardo is witty, but not when he wants to be taken for a serious man. If we tried to start a conversation with him, he would respond with a grin, a somersault and a bunch of lies... and he would not even make us laugh.

Justice! [from *Les Temps Nouveaux*]

Translated from "Giustizia!" La Rivoluzione Sociale (London),
no. 3 (November 1, 1902)

[*The article in* Les Temps Nouveaux *supports the theory that the Mano Negra anarchist group, which for several months in 1883 kept the police and courts of Andalusia busy, was a police hoax. Echoing the Madrid-based anarchist newspaper* Tierra y Libertad, *which has taken on the task of restoring the truth on the matter,* Les Temps Nouveaux *announces the plan of retracing the entire sequence of events, immediately launching a call for the liberation of the trial's victims who are still in jail. The following note from the editors of* La Rivoluzione Sociale *follows the article from* Les Temps Nouveaux.][118]

In order to echo the campaign that the Spanish anarchists are leading for the liberation of the Andalusian Internationalists condemned in 1883, and to respond as we can to their call for international solidarity, we have started by translating the call launched by French comrades, who already contributed mightily, with the general indignation that they were able to arouse, to the liberation of the martyrs of Montjuich.

We too shall publish the true story of the "Mano negra" trial.

Can we hope that in Italy the work of the anarchists, upon which we rely, will be joined by socialists and republicans? Though their erroneous strategy has led them to all sorts of transactions with power, will they be able to show that at least their hearts remain good and can beat for the pain of the martyrs of an ideal?

---

117   "Goliardo" was Guido Podrecca who, along with Gabriele Galantara, edited the satyrical magazine *L'Asino.*

118   The original article, entitled "Justice!," appeared in *Les Temps Nouveaux* (Paris) of November 1–6, 1902.

And will the example given by the comrades of Spain help to revive the campaign for Paolo Schicchi and those in forced residence?[119]

"The Young Guards"

Translated from "'Le giovani guardie.'" *La Rivoluzione Sociale* (London), no. 3 (November 1, 1902)

Here is a word that may be ill-chosen but serves a good purpose. In Belgium this name is used by organizations of young socialists who, being less than twenty years old, are subject to the military draft. The main purpose of these groups is anti-militaristic propaganda for the abolition of mandatory military service, "the blood tax." The best propaganda is understandably made among the conscripts who, harangued by talented speakers in the streets and in the very stairways of the areas where draft operations take place, come to pull out their number while singing anti-militaristic hymns, etc.[120] In Belgium there are already 120 groups, with 15,007 members and the effect is such that the government does not feel confident in the troops.

In Italy too, according to the socialist "Verona del popolo," in Alessandria, Valenza, and other places, groups of "Young guards" have been formed, calling comrades to follow their example; and so far very well! I only have one piece of advice for the young guards: do not delude yourself too much. Drafted soldiers are replaced by mercenaries. The very England that does not have a drafted army, in extreme moments trots out hired cavalrymen against the proletarians, not to mention the legions of policemen and detectives.

We anarchists, even before the "young guards" existed, wrote a little book which the Turati supporters of that time found impudent. The important issue is that the "Young guards," more than human propaganda and more than disarmament and the blood tax, enthusiastically see to preparing themselves with the means to counter force, given the very possible case of having to face the aforementioned mercenaries!

---

119   Sicilian anarchist Paolo Schicchi was condemned in May 1893 to over eleven years in prison for various crimes, and another year was added because he called the judges "oafs." He left prison in May 1904, after refusing a royal pardon a few months earlier.

120   In Belgium, military recruitment took place through a lottery-based draft.

The New International Workingmen's Association

Translated from "La nuova Internazionale dei Lavoratori," *La Rivoluzione Sociale*
(London), no. 4 (November 15, 1902)

The grandiose labor movement that is emerging throughout the civilized world, and the increasingly apparent need for solidarity between workers of all countries so that they may stand up to the progressive internationalization of capitalism, naturally had to generate, and in fact has generated in the minds of many, the idea of establishing a new International Workingmen's Association. And the international Federations established between labor associations of workers in certain trades, such as the coal miners and the transport workers, are already a start for the general union of all workers conscious of their class interests.

For this reason it might be useful at this point to recall the lessons of past experience, scrutinizing what the task of the old International was and the reasons that led to its demise.

The life of the renowned International Workingmen's Association was brief but glorious. Born into a time, similar to the present, of labor awakening, it died quickly and truly succeeded in shaking the world. It weaned the workers off of following bourgeois parties and gave them a class consciousness, a program of their own, and politics of their own; it broached and debated all the most essential social issues and devised the whole of modern socialism, which some writers then claimed was the product of their own heads; it set the mighty quaking, roused the ardent hopes of the oppressed, inspired sacrifices and heroism... and, just when it most looked destined to lay capitalist society to rest, it disintegrated and perished.

Why?

The dissolution of the International is usually attributed either to persecutions, or to personal antagonisms that emerged within its ranks, or to its method of organization, or to all of these causes together.

I believe otherwise.

Persecutions would have been unable to break up the Association, and often fostered its popularity and growth.

Personal antagonisms were actually only a secondary concern, and, as long as the movement was vibrant, they rather helped to spur the various factions and most prominent individuals into action.

Its method of organization, having grown centralistic and authoritarian by the handiwork of the General Council in London, and especially of Karl Marx who was the driving force behind it, actually led to the International splitting into two branches: but the federalist and anarchist branch that included the federations from Spain, Italy, French Switzerland, Belgium, southern France, as well as individual sections from other countries, did not long outlive the authoritarian branch. It will be argued that even within the anarchist branch, the authoritarian blight endured and that, there too, a few individuals were able to do and undo in the name of the masses who passively followed them. And that is true. But it is worth noting that in this case, authoritarianism was unintended and did not derive from the organizational form nor from the principles informing it, but was a natural, necessary consequence of the matter to which I chiefly ascribe the dissolution of the Association and which I am about to spell out.

Within the International, founded as a federation of resistance societies in order to provide a broader base for the economic struggle against capitalism, two schools of thought very quickly surfaced, one authoritarian, the other libertarian. These split the Internationalists into two hostile factions, which at least in their extreme wings, were associated with the names of Marx and Bakunin.

One group wanted to turn the Association into a disciplined body under the command of a central Committee, the others wanted it to be a free federation of autonomous groups; one group wanted to subjugate the masses and do their good by force, according to the obsolete authoritarian superstition, the others wanted to raise them up and persuade them to set themselves free. But the inspirations behind both factions had one distinguishing feature in common, and that is that each side passed on their own ideas to the body of the membership, reckoning that they had converted them when they had actually only secured their more or less unconscious acceptance.

Thus we see the International quickly turning mutualist, collectivist, communist, revolutionary, and anarchist at a rate of development documented in the proceedings of its congresses and in the periodical press, but which could not represent any actual and simultaneous evolution in the vast majority of members.

Since there were no separate organs for the economic struggle and the political and ideological struggle, and every Internationalist did all his thinking and fighting activity within the International, the inevitable outcome was either that the most advanced individuals would have had to stoop to and stay at the level of the slow-moving, backward mass or, as happened, stride ahead and proceed on their way with the illusion that the masses understood and were following them.

These more advanced members pondered, debated, discovered the needs of the people, they framed the vague intuitions of the masses into concrete programs; they affirmed socialism, they affirmed anarchy, they predicted and prepared for the future; but they killed the Association: the sword had worn out the sheath.

Not that I am saying this was a bad thing. If the International had remained a simple federation for resistance, and not been buffeted by the storm of ideas and partisan passions, it might have survived as the English *Trade Unions* have, useless and perhaps even harmful to the cause of human emancipation. It was better that it should have perished and tossed its fertile seeds to the winds.

But I say that today the International of the olden days cannot, and should not, be remade. Today there are thriving socialist and anarchist movements: the illusion and the error that sustained the old International are no longer possible today. The factors that ultimately killed off the old International, namely opposition between authoritarians and libertarians on the one hand, and the gulf between the thinkers and the semi-conscious masses driven only by interests on the other, are today likely to thwart the birth and growth of a new International, should it be, as the first one was, simultaneously a society for economic resistance, a workshop of ideas, and a revolutionary association.

The new International can only serve as an association designed to bring together all workers (which is to say, as many workers as it can) without regard to social, political, and religious opinions, for the fight against capitalism. Thus it must be neither individualist, nor collectivist, nor communist; it must be neither monarchist nor republican, nor anarchist; it must be neither religious nor anti-religious. A single shared idea, a single condition for entry: the desire to fight the masters.

Hatred of the ruling class is the beginning of salvation.

If later on, enlightened by propaganda, educated by the struggle in tracing the causes of suffering and searching for radical remedies, encouraged by the example of revolutionary parties, the bulk of the membership were to burst into socialist, anarchist, and anti-religious assertions, so much the better; since then progress would be real and not illusory.

Naturally, it is not that I would not like the new International Workingmen's Association to be socialist and anarchist: I would just like it to be genuinely so.

And so that it can become so, it needs to happen freely and gradually, as consciousnesses expand and understanding spreads.

AN OLD INTERNATIONALIST.

"The Armed Nation"

Translated from "'La nazione armata,'" *La Rivoluzione Sociale* (London), no. 4 (November 15, 1902)

Here is the ideal that authoritarian socialists and republicans boast of… when they go so far as to yearn for the abolition of permanent armies. And initially it would seem to be acceptable even to lovers of freedom, given the elastic meaning of the word and the various ways in which it can be interpreted.[121]

But they ordinarily make haste to cite the example of Switzerland, and this reveals and defines their thought: and induces us to reject the system of the armed nation as even more reactionary, if that is possible, than the military organizations prevalent today.

In practice, armed nation means that everyone is a soldier, everyone is at the disposal of the government, bound to the obligation of military service for most of his life.

It is the dream of the reactionaries—the militarization of certain categories of workers—extended to the entire population. A call to duty is issued and, lo and behold, the nerves are cut on a dangerous strike or a menacing popular riot:—what better weapon of repression could a government desire?

Under the regular conscription system, a soldier feels the violence he endures and serves reluctantly and therefore has the tendency to rebel, and on the other hand the civil population realizes that the army is organized to control them and could oppress them with impunity; whereas with the armed nation everyone believes he is free and only serves the common interests of the people—and the citizen-soldier is two of a kind with the voter, who believes he is being governed by the laws he himself made.

Switzerland is proof of what we say. In no other country is the government so safe from insurrections, and can with so much tranquility shoot strikers; in no other country are the subjects so sincerely convinced of being sovereign and are so ready to side with the police.

But, they will say to us, do you therefore want to remain defenseless, exposed to all prevarications? Certainly not. As it is necessary today for revolutionaries to procure the material means to resist the government's

---

121 In the debate on how the army should be structured, a debate that has accompanied the history of unified Italy, the "armed nation" was the model that federalist and democratic forces opposed to that of the permanent army at the sovereign's service. Under this model, military education was to be extended to all citizens and, instead of spending a long period of time in the barracks, training was given starting from school and then through short-term exercises at regular intervals.

armed force, so it will be necessary for the people to be equipped with weapons of defense as long as there is the danger that others will want to use violence with weapons against them; but this has nothing in common with the system of military organization that is commonly called an armed nation. With the latter system the government can leave rifles at the homes of soldiers, or keep them in the barracks and only entrust them to the soldiers during periods of actual service, according to the public's state of mind; but with or without a rifle at home, the soldier is always a soldier, obliged to show up when called and fight for the purpose which the government wants to make him fight for.

We instead want everyone to be free to bear arms or not. We want neither a government that commands, nor a military hierarchy that enforces the government's orders, nor anyone, in short, who has the right to obligate a citizen to take up arms and use them for a reason for which he is not willing to fight.

The "Lanistae"

Translated from "I 'lanisti,'" *La Rivoluzione Sociale* (London), no. 4 (November 15, 1902)

The ancient Romans used this name for those unfortunate men charged with removing gladiators who had fallen wounded in the circus arenas, and finishing them off with the so-called "coup de grâce."

Times have changed and today, in place of the "lanistae," we have foremen, who ordinarily are not the most skilled at work: little cowards, who are unable to do anything else but act as spies and tyrants, they are traitors to the worker's cause. In the narrow minds of these hounds teems the microbe of profiteering, and where they settle you see them soon get to work, creating an inn, a dive, or an eatery—anything with which they can exploit the wretched workmate.

And woe to those they cannot profit from! They always prefer bachelors, whom they dress, lodge, feed and... fleece out thus of all the money they earn. If one then has a family, mother or other commitments or does not want to subject himself to exploitation, the foreman will have no pity for that family man who is not "profitable," and will do anything to have him replaced by some bachelor glutton.

These "Shylocks"[122] are everywhere, in France, in Switzerland, in Germany, in England, etc. Our objective as workers who fight to free

---

122   Shylock is the usurer who, in William Shakespeare's *The Merchant of Venice*, requires a pound of the debtor's flesh to guarantee a loan. [Publisher's note: The depiction of the character is based on a stereotype that is antisemitic.]

ourselves, is to also abolish these exploiters who disguise themselves as protectors of workers. And we must boycott them and force masters to choose among the most skilled at work and to let them keep no sinecure beyond their position. And where we find a supervisor who tells us: "I have a boarding house," answer him that he is not our comrade but rather an innkeeper, and leave him to practicing his own trade.

Facts and Opinions

Translated from "Fatti ed Opinioni," *La Rivoluzione Sociale* (London), no. 4 (November 15, 1902)

ROMAN RAVINGS.—Giovanni Bovio, in the commemoration of Émile Zola held in Rome on October 29th, uttered the following address:[123]

> You (or Zola) must have intuited that the pope is either in Rome or is not there: that only in Rome, before the greatness of the Vatican, a new lay power is possible; that the ancient conflict comes to an end in ample Roman freedom; that if, in short, today no doctor, no Council can build new dogmas, here only the free evolution of the whole dogmatic construction is possible, here before the State that will be Roman only on the condition that it interprets all of modernity and must intuit at the same time that Rome loves Paris with a maternal love; for this precisely no element of modernity is born vital if it is not baptized in Paris.
> (*Italia del Popolo* of October 31st.)

And the audience, naturally, enthusiastically applauded the talented speaker.

But, prithee, what does all this jumble of words mean?

Perhaps it is because we are not philosophers, nor geniuses, nor republicans, nor anything that comes close to it, but we would truly be happy to see these concepts translated into vernacular terms, accessible to humble people like us.

Perhaps then, even the audience that usually applauds big words, and applauds more the less they understand, would realize that underneath the pompous phrases, there is only the rancid prejudice of Rome's providential mission.

Ah, if only the "philosophers" deigned to speak clearly!... how little philosophy would be often found in their chatter!

---

123   Giovanni Bovio was a philosopher and republican politician. October 29th marked the first month after Émile Zola's death.

***

AGAINST MILITARISM. —*La Voix du Peuple* ("The Voice of the People"), organ of the "General Confederation of Labor" of France has published, when the conscripts were being called up, a very successful special issue. It is adorned with beautiful evocative drawings, capable of showing, even to less developed intellects, what the eminently anti-worker role of the army is, and how the barracks are a school of degradation. And it contains excellent articles aimed at young soldiers, which explain to them the purpose for which the government arms them, and what they must do to not become the butchers of their brothers.

This is good and healthy propaganda to which all anarchists, all socialists, all friends of freedom and progress should dedicate their efforts; quite unlike the propaganda of the "democrats," who ask for decreased military expenses while professing love and respect for the national army and arguing that they want a reduction in the number of corps, because that way the army would gain in force and cohesion, while less would be spent. And quite unlike the propaganda of certain socialists (Enrico Ferri for example) who declare that militarism is the degeneration of the army.

For us, it is truly the very existence of the army that we want to destroy, however it is organized. It is loathing for the role of soldier—the role of slave and cop combined—that we must inspire in the spirit of the people and especially of the youth.

Gennaro Rubini

Translated from "Gennaro Rubini," *La Rivoluzione Sociale* (London), no. 5 (December 1, 1902)

We do not really know what to think of the Brussels episode.[124]

The strange and suspicious character of the actor—so different from the beautiful types of rebels and martyrs who are generally the ones that choose to die in an act of damnation against the oppressors of the human race—gives rise to all kinds of conjectures.

Is this simply a farce organized by the police to restore an aura of popularity to that old crook Leopold and provide a justification for persecutions? We do not believe so, since it would seem too foolish for the throne's defenders to provoke an attack that, as often happens, could

---

124   Gennaro Rubino (or Rubini, as he was commonly called) was a spy exposed by the London anarchists in May 1902. On November 15th of the same year, Rubino unsuccessfully tried to kill King Leopold of Belgium in Brussels.

then find sincere and determined imitators, but we admit that there are many signs that contribute to making that hypothesis plausible.

Or are we rather in the presence of a man who, put into a bad position, perhaps with not entirely perverse intentions, has become a target of everyone's contempt and, squeezed by poverty, tormented by spite and by remorse, decides to end it all with an act that can make his sincerity believed and lift him up in the regard of those who were or believed themselves to be betrayed by him?

We prefer to hold our judgment and wait for the unfolding of the trial to shed light (should it shed any) onto the mysterious affair.

Meanwhile, since it was in London and amongst us that Rubini performed the odious role he is rebuked for, and comrades are waiting to hear the truth from us about his previous history, we, although reluctant to harshly punish someone who already finds himself in the claws of those bourgeoisie's jackals that are called judges, we feel obliged to say what the facts are.

Rubini, since he came to London, had always claimed to be a legalitarian socialist, and had always frequented socialist circles. Moreover, despite his real or apparent financial constraints, he very quickly aroused suspicion, and there was no shortage of people who more or less openly called him a spy.

Then he left London and went to Glasgow, where he also frequented the socialists and seemed to actively participate in propaganda. We know that from there he wrote to one of our comrades, an author of a propaganda pamphlet, telling him of his intention to translate that pamphlet into English and asking him for permission, naturally denied, to remove references to anarchy from that pamphlet, leaving only the part that dealt with the economic question.

After a few months of living in Glasgow, Rubini returned to London well-equipped with money, and started to mix with the anarchists and to come to our meetings. But his language and his proposals were always those of a socialist, so much that several times he was asked why he insisted on coming to our groups since he did not have our ideas, until he was finally shown the door over a personal incident. He who, while he tried to be with us, had never broken relations with the socialists, continued, after being chased out of our group, to frequent socialists and anarchists. The man was unpleasant and suspicious to almost everyone, but there was nothing certain against him and he was tolerated.

But then we got our hands on some letters, dated from Glasgow and attributed to Rubini, which, if authentic, would prove that their author was a spy.

We then invited Rubini to come to a meeting that was meant to be about something that personally concerned him. Guessing what it was about—or having been informed, anyway—he did not come and instead sent a long letter which said that he had received an offer from Inspector Prina to join the police and had accepted, but had done so with the objective of siphoning money from the government and being of service to the anarchist cause by discovering who the real spies were amongst us.

We did not believe in his excuses; nor, if we had believed them, would we have approved of the dangerous and dubious method, and we denounced Rubini as a police agent.[125]

Then Rubini wrote again, protesting against the "pontiffs," the "courts," etc. and saying that even if he had used the considerable amounts received from Prina to buy himself a house and live well, he had still used a part to assist comrades in need: and he gave a very detailed list of the aid given, which boiled down to a few shillings given to this or that person and marked with scrupulous care, which would have been enough to demonstrate that the money had been given with an ulterior motive.

And the matter would have ended there, if the Brussels episode had not come to reopen the issue.

Waiting, as we said, until later to express our view on the Brussels attack, for now we would like to state that the Rubini episode cannot be used to suspend our judgment of others who, discovered to be in relationships with the police, put forward the excuse of doing it to serve the cause, as recently happened with Donati of São Paulo in Brazil.

The excuse would be too convenient: and we cannot in any way admit that someone be a spy in jest.

If someone wants to play the game, may he know that he risks his own honor, and that, until clear proof to the contrary is provided, he will be considered and treated as a spy for real.

Regicide

Translated from "Il regicidio," *La Rivoluzione Sociale* (London), no. 5 (December 1, 1902)

The attack, or pseudo-attack as it may be, in Brussels gave the bourgeois press and the so-called socialist press an opportunity to once again repeat the usual rubbish, and to demonstrate the usual hypocrisy.

If it were worth the effort and time would allow, we could assemble, with what has been written in these past few days about the regicide, an

---

125   See the article "On Guard" on p. 97 of the current volume.

entire anthology of stupid things that could be a document of the moral and intellectual decadence of the bourgeoisie.

Il "Secolo" says that Rubini was born in Italy, but since, in addition to a failed regicide, he was also an international spy, he is not Italian, he is not from any country. Bravo! But could the patriotic newspaper of the Milanese grocers ever say that Caserio, Angiolillo, and Bresci were not Italian, and before them, Agesilao Milano, whose family Garibaldi gave a pension to, and Felice Orsini, whose memory is honored in Italy with marble busts and commemorative plaques? Would it say that these regicides were not Italian... because they were not spies for their homeland's government?

And if spies are not from any country and are therefore outside of humanity (a theory that does not displease us), would not the rulers who hire the spies and the bourgeoisie that benefits from them also be outside of humanity? Oh imprudent idiots!

"L'Indépendance belge" demands that its insulted king be avenged by ferocious repression, because, it says, "blood calls for blood," and does not consider—imprudently, again—that if proletarians accepted and applied its barbaric maxim, all bourgeois and royal blood would not suffice to avenge one-hundredth of the people's blood the dominators shed to defend their privileges.

"L'Italia del popolo," which occasionally glorifies Oberdan, and by specific mission is the enemy of kings, talks about the abolition of the death penalty, as if the matter were the right to punish and not, rather, the right of defense against a triumphant enemy which, strong in bayonets and canons, keeps the workers in subjugation and takes away their bread and freedom.

And everyone speaks of the inviolability of human life, with an agreement that would be touching if it were sincere: everyone, from the landlord who chases a mother with her children onto the frozen pavement to die from the cold, because of a few liras of back rent; from the industrialist who shortens the lives of his workers in a thousand ways, to save on the expenses involved in implementing hygienic precautions; down to the patriot who dreams of wars, conquests, and massacres for the greater glory of his country; and to the republican who only yesterday went to kill the Turks to "free" the Greeks.[126]

So, is it so difficult to have a little bit of reason and a little bit of sincerity? Can fear among some and passion of servility among others, do so much as to make one lose common sense and all self-respect?

Let us try to reason, even if there is little hope of convincing our

---

126   This is a reference to the 1897 Greco-Turkish war, in which groups of Italian volunteers fought on the Greek side.

opponents, since it is a constant, and, perhaps, beneficial fact proven throughout history that the privileged classes degenerate, turn beastly, and die, but do not correct themselves.

It is useless, at least we hope it is, to demonstrate the absurdity of the divine right of kings and heads of state in general. No one believes it anymore: there are at most a few republican fossils and republicanized socialists left who believe in the divine right of the "people," meaning of the legal majority!

A king, a president of the republic, a parliament, cannot be considered anything but men in special positions, subject to all the responsibilities and all the risks of their position.

If some bandit, armed with a rifle and a dagger, extorts his fellow countrymen and, to get his revenge and maintain his prestige, murders someone from time to time, everyone will deem it good if the people seeks to get rid of him by all possible means, and will be cheered by his death, if someone daring takes a well-aimed revolver shot at him. Nobody will say then that human life is always sacred: rather it will be argued, and rightfully so, that the principle of the inviolability of human life justifies the suppression of that bully who made attempts on the life of others.

But if that bandit becomes stronger, extends his domain, buys the complicity of a certain class of people, obtains assent through fear or through habit from some of the people, changes his robbery methods to more refined ones and, instead of using a rifle and dagger with his own hands, makes use of hired or forcibly enlisted people to carry out his bloody work, will he stop, because of this, being a bandit and being subject to all the natural penalties that threaten the violent?

There is indeed a doctrine, which has gained fame from the literary value and personal prestige of one of its apostles, Leo Tolstoy, which negates the right to any resistance, unless passive, against violence: but it is an ascetic, antisocial doctrine that has no possibility of success because it is a negation of nature and life. The bourgeois would be very happy to see the proletariat adopt it, but certainly would not adopt it for themselves. Tolstoyans aside, everyone accepts the right to defense, everyone glorifies war when it is waged for a good cause. The only difference is that everyone believes their cause is good and their opponent's cause is bad. So indeed our adversaries fight against anarchism, they try to demonstrate that our ideal is bad, unjust, harmful to humanity; or (something that will be much easier for them) they frankly say that we annoy them because we threaten their privileges and their ambitions. But may they leave alone the inviolability of human life and all the usual sentences repeated by the courtiers when kings have diarrhea. Otherwise, they will look like idiots and hypocrites, not just before us, but also before each other.

There is also no need to be more royalist than kings.

Humbert of Savoy, after an unsuccessful attack against his person, said that it was a risk of his profession; and Wilhelm of Germany, who like all people who talk a lot would sometimes let slip compromising confessions, said that Carnot, shot to death by Caserio, had fallen like a general on the battlefield.

The modern world is divided into two camps: that of the bourgeoisie, which brings together all oppressors, all exploiters, all scammers who fight in favor of privilege, and that of the proletariat that fights for justice, for freedom, for the well-being of all. Sometimes a soldier of the proletariat advances and hits a leader of the enemy army; sometimes the enemy catches one of ours and hangs him or sends him to prison. What can one do about that? Let us bury the dead and continue the battle!

A more serious question would be about the utility or lack thereof of these attacks, since, as unfortunately tyrants are human too, the right to defense would not be enough to justify attacks against their lives when it is useless or harmful to the defense itself.

But it is a question that the anarchists do not have a practical reason to discuss, since they do not propose to prepare, organize, provoke attacks.

Despite all the inventions of the police, who dream up plots, mandates and selections by lot, all anarchist attacks are merely spontaneous explosions, unpredicted and unpredictable, by a rebel too sensitive to stand the abominations of present-day society and too impatient to wait for its fall. It is social injustice, it is the arrogance of the dominators that naturally, necessarily sparks the avengers.

Useful or useless, rebellions are the consequence of oppression. The oppressors have the remedy in their hands: may they stop oppressing.

Arbitration

Translated from "L'arbitrato," *La Rivoluzione Sociale* (London),
no. 5 (December 1, 1902)

Every now and then the bourgeois, and especially the "reformer" bourgeois, discover a remedy to resolve the social question: all lies, obviously, to dupe the simpletons and continue to sponge off of them.

Today the fashionable remedy, among the "friends of the workers," like those of the newspaper "Il Secolo" and certain "socialist" ministers and aspiring ministers, is arbitration. And the aforementioned bourgeois have so much faith in arbitration as a means for resolving conflicts between capital and labor that, to taunt the workers, they would like to make it obligatory.

Merely look at which pulpit the sermon comes from and put your defenses up. "I fear the Greeks even when bearing gifts," the ancients said: "I fear the bourgeois, especially when bearing gifts," the workers should say. After all, Zanardelli's arbitrament in the Genoa strike, that of Waldeck-Rousseau in the Creusot strike and a hundred other recent cases should suffice for experience.

But the people are unfortunately the most gullible beast imaginable and, worse than skylarks, it rushes to the baits of all bird catchers. Therefore among the workers there are plenty who believe in arbitration and would like for it to be officially recognized by labor organizations as a means of resolving issues between masters and workers and to avoid or end strikes. For this reason it is worth dealing with it.

However, let us set aside the so-called mandatory arbitration, which seems to us a sinister absurdity beneath any discussion, and let us speak only of true arbitration, that is, arbitration freely accepted by the disputing parties.

In general, arbitration is certainly the most civil method known to resolve conflicts that arise in society; but only when this concerns the interpretation, application, resolution of rights that the parties mutually acknowledge. Otherwise it is a case of war and not of arbitration.

Who would dare, for example, propose the creation of an arbitration commission to resolve a conflict between the killer and the designated victim? What people who aspire to independence, or want to keep their independence, would submit to arbitration of the issue of their national existence? And would property owners submit the difference that they have with us, who want to expropriate them, to arbitration? Would the king subject his crown to the fate of an arbitrament?

Now, what the workers challenge or should challenge masters about, is the right to be masters. Waiting for the day when they can destroy them, they meanwhile seek to be robbed as little as possible. What do arbitrators have to do with it, and what could they decide? It is as if, dealing with a common thief, an arbitrator should decide what he can take: in fact and in reason the person robbed calls for help and defends himself if he can, and if not he lets himself be robbed; but he does not really think about arbitrators. The thief could think about them, when he has accomplices that, with the pretext of resolving the issue amicably, would try to paralyze the resistance of the victim.

There is a war between workers and masters, and as in all wars, it is a question of force.

May the workers see about becoming stronger. There is no other way to win.

Useless Retaliation

Translated from "Rappresaglie impotenti," *La Rivoluzione Sociale* (London),
no. 5 (December 1, 1902)

The increasingly relevant labor unrest carried out in multiple strikes that often spread quickly in major industrial centers, the feeling of international solidarity that grows more and more pronounced, and the ever increasing understanding of the necessity of revolutionary action exhibited by the masses do not reassure the bourgeoisie, which, not for nothing frightened, has made recourse to extreme weapons of defense.

The police scum and, when they are not enough, the army, are used to massacre the strikers, even the most peaceable, and the judges are called to carry out, more insolently than usual if that is even possible, their role as guardians of the privileges of a few parasites against the just demands of the large working masses.

This is what recently happened in Paterson and Geneva.[127] There the anarchists had been able, with incessant propaganda, to awaken the spirit of resistance and rebellion among the workers against the forces the bourgeoisie had at their disposal. Now that the strike is over and the uprising has been quelled by the army's brutal and still unconscious force, the bourgeoisie has the most active and most intelligent of our comrades arrested, expelled, condemned to exorbitant penalties, thus hoping to destroy our movement, to suppress our periodicals, to end our action among the working masses.

Yet the rulers, the capitalists should have realized that such retaliation is useless. It instead serves to make the ideas, which they want to repress, more widespread.

Did the hangings of the Chicago anarchists in 1887 suffice to smother anarchist ideals, when the American judges, on the payroll of the billionaire capitalists, tried to strike down the nascent and already promising labor movement by striking down these active, indefatigable agitators?[128] Since then, through persecution, the fighters of anarchist

---

127   Between April and June 1902, a silk workers' strike took place in Paterson, New Jersey. On June 18th there were clashes with the police, during which the Italian anarchist Luigi Galleani was wounded by a police bullet. In Geneva, unrest among tram drivers turned into a general strike on October 8, 1902. The troops available in the canton were called back to duty and on October 9–10 there were repeated clashes with the strikers, which injured hundreds.

128   The reference is to the well-known "Chicago martyrs," the five anarchists condemned to death for murder after a bomb was thrown by an unknown person, on May 4, 1886, during a demonstration by workers in Haymarket Square of Chicago, killing several police officers.

socialism have multiplied and everywhere put their unselfish activity at the service of the proletarian cause.

And in response to the verdicts of the republican judges of Paterson and Geneva, comrades in America and Switzerland are doubling their activity.

The latest issue of Geneva's *Il Risveglio*—which promises to continue, despite the expulsions and sentences that have hit its editors—provides a summary of the trial endured by Bertoni, Steinegger, and Croisier, and Bertoni's self-defense spoken before the jury, which constitutes a splendid reaffirmation of the goodness of anarchist principles and the revolutionary method, a gauntlet thrown in the face of the ruling classes rendered ferocious out of fear of seeing their privileges stripped away.[129]

That the method we advocate is the only one able to seriously undermine the base of the bourgeois framework, and to pave the way for the advent of an era of justice and well-being for all, is proven to us by the diligence by which rulers in all countries—whether monarchies or *free* republics—hasten to persecute us. And this must encourage us to persevere with increasing audacity in the struggle undertaken, fighting the people's lullers, unmasking the traitors of their cause, participating actively in labor demonstrations and showing workers the way to achieve their common rights.

Facts and Opinions

Translated from "Fatti ed Opinioni," *La Rivoluzione Sociale* (London), no. 5 (December 1, 1902)

ANARCHY AND ASSOCIATION.—As we have already had an opportunity to state, we do not like to squabble about words. As regards what our comrades, who are not completely in agreement with us, say and write, we are willing to consider more the substance of their thought than the form in which they prefer to express it. But there is a limit to everything. We are unable to abstain from protesting when anarchists say, as if they were ideas common to all anarchists, things which would negate anarchy and common sense, if understood within the context of the vernacular vocabulary.

Speaking of an allegedly anarchist attack committed in Cologne, Germany, *Le Petit Journal* wrote: "Everything seems to indicate that the

---

129   Luigi Bertoni's speech is found in *Il Risveglio Socialista-Anarchico* of November 23, 1902. John Croisier and Karl Steinegger were respectively sentenced to three and eight months of prison, both with the application of a conditional sentence, while Bertoni was condemned to a year.

people responsible for the attack acted according to a plan a long time in the making, and that they are affiliated with a revolutionary organization."

Le Libertaire of November 15–22, noting the reactionary newspaper's treacherous words, says that all of this will serve as a pretext, as usual, to harass the anarchists of Germany, and adds: "Would it therefore be necessary to continuously repeat that there can be no association among people who love, like the anarchists do, their complete autonomy and the complete development of their character?"

We confidently assert that the comrades of *Le Libertaire* must mean something different from what their words express, since the mere fact of making a newspaper already presumes an agreement, a concerted activity, an association that they must consider consistent with their anarchist ideas. Nevertheless the principle of association is negated in plain language and adversaries could rightly make use of that text to justify the nonsense and slander they usually have to say about anarchy and anarchists.

How, then, is it that anarchists—protective of their autonomy—should not, could not, without ceasing to be anarchists, associate with others when they want to do something that one man alone is not enough to do?! Do they not see that this is like committing suicide out of a fear of dying?!

"Anarchists want the complete development of their character." Certainly: but isn't association, society, the necessary environment for human character to establish itself and reach the maximum development possible?

In modern society, and in almost every association that lives within society, there is authority that crushes individuals, and makes slaves or puppets out of people who should be members: and this is the authority that the anarchists want to radically destroy, to ensure that what today we call society, and is nothing but forced submission of servants to masters, becomes a true society of equals, in which each individual finds not an obstacle, but assistance in his own development.

Saying that anarchists do not associate is a defensive expedient, of dubious taste and even more dubious result, when the police drag us to court with accusations of true or false plots. As for us, we do not hatch plots… because it does not suit us to hatch them. Accused of conspiracy, we would deny the fact, even if it were by chance true, and we would leave the burden of proof to the prosecution; but we would not want to deny, not even to avoid prison, the right to unite with whomever we want to do whatever we like. Now, union among men to do something the law could not prohibit is simply called an association: if the union is instead to do something that has been declared illegal, in the interest of the dominators, it takes on the frightening name of plot.

Let us repeat, we do not hatch plots; but we lay claim to the right to hatch them, should we believe they are useful: and we find it strange that this right of ours would be challenged precisely by anarchists and in the name of anarchy.

Letters from Abroad

Translated from "Lettere dall'estero," *Il Grido della Folla* (Milan) 2, no. 2 (January 8, 1903)[130]

. . .

London, December 29, 1902.

(ARNALDO BRUNO).—Organized by the editorial group of the newspaper "La Rivoluzione Sociale" and for the benefit of the same, a charming and very successful propaganda celebration was held at the "Atheneum Hall" on the evening of this past 27th. The large hall overflowed with male and female comrades of all races and nationalities.

. . .

Invited by those present, comrade Malatesta spoke, outlining the character of doctor Stockmann;[131] he demonstrated with the convincing logic he is known for, how it is natural that those who fight to defend truth and justice be called, by the same people that they defend and whose human dignity they wish to raise, their enemies and wrongdoers.[132]

He went on to quickly review the main causes that constitute the foundation of the current order of affairs; and lucidly demonstrated how the goal of all other parties is summarized by the phrase *you come down, so I can go up*; he finished by inviting all workers to fight not for palliatives, but for the full conquest of every right.

. . .

---

130   A very similar report also appeared in *L'Agitazione* of Rome on the next day.

131   During the evening, the second and fourth acts of Henrik Ibsen's *An Enemy of the People* were performed. Dr. Stockmann is the protagonist of that theatrical work. For Malatesta's critical opinion on this character, see his speech on organization given at the Amsterdam Congress, on p. 234 of the current volume.

132   This last sentence is quite obscure in the original text, probably because of a few typos. In its place, we have translated the corresponding sentence from the report in *L'Agitazione,* which is very similar but more fluent and grammatically correct.

Condemned Society

Translated from "Società condannata," *La Rivoluzione Sociale* (London),
no. 6 (December 29, 1902)

Winter has come, and with winter, the suffering of the poor has intensified to the extreme.

One cannot open a newspaper without finding it full of heart-wrenching stories; one cannot take two steps in the popular neighborhoods without seeing a thousand pieces of evidence of the most painful, most brutalizing poverty.

The number of people unemployed has grown disproportionately: to give an idea of the size of the crisis, it suffices to say that the factories of the "Great Eastern" railway company have laid off 30 percent of workers, and that the "Thames Ironworks," which ordinarily employ 4,000 men, now provides work to only 800.

Groups of women and children rummage through the market trash at night, and lucky is he who can nab some cabbage leaves or a few rotten potatoes thrown away by the greengrocers. People anxious to pawn the last shirt must wait in line for hours before the pawnshops, so great is the throng of the needy. Robust men, wanting to work any job, for any price, must settle for penny soup sold by special institutions... when they manage to find a penny. The "Salvation Army" with prudent concern, during cold nights, lights fires in the streets around which those who do not have shelter gather; and around each of these fires up to 400 people have been counted.

Hence, without mentioning the ordinary, chronic poverty of a large part of the working class, a notable fraction of the population (at least 10 percent) absolutely suffers from hunger and cold. Nothing to eat, nothing to protect oneself from bad weather, not a hole to spend the night in. It is this poverty that, suffocating every human feeling, reduces a man to the state of a frightened and hungry beast; poverty that dehumanizes without even rousing the desire to bite and kick.

And this is not primitive Russia, nor feudal Italy. This happens in civilized England, in the richest country of the world, in the capital of international commerce.

Here labor organizations are strong; here the philanthropic spirit is fervid, and in particular thousands of women from wealthy classes can be seen dedicating themselves with admirable zeal to a thousand clever expedients to alleviate the conditions of the impoverished. But it is all useless: when read in figures the aid seems considerable, when distributed among the innumerable needy it has the effect of a glass of water thrown upon an immense desert of burning sand.

A philanthropic society distributes blankets to the poor, that is, to a certain number of the poor; but soon it realizes that the blankets go directly to the institutional pawnbroker, and the society is forced to mark them and loan them out, so that the pawnshops cannot accept them:— this means that ways must be invented so that the poor do not give up a garment indispensable for facing the season's harshness for a crust of bread. Either cold or hunger! when it is not cold and hunger at the same time.

Meanwhile three quarters of the land of Great Britain is uncultivated, and around London there are large fields that thirty or forty years ago gave abundant harvests of wheat and now lie abandoned because the owners gain no personal benefit in having them cultivated!

Well, a society that cannot ensure its members at least the minimum strictly necessary for material survival, a society whose structure prevents the use of man and nature's productive capacity, and condemns to demoralizing poverty those who could live a happy and comfortable life, is a condemned society. All remedies compatible with the current social constitution have been tried, and all in vain.

Charity, philanthropy, political reforms, legal resistance organizations, even science, everything has been useless.

After so many struggles, after so many discoveries, after so many and so much vaunted civil and technical advances... people die of hunger in the street!

The suffering is too great for it to be remedied by small means: its roots are too deep for it to be destroyed with small, superficial reforms.

The only reasonable method that comes to mind is destroying the monopoly over the means of production. When these means are available to all, every man can provide for his own needs, and none will live in poverty any longer.

And this is the way that will end up being accepted by all men with heart, who truly desire the well-being of their fellow humans.

The Degeneration of the Socialist Party in Spain as Well as Italy

Translated from "La degenerazione del partito socialista nella Spagna come in Italia," *La Rivoluzione Sociale* (London), no. 6 (December 29, 1902)

Two Dates and the "El Socialista" Newspaper.

It was February 1888 and Sagasta ruled. The population of Rio Tinto was dissatisfied and upset, because the mineral calcination practiced by a mining company was detrimental to cultivated fields. All protests and petitions addressed to the authority had turned out to be useless, so they decided to address the Municipal Council with a large demonstration. The Council met, but did not decide on assertive action, because this concerned a very powerful Company. The governor came to the town hall; a commission of demonstrators addressed him and was poorly received. He went out to the balcony, harangued the crowd to disband, not without telling them he was determined to maintain order at any cost; and at the end of his speech a horrible bang sowed fear. The soldiers, the sons of the people, had fired on that unarmed crowd. Once the panic of the first moment passed, 45 dead and 100 injured were seen lying on the ground.[133]

Throughout Spain the indignation elicited by that killing was unanimous. The labor periodicals opened subscriptions for the victims and their pages screamed for revenge.

El Socialista published a resonating article entitled "MURDERERS!" from which I am copying the following paragraph:

"Workers, those who, cowardly murdered, have fallen forever in Rio Tinto, were your workmates, your brothers. The blood that was shed there is your blood; the bones broken were your bones. Consequently, to prevent this from happening again with impunity and to avenge the tremendous wound they inflicted upon you, unite, form tight battalions, prepare yourselves well to fight your tyrants, and when you are ready, resolutely embark upon the conquest of your economic emancipation, getting rid, with iron, with fire, with what you find most effective, of the paid killers who stand in your way."

We are in September 1901 and Sagasta rules. In La Linea, several workers have been murdered by the Montjuich benefactors, aided in the sad task by soldiers who, tomorrow, will be gunned down in turn. The deaths rise to fourteen: it is impossible to know for sure the number injured.

The proletarian masses, outraged, prepare to offer moral and material help to their brothers. The labor periodicals publish assertive articles against the triumphant bourgeoisie.

Describing the events, "El Socialista" comments on them in the following manner:

"It is evident: on one side there is the workers' ignorance, exploited by people without consciousness who make them believe that it is easy to resist public force, and on the other, the improvidence and stupidity of authority."

---

133   The town and the river named after it are in Andalusia. The massacre, after which 1888 went down in history as the "year of gunshot," happened on February 4th.

The Spanish comrade observing these different attitudes at different times in Pablo Iglesias' newspaper adds sarcastic comments.[134]
We believe that the documents already speak eloquently enough on their own.

So What?!

Translated from "E allora?!" *La Rivoluzione Sociale* (London), no. 6 (December 29, 1902)

In Ravanusa (in Sicily), since elections must be held, the outgoing provincial councilor and mayor bribe and threaten voters and go as far as to abduct people and make use of stabbers.

The town's socialists are unable to do anything but telegraph the facts to Bissolati and shout "Do something!" at him.

Bissolati responds that it is useless for him to ask the government, because he is certain it would take the side of the corrupters, when the necessary reaction against corruption and violence is lacking even among the socialists.

And then, writing about the issue, he says:

Unfortunately this telegram reveals where the deep roots of the mafia lie. It is in the caution—let us call it thus—of the honest people. The bullies have free play, for the simple reason that the inclination to let oneself be overpowered prevails around them. Look here: these capable socialists of Ravanusa are faced with kidnappings and threats from stabbers. And instead of telegraphing us the news that they were finally able to get their hands on the brutes and break the heads of the stabbers, they are unable to do anything but telegraph a whimper: "do something!" You start doing something yourselves! Do you have the socialist Circle? Make it into a team of citizens ready to manfully defend the law and jurisprudence. Do you like to sing: the redemption of labor "will be the work of its children?"[135] Sing it, but also start acting out the refrain from our hymn, when it is a matter of delivering your town from the shame of corruption and violence by your work.

---

134 In 1879, Pablo Iglesias founded the *Partido Socialista Obrero Español* and in 1886 he founded its organ *El Socialista*. Iglesias remained at the helm of both until his death in 1925.

135 This is a line from "Canto dei lavoratori" (Workers' song), written by Filippo Turati in 1886.

Words of gold! But then what use is it to appoint deputies? In reality what Bissolati says is a severe critique of all parliamentary politics adopted by the socialists and also of the entire authoritarian constitution of society. If people are not capable of taking care of their interests and defending their rights by themselves, the government will be on the side of the oppressors and socialist deputies will not be able to do anything about that. If, instead, the people act and make themselves respected by their own initiative, those who would have the desire to oppress will let it pass, and the socialist deputies will brag about something they do not deserve. Meanwhile, preaching the utility of electoral battles and being nominated deputy only serves to extinguish that much energy and initiative the voters could have had, and to accustom them to consider the elected person as the godsend that can and must save them.

May Bissolati continue, if it so suits him, raising sheep, but do not be amazed if later there are no lions.

The Death of Classic Unionism

Translated from "La morte dell'Unionismo classico," *La Rivoluzione Sociale* (London), no. 6 (December 29, 1902)

With the jury's verdict in the Taff Vale case, in which the owners of a railway network demanded compensation from the Union of railway workers for losses caused by a workers' strike, the maxim recently established by the Chamber of lords has begun to be practiced. By this maxim, labor unions are required to take responsibility, using their social funds, for "breaches of contract" by their individual members, when these were encouraged, approved, or simply supported by the union.[136]

This is a mortal blow—and the capitalistic press openly says so—to the way workers have been fighting for many years in England.

If up until now the struggle by dint of money, using resistance reserves slowly put together over years of dedicated contributions, and then quickly spent in a few weeks of strike, was an inadequate means for facing the capitalists' financial force, with the new jurisprudence today, it has become absolutely impossible. The funds workers will collect, with a thousand hardships, will regularly be devoured by the people of the court in the thousand trials that owners, with all sorts of legal quibbles, will file against the unions.

We do not regret this.

---

136   On the importance of this verdict, see note 113 above.

At this point, English unionism, which has a revolutionary origin and owes its successes to the revolutionary spirit, rather than a means for collective emancipation, has become a source of personal and corporate selfishness. The master is no longer considered the enemy, the oppressor, to be endured by necessity when one really cannot do without but to whom no forgiveness is granted. Instead, his capitalist position is acknowledged as legitimate, and he is treated as a partner in industry with whom they have, from time to time, quarrels over interests, which are resolved in a more or less courteous manner. And more than class struggle against the bourgeoisie, there is struggle between workers themselves.

The typical unionist, who has regular and rather well paid work, scorns the poorer worker and hates the foreign worker. The Union "officials," former workers who fear nothing more than having to go back to work, are generally politicos who serve the cause of the capitalist order.

If the masters' greed and the blindness of the reaction tear useless weapons from the hands of the labor unions, weapons with which they have frittered their time away, so much the better.

The most favored workers will understand that, even for them, there is no salvation other than in solidarity with all of the oppressed and in the establishment of a new social order.

And the English labor movement will get out of the dead quagmire and will enter a new phase of fecund life, becoming, at least we hope, revolutionary and socialist.

Persecutions

Translated from "Persecuzioni," *La Rivoluzione Sociale* (London), no. 6 (December 29, 1902)

Apparently we are being threatened by an intensification of international persecutions.

Switzerland prepares special laws against anarchists, Spain grabs at strike organizers, Argentina expels our comrades by the dozens and sends them back to Europe, where the vigilant and malevolent eye of the police awaits them...

Anarchism, which every other day the governmental socialists say is dead and buried, will once again be exterminated.

The matter leaves us cold. We are already used to being destroyed... and finding ourselves healthier than before.

We are not among those who believe that persecutions are *always* powerless in suffocating the idea and *always* benefit, instead, its propagation and triumph. We do not believe in the philosophy of professor Bovio, who, elevating a well-known popular proverb to the status of a scientific truth, says that every rosebush necessarily blossoms, since we have too often seen tender seedlings trampled and killed by the brutal foot of the wayfarer, and we know many good ideas, many benevolent initiatives suffocated by the adverse or indifferent environment.

But we affirm and we are deeply convinced that all the joint forces of the reaction, State, Church, and Property, with all their instruments of deceit and repression, priests, professors, magistrates, police officers, soldiers, prison officers, etc., will not succeed in preventing the seed of rebellion, which anarchists are sowing around the world, from producing its fruit of freedom and well-being for all.

They will not succeed, because they realized the danger too late, and sought a remedy when there was no longer any remedy.

They will not succeed especially because the modern spirit and living conditions of our times no longer lend themselves to systemic, logical, continued repression.

The Catholic Church managed, during the inauspicious times of blind faith, to impose its dogma of death via persecutions and delay the explosion of free thought by several centuries, because it represented an entire, complete, and logical system of human annihilation and had available blind, devoted, believing instruments. It had Torquemada in its service, who burnt the heretics, in good faith, convinced of serving a terrible and omnipotent God and of thus earning his own salvation and the salvation of humankind: and this was his great strength.

Instead, today everyone, even the most reactionary, wants freedom for himself; and it is in the nature of freedom that the violation of someone else's freedom endangers one's own. All the bourgeois, and even the governmental socialists, would like to see the anarchists' freedom suppressed, but then they realize that, for those in power, any enemy is an anarchist, and to protect themselves they become "liberals" again.

On the other hand, no conservative believes anymore in the sanctity of the institutions he defends, and all are ready to abandon them for the minimum personal advantage. Today the priest plots with the Jew, the patriot swindles the State, the treasurer runs off with public or private money, the voter sells his vote to the deputy and the deputy sells it to the government, the influential man sells and buys the decorations that symbolize and guarantee honor, the man of weapons woos the businessman, the head of police holds the bag for fat thieves, and the unsatisfied petty police officer sometimes turns on a sovereign. Every day the grass snake bites the charlatan.

With these elements, how can the bourgeois seriously think about repressing anarchism?

If they had any judgment, they would seek, with moderation and tolerance, to make the already inevitable social transformation less tempestuous.

Instead, they get worked up over useless persecutions.

Thus, after making themselves ridiculous as well as odious, they will attract lightning that perhaps they could have avoided.

So much the worse for them!

The "Black Hand"
[from *Les Temps Nouveaux*]

Translated from "La 'Mano Negra,'" *La Rivoluzione Sociale* (London), no. 6 (December 29, 1902)

[*The following editor's note appears after the article from* Les Temps Nouveaux, *which we are omitting.*]

We have reproduced the last part of the story documenting this unjust police hoax, which is going by the name of the MANO NEGRA affair.[137]

The truth begins to clearly show through the dense intrigue of lies that for twenty years were forced upon public opinion and even upon revolutionaries from different countries.

The sinister figure of D. Tomaso Perez Monforte appears before us in all his unsightliness, in the act of devising and making honest workers suffer the most infamous torments, the cruelest torture, to force them to confess their guilt for imaginary crimes and admit they were affiliated with a nonexistent secret society.[138] Mass arbitrary arrests, intimidation, beatings, and inconceivable maltreatments, feigned or completely made-up crimes and episodes falsely attributed to those arrested, and finally the execution of some and the incarceration of others: here are the means by which authority and the bourgeoisie try to suppress, to kill the movement and organization of Andalusian workers once and for all. The mighty present-day labor movement in Spain tells us how they succeeded. Workers have been able to remain loyal to the revolutionary method and libertarian principles, providing frequent proof of fraternal

---

137   On this serial story taken from *Les Temps Nouveaux*, see the introductory article "Justice!," on p. 141 of the current volume.

138   Tomás Pérez Monforte was the head of the *Guardia Rural* of Jerez, which conducted the investigations. The trial against the presumed members of the secret association *Mano Negra* ended with seven of the accused being sentenced to death, performed by garrote in Jerez de la Frontera on June 14, 1884. Another eight accused were condemned to long prison sentences.

solidarity, of class consciousness, of courage and perseverance in the struggle.

Today, after twenty years of suffering and oblivion, the survivors of that horrible police-legal drama are reestablishing the truth of the matter and, through the prison walls, beg for justice from their brothers in Spain, from the civilized world. The Spanish labor Unions and labor periodicals have taken up the call and, with all their energy, they prepare to lead uprisings for the liberation of the eight convicted people who are still alive.

But it is necessary for all who, in different countries, nurture sentiments of justice and ideas of freedom, to join in their protest against the abomination committed, demanding the immediate release of the surviving victims. It is necessary that the results of the investigations, performed by the willing people who first took up the call, find the greatest publicity, so that everyone knows what infamous contraptions the bourgeoisie, at the end of the last century, dared to use to repress the proletariat's ideas and demands.

Up until now, the agitation begun by Spanish labor newspapers and picked up by many French and English newspapers, in Italy, has been joined by only one newspaper, the republican *Italia del Popolo,* besides our periodicals. Will *Avanti!* and all the minor organs, which take their cues from the major organ, find a little spot in which they can address this very serious and urgent issue?

Facts and Opinions

Translated from "Fatti ed Opinioni," *La Rivoluzione Sociale* (London), no. 6 (December 29, 1902)

For a Regicide.
Il Secolo of Milan published the following public announcement on December 20–21:

"The public lecture by the honorable Socci, which was to have taken place next Sunday in the Verdi theater to commemorate the twentieth anniversary of the magnanimous sacrifice by Guglielmo Oberdan, has been prohibited by the authorities, which wanted to thus earn the indulgence of their lukewarm friend, Austria."

And it adds: "No comment."

We shall make the comment.

Oberdan wanted to kill the emperor of Austria to avenge the Italian patriots murdered by Franz Joseph, and to advance the cause of Trieste and Trento's Italian status.

Bresci killed the king of Italy to avenge the Milanese people murdered by the incitement, and with the applause of, Humbert, and to advance the cause of human emancipation.

Socci and all the patriotic and democratic bourgeois call Oberdan's attempt a magnanimous sacrifice, and praise him and commemorate him, and then they appear to be so scandalized by Bresci's act.

This proves yet again what we always repeat when some magnanimous person makes an oppressor eat dirt and the bourgeois shout vituperation, proclaim the inviolability of human life, and invoke the extermination of anarchists. For the bourgeois, violence in all its forms, including regicide, is good, noble, holy, when it is used to support their interests and their ideals; it is bad, hideous, uncivilized when it aims to serve the interests and ideals of the workers.

New Wave Socialism

Filippo Turati says: The South of Italy is sick. There the government gives free reign to the reaction and makes use of criminal rackets. Must we of the North, more evolved, who under this government enjoy a certain freedom and abundance of life, must we make common cause, to our detriment, with the Southerners against the government?

And he responds: We must, for the benefits given to the North continue to support the Cabinet which causes so much harm to the South.

For us, a party that calls itself socialist and does not throw out, with a belch of disgust, a man who, in the name of socialism, so shamelessly repudiates every most elementary sentiment of human solidarity, is a party definitively judged.

Meanwhile, when we say that parliamentarism corrupts, the socialists continue to protest!

The New Republic

The news coming from Cuba shows that there, too, and earlier than one would have believed, the eternal, mournful story recurs. With the changing of the political regime, the people only change their masters and experiment at their expense that the new masters are as good as the old.

In Havana, cigar factory workers go on strike. Despite the fairness and modesty of their demands, the masters resist, to the point that all labor corporations, with the exception of the electric tramway staff, express their solidarity with the cigar makers and proclaim the general strike.

The rulers of the new republic, who just yesterday called themselves revolutionary and came to power thanks to the people's blood shed in the struggle against the Spanish oppressor, act precisely as the Spanish rulers did and put governing influence and force at the service of the masters.

A police chief, a certain Cardenas, famous for his brutality, hurls his henchmen against the strikers, but they resist energetically, until the government gets scared and to calm people down dismisses the imprudent police officer.

Later the *alcalde* (the mayor) summons the strike Committee and offers his mediation; but the workers, who know who they are dealing with, turn him down.

Then the government throws off its mask and the regime of terror begins.

On Monday November 24th, as the strikers tried to persuade the tram workers to stop working, a squad of police officers shot at a group of workers: the latter responded with stones and a few pistol shots, and many wounded and dead remained on the ground. Two other points of the city were the scenes of actual field battles, with the result of many wounded and quite a few dead.

Other skirmishes occurred here and there; but the worst is what happened at Campo di Marte. There was a collision between an electric carriage and a firefighters' wagon, the people agglomerated around the scene of the disaster, seeking to assist the firefighters in danger. The police, probably without understanding what was happening, immediately fired on the group, injuring and killing many. Not yet satisfied with this, they continued shooting at a number of people they saw in the vicinity. The latest news we received reports ten or twelve dead and 203 injured.

Naturally the bourgeois newspapers, great patriots and great enemies of... Spanish tyranny, blame the anarchists for everything. To which the anarchist newspaper *Tierra* responds: "If we had the influence over the people that you attribute to us, you would not be able to oppress them, deceive them, and massacre them as you do!"

Comrades Planas, Arturo Juvanet, and Sebastiano Aguiar were arrested, held a whole day without eating and then handed over to the judiciary under the accusation of sedition. And this was because Juvanet was caught in the act of reading Aguiar a report of the events that took place on Monday the 24th.

Not bad for a newborn republic!

To Comrades!

Translated from "Ai Compagni!" *La Rivoluzione Sociale* (London),
no. 7 (January 27, 1903)

Once again financial difficulties force us to publish two weeks late.

In undertaking the publication of this periodical, we intended to fill a gap in the Italian-language anarchist press. The newspapers that come out in Italy are ineluctably obliged to castrate their thought, to mitigate their comments with regards to daily events.

And we—who are devoted here to expressing our ideas without euphemisms, and who wanted to pit our frankly anarchist and decidedly revolutionary criteria against the evident signs of a deviation in the Italian anarchist movement and the corruption increasingly invading the so-called popular parties—we counted on help from comrades who share our aims and consider our initiative useful, to make it viable and long-lasting.

The terrible crisis England is experiencing at this moment and the consequent aggravation of unemployment and poverty allow us to shoulder only partially—sometimes minimally—the considerable expenses required for a periodical publication.

Moreover we relied on the active collaboration of comrades from abroad. There are many comrades scattered about different countries, who, driven by the same objectives as we are and able to write, could send us articles and correspondence suitable for the nature of the newspaper, thus greatly facilitating the task we took on.

So far—except for some intermittent submissions of money and a few texts we have received from abroad—our expectations have been disappointed. We therefore again turn to comrades, urging them to help us morally and materially, so as to permit us to continue publication.

If our plea produces no effect, it will mean that they do not feel this periodical is a necessity: all we will have to do then is address our modest efforts towards more vital initiatives.

THE EDITORIAL GROUP.

The War against Foreign Workers

Translated from "La guerra contro i lavoranti stranieri," *La Rivoluzione Sociale* (London), no. 7 (January 27, 1903)

Unemployment and poverty are all the rage in London; and part of the press takes the occasion to launch a cry of alarm against "the foreign invasion," blowing on the malcontent that native workers already on their own feel against the proletarians from other countries who come here in search of work, chased from their native countries by hunger or political, religious, or racial persecution.

The phenomenon is not unusual, and is found during all time periods, especially those of recrudescent poverty, and in all countries, especially those with strong immigration.

The general sentiment among workers is that those who come from outside to seek work, come to take the "bread out of their mouth." And this sentiment is so strong and so blurs a correct view of social phenomena, that many see in "foreigners" the cause of economic distress and believe that some *good laws* against immigration of foreign proletarians would resolve the social question, creating abundance for all... the natives.

This is evidently a stupid error, which is well explained by the fact that the damage, in terms of lack of work or decreased wages, each individual suffers or could suffer due to competition from immigrants, is immediate, direct, easily perceived damage; while the general damage that is caused by failure to acknowledge solidarity among workers of any origin and would be caused by a forced stop of immigration flows, is a complex phenomenon, poorly understood without a bit of intellectual effort.

Without considering political and moral matters for the moment, and limiting ourselves to strictly economic considerations, it is certain that the phenomenon of immigration, even if it creates temporary imbalances and therefore real disadvantages for individuals who are defeated by competition, does not, in terms of general and permanent effects, cause a lack of work or a lowering of wages. Rather, the contrary takes place. Countries which receive many immigrants are either countries that still have a lot of free land and can therefore absorb a lot of people without damage and instead to the advantage of those who are already there, as is the case in North America and Canada; or are countries that export a lot of manufactured merchandise, as is the case of England. Now, for example, if England closed its doors to workers from other countries, those countries, either due to political retaliation or by the natural effect of economic competition, would remain closed to English merchandise. Therefore, even though the offer of labor in the labor market would be considerably lower than now, there would also be much less demand and unemployment would increase and with this wages would drop. If proletarians from countries with high emigration no longer had the chance to go abroad, wages in those countries would drop even more, and their capitalists would find themselves in a more advantageous position to compete with capitalists at high wages and to chase away the latter's merchandise from the international market. The same English or North American capitalists would establish themselves where labor is cheap, as they are already starting to do, and would leave their compatriots without work.

In the conflict between property owners and proletarians, which is an inevitable consequence of the current social order, the interests of workers around the world are in agreement. Relationships of all types among the different countries have become so numerous and frequent, and isolation from the rest of the world so impossible, that the price of everything, including the price of the labor force, tends to rapidly equalize everywhere. Conditions for workers in one country are more or less bad based on how more or less bad conditions are for workers in other countries.

And given that emigration naturally goes from countries where people suffer more to countries where people live better; that emigrants upon changing countries get used to higher standards of living and learn to have greater demands; and that, by decreasing the supply of labor in countries that they leave, wages there increase, the general economic effects of migratory currents are favorable to the proletariat and to civilization in general.

But we understand that these considerations cannot win over starving people. When, as is happening now in London, the crisis is all the rage and hundreds of thousands of people are without work and go about the city in lamentable processions asking for handouts; when whoever has a job that gives him a crust of bread fears losing it and being reduced to suffer hunger together with his family and spending winter nights outside, then economic science loses its entitlements, and it is no marvel, nor a reason for reproach, if the unemployed, or those who fear becoming so, do not think about what they could have tomorrow, and look with antipathy, perhaps with hatred, at every new competitor.

And we even understand that the capitalists, while they take advantage of the immigrants' poverty and ignorance to snag them into work under conditions they would not dare offer workers in their own country, seek to keep the latter calm by means of their press and agents, deflecting their righteous anger into a stupid and fratricidal fight against the "foreigners." They are following the logic of their unfair situation, and we do not expect that they would want to point out the true causes of suffering and the true remedies to their victims.

But what we do not understand, what outrages us, is to see many who call themselves socialists, and hold among socialists an influential position such as members of parliament, speakers, and journalists, entertain the popular prejudice and even themselves contribute to distract the workers' attention from the true cause of their suffering, inciting them, with more or less hypocritical methods, against their brothers born in other countries.

When "socialists" were truly socialists and not the vulgar vote hunters of today, they preached brotherhood among workers of all races; they recommended to welcome foreign comrades, to offer them solidarity and ask for reciprocity, and to do whatever possible to prevent them from falling victim to the capitalists and accepting wages lower than the current wage.

Today… today, to cite a few examples, the *Labour Leader*, organ of the "Independent Labor Party," and more specifically of the socialist member of parliament Keir Hardie, praises a ministerial candidate because he wants the number of foreign sailors allowed on English mercantile ships to be limited by law, and the French socialist member of parliament Coutant proposes a law which establishes that the number of foreigners employed in factories cannot be over 10 percent of staff.

Is this not like telling workers that the cause of their poverty is foreigners and that the remedy is in excluding them?

In the study preceding his draft bill, Coutant says that "the government cannot lose interest in the French workers who contribute to all State taxes and whose earnings are the lifeblood for domestic trade, to the benefit of foreign workers who neither for trade nor for the State are elements of vitality."

Oh, days of the International Workingmen's Association, how far away you are!

How many times will we have to exclaim: poor socialism!

The Violence of Anarchists and the Meekness of Socialists

Translated from "La violenza degli Anarchici e la mansuetudine dei Socialisti," *La Rivoluzione Sociale*, (London), no. 7 (January 27, 1903)

Under the title **A Socialist from Imola Stabbed by an Anarchist,** *Avanti* of Rome prints:

> We receive the news and details of a revolting episode of anarchist violence, which took place on Christmas day in Imola, from other newspapers, since we have no word from our correspondent.
>
> Adamo Mancini, an anarchist from Imola, writing to the anarchist leaflet of Milan *Il Grido della Folla*, had several times attacked Dr. Rosolino Cenni, socialist, member of the Imola Congregation of Charity, a highly respected person, calling him with disdain doctor Musolino.[139]
>
> On the morning of the 25th, doctor Cenni, meeting Mancini, told him that he wanted to be called by his name and not otherwise. Mancini responded with insults and Cenni replied by giving him a slap.
>
> It all seemed to be over. Cenni walked away. Mancini, a little perplexed, suddenly drew a dagger and, running straight at Cenni without

---

139   Giuseppe Musolino was a famous Calabrese bandit, active from 1889 to 1901, the year he was arrested.

the latter realizing, stabbed him, in the shoulder, in a cowardly manner. Then he ran away; and now is at large. Cenni, despite the serious wound penetrating the cavity, is out of danger.

And *La Lotta*, a socialist periodical of London, reproducing the above from *Avanti*, adds:

Now it is no longer enough for the republicans to murder the socialists, but the anarchists also join in.

Will *La Rivoluzione Sociale*—so scrupulous to note Turati's words and shape them in their way—not note this brutal violence? From the words of only one man from the Italian socialist party, it draws considerations on the entire party and the essence of socialism, so much as to print in bold letters: NEW WAVE SOCIALISM; will it not draw any consideration from this event on violence by a dagger and on the inviolability of human life?[140]

Think about what is right, fellow paper: facing the sad event we stigmatize the man, the individual, and do not print: NEW WAVE ANARCHISM.

We remember on good account that the enemies listed by Malatesta at the libertarian celebration are also our own, and we bring our attacks against them without falling into a ridiculous attitude of competition.[141]

We shall say nothing of *Avanti*, because it has already demonstrated its bad faith on many occasions. If it already had the habit of defacing anarchy and slandering anarchists when it itself was a *subversive* organ, how could greater equanimity ever be expected from it now that, attacking us, not only does it satisfy its partisan spite, but moreover acquires further new titles by the good graces of the government?

To *La Lotta*, whose sincerity we have no reason to doubt, we will say that if they really wanted to start a polemic with us, there would have been no lack of subjects on which discussion would be generally useful, without compromising itself so clumsily with an attack that would fit better in *La Tribuna* and similar filth.[142]

It says, for example, that we "shaped" Turati's words in our own way, thus invalidating the conclusions we drew from them. Instead of so gratuitously asserting the inaccuracy of our citation (which we literally

---

140   See "Facts and Opinions" (December 29, 1902) on p. 168 of the current volume.

141   This is probably a reference to the libertarian celebration of December 27, 1902, summarized in "Letters from abroad," on p. 159 of the current volume.

142   *La Tribuna* was a newspaper founded in Rome in 1883. In previous years it had been a strong supporter of Italian colonialism.

got from *Il Secolo nuovo,* a socialist newspaper from Venice, not suspected of preconceived aversions to Turati), why did *La Lotta* not print
the claimed inaccuracies, restoring Turati's words in their authentic version? It would be seen if our attacks against socialists are inspired by
pressure and bias, rather than love of the truth.

But no; *La Lotta* preferred to pick up from *a variety of events* a painful personal episode, just to involve us and anarchism.

On the streets of Imola, following an altercation, a man slapped
another man and the latter responded with a stab. A disgracefully banal
thing, given the customs of our sweet homeland. But it happens that
the slapping man is a socialist and the stabbing man is an anarchist:
and here are the newspapers shouting about anarchist violence, taking
on the attitude, like *La Lotta,* that they are doing us a special favor if
they do not directly say that anarchism, new or old, consists of stabbing
people.

Did we remember that Murri was a socialist when we read that he
murdered his brother-in-law?[143] When we look over the crime blotter,
do we concern ourselves with the political, social, religious, artistic, etc.
opinions of the criminals and say: homicide committed by a monarchist, rape done by a Catholic, forgery perpetrated by an enthusiast of
Wagner's music, and so on?

It is a deplorable fact, but a well-established fact, that the ideas an
individual professes only have a very limited influence on their conduct:
they are certainly a guide, a brake or a spur, but hardly, and rarely, they
succeed in overcoming the influences of heredity, education, and the
environment. Neither have we ever claimed that anarchists as men, are
better than the others.

We do not know with certainty how things truly happened. But let
us suppose that they happened as *Avanti* presented them, let us grant
(and it is a lot to grant) that all the wrong was done by Mancini: the matter still boils down to a vulgar brawl. What does this have to do with our
attacks against Turati?

Turati is a public man with a large following. His words and acts,
while they are an index of a party's leanings, influence in turn those
leanings and confirm them or modify them. He, in the name of socialism, says and does things that are the negation of socialism; and we, in

---

143   On September 2, 1902 the cadaver of count Franceso Bonmartini was found in
        Bologna. Bonmartini was the husband of Linda Murri, daughter of the famed
        doctor Augusto Murri. The latter denounced his son Tullio, attorney and
        socialist municipal council member in Bologna, for the homicide. The case,
        which also involved Linda and various other people of the upper bourgeoisie,
        roused a great deal of interest in the press, developing tones of an ideological
        controversy on the materialistic education Augusto Murri taught his children.

defense and in honor of true socialism, stigmatize him and with him we stigmatize those who by following a man repudiate their ideas and their best sentiments.

If *La Lotta* does not approve and does not follow Turati, our attacks against Turati and his people do not concern it and do not affect it.[144]

But since we are on the subject, it will not be useless to more closely examine the events of Imola, as shown in the same report in *Avanti*, and see if it has so much of a right to shout against Adamo Mancini's violent act, making it appear as if Rosolino Cenni is an angel of meekness.

Mancini, within his rights as a citizen, attacked Cenni as a member of a public administration. Now it does not matter if the attacks were justified or not: naturally he who is attacked always finds that he was so unjustly, and it would be a curious freedom to be able to criticize authority only when authority estimates that the criticism is correct.

Cenni confronted Mancini in the street and, not obtaining satisfaction gave him a slap. What should Mancini have done, he who, it is well known, is a small man with a scrawny build?

Put up with the slap? In that case he would have had to renounce his freedom as a writer and his dignity as a man: a slap, as usually happens, would be followed by others every time he opened his mouth; and *Avanti* would not fail to slice up disregard and disdain for the "slapped" Mancini. These are the customs of Italy, and Mancini cannot be called responsible for them. Or would the socialists have preferred that Mancini, rather than yielding to the impetus of the moment, had attempted to kill Cenni in cold blood in a duel performed according to the rules?!

Certainly weapons are primitive things; but if slaps are allowed, weapons become a useful and necessary brake: otherwise freedom would not exist for those of weak physique, and the golden age would come for prevaricators with a strong punch.

We could blame Mancini; because in our opinion the slap given by Cenni only dishonored Cenni himself.

Avanti and *La Lotta* have no right to blame him, as they find not a single word of reproach against the bully who wanted to use brutal violence to suffocate the voice of an opponent.

---

144   On this subject see also "Ideas and Persons: An Explanation," on p. 95 of the current volume.

The Proposed Antimilitarist Congress

Translated from "Il proposto Congresso antimilitarista," *La Rivoluzione Sociale* (London), no. 7 (January 27, 1903)

Some French individuals and groups, of "progressive" opinions, have proposed holding an *antimilitarist Congress* in London, and a provisional Committee has been established in London to support and carry out this initiative. The Committee has invited several organizations known to be against militarism to appoint delegates to form the definitive Committee, which should convene and organize the Congress.

As we too have been invited to contribute to these efforts, we should, to avoid any doubt, say what we think on the subject. And we say immediately, frankly, that we have no sympathy for this kind of fragmentary agitation that tends to divert attention from the fundamental causes of social evils, and to make classes and parties fraternize while they are or should be enemies.

It is superfluous to say that we are antimilitarists in the most complete sense of the word. We are not enemies of this or that form of military organization; we are sworn enemies of any armed force whatsoever in the service of any authority. We are enemies of the army, enemies of the police, enemies of the system known as the armed nation.[145]

Yet we know that armed force serves to defend the privileges of capitalists and rulers; that it would not exist if there were no capitalism and no governments; and that, under one form or another, it will always exist as long as there are oppressors who need it to carry out their violence and defend themselves against the demands of the oppressed. And for this reason we find laughable the antimilitarism of the bourgeois who, wanting to preserve the fundamental bases of the current institutions, individual ownership and authority, must also want the means necessary to preserve them.

And in fact the antimilitarism of these gentlemen boils down to a simple question of manners and people: some want to reduce the number of army corps, others want to change the method of recruitment, others want to "raise the moral standards," "republicanize" the army, others want the "armed nation" to replace permanent armies: but all, as they are bourgeois, want enough soldiers and police for "order" to be guaranteed and force to remain with the law.

Now, together with anarchists, socialists, and workers in general, all

---

145   As regards this last concept, see the article entitled "The Armed Nation," on p. 146 of the current volume.

the bourgeois, "progressive" journalists, and members of any "society of peace" that calls itself antimilitarist should take part in the proposed congress.

What could be achieved together by people who have diametrically opposed opinions and interests?

That such a Congress be held is not something that would displease us when it is convened and organized either by bourgeois or by neutral men, as there are many, full of good intentions and empty of any specific idea. If allowed to participate in it, we would do so to tell the bourgeois what we think of their false antimilitarism and seize the occasion to make propaganda.

As for us summoning the bourgeois to a congress and demonstrating that we believe it is possible to abolish militarism in agreement with capitalists and without abolishing capitalism, one hundred times no.

Certainly, it is not due to hatred or personal antipathies that we wish to have nothing in common with the bourgeois and strive to dig an abyss between the class of the proletarians and the class of the capitalists: it is due to the conviction that social regeneration must be born from conflict between these two classes, and that any agreement between them tends to perpetuate the social injustices that we wish to destroy.

We know well that there are individuals of bourgeois origin who sincerely deplore the suffering of the proletariat and would like to find a solution, and we are delighted to accept their involvement when they break with their class and begin to decisively fight together with the workers: if instead they preach harmony between classes and understanding between rich and poor, between masters and workers, they could be very well intentioned but remain practically enemies of the proletariat and supporters of the current society.

Already in 1868, at the League of Peace and Freedom Congress that took place in Berne, Bakunin told the Congress participants: If you truly want peace and freedom, you need to seek it in social justice—and recommended they dissolve the useless League and enter the International Workingmen's Association to fight on the side of the workers for total social transformation.

If the antimilitarist Congress took place and we were admitted, we would repeat in substance what Bakunin said thirty-five years ago: may he who is sincerely antimilitarist fight with us against capitalism and against governmentalism; he who does not do this and says he is antimilitarist, is either deceiving himself or seeking to deceive others.

The Candela Murder

Translated from "L'Assassinio di Candela," *La Rivoluzione Sociale* (London), no. 7 (January 27, 1903)

The epilogue to the bloody drama is taking place these days at the court of Lucera. At this time, the outcome is unknown.[146]

We really do not care to know it, because it can easily be predicted; in a country such as Italy where the judiciary is subservient to the police and is exclusively, except for rare exceptions, an instrument of reaction and oppression towards the working classes, it will certainly come as no surprise that the poor workers, in addition to being paid with the grape-shot that laid seven or eight of them out on the ground, also get a few months and perhaps more of imprisonment. Instead, it is important and necessary to draw a lesson that can be used to train workers for the future and to show them how much injustice is committed with impunity by the bourgeoisie, so that in future struggles for the gradual conquest of their own rights, they will no longer have to regret the deplorable fact of a proletariat that indifferently witnesses the violent massacre of poor workers.

Therefore it is useful to briefly recall the past and, without going back through the years and again portraying the agonizing spectacles of the poor murdered people of Conselice, Caltavuturo, and other places, it will suffice to recall the despicable massacre of Berra, which shook all of Italy's workers into a deep howl of anguish and protest.[147]

But the howl went unheard and the protest, although unanimous, was fruitless! Why? Because it was done in a childish way. Barely a year later, the bloody drama happened again in Candela!

And it will happen again—it would be nice if it did not—it will happen again.

The workers' struggle to assert human rights against the Bourgeoisie continues, tenacious, incessant, and inasmuch as this conflict of opposing interests exists in a state of action, these attacks on human life will happen from time to time. As long as the Bourgeoisie holds the force in its hand, it will oppress, it will always crush the weak, and no protest in the world will be enough to stop this homicidal rampage if the worker has not acquired that strength of resistance, which only comes from a precise

---

146   See note 100 above on the events concerning Candela. The trial involved eighty-two accused, most of whom were being arraigned for attacking the freedom of work and for assailing and resisting police agents.

147   In Conselice, Emilia-Romagna, three workers were killed on May 21, 1890, while in Caltavuturo, Sicily, on January 20, 1893, the police killed eleven farmers during a demonstration. For information on Berra see note 100 above.

understanding of his rights, and developed within himself the revolutionary spirit, the spirit of rebellion against all subjugation and violence.

Instead!

After Berra, large assemblies in which more or less apt, more or less elegant speakers wove together the great tragedy in somber colors before the trembling people, numerous protest agendas, then nothing more, oblivion!

And true revolutionary action, which instills the spirit of resistance in the worker's soul and consciousness, the true method for shaping the serious protest, which would have brought together a phalanx of workers ready to oppose such hideous violence, were not at play, nor are they coming about in the field of organization. Every day people move closer to legality, every day they further acclimatize to quiet living, to small concessions that muffle the enthusiasm in the worker's spirit.

What happened in Berra, happens in Candela, and the silence among the people of Italy is identical.

The wrong is therefore in the method of propaganda being made amidst workers in Italy.

It is therefore necessary to return to the practical revolutionary method, to seek to infuse that spirit of true resistance against the bourgeoisie within the organized proletariat of Italy, which will lead them to real and deep conquest after conquest, to their complete emancipation.

The poor peasants of Candela will perhaps be sentenced; hunger, bullets will not be enough: prison too shall lock away the best of them. The people of Italy, supine and head down, will listen to this sentence in silence, just as it ignored the howls of pain and kept silent before the supreme torture: praise to Centanni!! Who will wake them up?[148]

Facts and Opinions

Translated from "Fatti ed Opinioni," *La Rivoluzione Sociale* (London), no. 7 (January 27, 1903)

JOKE REFORMERS. —Apparently there exists an international League against dueling, that has an Italian section, to which a Lombard Committee belongs.

We do not know anything about the general operations of this League, but we found out that the Lombard Committee is collecting,

---

148 The brigadier Centanni held the most responsibility for the Candela slaughter, having shot twenty-four of the total fifty-nine shots fired. He was the aggrieved party in the Lucera trial, in which twenty-two of the accused were sentenced to punishments from two to seven months.

through the copious diffusion of forms, membership from every order of citizen, warning that "membership is not binding until honor has been defended in a more effective and adequate manner." This means that those who protest against the duel by speaking will thus continue to fight as before; rather the Committee's warning could very well be interpreted to encourage dueling, as it implicitly states that, lacking "more effective and adequate" means, those who refuse to fight are poorly defending their honor!

Truly, it is not with a half-consciousness and a half-character, as possessed by the gentlemen of the Committee and those who endorse a protest declared invalid by the very act in which it is announced, that one will succeed in uprooting the habit of the duel or any other prejudice.

He who seriously wants to see the duel disappear must begin by never provoking nor accepting challenges, and thus contribute to shaping public opinion to disapprove of the duel and to consider honor as something that lies in the integrity of life, and not in barbaric prescriptions of so-called chivalry.

Instead, it seems as if they want to add a few new articles to the Zanardelli code, already so favorable to instigators. Perhaps these punctilious defenders of "honor" would like it to be easier to be paid in cash for insults received, so that insults can be provoked with the premeditated purpose of receiving indemnity in farthings, as is rather common practice in England!

The socialists took an important step toward abolishing the duel when they considered it shameful for anyone who fought in duels to belong to their party; but then even this vanished in their general abandonment, more or less disguised, of their entire program.

Anarchists, always diligent to match their behavior to their ideas as much as possible, are against dueling and therefore do not fight: an anarchist who was tempted to do so knows he would lose the respect of his comrades and be ridiculed. If the members of the League against the duel truly want what they say they want, may they do as the anarchists do: refrain from fighting and disapprove and ridicule those who do. And as they are influential people precisely within the class that practices the duel, they can be sure of success.

FREEDOM! —Two of our comrades, Antonelli and Malighetti, exiled from the country so dear to the aspiring minister Turati, have now come to London asking for the hospitality they were denied by the very republican republics of the Millerands and the Thiébauds.[149] Indeed the latter

---

149   The anarchists Adolfo Antonelli and Carlo Augusto Malighetti had both

republic, which for some time has seemed to be trying to collect attestations of merit from the most reactionary European States, in this moment is completing one of the most cowardly attacks on freedom by again sending Russian nihilist Nackacidze to the border, as the bourgeois... and republican journalists cry crocodile tears and get emotional over his persecution![150] This is nothing new; government means class domination, oppression and subjugation of people, and for it, the measures of repression employed to guarantee its existence are perfectly excusable. As long as there is government, we will never be free; only Anarchy will bring true freedom.

*
**

REPUBLICANS? —Though with little surprise, we read in the newspapers of Italy that the republican attorney Golinelli, mayor of Bologna, sent, on behalf of his town, new year greetings to the king and called him "the interpreter of the mission of Italian thought."

For a republican who, at least presumably, wants to destroy the monarchy and with it and first of all the prestige of the monarch among the people, this is not so bad!

And here is the best part; as this telegram rightly provoked many different comments, Golinelli's political friends unbelievably reconfirmed their full trust in him, and he himself declared in an interview, with the most brazen cheek in the world, that he did not, through that act, fall short of his republican beliefs and that he remained republican!

This brief incident may seem to some like a simple personal act, nothing outside of the usual courtesy, but it seems like much more to us. This is truly the logical consequence of that which we have been fighting against for so long: the conquest of public powers that inevitably leads to negating, little by little, one's own ideals and adapting oneself to the system which, before, one fought against so fiercely.

---

endured convictions in Italy and, after living in Switzerland, moved to France, from where they were expelled in December 1902, to finally land in London. Until a few months prior, French socialist Alexandre Millerand had been minister in the coalition government of Pierre Waldeck-Rousseau. Since 1897 Fritz Thiébaud had been the first Swiss socialist to participate in a cantonal government.

150   In 1890, Viktor Nakashidze was sentenced in Paris to three years of prison for having participated in a plot against the tsar, actually devised by an agent of the Russian police. Over the next few years he was expelled from several European countries, including Italy, where in 1901 he was arrested for violating a previous expulsion order. At the time of this article, he had recently found the same fate in Switzerland.

Production and Distribution

Translated from "Produzione e distribuzione," *La Rivoluzione Sociale* (London),
no. 8 (February 20, 1903)[151]

In a lecture recently held in Milan, Arturo Labriola, the celebrated Italian intransigent socialist director of the newspaper *L'Avanguardia Socialista*, demonstrated—according to the summary we find in *Il Grido della Folla*[152]—that "the real issue that must be resolved is not the issue of wealth distribution, but that of the rational organization of production."[153]

Since Malthus, conservatives of every hue have argued that poverty is created, not from the unfair distribution of wealth but from limited productivity or inadequate human industry.

In its historical origins and fundamental essence, socialism is a negation of this theory; it is an emphatic assertion that the social problem is primarily an issue of social justice, a distribution issue. But ever since socialists began whoring[154] with power and with the propertied classes, that is, ever since they stopped actually being socialists—they too have, in a slightly more modern form, begun to support the conservative theory.

If that theory were true, it would be wrong to say that the antagonism between masters and workers is irreconcilable, since the solution to it would be the shared interest that masters and wage earners have in

---

151   This article was reprinted, with Malatesta's signature and without any mention of the original article, in *Il Pensiero* of Rome on May 16, 1905, under the title "Bourgeois Seepage into Socialist Doctrine." We have provided notes on the significant differences between the two editions. The main difference is that the following introduction was added to the beginning of the second edition:

> For some time now, reformist socialists, to justify the paths of renunciation which they have embarked upon, have begun modifying socialism's theories in addition to its tactics. Thus, a little bit at a time, a number of essentially bourgeois moral, political, and economic ideas, and even prejudices, have infiltrated socialist doctrine.
>
> You can immediately understand how serious this phenomenon is, if you consider that it is already being exhibited not only by the more moderate parts of the democratic socialist party, but is also beginning to undermine the other parts which are proud of being more revolutionary and intransigent.

152   The summary appears in the January 29th issue, in the "Cronaca Locale" column.

153   In the edition of *Il Pensiero*, the following paragraph is added here:

> This is so wrong, that we would do well to dwell upon it, because it compromises the very foundations of socialist doctrine, and the conclusions that can logically be deduced from it are anything but socialist.

154   *Il Pensiero* has the verb "negotiating" here.

increasing the quantity of products: or rather socialism would be wrong, at least as a modern means of solving the social problem. And in fact, we have already heard Turati argue that during strikes the workers must take care not to ruin the master and his industry; and, before Turati, Ferri had said that socialists should help the bourgeois enrich themselves; and all the most distinguished representatives of Italian democratic socialism thunder in our ears about Italian proletarians' supposed interest in being governed by a wealthy, civilized, "modern" bourgeoisie.

This new sermon by the socialists, which aims to make the conscious proletariat turn away from the main path of class struggle and be herded down the blind alleys of bourgeois reformism, is especially dangerous in that it takes a genuine fact as its premise: that current production is not sufficient for meeting even a narrow range of everyone's needs. After stunning the public with a demonstration of this fact, with a slight sophist expedient the argument turns effect into cause and, without seeming to, draws the incorrect conclusions that serve its purposes.

We need to lift the veil off the system.

It is certain that production as a whole, especially production of basic necessities, is meager, inadequate, almost laughably small compared to what it should and could be.

The starving person passing large stores bulging with foodstuffs, he who lacks everything and sees the lengths to which shopkeepers go to sell off goods in surplus to public demand, may believe that there is enough stuff in abundance for all, and that all that is missing is the means to buy it. Some anarchists, bedazzled by the more or less mystifying figures of statistics, and perhaps also to have an impressive argument in their propaganda that can easily be understood by the ignorant masses, have been able to contend that actual production is far in excess of all reasonable need, and that the people have merely to assume possession of it all, so that all can live in the land of abundance.[155] And the recurrent crises of so-called over-production (meaning that work is in short supply because the masters cannot find a market for the goods they have accumulated) help embed such superficial impressions in the public mind.

But a little cool-headed critique soon makes one understand that this alleged wealth must be a delusion.

What the great mass of the people consume is not enough to satisfy the most basic needs; the vast majority of people eat little and poorly, are poorly clothed, poorly housed, poorly provisioned in everything; many die directly of hunger and cold. If enough is really being produced to meet everyone's needs, and since the majority do not consume enough,

---

155   This refers to the theories presented in the pamphlets *Les Produits de la Terre* and *Les Produits de l'Industrie*, originally published between 1885 and 1887. See also note 247 below.

where on earth would the yearly surplus production be stockpiled? And by what unimaginable aberration would capitalists who produce to sell and to make a profit, persist in producing that which they cannot sell?

Due to inter-capitalist competition and mutual ignorance concerning the quantity of goods that others might be able to put on the market at any given point, due to the spirit of speculation, due to the greed for gain and due to mistakes in planning, it may be and very often is the case that, especially in the manufacturing industries where productive potential is more elastic, production exceeds demand at a certain point; but then the crisis promptly arrives, work is suspended to restore the equilibrium:— and usually, in the long run, production does not outstrip demand. It is demand that governs production and not the other way around.

Besides, in regard to foodstuffs, which are the most vital necessities, one has only to look at the terrible consequences a failed harvest has upon a farming region, to be convinced that, even eating as poorly as most people do, barely enough is being produced for survival from one year to the next.

If the sum of the wealth produced annually, of which today over half goes to a tiny number of capitalists, was equally distributed among everyone, it would bring little improvement in the conditions of the working man: and still, his share would be increased, not in terms of necessities but in the thousands of virtually useless, if not positively harmful trinkets. As to bread, meat, housing, clothing, and other basic necessities, the share the rich overconsume or squander, distributed amongst the countless masses, would make no discernible difference.

Therefore production is insufficient and needs to be increased: on that we agree.

But why is more not being produced today? Why is so much land left untilled or poorly worked? how come so many machines are inoperative? why are so many workers unemployed? How come homes are not being built for everyone, clothes not being made for everybody, etc., when there is plenty of material for doing so and men able and eager to put those materials to use?

The reason is obvious and should not come as a surprise to anyone who calls himself socialist. And it is that the means of production, soil, raw materials, instruments of labor, are not in the hands of those who need what they can produce, but instead are privately owned by a small number of people who use them to make others work for them, and then only as much and in the manner that suits their own interests.

Today a human being has no right to any share in production by the mere fact that he is a human being: if he eats and lives it is only because the capitalist, the owner of the means of production, has an interest in putting him to work in order to exploit him.

Now, the capitalist has no interest in developing production beyond a certain point. Rather, his interest always lies in preserving a relative shortage. In other words, he runs production as long as the product can be sold for more than it costs to him, and increases production as long as the increase in his profits can keep pace. But once he sees that in order to sell his goods he might have to cut his prices too much, and that abundance would lead to an absolute decrease in profits, he stops production and often—and there are thousands examples of this!—destroys some of the products available in order to increase the value of the rest.

So, if we want to see production grow in order to be able to fully meet everyone's needs, it needs to be tailored to the needs that require satisfying, rather than the private profits of the few. Everybody must have a right to enjoy products; everybody must have a right to use the means of production.

If somebody suffering from hunger had the right to take bread, we would need to see to it that there is enough bread to fill us all; and the land would be put to work, and outmoded methods replaced by more productive farming methods. On the other hand, if, as is the case today, existing wealth in the form of means of production and stockpiled goods belongs to a special class of people, and this class, being blessed with everything, can have the hungry gunned down when they shout too loudly, production will keep stopping at the line set by capitalist interests.

In conclusion, the reason for meager output today is limited distribution; and if we want to destroy the effect, we need to destroy the cause.

In order to produce enough for everyone, it is necessary for everyone to have a right to consume enough.

Thereby the socialist thesis is proven, that the poverty problem is first and foremost a question of distribution.

We shall revisit the issue.[156]

A Protest

Translated from "Protesta," *La Rivoluzione Sociale* (London), no. 8 (February 20, 1903)

Dear friends,

A circular was sent round inviting people to participate in an "international antimilitarist Congress" to be held in London, and was signed by a Committee. Among the committee members my name is shown as a member for England.

---

156   This concluding sentence is missing from the edition of *Il Pensiero*.

I am against, for the reasons presented in the previous issue of *La Rivoluzione Sociale*,[157] anarchists taking any part in the Congress initiative, to which all "antimilitarists" are invited without distinction of school or party. In other words, even advocates of capitalism and of government, who might very well want reforms in the organization of the armies, must also want an armed force to defend institutions against attacks by the exploited and oppressed.

I have expressed this opinion of mine repeatedly in public and in private and to those very people who made themselves propagators of the idea of the Congress in London: and I do not understand how my name could have been put under the aforementioned circular.[158]

To avoid misunderstandings and for the propriety of our customs, permit me to publicly protest against this strange habit (of which this is not the only example) of using someone's name not just without consulting them, which is already rather bad, but also against their express will, and for things that he disapproves of, which is truly unspeakable.

Yours
ERRICO MALATESTA.

Our Aims

Translated from "I nostri propositi," *La Rivoluzione Sociale* (London), no. 8 (February 20, 1903)

Someone said that our newspaper signals a change of tactic, almost a repentance for what we had done and propagated before.

Maybe not for the people who said such things, but certainly for the public and for our comrades a few explanations are useful.

We never felt it was reprehensible and shameful to change ideas,

---

157 See "The Proposed Antimilitarist Congress," on p. 178 of the current volume.
158 The congress initiative had already been started in December 1902 by a group of French figures, including Laurent Tailhade, Charles Malato, the socialist deputy Francis de Pressensé and Ch. Vallier (pseudonym of Charles Chevallier), founder of the *Ligue pour la Défense du Soldat*, recently established. The secretary of the London provisional committee was Henry Cuisinier, while among the Italian exiles in London, Carlo Frigerio was active from the start. According to a French police spy, during a meeting on January 6, 1903 Malatesta and Frigerio were appointed delegates to a later meeting for the establishment of the definitive committee. According to another French spy, Malatesta actually participated in a meeting held on January 11th, where he expressed his opposition to the congress. The circular in question was subsequently printed in Paris. The congress was then postponed and was held the next year in Amsterdam.

when change is motivated by new, sincere, convictions and not by dubious personal aims. Continuing to profess and defend earlier ideas, when study and experience have convinced us we were wrong, would seem like the stubbornness of donkeys or the tenacity of vain people, or even bad faith. Therefore if our ideas had changed, we would say so frankly, presenting the reasons, and we would gladly believe we have made a step forward toward the truth.

But whether good or bad, the fact, the simple fact, is that our ideas, since we have been doing the work of propagandists, have not changed at all, and that today we aspire to the same ideals we aspired to yesterday, and we support the same tactic as we did yesterday. If there is a difference in tone, and we believe that there is, between this publication and other prior publications of ours, if the matters that we prefer to address are not those of another time, this is simply because, in our opinion, the current necessities of propaganda have changed, and the errors that now prevail, and that one must fight, are different from those that prevailed at other times. And the essential difference is this: that before the majority of Italian anarchists did not understand how organizing workers into resistance societies could be useful for popular education and revolutionary preparation, and they hoped to start the revolution with only conscious anarchists relying upon general malcontent and the rebellious instincts of the masses; while today, jumping from one extreme to another, they hope for everything from worker organization, and think little or nothing more of revolution and the necessary material preparation.

One of the difficulties found in propaganda is the tendency people have to pay little mind to that which someone actually says, making them say what they want them to say. If someone is your friend, and you have the misfortune of enjoying celebrity and influence, the friend will brag about you saying all the things that seem good to him; if he is your enemy he will make you say all possible blunders, and when you, by dint of persistence, finally succeed in overcoming misrepresentation and making your true thoughts known, then with a triumphant air he will say that you have changed your mind about your errors and that finally "you agree"… with him.

But the worst is that, most of the time, this is sincerely done in full good faith. The friend has you say what he thinks, not because he intends to give authority to his ideas by using your name but because, starting from some of your statements taken in isolation, he draws, using his logic, the consequences that seem to him correct. To him, it seems that you must necessarily arrive at the same conclusions as him. And the enemy attributes to you ideas that are not yours, not out of a desire to slander you (at least we like to hope so) but because he too, blinded by his prejudices, believes that you truly profess those ideas.

At heart, the cause of these errors and misunderstandings is the difficulty that many have in seeing different sides of the matter at the same time, and the tendency to draw final consequences from any premise without taking into consideration the thousand factors that gradually limit the value of that premise. Thus, you speak of the necessity of violent revolution and the material means necessary for it, and at once you find someone who has you saying that all human evolution is reduced to a few primitive brawls and that all of our work is reduced to provoking insurrections without moral preparation and without a determined purpose. You speak of education, of breaking through to the working masses, of worker organization, of small and everyday fights that should serve as training for the major and decisive battle for full emancipation, and they will say that you are deluded by the apparent strength of the *Trade Unions* and that you are not revolutionary. Preach organization and especially the spirit of organization and they will say that you are authoritarian; protest against the authoritarianism observed in organizations that are not imbued, or not imbued enough, with the anarchist spirit, and they will say that you are saying *mea culpa*. Preach association and they will say that you want to suffocate the spirit of initiative and violate individual autonomy;—point out that the first source of any force and the ultimate purpose of every activity is the individual, seek to spark individual energies and they will say that you renounce the principle of association. Criticize an individual action that seems to you bad or foolish, even if done in the name of anarchy, and they will say that you are against individual actions and that, according to you, in order for an act to be acceptable it must be contributed to by a given number of people; then, on another occasion, praise another individual action, of a different nature and done under different circumstances, and they will say that you have converted and that you repent of your past criticism.

We would like our readers, and especially comrades, to not make us say anything other than what we really say and to not draw from our premises, on our behalf, consequences other than those that we draw ourselves. It is understood that anyone can, from what we say, take and leave what he wants, and draw all the conclusions that seem right to him, but on his own behalf, and not in our names.

We do not intend for this note, provoked by unjust remarks that have reached us, to present our entire program, which would then be equivalent to a presentation of anarchist socialism. We rather want to say something on the specific purpose of this publication of ours and the special role we intended to assume by coming to take a place in the midst of the anarchist press.

As we have already said and repeated other times, once anarchists stayed aloof from the labor movement and common people's life and only thought about starting the revolution. Some observed that revolution could not be done without the masses and urged anarchists to keep in touch with the masses and take an active part in the labor movement; and they won:—but they won too much.

The flaw of seeing things from only one side made it so that anarchists who entered the labor movement (we are particularly speaking of Italy) became too absorbed, almost mistook the means, or one of the means, for the end, and—in practice if not in theory—they forgot revolution, which nonetheless remains an essential necessity imposed upon us by the entire environment.

We launched this periodical to call our comrades back to the consciousness of this necessity and to remind them that the government—more or less tolerant as long as it does not fear danger and sees the labor movement as an innocuous pastime or a provident distraction—will use the soldiers as soon as it truly feels threatened, for itself and for the bourgeois class; so, if we do not want to periodically see any movement that starts to become effective suffocated in massacres and prisons, it is necessary to be morally and materially prepared to greet the soldiers fittingly.

In the next issue we will discuss practical methods for enabling ourselves to resist soldiers and start the revolution, in its material part.[159]

Today we will only say that we do not intend to propose a general conspiracy among anarchists of action, something that would excessively expose us to the blows of the police, and that would seem anyway to poorly match the spirit and temperament of our comrades. But we would like for every anarchist to always bear in mind that one day or another he will need to come to blows with armed forces, and therefore make agreements with the comrades closest to him who inspire the most confidence and sympathy in him, to prepare themselves for all possibilities.

And thus from neighbor to neighbor, without formal organization, especially by virtue of a shared spirit, come to build a network of relationships and to have available an abundance of means that would allow us to successfully respond to the government's attacks, or ourselves take the initiative to attack.

---

159 The next issue of the periodical came out on April 5th. In that issue "The Armed Insurrection" appeared, published on p. 196 of the current volume, which included a discussion of the matter in question.

Polemical Digressions.
The Principle of Association

Translated from "Divagazioni polemiche. Il principio di associazione,"
La Rivoluzione Sociale (London), no. 8 (February 20, 1903)

Le Libertaire of Paris, responding to a police insinuation from a bourgeois newspaper, wrote:

"Would it therefore be necessary to continuously repeat that there can be no association among people who love, like the anarchists do, their complete autonomy and the complete development of their character?"

And we, convinced that comrades from *Le Libertaire* wanted to say something other than what the aforementioned words literally mean, deplored the habit of writing in a way that lends itself to false interpretations and intentional slander by enemies.[160]

This was disliked by a contributor to *Il Grido della Folla* and caused him to respond to us, in a bitter and indignant tone, with two columns of prose that... do not respond to us.[161]

He says that "we do not want to understand what difference there is between the natural reality of an ordinary shared understanding in the multiple relations of human life and the associations that ineluctably are based on authoritarianism..." And he adds: "Was it ever said that men are not free to come to agreements among themselves? But the associations we fight are certainly not born from this agreement, which is a need."

This means that our contradictor calls "understanding" what we call "association" and that he does not actually fight against association in general, but certain determined forms of association.

Is it not the case to once again deplore the urge to express oneself in a paradoxical manner, in order to then argue about words?

Such skirmishes made of saber strokes in the air seem so pointless to us, that we would not even have heeded the article from *Il Grido della Folla*, if its writer had not interpreted a sentence we wrote as an insult and an insinuation, which were far from our intention.[162] And we wrote this note especially to lay claim to our right to freely express our

---

160   See "Facts and Opinions" (December 1, 1902), p. 157 of the current volume.

161   The article, signed by "Victor" and dated "Cairo, January 9, 1903," appeared in *Il Grido della Folla* of January 22, 1903 and was entitled "Ancora dell'Associazione" (Again on association).

162   In the previous article Malatesta had written: "Saying that anarchists do not associate is a defensive expedient, of dubious taste and more dubious result, when the police drag us to court with accusations of true or false plots." The contributor to *Grido della Folla* had replied: "And here it is insinuated, without seeming to, that those who are not associated sheep are nothing but cowards."

opinions, without any need on the part of those who disagree with us to take offense.

When we want to insult someone we know how to do so openly, in clear language, and we never make use of veiled or cowardly insinuations.

Facts and Opinions

Translated from "Fatti ed Opinioni," *La Rivoluzione Sociale* (London),
no. 8 (February 20, 1903)

THE END OF UNIONISM.—Another ruling by English magistrates has come to show that workers are always wrong in the legal field, and cannot put up serious and effective resistance against capitalist tyranny.

The Denaby miners are on strike and should receive assistance from their union, in view of which they contributed to build up resistance funds through their weekly contributions.

But a member of the union—just one, paid and directed by the masters—asks the judge to prohibit the union from supporting its striking members; and the judge, drawing from obscure and insidious legal texts, orders the union's representatives to comply with the requested prohibition.

At this point, if the union keeps right on going and provides assistance, it is subject to a criminal trial for contempt of the magistrate's ruling and a civil trial for compensation of damages inflicted upon the owners, which means that a few people will go to jail and the social funds will be consumed in trial expenses and payments of fines and compensation.

And after this, if workers do not understand that in order to win they have to leave legality behind, it is truly not the fault of the masters!

*
**

INFIRM MILITARISM.—Belgium's minister of war has declared that socialism is making great progress in the ranks of the army and that if he can count on the soldiers in the event of an invasion, it is very doubtful that they can be used to repress an uprising by the people.

And this will probably be the reason why the governments will end up implementing the wish of the "antimilitarist" bourgeois, to decrease the number of soldiers... and increase the number of police officers. A reason certainly not to the liking of the bourgeois but therefore very much to our liking!

*
**

INTRANSIGENT SOCIALISTS. —Since there are those who ask us, we frankly say that we have little sympathy for intransigent socialists, so-called revolutionaries, led by Ferri, Labriola, Soldi, etc.[163]

And this is because, despite a vague hope that the best among them, realizing the corruption that authoritarianism and parliamentarism have brought to socialism, can become anarchists, we greatly fear that, speaking and acting as a few years ago Turati and Bissolati spoke and acted, they must end up the way Turati and Bissolati have ended up.

Perhaps, since it is also necessary to save appearances and somehow distinguish oneself from one's opponents, they will wait until the monarchy has given way to the republic to become ministerial supporters and candidates, but for us this does not make a big difference.

After all, it would not be difficult to recall acts and words from some of these "revolutionaries" that show them to be even less revolutionary and less socialist than their comrades of the other trend: which is truly no small feat.[164]

The Paris Commune and the Anarchists

Translated from "La Comune di Parigi e gli anarchici," *La Settimana Sanguinosa 18 marzo–24 maggio* (London), single issue (March 18, 1903)

For many years anarchist critique has scrutinized the events known under the name of the Paris Commune, and little or nothing remains of the communalist regime, as it was understood in 1871 Paris, that can be accepted and given in example by the anarchists.[165]

The Commune was a parliamentary government, and like all governments it was obliged to be authoritarian and paralyze the people's energy, perhaps against the intention and will of its constituents.

The social reforms that were part of the announced program either remained platonic desires or, if decreed, amounted to nothing because they were made, or intended to be made, into laws when what was needed was action, immediately and directly performed by the people.

---

163   See note 101 above.

164   We omitted the next section of the column, signed by "Nolano."

165   The Paris Commune was the municipal government that arose on March 18, 1871, from a popular uprising against the government of Adolphe Thiers, who came to power after France's defeat in the Franco-Prussian war. Thiers, who took refuge in Versailles, unleashed a ruthless repression in the week of May 21–28, 1871, known as the "bloody week," referenced by the title of the single issue in which this article was published. For more of Malatesta's analysis of the Paris Commune, see "The Paris Commune," in the volume covering years 1899–1900 of these *Complete Works*, pages 238–244.

The fight against reactionary plots turned out odious and ineffective because they made use of the usual police weapons—suppression of the press, persecutions, arrests, shootings—rather than leaving everyone the widest liberty and, to weaken their enemies, counting on winning the support of the masses through the goodness of actions favorable to them.

And the Commune was not only a government, but it was also a bourgeois government, since, despite high-sounding statements, it respected and defended bourgeois privileges.

Therefore it fell, honored by the sublime heroism of its own, but to the indifference of the majority, who saw no considerable difference between it and the governments that had preceded it.

Despite all this, and even more that anarchists have said and could say against the Paris Commune, they continue to commemorate it and honor its memory.

This is because it was an insurrectionary act.

Today, as even among us some express the tendency to wait for legal or quasi-legal means to give more than what they can humanly give, it is good to remember, through the example of Paris, how to tear the oppressing yoke off of one's neck.

E. MALATESTA.

[Speech Given in London on March 18, 1903]

COMMUNE MEETING
Freedom (London) 17, no. 175 (April 1903)

The meeting to celebrate the thirty-second anniversary of the Paris Commune was held this year at the Athenæum Hall, and considering the disadvantages we laboured under it was a decided success.[166]

...

Malatesta urged the importance of revolutionary action and lamented the fact that the workers of Milan, in 1898, limited themselves to throwing stones at

---

166   In addition to Malatesta, speakers included Louise Michel, Lothrop Withington, Fernando Tárrida del Mármol, Frank Kitz, Edward Leggatt, Seraphine Pajaud, and Jenny Atkinson. Two other speakers, Shepherd and Wess, opted out of speaking due to scheduling problems. Kropotkin, convalescing, could not participate but sent a letter. The session was presided over by Harry Kelly.

the troops who were shooting them down, instead of turning their guns on them.

...

LETTERS FROM ABROAD

Translated from "Lettere dall'estero," *Il Grido della Folla* (Milan) 2, no. 11 (April 2, 1903)

London, *March 19.*

(CH. BERRUTI). Yesterday evening a tribute to the Paris Commune was held at Atheneum Hall. After the very long speeches by several Englishmen and Louise Michel's impassioned words, Enrico Malatesta took the floor. Starting to speak about the Commune, he found a way to graft a statement we liked into his speech, as we are always pleased to see the truth acknowledged.

Essentially, Malatesta stated, to our great amazement, that after having fought for so many years for organization—the much vaunted organization—he has now realized that the fruits organization has given are far from what could have been expected. In fact he remarked that following this tactic, the more legalitarian tendencies are infiltrating within the element that is called anarchist-socialist.[167]

...

The Armed Insurrection

Translated from "L'insurrezione armata," *La Rivoluzione Sociale* (London), no. 9 (April 5, 1903)

Despite the fact that our governments show more and more clearly everyday their firm intention to drown in blood any popular action that seriously threatens the current social establishment, many who want to tear down this establishment, comrades of ours, continue to consider the question of means for material struggle to be insignificant, and to put all

---

167   The report evidently stretches Malatesta's arguments from an anti-organizationist perspective. In fact, a polemical reference to the trend, that also appeared among anarchists, "to wait for legal or quasi-legal means to give more than what they can humanly give" was also present in the previous article on the Commune that appeared in *La Settimana Sanguinosa.* However, it is probable that Malatesta's actual argument instead followed what was expressed in the circular "To the Italian-Language Anarchists," reproduced on p. 101 of the current volume, in which a self-critique was performed on behalf of organizationist anarchism.

of their hopes in one hundred forms of agitation: economic organization of workers, refusal to pay taxes and rent, refusal by farmers to deliver the products of the earth to the masters, general strike—all excellent things, but either useless or impossible if they cannot count on the intervention of good rifles or equivalent arms.

It has even become commonplace to say that today, with the improved weapons soldiers have available and with the quick means of communication, a victorious insurrection is no longer possible, and that making barricades and '48-style uprisings would be exposing oneself to a certain and useless defeat: and so we have arrived at this absurdity of wanting to preach revolution by making propaganda of fear.

The article by comrades Baldazzi and Chiesa that we are publishing in this issue is proof of the tendency we herein deplore.[168] They propose good things, but they are wrong in presenting such things as replacements for the violent struggle, when instead such things cannot even begin to be achieved without precisely bringing about the violence they want to avoid.

Power of rhetoric! It began with saying that workers could starve the bourgeoisie by merely folding their arms, which was a way of emphasizing that the workers produce everything and that the bourgeoisie lives as a parasite on the product of the efforts of others; and then it finished with the belief that if workers really came to an agreement and stopped working, the bourgeois would immediately capitulate, or they would calmly die of hunger and free the world from their presence without much ado!

Instead, the clear and evident truth is that if workers go on strike and wish to respect the law—that is to say, if they leave the bourgeois the things that are lawfully theirs—these workers would be the ones to have to surrender, or they would die of hunger, long before the masters lacked anything:—therefore it is an absolute necessity to proceed with the immediate expropriation and sharing of at least foodstuffs, which implies an inevitable conflict with the armed force that defends the property of the lords. In fact, as has already happened other times, fearing that strikers will make an attempt at the rights of the masters, authority will seize the initiative of violence and end the matter with gunshot and arrests.

Therefore it is clear that we must either be resolved to fight, and thus be prepared to do so at an advantage, or resign ourselves to being eternally defeated.

---

168   The article, sent by the Bolognese Giovanni Baldazzi and Pietro Chiesa, was entitled "Lo Sciopero Internazionale" (The international strike) and proposed the extension of the general strike to the international sphere, starting with forms of agitation like those listed by Malatesta in the beginning paragraph of his article.

Furthermore it is not true that the improved weapons governments have available today make them invincible. It is sufficient that revolutionaries only know how to adapt their strategy to current conditions. And a hundred modern events show that if authority easily remains victorious in conflicts with the people, it is not because it is invincible but because the people in general and revolutionaries in particular always allow themselves to be caught off-guard by events.

The first consequence resulting from the increased power of the repressive means of governments is that today, except for cases of fortunate combinations of circumstances that cannot be relied upon, it is not possible to rise up and win if one is not prepared. The rapidity of means of communication that allow the government to quickly concentrate troops at threatened points, imposes upon revolutionaries the necessity of simultaneous, large movements. And for this purpose large strikes, and better still a general strike, offer precious opportunities.

Improved weapons impose the necessity of equipping oneself with the means capable of resisting them. Chemistry and mechanics must not be advanced only for the oppressors.

There is a part of the work that can and must be performed by the large masses: there is another that can only be done by groups properly organized and prepared in advance.

Strikes, resistance to government orders, protest against an injustice that upset the public can be, or can be made to be, occasions to provoke conflict with authority and push the people to revolution.

But for this to succeed, it is useful that there are groups that possess weapons or know where to go and get them; groups that already have a battle plan ready and are prepared to execute it; groups that know how to opportunely make use of iron, fire, explosives; groups that have the necessary contacts to widen and spread the revolt; groups that know the residences and gathering places of officials in order to stop them at the right moment from reaching their regiments; groups prepared to take all initiatives useful to involving the masses of people and unraveling the government's resistance.

Since war is necessary and inevitable, let us insist on its difficulties only to find the ways to overcome them.

Facts and Opinions

Translated from "Fatti e Opinioni," *La Rivoluzione Sociale* (London), no. 9 (April 5, 1903)

Symbolic. —A Hungarian minister and a Hungarian deputy, wishing to fight each other in a duel, go to do so in the officials' barracks.

This being a matter of killing, it is natural that they go to the butchers' house.

And since the killing is taking place among men, they chose the butchers of human flesh.

*
**

Causes and effects. —In the latest administrative elections of Ancona (in which the monarchists won), the anarchists did not publish their usual abstentionist manifesto.

A correspondent from *L'Agitazione* cast suspicion that they refrained from doing so in order to not cause grief for the republicans, their allies in the Chamber of Labor, and to ingratiate themselves with the latter for the upcoming executive Commission elections.

We do not know what grounds such a suspicion is based upon; but to us, the mere fact that such a presumption has become possible seems to prove the terrible slope that these anarchists have embarked upon, accepting and soliciting positions in labor organizations.

It begins with joining forces with other parties; then one sacrifices a little of his own ideas and his own strategy for good relations with allies; then...

And then you know where it ends!

Parliamentarism, with its lies and its corruption, is also found outside of the legislative halls.

*
**

Police officers. —The Italian Consulate in London continues, naturally, to be nothing else than a police bureau.

A new spy has been discovered, a certain Luigi Beffagnotti, who tried to pass himself off as an anarchist.

The Consulate may continue; its agents are not the ones who draw us into traps.

Its plots are only useful in making every honest person consider it a dishonor to have any relationship with it.

SECTION IV
Anarchists at Congress

[Private Conversation, London, June 1903]

Translated from a report by "Virgilio" to the Ministry of the Interior, London, June 17, 1903[169]

As I have previously written you, Malatesta was supposed to speak at the Rally for those incarcerated in Spain. Instead, he did not speak and this shows you what diffidence he finds himself facing. I had a long conversation with him that I deem suitable to reproduce almost verbatim.[170]

"It seems to me," Malatesta said, "that rallies and verbal propaganda are now nothing but a waste of time: I no longer believe in these things and therefore I stand back and watch what the others will do."

Question: But why are these things useless if they help propaganda?

Answer: "Propaganda made from chit-chat. It takes action!"

Question: And why did you not go to preach your theory of the deed?

Answer: I have been preaching it for decades, but it leads to nothing.

Question: Yet the anarchist movement has never been as widespread as it is today.

Answer: A movement that is worth nothing, or better, I do not believe in it.

Question: But look, for example, at the outpouring of support and the numerous contributions for "Il Grido della Folla": does not this seem something to you?

Answer: I am telling you, I do not agree with anyone. "L'Agitazione" and "L'Avvenire Sociale" have become too bourgeois. "Il Grido della Folla" is scatter-brained. Furthermore I especially disagree with those from "Il Grido della Folla" because I do not see that they have a clear vision of their objective, they repeat what has already been done and said thirty years ago, they have their heads in the clouds, and they have all the shortcomings and uncertainties taught to them by Gavilli.[171] You say they are young? And I tell you they are old; when we met them here, they were among those who did not know what they wanted; they brought misery and confusion. Now they have gone to Italy and they seem to have become luminaries in social science.

---

169   Manuscript, Archivio Centrale dello Stato, Rome, Casellario Politico Centrale, box 2949.

170   "Virgilio," whose true name was Ennio Bellelli, was the spy directly assigned by the Italian government to report on the activities of anarchists in London. A report of a private conversation by a spy, who possibly at that time had already raised suspicions, obviously needs to be considered with even more caution than what spy reports generally require. However, we decided to include it in this collection because, aside from the language being used, the ideas reported, as a whole, seem to be in line with those expressed elsewhere by Malatesta and may contribute to shed light on his relationship with the Italian anarchist movement in this period.

171   See note 107 for information on Gavilli.

Question: It seems to me that you are exaggerating the issue.

Answer: That may be, but I do not agree with anyone and nobody agrees with me anymore. I therefore stay on the side (bitterly). And then I can only be a party leader; not being in agreement with the others I remain on the side and watch. I cannot be a follower. I preach and I have preached that it is useless to chit chat and that violence is necessary. (With rage) I need to go to Italy. Ah if I had the money, I would go to Italy! But I do not only need travel expenses, you understand me? Now the time is good and I would show what I can still do. I have been looking for money for a while. At one time, two or three years ago, it seemed that I had found an arrangement but then everything fell apart. There was a time that I thought highly of Morgari as well, but then I saw he was a buffoon. I do not believe in anyone anymore. Perhaps still De Andreis, Pirolini...[172] However there would still be a lot to do, and I will look for a way to get to Italy. For the time being I have an idea to make *incubators* for chickens etc. I could also make them for silkworms. In Italy I will try to send them to Maffei. Once, with the excuse of agricultural experiments, we agreed to obtain from the Government a certain quantity of dynamite that I would use myself. This too went belly up. As I tell you, I am disheartened. Among the youth, many approve of violence, they say that individual action is alright, but they say it the way someone repeats a sentence by ear without considering the meaning. They say so without feeling anything. None of them would be ready for a coup de main and this is what I need.

Question. You want to get there with organization. Yet you must see that for your purpose, with or without organization, you could reach the identical objective.

Answer. No, for me organization is not a question of tactics; it is a question of principle.

Question. It seems to me you are exaggerating. The principle is the anarchist idea; organization is a temporary phenomenon, at least with regards to the attitudes that it takes on under given circumstances. You yourself acknowledge that even the individualists are implicitly organized, without confessing it and even saying the opposite.

Answer: When they undertake an action, yes, they are and cannot be otherwise. (With rage) But then they fight me and organization in an indecent manner. Enough, I'll stay on the side and watch, meanwhile I will find money and tomorrow I will come see you and we will chat.

The conversation was then interrupted by the intervention of a third (Sabattini).

...

---

172   Oddino Morgari, socialist, had helped Malatesta escape forced residence in 1899; Luigi De Andreis and Giovan Battista Pirolini were prominent figures of the republican party, of whom the latter was secretary in 1897–98.

[Speech Given in London on September 6, 1903]

Translated from a report by police commissioner Mandolesi to the
Ministry of the Interior, London, September 8, 1903[173]

SUBJECT: *Forthcoming publication of a pamphlet by Enrico Malatesta*[174]

Sunday evening during a meeting held at Galassini's home, Malatesta read the main points of the pamphlet I reported about in my previous dispatch dated August 10th.[175]

He is set on the goal of persuading anarchists to enter labor associations of whatever political color they are, to fight individuals who use associations as their own tools, to foment the spirit of rebellion and to facilitate propaganda and thus increase the number of rebels and expedite the day of social demands.

He hopes this pamphlet will appear within fifteen days at most.[176]

[Letter to Italian Anarchists in the United States, London, before February 8, 1904]

Translated from a report by the Italian Consulate of New York to the
Ministry of the Interior, February 8, 1904[177]

Malatesta Enrico, anarchist[178]

A printed letter by the anarchist Malatesta Enrico is circulating among the anarchist groups of New York and New Jersey. In the letter he deplores the

---

173 Manuscript, Archivio Centrale dello Stato, Rome, Casellario Politico Centrale, box 2949.

174 Note in text margin.

175 This meeting took place on Sunday, September 6th. Antonio Galassini was one of Malatesta's closest collaborators, having been a manager and editor of *La Rivoluzione Sociale*. In the previous dispatch Mandolesi refers to, he had written that, during a meeting held on August 8th, Malatesta proposed releasing a pamphlet entitled *What Anarchists Should Do in Organizations*, that he was going to write and submit for discussion in a forthcoming meeting. Malatesta had already tackled the subject the year prior in the article "Anarchists in Labor Unions," reproduced on p. 110 of the current volume, announcing that he would soon address the subject as thoroughly as possible.

176 The September 29, 1903, issue of *L'Avanguardia Libertaria* of Ancona announced that a pamphlet by Malatesta entitled *The Action of Anarchists in Labor Chambers* would soon be released. In a report dated December 9th, the spy "Virgilio" wrote that Malatesta "is still due to publish his pamphlet," which nevertheless seems to have never been published.

177 Typescript, Archivio Centrale dello Stato, Rome, Casellario Politico Centrale, box 2949.

178 Note in text margin.

inactivity that has for some time stricken revolutionary anarchy and calls the newspapers fruitless and the protests based on manifestos ineffective. In the aforementioned letter Malatesta regrets that the year 1903 has ended, as he says, *"without a shout of revolt, without a step forward and without the fall of a tyrant."*[179]

. . .

Letter from Malatesta

Translated from "Carta de Malatesta," *Heraldo de Paris* 4, no. 65 (March 10, 1904)

Dear friend: I received your postcard too late; probably because you got my address wrong.

I am sorry I have not been able to see my friend Bonafoux. Please let me know me what the matter is and what decision was taken.

Yours, MALATESTA[180]

---

179   In the latter part of the report the author specifies: "To date it has been impossible for this Office to obtain a copy of the aforementioned letter." In a report dated March 1st the London Consulate excludes the possibility that this letter was printed in London and instead speculates that it was a letter written by Malatesta to some of his friends in America who then printed it to distribute among the anarchists.

180   The recipient is in all likelihood Baldomero Oller, the editor of the London section of the *Heraldo*. The same page on which the letter appears contains summaries of two recent events presided over by Bonafoux in London, neither of which Malatesta seems to have attended. The first was the public inauguration of the London newsroom of the *Heraldo*, on February 17th. The second, to which Oller's invitation probably refers to, was a "meeting of representatives and figures from the international revolutionary party," which took place on February 21st. A disagreement took place at the meeting between those who, like Bonafoux and Oller, asked for immediate public support for the solidarity campaign on behalf of those tortured at Alcalá del Valle, and those who, like Tárrida del Mármol, Cherkezov, and Kelly, wanted to postpone the initiative until the demonstration that was going to take place on March 18th. An agreement was not reached and Bonafoux, together with others, left the meeting. In Alcalá del Valle, in Southern Spain, a general strike on August 1, 1903, had given rise to clashes with the Civil Guard. The subsequent mistreatment of the many arrested people had stirred up an intense protest campaign.

[Speech Given in London]

Translated from Giuseppe Sinicco, *Le memorie di un calzolaio da Borgnano a Londra* (Udine: A. Pellegrini, 1950), p. 78–79

[The author talks about the activity of the London section of the Italian Socialist Party and recalls that "from 1905 to 1919 it only gave signs of life when some big shot came to London: a deputy or a famous person."]

The first big shot hosted was Nicola Barbato. During his lecture he claimed that science was in our favor; but Malatesta stated the opposite. After some discussion, naturally lively, they ended by deciding to hold a debate.[181]

Barbato spoke first demonstrating how the future society had to be collective and international, also because science was increasingly turning peoples into brothers, while the development of mechanization increased unemployment and created the discontent that would end up toppling over the capitalist system. Malatesta instead argued that science was against us because it helped the bourgeoisie to remain in power—creating new instruments of war and increasing its strength—and put it in a more favorable position against the revolutionaries.

. . .

[Speech Given in London on January 27, 1905]

LATEST TELEGRAMS

Translated from "Últimos telegramas," *Heraldo de Madrid* 16, no. 5180 (January 28, 1905)

. . .

MEETING AT WONDERLAND. —LEAGUE AGAINST TYRANTS. —A SOLDIER'S PROPHESY.

---

181 Nicola Barbato, socialist representative known for taking a leading role in the Sicilian Fasci movement of 1893 and deputy from 1900 to 1904, emigrated to the United States in 1904, after finishing a lecture tour in Europe among Italian emigrants. Since Barbato spent several years in the United States, while Sinicco states he was the first famous guest during the period he indicates, the debate in question must have taken place before Barbato left for the United States, therefore, at the latest, in 1904.

London 28 (9.10 in the morning)

In the meeting held yesterday at Wonderland, in addition to Tchaikowsky's proposal, the enormous audience that attended the meeting unanimously approved Malatesta's amendment on the necessity of organizing a global movement of the proletariat against tyrants in all countries.

This amendment was supported by German, Turkish, Russian, Spanish, French, Jewish, Italian, Yankee, and English speakers, whose energetic speeches aroused great enthusiasm.

The Russian lieutenant Serebrjakov, army deserter and refugee in London, prophesied that the majority of troops currently in Manchuria will rebel as soon as they return to Russia.[182]

...

TRANSLATION FROM "RELAZIONE SUL MOVIMENTO ANARCHICO E SOVVERSIVO NEL MESE DI GENNAIO," BY POLICE COMMISSIONER MANDOLESI, LONDON, FEBRUARY 1905[183]

...

Protest rally against the Russian massacres[184]

On January 27 at Wonderland Hall, Whitechapel, a rally was held to protest against the Russian massacres.[185]

The large hall was packed: no less than 4,000 people were present, the majority being Russian, Polish, and Jewish. Only a dozen Italians.

Malatesta spoke in French, which is a language generally understood by all revolutionaries.

Speaking of the general strike he said that, whether it happens in Russia or in Italy, it has only one way to succeed: that of being violent. All peaceful

---

182   In February 1904, war had broken out between Russia and Japan for imperial domination in Manchuria and Korea, during which Russia suffered a series of heavy defeats. In January 1905 anti-militarist demonstrations against the war took place in several European cities.

183   Manuscript, Archivio Centrale dello Stato, Rome, collection "Divisione affari generali e riservati, Archivio generale," series 1905, box 22, folder 377, subfolder 2.

184   Note in text margin.

185   Demonstrations against the tsarist government, which had grown in intensity after the defeats in the Russian-Japanese war, culminated in St. Petersburg with the mid-January strikes and the demonstration of January 22, 1905, organized by Pope Gapon to present a petition to the tsar: the unarmed demonstrators were massacred by the hundreds before the Winter Palace in what went down in history as "bloody Sunday" and which is considered the starting point of the 1905 Russian revolution.

strikes, he said, will only lead to useless massacres of the people... However he had reason to feel comforted by the fact that the friends of the Russian people had faced the danger of reactionary vendetta pushing the masses toward emancipation, although he did not share the ideas under which the strike was organized.

He identified the reason for the lack of success in the fact that the people were made to hope for justice from the Tsar, with the result that the government had enough time to arm itself, assembling loyal soldiers and thereafter confidently proceeding to massacre.

He continued his violent speech demonstrating that armed rebellion is necessary always and everywhere.

Strikes, he said, starve the workers, not the rich, but if the strikers responded to gunshot with bombs and other means more lethal than rifles, the outcome would be different. Hence, if the Russians had brought bombs with them, the Cossacks, out of a fear of death, would have escaped as they escape before the Japanese or would have refused to shoot at the people.

He concluded saying that it is time to stop producing and start taking, as the raid is the proletariat's only insurrectional form, and finally that the *fall of the Romanoff dynasty is the bell that awakens all of Europe to consciousness and to revolt.*

Of course he was continuously interrupted by applause and at the end was the object of a warm tribute.

An agenda sounding protest against Russian barbarism was approved with furious enthusiasm.

...

[Speeches Given in London on February 25 and 26, 1905]

Translated from "Relazione sul movimento sovversivo in Londra nel mese di febbraio," by police commissioner Mandolesi, London, March 1905[186]

[*A section of the report is dedicated to the February 25th inauguration of the Popular University at Euston Buildings, Euston Street. First Tárrida del Mármol spoke, explaining the importance of education in shaking off the capitalistic yoke.*]

Malatesta was more clear. After encouraging the audience to attend classes, he said that the Popular University will be a center of mutual education, that it

---

186   Typescript, Archivio Centrale dello Stato, Rome, collection "Divisione affari generali e riservati, Archivio generale," series 1905, box 22, folder 377, subfolder 2.

will benefit the workers and show them how progress in science, mechanics, but especially in chemistry, can be used to shake off the yoke of capitalism. Clearer allusions to instruction on how to build bombs could not be made. And in fact Malatesta reserved for himself the teaching of physics and chemistry.

[*Later the report contains a brief summary of a lecture given at the Popular University on the following day, February 26th, by Varlaam Cherkezov, on the conditions of the Russian people.*]

After a brief summary of the speech Malatesta came to conclude that the only way to win would be to make recourse to the general strike provided that it was violent.

Advance notice of a pamphlet by Malatesta on the general strike[187]

The same Malatesta conveyed to his friends a desire to publish a pamphlet or at least a manifesto on the general strike, seizing the occasion of what has happened in Russia and then going back to what happened in Italy. The purpose would be to incite the Italian working class to timely equip itself with weapons and then proclaim the general strike. He would like to flood Italy with his manifesto and for this he would ask his comrades to help collecting the necessary amount.

. . .

Revolutionary London: Assembly of Russian Terrorists [by Luis Bonafoux]

Translated from "Londres revolucionario: Asamblea de terroristas rusos," *Heraldo de Madrid* 16, no. 5224 (March 13, 1905)

[*The article, dated London, March 10, summarizes a meeting of Russian revolutionaries organized by Varlaam Cherkezov, so that they could present their opinion on the situation in Russia to Bonafoux. The central part of the article reports statements made by Cherkezov himself.*]

. . .

A few minutes before Tcherkessoff finished, a figure entered the hall. Tormented and tempestuous, he could not be mistaken for anyone else. More sallow and bilious than ever; more wild, withered and pallid—with the avenging whiteness of lightning, that seemed to bury itself and then resurface in his very black tousled head –; his pupils blazing more than ever with chaotic blackness, Malatesta, his body still suffering from recent physical illness, but with his spirit always keen and tough, told me:

---

187   Note in text margin.

— My presence here is useless. But I heard that you were here, and I have something to tell you. Not now, later...

— For many reasons—I answered him—I am happy to see you. Seems that the situation in Russia...

— Yes, it is progressing, although with some slowness. We sent a few comrades there, very determined, who succeeded in crossing the border. They are good lads. They will do good work...

[Classes Held at the Popular University of London, March–April 1905]

Translated from "Relazione del movimento dei sovversivi in Londra nei mesi marzo ed aprile," by police commissioner Mandolesi, London, May 1905[188]

[*A section of the report is dedicated to the Popular University and describes its collapse, due to the lack of funds, which had culminated in a fundraising concert planned for April 29th that turned out to be a failure.*]

Malatesta, who under the auspices of this University hoped to find new followers, is very saddened.

He had set to work with great enthusiasm and at the beginning his school had a greater attendance.

From the first classes he had sought to demonstrate that physics and chemistry provide a clear demonstration of the logical precision of anarchist thought.

Speaking for example about chemical affinity, he alluded to the mutuality that should exist in human relations. Speaking about the diagram of divergent forces, he explained how this reasoning can be nicely applied to sociology. Supposing that one force is the bourgeois tendency and the other the revolutionary tendency—divergent by nature but acting on the same point, present-day society—it is clear that the resultant, if there will be any resultant, is the direction that society will take under the influence of two forces. The revolutionary force must exceed the other force in proportion to the change we want to effect on society, since the new society will not be that which we asked for, but the resultant of ours and the opposite force etc.

As you can see Malatesta's classes, in reality, are just classes in anarchy.

During the last class he spoke of explosives, explaining their physicochemical causes, and of the production of ordinary gun powder and flash cotton, describing the heating properties of certain chemical combinations.

---

188 Typescript, Archivio Centrale dello Stato, Rome, collection "Divisione affari generali e riservati, Archivio generale," series 1905, box 22, folder 377, subfolder 2.

If he could have continued his classes, he would have openly taught the methods for producing bombs.

. . .

[Speeches Given in London on September 20 and 27, 1905]

Translated from "Relazione mensile, del Mese di Settembre 1905," by police officer Frosali, London, October 9, 1905[189]

. . .

Lectures by Malatesta Enrico.[190]

The anarchist Circle that the Germans opened early last month at 107 Hampstead Road, N. W. and that now counts 74 members, has twice, during the month of September, invited Malatesta to give Lectures.

Malatesta accepted and spoke last September 20 and 27, the first time in the presence of only 10 or 12 people "about the possibilities of making propaganda in London among the indigenous and foreign elements."

The topic was suggested by the fact that during the last month, formation of a resistance society among waiters had been attempted, particularly using the French element as a foundation.

Malatesta summarized what had already been done and attempted in London, observing how almost always personal issues had prevailed and destroyed everything that one had been able to accomplish over long months of patient work. The high rent for the space in which the Club's formation had been attempted, he said, almost always forced the initiators to count on the consumption of drinks to keep the Club going. This always backfired to the disadvantage of propaganda and the education of members.

Although not a "teetotaler" he nevertheless would desire that the club in which he spoke only sold non-alcoholic beverages.

He discussed alcohol abuse, from the social point of view. More than a lecture it was a friendly "causerie."

In the second lecture Malatesta was expected to present the history of the International.

This time as well few people attended the lecture.

Malatesta spoke in French, and not all the German members understand that language.

---

189   Typescript, same archive reference.
190   Note in text margin.

Malatesta limited himself to making a parallel between the current socialist movement and what the workers' International preconized.

He noted how each day the socialist party further forgot the promises that it had made through its most influential representative, Karl Marx, in the Communist Manifesto. He recalled how this publication, which up until a few years ago had been considered original, had been shown to be just an impudent plagiarism Marx had made of the work of the French writer "Considerant," as was very well shown by the articles of comrade "Tcherkesoff" in the newspaper "Les Temps Nouveaux" of Paris.[191] He even mentioned how recent further research by the same comrade uncovered that the famous book by "Engels," friend and collaborator of Marx, titled "Conditions of the English proletariat," released in 1848, was in turn an equally impudent plagiarism, to the detriment of another French writer. Tcherkesoff soon will publish the results of his research in the same Paris newspaper.

Thus the honesty of the socialist party not only in political matters, but also in literary matters, comes to be discredited.[192]

In summary, it was a rather uninteresting lecture on the past, which nevertheless the German audience really liked.

. . .

[Speech Given in London on October 22, 1905]

Translated from "Rapporto Mensile del Mese di Ottobre 1905," by police officer Frosali, London, November 7, 1905[193]

. . .

Lecture by Barsanti Torquato and Malatesta Enrico.[194]

During the past month, in the Socialist Circle of the German Anar., the Italian Socialists organized a lecture on the theme "Socialism and Religion," given by Torquato Barsanti, who arrived from France, whence he was recently expelled.

---

191   In the article "Un plagiat trés scientifique," published in installments by *Les Temps Nouveaux* from April 14 through May 26, 1900, Varlaam Cherkezov argued, with a plethora of details, that the 1848 *Manifesto* by Marx and Engels was plagiarized from *Manifeste de la démocratie au dix-neuvième siècle* by Victor Considérant, published in its second edition in 1847.

192   This sentence is enclosed in quotes, added by hand.

193   Typescript, Archivio Centrale dello Stato, Rome, collection "Divisione affari generali e riservati, Archivio generale," series 1905, box 22, folder 377, subfolder 2.

194   Note in text margin.

The Lecture having been planned for Sunday,[195] about 50 people were present, all Italian and socialist, with the exception of several anarchists who participated in the company of Malatesta.

The Lecturer, who said he had given many lectures in France, was instead very ineffective here in London. He made some unfounded statements about the anarchists, though he declared that he admired and approved Bresci's act. The observations made against the anarchists' tactics caused Malatesta to respond.

Malatesta, reiterating what he has already said in public a number of times, gave a precise critique of the alleged reforms demanded or sometimes obtained by Anar.-socialist parties[196] in several countries and attempted to demonstrate that these reforms have never definitively improved the conditions of the Workers. As regards religion, Malatesta stated he agreed with the lecturer on many points, but said that religion—and the clergy, as the representative of religious formulas—can only exist in a society in which there are the poor and the rich, in which there is Capital and the right of ownership.

. . .

[Speech Given in London on November 16, 1905]

Translated from "Rapporto mensile del mese di Novembre 1905," by police officer Frosali, London, November 30, 1905[197]

. . .

Malatesta Lecture[198]

Thursday, November 16 in the aforementioned place,[199] Malatesta gave a lecture "On the Origins of the World" explaining Darwin's theory, supplemented by his considerations concerning the well-known point: "struggle for life and survival of the fittest."

He attempted to demonstrate that the fittest is not always the best, neither in the way the advanced parties understand it, nor in the way they understand the race in its need to reproduce and improve. The Lecture was given in French and was received rather well.

. . .

---

195 According to an October 24th report by the spy "Virgilio," the lecture took place on October 22nd.

196 It is evident from the context that Malatesta must have instead been referring to democratic socialist parties.

197 Typescript, Archivio Centrale dello Stato, Rome, collection "Divisione affari generali e riservati, Archivio generale," series 1905, box 22, folder 377, subfolder 2.

198 Note in text margin.

199 Wonderland Hall, Whitechapel Road.

[Speeches Given in London on December 2 and 3, 1905]

Translated from "Rapporto mensile del Mese di Decembre 1905,"
by police officer Frosali, London, February 7, 1906[200]

. . .

In the same place,[201] on Saturday, December 2, 1905, small informal concert during which the events in Russia are discussed in a lively manner. Malatesta hopes that Tsarism soon falls.

. . .

During the evening[202] Malatesta spoke at the German Club, in French, on the Topic: The Resistance Society Movement, in France, Italy and England.

He aims to demonstrate that the spirit of class struggle has not yet penetrated the spirit of workers so strongly in England, as it has in Latin countries.

He speaks of what is now customarily called direct action. At several points Malatesta's speech repeats the theoretical part of the enclosed article by Kropotkin, which first appeared in the newspaper *"Les Temps Nouveaux."*[203]

. . .

Dear Comrades of the Board of Directors

Originally published as "Verte genosn fun fervaltungsrate," *Di Fraye Arbayter Velt* (London), no. 4 (December 22, 1905).[204]

We hope that you can give us a little space in our newspaper "F. A. Velt" to publish this little piece of correspondence, as well as comrade Malatesta's letter, which we have not been able to publish until today.

Comrades near and far!

It is indeed unpleasant for us to reopen old wounds, but for us it is an urgent necessity. Already twice the Arbayter Fraynd has given the news that

---

200   Typescript, Archivio Centrale dello Stato, Rome, collection "Divisione affari generali e riservati, Archivio generale," series 1905, box 22, folder 377, sub-folder 2.

201   German Club of Hampstead Road.

202   The day is Sunday, December 3rd.

203   Kropotkin's article "L'Action directe et la Grève générale en Russie" had appeared in the December 2nd edition of *Les Temps Nouveaux.*

204   This English-language translation was based on the Italian translation, performed by Furio Biagini and Marisa Ines Romano, of the original Yiddish version.

*a Frayheyt group is publishing Kropotkin's autobiography and that, beyond
all the rest, representatives of the old Frayheyt group are being solicited to
settle their debts with the people who on March 13, 1905 acted in conspiracy
to take possession of all assets of the old Frayheyt group. Such people subsequently called themselves the "Frayheyt" group, ignoring the fact that the old
Frayheyt group survived the betrayal and continues its work. Consequently
we are calling upon all those who have incurred debts with the old Frayheyt
group through March 13, 1905, so that every single penny they owe is rightfully paid to the old Frayheyt group, otherwise they would end up participating in that shameful act. To confirm our claim, we present a letter from
comrade E. Malatesta, so that our representatives and comrades in general
know how to behave.*[205]

Regards.
"Frayheyt Group"

London, December 20, 1905

*
**

112, High St., Islington.
London, N.
6/4 1905.

To the London "Frayheyt Group."

Dear Comrades!
I refrained from responding to your letter concerning the dispute
with the Ar. Fraynd group as long as possible, because it makes me

---

205   *Der Arbayter Fraynd* (The workers' friend) was the Yiddish-language news-
       paper edited by German anarchist Rudolf Rocker. Most Jewish anarchists in
       London belonged to the group that ran the newspaper. In 1901, the dissident
       group *Frayheyt* (Freedom) originated, which several former collaborators
       of the *Arbayter Fraynd* joined, including L. Baron. The divergence of ideas
       between the two groups overlapped with the financial diatribe to which this
       correspondence refers. According to the members of the *Arbayter Fraynd*
       group, the funds used to acquire the typographic material for the *Frayheyt*
       group rightfully belonged to their newspaper. Later a split developed within
       the *Frayheyt* group, provoked partly by members infiltrating from the out-
       side. During a nocturnal blitz, the dissident faction took possession of the
       Frayheyt group's typographic material, with the intent of returning it to
       the *Arbayter Fraynd* group, which knew and approved of the plan of action.
       After the fact, Baron and his collaborators invited Cherkezov and Malatesta
       to express their opinion on the matter. While the former was in favor of the
       Arbayter Fraynd group, during a meeting held in June 1905 Malatesta took
       the side of the *Frayheyt* group, based on the reasoning developed in the letter
       reproduced herein.

uncomfortable to meddle in a war between comrades. I think rather that it would be best to resolve these problems by mutual agreement instead of involving people from outside, and for this reason I had hoped—since all, both one and the other, are ultimately anarchists—that the spirit of justice and tolerance would triumph in the end and the issue would be sorted out peacefully.

But as it seems that this has not yet taken place, that you insist upon my response and that other comrades ask for my opinion on what happened... I cannot hold back any longer and I must write black on white what I think, so that anyone can analyze it for what it is worth.

As far as I know and mainly for the recognition of others, personally I am absolutely of the opinion that an injustice has been committed against you, because, through a scheme organized with the direct participation of the Ar. Fraynd group, you were robbed of the resources for propaganda that you had collected, which were then given to a rival group, in this case to the same Ar. Fraynd group. As far as I am concerned, I find no justification for this behavior.

To say, as it has been said, that this was an act in the interest of propaganda is not, in my opinion, a justification, not even if the Ar. Fraynd group succeeds in convincing us that it has good reasons to fail to recognize your propaganda from an anarchist point of view.

Recurring to a swindle to prevent someone from making propaganda, just because we do not like it, is an action worthy of a regime or an authoritarian party seeking to take the power for themselves.

But we anarchists can only fight propaganda with propaganda; we can use force only to defend ourselves and only as defense against those who oppress others with violence.

The freedom which we fight for must be valid for the individual and for all, and not for ourselves and our friends.

You surely have the right to defend yourselves from the accusations made against you, to defend your honor before comrades, but I hope that when you do it you will avoid publicity and scandals, which would only work to the advantage of our common enemies. There are things that it would be much better to forget.

With fraternal regards,

Yours
E. Malatesta

Towards Emancipation

Translated from *Verso l'Emancipazione* (Paris), single issue (May 1, 1906)[206]

In the arduous and gory path that humanity laboriously travels, this May First will stand as a milestone, indicating one of the phases in the process by which the proletariat, achieving consciousness of human rights, finally succeeds in breaking its chains and inaugurating the new era of freedom and well-being for all.

This is the grand event: the French workers—unfortunately still poorly supported by comrades from other countries—attempt an organized effort to win the eight-hour day by direct action, and propose to confront and conquer the resistance of the masters through the general strike.

It is not the demanded reform that lends special importance to the movement in question.

This reform, like all reforms that leave the fundamentals of capitalist society intact, has no substantial value.

To work for a master for only eight hours is certainly better than working nine, or ten, or twelve; but the worker would continue to be exploited, and it is moreover quite doubtful that this limit could apply to all categories of workers, under the current system of production and exchange. Conversely, it is certain that the capitalists would first offset the lesser duration of work with increased intensity and then would seek to return to the old schedule, while continuing to demand the greater intensity reached;—and it would always be probable that they would succeed despite the workers' resistance, as masses of unemployed people are at their disposal, and their numbers are destined to continually grow, insofar as the productivity of human labor grows with advances in technology.

Partial reforms, that of the eight-hour workday like all the others, have a tendency to establish privileged categories of workers in hostile conflict with the more miserable masses, and often end up doing more bad than good:—if they improve the position of some, they tend therewith to worsen the condition of others; if they manage to make the life of workers more tolerable, by the same token they tend to consolidate the whole of bourgeois society.

---

206   The single issue, which bore the subtitle "Publication by a Group of Anarchists," was printed at the same time as the May First demonstration in Paris and was distributed free of charge. The single issue's collaborators included, among others, Amilcare Cipriani, Charles Malato, and Felice Vezzani. As Luigi Fabbri recalls, Malatesta traveled incognito to Paris for the occasion, as he was affected by an expulsion decree. At the time French revolutionary syndicalism, in which the anarchists played a predominant role, was at its height, and therefore May First was going to be an opportunity for a field battle around the eight-hour workday platform.

But this does not mean that, if we cannot immediately start the revolution and change the social establishment from top to bottom, we must remain inert, and content ourselves with simple theoretical propaganda. Nor does it mean that the movements of the masses—which are still unable to understand the concatenation of factors that holds them in slavery, yet grow intolerant of their pain and seek, perhaps by the wrong paths, to remedy it—are useless and must be opposed or neglected by he who has a more complete understanding of social matters and thinks of more radical remedies.

After all, human institutions are merely the external forms which house, more or less uncomfortably, whatever men can and want to put in them. While abstractly having their own logic, that is to say a tendency to produce certain determined effects, in the complex reality of life institutions can produce different results and even results that are the opposite of what would be in their nature. Their content and scope change, up to a certain point, with the ideas, feelings, activities, and resistance of men who make and unmake them, benefit or suffer from them. And when they finally become incompatible with general desires, they die,—by means of a violent revolution, if they use violence to sustain themselves.

Anything is useful, which develops the desire for freedom, well-being, and justice, and thus hastens the moment when the incompatibility between old institutions and new needs becomes evident.

Today's capitalistic and authoritarian society, a result of the centuries-old struggle that men have fought amongst themselves, continues to be a battlefield in which each class and each individual seeks to ensure the best possible conditions without bothering about the others, nay, considering the others as material to exploit and dominate. Whatever social forms derive from the contrast of interests and passions, each person's actual conditions are those he has been able to win and defend with the force he has available. Therefore the only value of reforms is to indicate the force of those who won them; this goes to say that they only represent real progress, a step on the way to emancipation, when they are seized from the oppressors by the force of the oppressed, which, far from accepting them with a grateful spirit and being satisfied with them, see in the concession a sign of the enemy's weakness and take advantage of it to demand increasingly more.

*
**

What makes the current movement so interesting and thus full of promise is the spirit that animates it, the method that it follows.

So far, except for particular cases, workers, unconscious of their rights and the force they could find in the union, have hoped alleviation of their suffering would come from others.

They hoped for the aid of a chimeric god, and their naive belief only served to hold them submissive and to feed one of the worst classes of parasites and scammers, the priests.

They trusted in the spirit of justice and in the goodness of the masters, and they were always ferociously mistreated.

They hoped for protection from the rulers, and these, exploiters and oppressors themselves, were natural allies of masters and the most effective instrument of oppression.

They followed the middle classes in the fights against the nobility, and only succeeded in creating new oppressors.

They supported this or that political party, shed their blood to replace one government with another, and only served as springboards for the worst adventurers.

Finally understanding they could hope for nothing from other classes and that *the emancipation of the workers must be conquered by the workers themselves*, they chose from among their ranks those who they believed were most capable and most devoted, and asked these people to fight for them. They pushed them up, they succeeded in sending them to the legislative bodies, thus believing to penetrate the enemy fortress, and were again betrayed: the workers who became members of the ruling class provided the best evidence of what poor people who become rich usually do; and if somebody remained personally honest, he was, naturally, completely powerless to be of use to the workers' cause.

And here today, finally, they, the workers—or rather the most energetic and intelligent, who in the end are the ones who decide the fate of battles—tired of disappointments and betrayals, reflecting that throughout history the oppressed have never achieved anything beyond what they were able to take, push away pimps and philanthropists and politicos, take their own fate in their own hands, and decide to act directly.

*
**

This May's movement is an affirmation—let us hope a grandiose one—of the new path the workers have set out upon as they fight for their emancipation. It will not mark a major win, perhaps it will not even be the occasion of a big battle; but it will certainly be a large experiment which must be learned from for the near future. It will serve as preparation and training for the decisive battle which will no longer concern partial and therefore ephemeral and illusory improvements, but will be fought for the definitive abolition of capitalism and authority. That battle will not be a matter of putting a limit on the exploitation and oppression by means of more or less general strikes but of demolishing political power and pooling the social wealth by means of revolution.

May all conscious workers, may all revolutionaries, take an active part in the movement, and may they make an effort to broaden it, prolong it, and make it produce the biggest outcome possible.

And when the acute period is over, and ordinary calm returns, may the work immediately begin to resume the fight soon under better conditions.

Errico Malatesta.

Source: International Institute of Social History, Amsterdam

Reformist Courage and Coherence

Translated from "Coerenza e coraggio riformista,"
Verso l'Emancipazione (Paris), single issue (May 1, 1906)

In Paris, there is a little congregation, comprised of a dozen members, that has given itself the title, neither brief nor modest, of: *The Italian Socialist Federation of the Seine.* Almost one word for each member.

This "Socialist Federation etc. etc." felt the need to publish, on the subject of May First, a short manifesto, dedicated to the Italian workers living in France, that is a monument of reformist prudence and eloquence.

After blabbing some nonsense on the debt of gratitude Italian workers owe the French and on forgiving insults; after speaking of dignity, pride, solidarity, and other beautiful things, it addresses these words to the worker:

"Foreigner, you are not allowed to participate in the struggle in an excessively conspicuous manner, but you are allowed and morally obligated to be in solidarity, to stop working after eight hours.

"Should you not feel the courage to do so, rather than showing yourself to be a coward, rather than enduring the insult and shame that fall upon traitors, *stay home that day, do not show up. And wait for the decision of the French comrades before going back to work.*

"This is the act of solidarity that you must perform and that you shall perform!"

Did you understand, Italian worker? You who work and suffer alongside the French worker, you are still a **FOREIGNER**! And it is the scientific socialists who tell you so. Lift your hat and shout: *Vive la Patrie! Vive l'Armée!*

And then you must also clearly understand that, to be in solidarity with French comrades, you just have to shut yourself up at home, because "you are not allowed to participate in the struggle in an excessively conspicuous manner," since you would need to obtain such a concession from the police or… the Italian Socialist Federation.

And with this they have the audacity to speak of courage, pride, solidarity: to launch tirades, curses, threats, and to spit out the supreme insult of *coward*!

You who tie on the name of socialist, may you learn dignity, pride, solidarity, before preaching it to others!

And may you learn that no one is a foreigner on the land where he sweats, works, and suffers; and may you learn what a coward is, before spitting this insult on others, if you do not want the spit to fall back upon you!

An Interview with the Anarchist Malatesta

Translated from "Un'intervista coll'anarchico Malatesta," *Il Secolo* (Milan) 41, no. 14404 (June 2, 1906), 2nd edition

We received the following by phone from London, 1, evening. (B.):

This morning I went to Islington, where the anarchist Malatesta, the well-known Italian anarchist propagandist, lives. I asked him for his impression of yesterday's attack.[207]

Although his interest lies simply in making doctrinaire propaganda and he lives mostly among books, Malatesta is very familiar with the militant anarchists of all countries, especially those of Spain, where he spent several months.

— What do you think of the Madrid attack? I asked him.

— The news, he answered me, did not surprise me at all, since it was to be expected.

— So do you think there was a conspiracy, and that this had been hatched in London, as the *Evening Standard* claims, on the eve of the attack?

Malatesta shrugged his shoulders laughing, then said:

— I do not believe there was a conspiracy, nay, there certainly was none; anarchists act almost always individually and each on their own initiative.

As regards the latest conspiracy described by the *Evening Standard,* this is a journalistic invention. In fact the newspaper, without naming names, let it be understood that Vallina had left weeks ago for Spain, where he committed the attack, while just yesterday evening he came to one of my lectures.[208]

— Do you know the perpetrator of yesterday evening's attack?

— The different names in the newspapers are absolutely unknown to me; when the police say for sure who the attacker is, I may recognize him.

— The Spanish police, I noted, do not seem to have been very shrewd, if it is true that the assassin had rented the room from where the bomb was thrown, for several weeks.

— What do you want the Spanish police to know and see! I was condemned to death in contumacy in Spain,[209] but I am certain that I could go back there without being disturbed. Believe it or not the indictment said that I was a tall

---

207   On May 31, 1906, in Madrid, the Spanish anarchist Mateo Morral threw a bomb at the wedding procession for king of Spain Alfonso XIII and his wife Victoria Eugenia. Dozens of people lost their lives in the attack, which the royal couple escaped.

208   Pedro Vallina was a Spanish anarchist who had come to London, according to what he writes in his own memoirs, in early May, after being expelled from France.

209   The presumed death sentence Malatesta is referring to concerns the peasant riot that took place on January 8, 1892, in Jerez, Andalusia. This was followed by indiscriminate repression, after which four anarchists were sentenced to

man, with a blonde beard, who wore gold glasses... and Malatesta, who does not wear glasses, who has a brown complexion and a dark black beard, laughed.

— What do you think will be the consequences of yesterday evening's attack?

— The consequences? Many arrests, many persecutions, many tortures... and another attack.

— What is the reason for this doggedness among anarchists in Spain?

— He who sows wind harvests storms. The monarchy's days are numbered in Spain: if not one day, it will be another, but the end of the monarchy is decided. The tortures of Montjuich and the Jerez hangings are too fresh in the people's memory, not to mention the terrible economic conditions, in which the majority of Spaniards find themselves in a country where to live, one must steal.[210]

"On the other hand, the anarchists in Spain form the strongest party. In Catalonia and in Andalusia the revolution could be started tomorrow.

"The socialists instead have no influence, they do not even have a representative in Parliament. Their leader, Iglesias, has remained a candidate for life.[211] Except in Bilbao and a few other industrial centers in the North, socialism does not matter in Spain; the popular movement in Catalonia and the entire terrorist and revolutionary movement in no country would have such a close collaboration as in Spain. Unlike other countries, the anarchist party is especially strong in the countryside. In Andalusia the peasants go by foot from *costico* to *costico* to communicate news, pamphlets, and newspapers. Elsewhere anarchists have abandoned the aggressive system of propaganda, in Spain no; you saw it yesterday evening, and you will see it again in the future."[212]

---

death. As Malatesta was in Spain on a propaganda tour at the time of the riot, he was attributed a role in the riot.

210   On Montjuïc and Jerez see, respectively, note 66 above and the note that precedes this one.

211   As regards Pablo Iglesias, see note 134 above.

212   As regards Mateo Morral's attack, Luigi Fabbri, who visited Malatesta in London in December 1906, narrates the following episode: "I remember that, Mateo Morral's attack on the king of Spain having happened only a few months earlier, Malatesta told me about the insistence of an editor from a major English reactionary daily to wring an interview out of him or at least a few words condemning the event. Malatesta had refused: 'You people are enemies, and enemies do not get explanations.' And since the other insisted and continued to speak of the innocents caught up in the explosion, Malatesta, impatient, at a certain point interrupted him: 'You are right, that poor fatally injured horse was entirely innocent.' At any rate, while leaving, the journalist told him: 'Alright, you did not want to grant me the interview; however I already did it, and I shall publish it all the same.' 'And then go and trust interviews!' Malatesta concluded" (*La vida de Malatesta*, Barcelona, 1936, 154). The episode is also recalled in Fabbri's interview with Malatesta published on p. 253 of the current volume.

Lecture by Enrico Malatesta on the Anarchist Attacks

Translated from "Conferenza di Enrico Malatesta sugli attentati anarchici," report by police officer Frosali to the Ministry of the Interior, London, July 16, 1906[213]

Malatesta's lecture at 107 Charlotte Street (see the enclosed manifesto)[214] was carefully listened to by about 100 subversives, many of whom do not normally attend meetings. Among others the following were noticed: Goldoni, Rossi, Magnoni, Tombolesi, Sinic[c]o, Panigatti, Mazzotti, Frigerio, Corio, and others.

This is a summary of what Malatesta said:

"Attacks have been a historical necessity, since war has existed between classes and between parties. Every party used violence: monarchists, republicans, socialists. Ancient history teaches us to consider its Brutuses as heroes. The streets of our cities have more monuments to soldiers than to other classes of people. Every party justified attacks, when they were advantageous to them; they therefore have no right to reproach us for it. But the anarchists' violence is the only self-defense, as they do not want the State, the organized form of violence.[215]

"Attacks are the product of the current conditions, which act upon individuals perhaps more intelligent, certainly more sensitive, more courageous, and perhaps a bit desperate.

"They are not the work of criminals, but of pioneers.

"Nobody will say that in the past violence was useless.

"Let us look at the war for Italian independence, at the French revolution. It is too soon to judge today's attacks; certainly Bresci's deed brought freedom to Italy; like Angiolillo's in Spain.

"Whether bombs or daggers are better is a matter to be decided in each single case. The means that reach an end are good.

"Orsini, while failing, killed 40 innocent people, nevertheless official Italy made him a statue.

"William of Germany said, when Carnot died by Caserio's hand: "He died on the battle field."

"Which is true. Today workers die in mines, tomorrow a King dies from an attack, and most often the best are targeted.

"Kings are criminals for their positions, and therefore will be exterminated."

---

213   Typescript, Archivio Centrale dello Stato, Rome, Casellario Politico Centrale, box 2949.

214   The manifesto could not be found. According to scholar Peter van der Mark, the lecture was held on July 13th.

215   In the original text, this last sentence is jumbled. Rather than translating it literally, we have taken the liberty of interpreting it in the way that seemed most sensible.

A Frenchman, and an Italian, Sinic[c]o,[216] said "they did not approve of the anarchist tactic of bombs, but while wanting almost the same objective, they believed they could achieve it with parliamentarism."

Malatesta then challenged parliamentarism saying that "it is a limitation of freedom and it is absurd because it always crushes the minorities."

The following spoke: Rossi Giulio, Mazzotti, Frigerio, and Bergia, approving individual deeds.

The lecture began at 8½, and finished at 12.

At the end of the lecture 30 shillings were collected, some to pay for the hall, and the remainder for the "Germinal" group.

The Recent Anarchist Attacks in Rome

Translated from "Les récents attentats anarchistes de Rome," note by the French police, Paris, December 3, 1906[217]

THE OPINION OF MALATESTA.
WHAT ROCKER SAID.

The London correspondent sends the following information:

"Met MALATESTA at the Italian club. I asked him his opinion on the subject of the recent attacks in Rome[218] and he answered me smiling (as always): oh! it is just an experiment, we anarchists we do not have the skill of the Russians and in my opinion, in the hands of Italians, the knife is the safest weapon, that does not take innocent victims."

...

---

216   This is socialist Giuseppe Sinicco, author of the memoir from which the summary published on p. 207 of the current volume was taken.

217   Typescript, Archives Nationales, Paris, collection "F/7 Police Générale," box 12905.

218   On November 14, 1906, a bomb exploded on the threshold of Caffè Aragno in Rome, slightly injuring one person; another explosion had taken place on November 18th in St. Peter's basilica, in front of Pope Clement XIII's tomb, without causing any damage.

Against a Law on Labor Exchanges

Translated from "Contro una Legge sugli Uffici di Collocamento,"
Revue (London) 2, no. 16 (December 1906)[219]

Our comrades working in the canteens perhaps will not like what we are about to say, but we are saying it all the same, because we think that the first duty of a friend is to tell the truth, even, and especially, if it is bitter.

We who have joyfully welcomed the symptoms of an awakening among a class of workers so oppressed and demoralized, we watch, with sorrow and a sense of disillusionment, how they handle the first action they are promoting, that against the labor exchanges.

Certainly, they have good reason to want to destroy these vampires, who in a thousand ways trick and exploit the poor unemployed and use shady maneuvers to provoke employment instability, among other things, since they benefit from every change. And they would merit the sympathy and solidarity of all men of progress if, in order to attain their rightful desire, they were able to work energetically and willfully, starting with a boycott of the aforementioned exchanges, and organizing their own free placement service for the benefit of all.

But what should we think of their state of mind and their likelihood of succeeding, when we see that they, eternal victims of all laws, are unable to do anything but ask for a new law?

Oppressed, robbed, scorned, they are unaware of the strength they can draw from union, solidarity, individual and collective initiative; and they wait for the improvement of their own conditions from the benevolence... of their lords!

Do they therefore think that the lords in Parliament, even if they were once workers, will take an interest in the matter of the employment agent who squeezed a few shillings out of the poor kitchen boy?

Do they not know that without the direct force of those involved, no oppressed class has ever achieved a real and lasting improvement, let alone emancipation?

Then again, let us look at the very nature of parliamentary roles.

Deputies are not deities, good or evil, free to do as they please, who can be moved by prayer and the spectacle of one's suffering. They are in Parliament to represent the dominating forces and interests in the country. Either they are dishonest (which is the case... sometimes), and will take advantage of the position to procure their own personal advantage at the expense of the public; or they are honest (as the word is generally

---

219   *Revue* was the multilingual organ of food service workers. It had been founded the year before by Italian anarchist Bergia, as part of a campaign to organize workers from that sector, in which Italians were numerous.

understood), and must act in the interest of their electors, or rather that part of the electors whose wealth, influence, material and moral force, in a word, decide the fate of elections.

Now, seriously, what material or moral force does the association of kitchen boys and servers represent in the national economy?

But the force that we do not have, one could respond, we can acquire with union and energy.

Absolutely; and this is indeed what we urge you to do. But if you can only obtain something from parliament once you have the force to oblige the public to consider your needs, this means that you would obtain the law when you no longer would need it, because by that time you could act on your own. In fact, much later: because it is obviously much easier to enable yourself to do without the leeching employment agents and obligate the masters to supply themselves with staff directly through or by means of your associations, than to elevate the matter to national importance and command the parliament's attention.

So, the only practical result you could obtain, putting your hopes in the prudent laws yet to come, will be to anesthetize your energy and extinguish the spirit of battle and sacrifice, without which a cause cannot triumph.

But there is another aspect of the matter to look at, and it is no less important.

Since we live in a legal regime, and the law is created for all, it is not possible to apply different criteria to each case and to each particular interest. If canteen workers, incapable of defending themselves on their own, ask for and obtain a law of special protection, all the thousands and thousands of conflicting social interests shall have the right to ask for and obtain special laws; and the government, which naturally has the tendency to increasingly expand the sphere of its responsibilities, would take advantage of this to invade and hinder, even more than it does now, all branches of human activity, and certainly not to the advantage of the weakest.

The canteen workers, instead of seeking improvement and emancipation through the routes to freedom, put their hopes in growing government regulation and interference.

Naturally should they persist, they will not receive sympathy from men of freedom, from those who believe that progress is achieved not through multiplying brakes and chains but through leaving the field free to all activities. And should they succeed, they would soon realize how foolish it is to entrust the powerful with the defense of their own interests.

In fact, if the government prohibits the industry of employment agents and thus creates a privilege for workers' associations, it would very much need to claim, in exchange, a right of surveillance over the same associations.

What would the workers gain from this?

They would no longer be able to meet as an association without the government's authorization, subjecting themselves to the regulations imposed by the law and the consequent police surveillance: and this would be necessary for the same purposes of the law, since otherwise the employment agents, with the support of a few scabs, could establish false associations and easily continue their trade, as today the unlicensed liquor merchants and the managers of gambling houses do, running their businesses through false clubs.

Then he who seeks employment would come to the association not in a spirit of solidarity, not because he desires to emancipate himself and seeks the means to do so in union with his comrades, but simply because he was forced to do so by the association's legal privilege; and he would therefore come in a bad mood, full of bitterness and suspicion.

Then what good would an association be anymore, as a means of education and emancipation?

We are familiar with the difficulties our comrades in the canteens are fighting against. We know that they are working in a class which finds itself in deplorable moral conditions, and that, practicing a trade for which no apprenticeship is generally needed, they must put up with the competition of new arrivals, who are often deaf to the feeling of solidarity, and are almost always obliged by urgent need to accept any condition.

But this does not take anything away from our arguments. It only adds the fact that the conditions of canteen workers, like those of all workers and even more so, are linked to the general state of society; and it makes you understand the need to fight, not just for the small immediate improvements that can be obtained, but also, and more so, for the radical destruction of suffering, that is, for a social transformation such that there will no longer be rich people who carouse in idleness and poor people who scrape by while enriching the others.

ERRICO MALATESTA.

[Conversations with Pio Baroja, London, Summer 1907]

Translated from Pio Baroja, *Obras Completas*, vol. 7
(Madrid: Biblioteca Nueva, 1949), p. 773 and 782[220]

. . .

Malatesta was not, as the English detective says he was, a fanatical and arrogant man, but quite the contrary: a simple and humble fellow.[221] This impression was so strong in me that I supposed he then found himself quite isolated and disillusioned by revolutionaries and, especially, revolution. Several times he told me:

— You writers are the ones who have a great task to accomplish: to give the people an ideal, and manage, in an attractive and artistic manner, to get them to appreciate culture.[222]

. . .

As I was in London, Tarrida del Mármol came from Paris. He was going to see Malatesta. We talked about Spain. Malatesta knew they had acquitted Ferrer,[223] and said with a certain air of sadness:

— Well. I do not know what I am going to do now, after having prepared a protest movement here.

— Surely—Tarrida murmured—this acquittal is a disaster for you. There is no other way than to see if we manage to get him jailed again.

. . .

---

220   The two conversations, from which Baroja takes these brief excerpts, took place during the Spanish writer's three-month stay in London. The first conversation took place at Malatesta's house, which Baroja visited while accompanied by Tárrida del Mármol. The narrative of the second conversation is taken from Francisco Iribarne's interview with Baroja, which the latter included in his memoirs.

221   Baroja had previously reported the imaginative description of Malatesta provided by Herbert Fitch, a former Scotland Yard inspector, in his memoirs.

222   A few years earlier, Malatesta himself had tried his hand at a theatrical work, *The Strike* (see the volume of pamphlets, programmes, manifestos and other miscellaneous publications of these *Complete Works*). It was performed in 1901, but afterwards he decided not to publish it. The theme of the relationship between anarchism and art was also touched on in a conversation Malatesta had in July 1901 with Ben Reitman, then a medical student visiting London. According to what Reitman reports in an October 1910 article in *Mother Earth*, Malatesta told him about "the great advance of Anarchism in Europe and of its influence on every phase of human thought, not so much in a direct as an indirect manner. He said Anarchism is exerting an influence on Socialism, trade unionism, on literature, the drama, and education."

223   Francisco Ferrer, Spanish anarchist educator and founder of the Modern School, was incarcerated in 1906, because he was suspected of complicity in Mateo Morral's attack against the king of Spain, and freed in June 1907.

August 25, 1907, Malatesta speaks in the Plancius garden.
Source: Centro Studi Libertari / Archivio Giuseppe Pinelli, Milan

E. Malatesta's Lecture
[by "The Irish Rebel"]

Voice of Labour (London) 1, no. 33 (August 31, 1907)

The first of a series of indoor meetings convened by the VOICE OF LABOUR group took place at the Bath House, 96 Dean Street, Oxford Street, W., on Wednesday, August 21, Comrade Malatesta was the lecturer, his subject being "The Labour Movement from the Anarchist Standpoint."

He first showed the fallacy of the general strike, as generally understood, pointing out that it was useless for the workers to come out on strike, but that they should remain in on strike against producing for the capitalist class, and go on producing for the whole community. He also dealt with the uselessness of the political machine, and said it was foolish to treat with the capitalist class in any other way but by direct revolutionary action. Showing the interest the audience took in the lecture, a number of questions were asked, and answered at great length by our comrade. There was also a good deal of discussion, which the lecturer replied to, and regretted his inability to be more clear in his delivery. But the audience were able to follow him throughout.

. . .

[Amsterdam Congress, Preliminaries
of August 24–25, 1907][224]

Translated from "Congrès Anarchiste tenu à Amsterdam, Août 1907," in
Anarchisme & Syndicalisme (Rennes and Paris: Nautilus and Éditions du Monde
Libertaire, 1997; original edition, Paris: La Publication Sociale, 1908), p. 137[225]

[*The congress participants begin to arrive in Amsterdam on Saturday, August 24th. On Sunday, August 25th an international meeting is held in the Plancius garden. The first to speak is Raphael Friedeberg, followed by Malatesta.*]

---

224   We are providing Malatesta's contributions from the congress proceedings, omitting brief exchanges and remarks concerning procedural matters.

225   There are numerous summaries of the Amsterdam congress in the anarchist press. Reproducing them all would have been too repetitive. We opted to use this summary, unanimously recognized as the most complete, as the main source, complementing it, in footnotes, with excerpts from other summaries, when these provide additional elements or report the same arguments from a different angle. We made one exception for Malatesta's speech on syndicalism and the general strike, of which we provided two entire summaries that we consider to be complementary.

MALATESTA, after greeting the revolutionaries of little Holland, stated that the people must not rely on anyone but themselves for their emancipation.[226] Human progress will only become possible again when worker violence destroys the economic, political, and religious oppression which characterize present-day society.

. . .

[Amsterdam Congress, Morning Session of August 26, 1907]

Translated from "Congrès Anarchiste tenu à Amsterdam, Août 1907," p. 140–41[227]

[In the Monday, August 26th morning session, Ferdinand Domela Nieuwenhuis, supported by Friedeberg and others, proposes replacing the part of the agenda about antimilitarism with mass participation in the 2nd antimilitarist international congress, scheduled for Friday the 30th.]

MALATESTA, soon supported by Marmande, Thonar, and Chapelier, vigorously opposed the Domela–Friedeberg proposal—Either, he says, Friday's congress will only bring together anarchists, and then it will be a redundant duplicate of this congress, and I do not at all see the need for that; or non-anarchist elements, even bourgeois and pacifist elements, will also participate in that Congress, and then our duty as anarchists is, before going there, to discuss right here, among ourselves and from our point of view, the issue of antimilitarism. And Malatesta asks, concluding, to move on to the agenda.[228]

[After further lively discussion and suspension of the session, Malatesta's proposal is accepted with 38 votes, against 33 votes for Friedeberg's proposal.]

226　In the September 21, 1907 issue of the Dutch periodical *De Vrije Communist,* Cornelissen reports the following words from Malatesta: "I will not say much, he shouted, just a few words: do not rely on saviors, on apostles who work for liberation on your behalf: you have to do that work yourself."

227　From this point onward we will cite this source in abbreviated form. For complete bibliographic information, see the previous article.

228　On Malatesta's position concerning antimilitarist congresses, see also the 1903 article "The Proposed Antimilitarist Congress," published on p. 178 of the current volume.

[Amsterdam Congress, Evening Session of August 26, 1907]

Translated from "Congrès Anarchiste tenu à Amsterdam, Août 1907," p. 154

[*During this session, a continuation of the afternoon session, reports were read on the state of the international anarchist movement. Malatesta gave the report for Italy.*]

ERRICO MALATESTA—A few brief words on the Italian anarchist movement. The movement is going through a crisis, entirely similar to that which has struck the Italian socialist party. Comrades are divided into organizationist and anti-organizationists on one side, into syndicalists and anti-syndicalists on the other.

Despite everything, the movement, though it has suffered a setback due to the effects of internal discord, has retained its strength: great in the North and Center where newspapers are plentiful; much less in the South.[229]

The Italian proletariat has always been inclined toward revolutionary action; for this reason it is unlikely that the socialist Party, organized according to the German model, will be able to lead it to parliamentarism. It is furthermore divided into different currents of which one, if it is logical, will come to anarchism (that is the one called syndicalist and anti-statist); therefore the anarchists have a bright future in front of them, if they can avoid the hurdles strewn along the way.

. . .

[Amsterdam Congress, Evening Session of August 27, 1907]

Translated from "Congrès Anarchiste tenu à Amsterdam, Août 1907," p. 166–69

[*During the Tuesday, August 27th evening session, discussion continued on "Anarchism and Organization" which had begun that morning with a report by Amédée Dunois and*]

---

229   According to the summary in the September 7, 1907, issue of *De Vrije Communist*, Malatesta said the anarchist movement in Italy was flourishing, with a strong presence in Northern and especially Central Italy. In some places the majority of the population was anarchist, while in other areas, like Sardinia, the movement was absent. Socialism was at that moment in a state of crisis. It was born anarchist in Italy, but then the parliamentarian degeneration happened. However, the people's spirit remained anarchist. In *Freedom* (London) of October 1907, Karl Walter, representative for England at the congress, indicates Ancona and Massa Carrara as the cities with anarchist majorities mentioned by Malatesta.

continued in the afternoon with a report by Hijman Croiset, who represented the individualist tendency.]

ERRICO MALATESTA.—I have listened closely to everything that was said before me on this issue of organization, and my very clear impression is that what divides us, are the *words* that we understand in different ways. We are looking to quarrel over words. But I am persuaded that we are all in agreement on the very foundation of the matter.

All anarchists, whatever tendency they belong to, are in a certain way, *individualists*. But the opposite is far from being true: not all individualists are anarchists, by a long shot. Individualists are divided into two very distinct categories: the ones demand the right to full development for all human individuals, themselves as well as others; the others only think of their own individuality and never hesitate to sacrifice the individuality of others. The tsar of all the Russias is among the latter individualists. We are among the former.[230]

It has been written, after Ibsen, that the strongest man in the world, is he who stands most alone!—Enormous nonsense!—Dr. Stockmann, in whose mouth Ibsen put this maxim, was not an *isolated man* in the full power of the term: he lived in an established society and not on Robinson's island.[231] The "alone" man finds it impossible to accomplish the smallest useful, productive endeavor; and if someone needs a master above himself, it is truly the man who lives in isolation. What liberates the individual and allows him to develop all of his abilities, is not solitude, it is association.[232]

---

230   In the summary in Russian, prepared by Nikolay Rogdayev and published as a pamphlet, Malatesta is instead attributed the idea that "all, even the most extreme individualists, are always communist in their actions." Perhaps the alleged statement should be interpreted in light of the concept, clarified further down by Malatesta, that cooperation is always indispensable for any practical work, while the isolated individual is powerless.

231   According to Emma Goldman (*Mother Earth*, October 1907), Malatesta also said that if doctor Stockmann were "a worker in some factory, at the mercy of poverty and exploitation, he would soon descend from his lofty pedestal." The character of doctor Stockmann had already been critiqued in a previous speech by Dunois. Max Baginski and Emma Goldman, instead, responded to Malatesta by defending Stockmann. For a previous critique by Malatesta of the character by Ibsen, who was very popular among anarchists, see "Individualism in Anarchism," on page 77 of the volume of these *Complete Works* covering the years 1897–98.

232   In the continuation (November 1907) of his report for *Freedom*, Karl Walter reports the following additional observation by Malatesta: "The very reason that we are not free is because we are not organised and the capitalists are. How can a single individual peasant free himself? He can only do it by organising with his fellows." In his autobiography (*En la borrasca*, Buenos Aires, 1949, 228), Rudolf Rocker, who participated in the congress representing the Federation of Jewish anarchists of London, instead summarizes Malatesta's argument on association thusly: "Malatesta stated that man is conceivable only

To accomplish truly useful work, cooperation is indispensable, today more than ever. Without a doubt, association must leave full autonomy to the individuals who participate in it, and federation must respect this same autonomy among groups: let us be wary of believing that the lack of organization is a guarantee of freedom. Everything demonstrates the contrary.

An example: there are French anarchist newspapers which block from their columns all those whose ideas, style, or simply appearance have had the disgrace of displeasing their usual editors. The result is that these editors are invested with a personal power that limits the freedom of opinion and expression of comrades.[233] It would be different if these newspapers, instead of being the personal property of this or that individual, belonged to groups: then all opinions could be discussed therein.

We talk a lot about authority, about authoritarianism. But on this point we should understand one another. We rise up with all of our soul and we will never cease to revolt against the authority incarnated in the State with no other purpose than to maintain economic slavery within society. But there is that purely moral authority which comes from experience, from intelligence or from talent, and, as anarchist as we are, there is nobody among us who does not respect that authority.

It is an error to depict the "organizationists," the federalists, as authoritarian; and it is another error, no less serious, to depict the "anti-organizationists," the individualists, as deliberately condemning themselves to isolation.

For me, I repeat, the quarrel between individualists and organizers is an unmitigated quarrel of words, that does not hold up under a careful examination of the facts. In practical reality, what do we see? We see that the individualists are sometimes better organized than the "organizationists," because the latter too often confine themselves to preaching organization without practicing it. On the other hand, it happens that one finds much more actual authoritarianism in groups that noisily demand the "absolute freedom of the individual," than in groups which are ordinarily considered *authoritarian*—because they have a committee and make decisions.

---

in society and that the individual does not represent a unit separate from his neighbor, but must instead be considered first and foremost a social species, who prospers and evolves only in community. Society, in which every day in a thousand ways mutual relationships among men are reinvented, is therefore the original image of any organization, which springs from the social conditions of life itself and therefore conditions human coexistence. It is not organization as such that is harmful; what is dangerous is rather the dead mechanization that aims to submit all human relations to a specific model. For this reason, anarchists have always fought political and social centralization and have proposed a federative association of independent groups whose objectives go in the same direction."

233   *Les Temps Nouveaux* and *Le Libertaire* are explicitly cited in the report in the October 19, 1907, issue of *De Vrije Communist*.

In other words, organizationists or anti-organizationists, they all organize. Only those who do nothing or very little can live in isolation and enjoy it. This is the truth; why not acknowledge it?

Here is proof to support what I have said: in Italy all comrades who are currently in the struggle claim to adhere to my ideas, the "individualists" as well as the "organizationists" and I truly believe that all are right, since, whatever theoretical divergences there are between them, all equally practice collective action.

Enough with quarrels over words; let us stick to actions! Words divide and action unites. It is time for us all to get to work together in exerting effective influence over social events. It pains me to think that, in order to tear away one of our own from the talons of his executioner, we had to turn to parties other than our own. And so, Ferrer would not owe his freedom to bourgeois free thinkers and free masons, if the anarchists, grouped into a powerful and feared International, had been able to take into their own hands the universal protest against the criminal infamy of the Spanish government.[234]

Let us therefore seek to finally make the anarchist International a reality. To enable us to rapidly call upon all comrades, to fight against the reaction, as well as to take, in due time, revolutionary initiative, our International must exist![235]

---

234   According to the report in the October 6–13, 1907, issue of *Le Libertaire* (Paris), signed by Henri Beylie, member of the French delegation to the congress, Malatesta explained that Ferrer's defense "should have been the work of the anarchists, if they had been organized, if they could have conducted, through said organization, a violent protection campaign in every country." On Ferrer's incarceration and release see note 223 above.

235   The final part of Malatesta's speech, summarized in the last two paragraphs, is reported by Karl Walter as follows: "As to the desirability of organisation in the Anarchist movement itself, the lack of it is a constant reproach to us. Take only as an instance, what happens when one of us is threatened with imprisonment. Is it the Anarchists who organise those monster demonstrations, which by sheer weight of public opinion force the authorities to withhold the sentence? No; we left it to the Freethinkers and the Socialists to liberate Ferrer. What is wanting among us is primarily the spirit of action. When that comes we shall organise, and no fear of authority creeping into our organisations will daunt us. While we do nothing it is only natural that our organisations fade, but when we see what there is to be done, and set out to do it, then the International will become a reality. It is not for propaganda that it is wanted—with or without international organisation the propaganda grows—but we need it for action. Whenever there is a revolutionary movement anywhere in the world, international organisation becomes necessary."

[Amsterdam Congress, Morning Session of August 28, 1907]

Translated from "Congrès Anarchiste tenu à Amsterdam, Août 1907," p. 172–73

[The discussion on "Anarchism and Organization" ends during the morning session of Wednesday August 28th. Dunois presents a motion, slightly amended by Emma Goldman and completed by Karel Vohryzek and Malatesta.]

DUNOIS MOTION:[236]

The anarchists meeting in Amsterdam on August 27, 1907,

Considering that the ideas of anarchy and organization, far from being incompatible, as it is sometimes presumed, complete each other and reciprocally enlighten each other, the very principle of anarchy residing in the free organization of producers;

That individual action, however important, cannot compensate for the lack of collective action, of an organized movement; no more than collective action could compensate for the lack of individual initiative;[237]

That organization of militant forces would instill a new impetus into propaganda and could only stimulate the penetration of the ideas of federalism and revolution within the working class;

That the labor organization, founded on the identity of interests, does not exclude an organization founded on the identity of aspirations and ideas;

Are of the opinion that comrades from all countries place the creation of anarchist groups and the federation of the groups already created on the agenda.

VOHRYZEK–MALATESTA ADDITION:

The anarchist Federation is an association of groups and individuals in which nobody can impose his will or curtail the initiative of others. Vis-a-vis present-day society, its purpose is to change all moral and economic conditions and, in this sense, support the fight with any adequate means.[238]

[Another motion is presented by Pierre Ramus. The Dunois motion receives 46 favorable votes and one against; the Vohryzek addition 48 favorable votes and none against. The Ramus motion receives 13 favorable votes and 17 against. Many congress participants abstain because the Ramus motion does not add anything to the previous one.]

---

236   [Author's note] The text of this motion was changed slightly in the French edition of the *Résolutions approuvées par le congrès anarchiste tenu à Amsterdam*. Here we are providing it as it was drafted and voted upon.

237   [Author's note] The emphasized clause summarizes Emma Goldman's amendment.

238   [Author's note] Same observation as for the Dunois motion.

[Amsterdam Congress, Afternoon Session of August 29, 1907]

TRANSLATION FROM "CONGRÈS ANARCHISTE TENU À AMSTERDAM, AOÛT 1907," P. 190–99

[*During the Wednesday, August 28th afternoon session, held privately, the decision is made to establish the anarchist International. During the evening session, discussion begins on the subject of "Syndicalism and Anarchism," with Pierre Monatte's report supporting revolutionary syndicalism. Due to time constraints, during the Thursday, August 29th morning session it is decided, per Malatesta's suggestion, that two similar subjects "Syndicalism and Anarchism" and "General economic strike and general political strike" will be combined into a single subject, "Syndicalism and General strike." Discussion of this subject will continue in the afternoon, while the rest of the morning session is taken up by discussion on "The Russian Revolution." The afternoon session begins with the approval of a resolution supporting the Russian revolution.*]

Once the session is open, EMMA GOLDMAN reads a resolution supporting the Russian revolution, proposed by comrades Rogdaëff, Wladimir Zabrejneff, together with Goldman, Cornélissen, Baginsky, Peter Mougnitch, Luigi Fabbri, and Malatesta. Here is the resolution that was naturally approved unanimously.[239]

Considering

a) That with the development of the Russian revolution, it is increasingly observed that the Russian people—the proletariat of the cities and countryside—will never be satisfied with the conquest of a vain political liberty; that it demands the complete suppression of political and economic slavery and uses the same methods of struggle, which, for a long time, have already been propagated by the anarchists as the only effective methods; that it does not expect anything from above, but endeavors to reach the realization of its demands through direct action;

b) That the Russian revolution does not only have national or local importance, but that the near future of the international proletariat depends upon it;

c) That the bourgeoisie of the old and new world has united to defend its privileges in order to delay the hour of its annihilation and has provided moral and material assistance to best support the reaction—the government of the tsar, which to the detriment of the Russian people, it supports with money and munitions;

d) That at the critical moment it is always ready to offer it the assistance of its cannons and its rifles (such is the case of the governments of Austria and Germany);

That intellectual support is reflected by the complete silence over the fight led by the Russian people, as well as over all the brutalities of the autocracy.

---

239 [Author's note] This text was published by the *Bureau International.* Nevertheless, we believed it appropriate to make a few grammatical corrections.

The Congress recognizes: that the proletariat of all countries must put forward the most energetic action coming from the worker's Anarchist International against all aggression by the Yellow International comprised of the united capitalists and governments of all kinds: monarchist-constitutional and republican-democratic; through this action they shall give proof of their solidarity with the rebelling Russian proletariat. In its own interest, well understood, it must categorically refuse all attempts that will be made to suffocate the strikes and insurrections in Russia.[240] Never must the foreign proletariat in uniform lend a hand to any action directed against his Russian brother. If the industrial proletariat, in case of a strike in Russia, does not have the opportunity to declare a general strike in the corresponding branch, due to local conditions, it should then make recourse to other methods of struggle, to sabotage, to the destruction or deterioration of products sent to the common enemy, to the destruction of the channels of communication, railways, boats, etc.

The Congress insistently recommends, to all those who share its point of view, the widest propaganda in favor of all means by which it could help to support the Russian Revolution.

[*The discussion on syndicalism and general strike resumes, with a speech by Christian Cornélissen, followed by a speech by Malatesta.*]

ERRICO MALATESTA—I wish to immediately declare that I am going to only elaborate on the part of my thinking that does not align with that of the previous speakers, particularly Monatte. To act otherwise would be to subject you to pointless repetitions that one can allow in meetings, when speaking to an audience of opponents or indifferent people. But here we are among comrades, and certainly none of you, hearing me criticize what can be criticized in syndicalism, will be tempted to take me for an enemy of organization and action among workers; otherwise he would know me rather poorly!

The conclusion Monatte reached is that syndicalism is a necessary and sufficient means of social revolution. In other words, Monatte declares that *syndicalism is sufficient onto itself.* And this, in my opinion, is a radically false doctrine. Fighting against this doctrine shall be the subject of my speech.

Syndicalism, or more precisely the labor movement (the labor movement is a *fact* that nobody can ignore, while syndicalism is a doctrine, a system, and we must avoid confusing the two), I say, has always found in me a resolute, but not blind, advocate. This is because I see it as a particularly propitious terrain for our revolutionary propaganda and, at the same time, a point of contact between the masses and ourselves. I do not need to insist on that. You must acknowledge that I have never been among those intellectual anarchists who, when the old International dissolved, gracefully retreated into the ivory tower of pure speculation; that I have not ceased to fight that attitude of haughty isolation wherever I found

---

240   The subject implied in this sentence is presumably the international proletariat.

it, in Italy, in France, in England and elsewhere, or ceased to push comrades down the path that the syndicalists, forgetting a glorious past, call *new*, though the first anarchists have already glimpsed and followed it in the International.

Today as yesterday, I want anarchists to enter the labor movement. I am, today as yesterday, a syndicalist, in the sense that I support the unions. I do not ask for anarchist unions, which automatically would legitimize social-democratic unions, republican, realist or other kind of unions and would have, at most, the effect of dividing more than ever the working class against itself. I do not even want *red* unions, because I do not want *yellow* unions. To the contrary, I would like unions widely open to all workers without regard for opinions, unions that are absolutely *neutral*.

Therefore, I am for the most active participation possible in the labor movement, but I am especially so in the interests of our propaganda, for which the field would then be considerably widened. But in no way can this participation be considered as the renunciation of our dearest ideas. In the union, we must remain anarchists, in the full strength and full breadth of the term. The labor movement for me is only a means—evidently the best among all means that are available to us. I refuse to consider this means as an end, and I would not even want it anymore if it caused us to lose sight of the entirety of our anarchist views, or more simply of our other means of propaganda and agitation.

The syndicalists, on the other hand, tend to turn the means into an end, and to look at the part as the whole. And in this way, in the minds of some of our comrades, syndicalism is becoming a new doctrine and is threatening the very existence of anarchism.

Now, even if it proudly adds the useless epithet of revolutionary, syndicalism is not and will never be more than a legalitarian and conservative movement, with no other accessible end—if that!—than the improvement of working conditions. I need not look for any further proof other than that offered to us by the great North American unions. After showing radical revolutionism when they were still weak, these unions became, little by little as they grew in strength and wealth, distinctly conservative organizations, solely concerned with making their own members into privileged people at the factory, in the workshop or in the mine, and are far less hostile to the masters' capitalism than they are to unorganized workers, to that ragged proletariat defamed by social-democracy![241] Yet this ever growing proletariat of unemployed people—which is of no matter for syndicalism, or rather it only matters as an obstacle—we, the anarchists, cannot forget, and we must defend it because its members suffer most.

I repeat: anarchists must enter the labor unions. First for making anarchist

---

241   The French original reads "à ce prolétariat en haillons flétri par la socialdémocratie." The term "prolétariat en haillons" translates the German "Lumpenproletariat," which Marx and Engels, in *The German Ideology* and later writings, used in reference to the sub-proletariat that they considered incapable of class consciousness, and to which Bakunin instead paid special attention.

propaganda; then because it is the only way for us to have available, on the longed-for day, groups capable of taking over the direction of production; finally we must enter them to energetically react against that detestable frame of mind that pushes unions to only defend specific interests.

In my opinion, the fundamental error of Monatte and all the revolutionary syndicalists comes from a too simplistic understanding of class struggle. It is an understanding according to which the economic interests of all workers—of the working class—would be in solidarity, the understanding according to which it suffices for some workers to take in hand the defense of their own interests to defend at the same time the interests of the entire proletariat against the masters.[242]

The reality is, in my opinion, very different. Workers, like the bourgeois, like everyone, are subject to that law of universal competition that descends from the regime of private property and that will only be extinguished with the latter. Therefore there are no classes, in the true sense of the word, since there are no class interests. Within the same working "class" there exist, just as there exist among the bourgeois, competition and struggle. The economic interests of one category of workers are irreducibly opposed to those of another category. And sometimes we see that some workers are economically and morally much closer to the bourgeoisie than to the proletariat. Cornélissen gave us an example of this from Holland itself.[243] There are others. I do not need to remind you how often, during strikes, the workers use violence against... the police? the owners? No: against the *Kroumirs*[244] even though the latter are exploited like the workers and humiliated even further, while the worker's true enemies, the only obstacles to social equality, are instead the police and the owners.

Nevertheless, moral solidarity is possible among the proletariat, even though they lack economic solidarity. The workers who isolate themselves in defense of their own corporate interests may not know it, but it will emerge on the day when a shared desire for social transformation turns them into new men. In

---

242 Concerning the argument that the ideas of anarchism are not exhausted in purely economic problems, Rocker provides the following report: "Malatesta in particular clearly expressed this point of view, stating that anarchism was not a matter of a specific class, but was a social view that embraced all domains of life. Therefore it was necessary to never forget that, in addition to economic problems, there are many other problems that not even the most revolutionary labor movement can exhaust. For this reason, the formula that syndicalism *is sufficient onto itself*, is not correct, because neither organizations nor ideas ever suffice on their own, but are constantly compelled to resort to loans from the exterior. Anarchism's absorption into syndicalism was therefore impossible and would not be beneficial for either party." (*En la borrasca*, 230).

243 Cornélissen had provided the example of diamond makers in Amsterdam and Antwerp who, after significantly improving their conditions through the practice of labor direct action, "made their corporation into a sort of closed caste, around which they raised a veritable Chinese wall."

244 [Author's note] This was the term for *scabs*, those who work during strikes, in Italy and Switzerland.

present-day society, solidarity can only result from communion within a shared ideal. Now, it is the role of the anarchists to incite the unions to the ideal, guiding them little by little to the social revolution, at the risk of damaging those "immediate advantages" which they seem so fond of today.

We cannot even dream anymore of denying that union action entails danger. The greatest of these dangers is certainly the acceptance by activists of positions in the union, especially when these are paid positions. The general rule is that an anarchist who agrees to become a permanent and salaried official of a union is lost to propaganda, lost to anarchism! At this point he becomes indebted to those who pay him and, since they are not anarchists, the salaried official, torn between his conscience and his interest, will either follow his own conscience and lose his position, or will follow his own interest and then, goodbye anarchism!

The official in the labor movement is a danger comparable only to that of parliamentarism: both lead to corruption and it is a short step from corruption to death!

And now we come to the general strike. Personally, I accept the principle that I have been propagating as much as possible for years. The general strike has always seemed to me an excellent means for beginning the social revolution. However, let us take care to not fall into the pernicious illusion that, with the general strike, armed insurrection becomes superfluous.

It is presumed that by abruptly stopping production, in a few days workers would starve the bourgeoisie, who, dying of hunger, would be obliged to capitulate. I cannot imagine a bigger absurdity. The first to die of hunger during a general strike would not be the bourgeois, who have all accumulated products available, but the workers who only have their labor to live on.

The general strike as it was described to us in the past is pure utopia. Either the worker, dying of hunger after three days of strike, will go back to the workshop, his head bowed, and we will chalk up another defeat. Or he will seize the products by force. Who will he find before him, to stop him? Soldiers, policemen, if not the bourgeois themselves, and then the issue will need to be resolved by rifles and bombs. It will be the insurrection, and victory will go to the strongest.

Let us therefore prepare ourselves for this inevitable insurrection, instead of limiting ourselves to advocating for the general strike as a panacea for all ills. Let us not argue that the government is armed to the teeth and will always be stronger than those who rebel. In 1902, in Barcelona, the army was not numerous. But nobody was prepared for armed struggle and the workers, failing to understand that political power was the true enemy, sent delegates to the governor asking him to make the owners yield.[245]

Even reduced to what it genuinely is, the general strike is still one of those double-edged swords that must be used with great caution. The provision of food could not withstand prolonged suspension. Therefore it will be necessary to seize

---

245   See note 86 above on the 1902 events in Barcelona.

by force the means of feeding people, and immediately, without waiting for the strike to develop into an insurrection.

Therefore, it is not so much to stop work that we must invite the workers, but rather to continue it on their own behalf. Otherwise, the general strike would soon transform into general famine, even if one had been energetic enough from the start to take possession of all products accumulated in warehouses.[246] Fundamentally the idea of the general strike has its origins in a totally erroneous belief: the belief that by taking over the products accumulated by the bourgeoisie, humanity can continue to consume, without producing, for an indefinite number of months or years. This belief has inspired the authors of two propaganda pamphlets published about twenty years ago: *Les Produits de la Terre* and *Les Produits de l'Industrie*,[247] and these pamphlets have done, in my opinion, more harm than good. Today's society is not as rich as one might believe. Kropotkin demonstrated somewhere that, in the event of a sudden interruption of production, England would only have what it needs to survive for a month; London would only have enough for three days. I am well aware of the well-known phenomenon of overproduction. But every overproduction has its immediate correction in the crisis that soon brings order back to industry. Overproduction is never more than temporary and relative.

Now I must conclude. I once deplored that comrades isolated themselves from the labor movement. Today I deplore that many of us, falling into the opposite extreme, allow themselves to be absorbed by that same movement. Once again, the labor organization, the strike, the general strike, direct action, boycott, sabotage, and the armed insurrection itself are only *means*. Anarchy is the *end*. The anarchist revolution which we want far exceeds the interests of a class: it proposes the complete liberation of humanity currently enslaved, from the triple perspective, economic, political, and moral. Let us refrain therefore from any unilateral and simplistic means of action. Syndicalism, an excellent means of action due to the labor forces that it makes available to us, cannot be our sole means. Much less must it make us lose our sight of the only end that is worth any effort: Anarchy![248]

. . .

---

246   In the aforementioned report by Emma Goldman for *Mother Earth*, Malatesta articulates the argument as follows: "It may be impossible and, in fact, inadvisable for *all* workingmen to join the General Strike—railroad men, sailors, carmen and others, holding the means of transportation in their hands, may serve the cause of labor infinitely more by carrying the necessities of life to their striking brothers."

247   [Author's note] Geneva, 1885, and Paris, 1887. These pamphlets, attributed to Elisée Reclus, are the work of one of his Swiss collaborators, currently retired from the movement.

248   In the September 3–10, 1907, issue of *La Guerre Sociale* (Paris), Malatesta's speech was summarized as follows:

> He says that unions are merely a means for getting to the Revolution, but fights syndicalism as "power" over individuals. He deplores the bureaucratization of the unions, which annihilates all energies, once their followers manage to use syndicalism as a springboard.

THE AMSTERDAM CONGRESS [BY KARL WALTER]
Freedom (London) 21, no. 223 (November 1907)

. . .

MALATESTA expected some comrades would be surprised to hear him speak against Syndicalism and the General Strike, against a certain conception of the General Strike, a pacifist conception that seems to be growing popular among Syndicalists. But first he desired to make it quite clear that he as much as any one regretted the isolation that is the fate of Anarchists who do not participate in the Labour movement. In the propaganda of Anarchist ideas we must, of course, support the mass movement. He was so far entirely in agreement with previous speakers. But he felt that the other side of the question had not been fairly put, so he would limit himself to bringing out what he considered the essential differences of opinion between Anarchists and Anarchist-Syndicalists. He had himself been such a strong advocate of entering the Syndicates that he had even been accused of being a Syndicate-maker. That was all very well at one time, but now we are confronted with "Syndicalism," the doctrine. He would have nothing to say against it if he could believe that Syndicalism alone could, as was claimed for it, destroy Capitalism. But who could expect to overthrow Capitalism while remaining a servant of capitalist production? Together with a solution of the unemployed problem, they might do it; but the fact of the matter was that as the Syndicalist organisation grew nearer and nearer to perfection, the number of unemployed grew greater and greater. Certainly, Syndicalism in this way can emancipate a part of the workers, but not all. It is only too obvious that the Syndicates make a serious division of the workers, and often enough without doing any harm to the capitalists.

Do not let us make any mistake about what we mean by "solidarity of the workers." It is often used as if there existed some natural economic solidarity among the exploited workers. But this class solidarity even is only an abstraction. The material fact of life under existing conditions is the personal antagonism between all workers. Solidarity is an aspiration, and in that alone lies its importance

---

— The union does not encompass everything, he exclaimed, there is more, and we must not forget that we are first and foremost anarchists, and that all methods must be used to hasten the insurrection, not by means of the general strike of folded arms, but by means of the "armed strike." He recalls that science makes available to everyone powerful and truly revolutionary means, whose use for defense purposes should be encouraged and approved.

Discussion then follows on the inadequacy of the general strike due to the subsequent shortage of consumer goods and lack of preparation to face repression.

An almost identical summary of Malatesta's speech appeared in the aforementioned report by Henri Beylie published in the October 6–13, 1907 issue of *Le Libertaire* (see note 234 above).

to the workers. It is an aspiration that is capable of transforming the economic conditions of a nation, for the differences of economic conditions are not due to financial causes, but to the varying spirit of the people in the different countries. Indeed we may as well confess at once that the purely economic struggle is not sufficient; it must be based on an intense moral struggle, for changes in economic conditions soon readjusted themselves where the moral conditions of the people remained unaffected.

Of one point about Anarchists in Syndicates he was quite certain,—that no Anarchist could take an official position in a Syndicate without placing himself in a false position. Indeed, he was not sure whether even the plain Anarchist member of a Syndicate would not before many years find himself in a false position, for he was only accepted until the Syndicates became really strong, and then he would be asked to go. He did not see why France should consider herself in a novel condition; English Trade Unionism began in just the same revolutionary tone, and look at it now!

He should like, in passing, to clear up a misunderstanding of terms. He often heard political action referred to as if it involved Parliamentarism. This was a great mistake. What, for example, was Bresci's act? Was it economic? No; it was political. Marx was responsible for this confusion. He approached the whole question from the economic viewpoint, and sometimes almost takes it for granted that the peasant enjoys paying rent to his landlord. This is manifestly absurd. No peasant—and no other worker for that matter—*likes* paying rent; he does so simply because of the force—the political force—that is behind the landlord.

He now came to the General Strike. What he objected to was the idea, so freely propagated by some Syndicalists, that the General Strike can replace insurrection. Some people fondly cherish the idea that we are going to starve the bourgeoisie. We should starve ourselves first. Or else they go so far as to admit that the General Strike involves expropriation. But then the soldiers come. Are we to let ourselves be shot down? Of course not. We should stand up to them, and that would mean Revolution. So why not say Revolution at once instead of General Strike? This might seem only a question of words, but it goes deeper than that. The advocates of the General Strike make people think they can do things without fighting, and thus actually spoil the revolutionary spirit of the people. It was propaganda of this kind that brought about such illogical positions as that taken up by the strikers recently at Barcelona, where they did fight the soldiers, but at the same time treated with the State. This was because they were under the delusion that it was only an economic question.

He considered that some of the pamphlets published on the General Strike did nothing but harm. In the first place, it was a fallacy to base their arguments, as some of them do, on a supposed superabundance of production. Not being much of a hand at statistics himself, he once asked Kropotkin what was the real position of England in this respect, and he was told that England produces enough for three months in the year only, and that if importations were stopped for four weeks everybody in the country would die of starvation. The modern possibilities of transport make it undesirable for capitalists to accumulate food. It was estimated that London was never provisioned for much over three days, in spite of all her warehouses.

In dealing with this question of the General Strike we *must* begin by considering the necessity of food. This is a more or less new base for the conception. A peasant strike, for instance, appeared to him as the greatest absurdity. Their only tactics were immediate expropriation, and wherever we find them setting to work on those lines it is our business to go and help them against the soldiers. And then he had read somewhere that we ought to go and smash the railway bridges! He wondered whether the advocates of such foolishness ever realised that corn has to come the same way the cannons come. To adopt the policy of neither cannons nor corn is to make all revolutionists the enemies of the people. We must face the cannons if we want the corn.

Let us realise that the General Strike is only one means of fighting the capitalists, and let us find out how it works in practice, how really to use it. If the Governments have perfected the arms of repression, we must set to work to perfect those of revolution. We need more knowledge; we want new methods of fighting; we need a *technique militaire*. In his own early days when they talked about the General Strike for the first time, every man had his own rifle and revolver, his plan of the town, of the forts, arsenals, prisons, Government buildings, and so forth. Nowadays nobody thinks of these things, and yet they talk on glibly about revolution. Look at what happened in South Italy. The Government shot down peasants by the hundred, and the only soldier that was hurt fell off his horse by accident. (It was this massacre that made Bresci take extreme action. He believed a telegram which was sent him from Rome saying that the King himself had ordered the soldiers to shoot without mercy.)

If we talk about revolution, then, let us at least be prepared for it. Unfortunately, the fight must be brutal. He would like to think otherwise—but how could it be? We cannot let ourselves be killed. These are a few of the things he would recommend the comrades to ponder and discuss.[249]

---

249 The August 30th issue of the *New York Tribune* thus encapsulated Malatesta's speech in a piece of correspondence of the day before from Amsterdam: "The members of the Anarchist Congress, which is at present in session here, are now exercising great care in the selection of the phrases they use in their speeches. For instance, Enrico Malatesta, one of the Italian delegates, delivered a speech to-day, in which he condemned the proposal for a general strike because the resources of the workmen are inadequate compared with those of the government, 'unless,' Signor Malatesta continued, 'they be aided by such scientific power as chemistry affords,' an undoubted reference to the use of bombs." The same piece of correspondence appears in the *Washington Post* of the same day, with the only difference that Malatesta is presented as a Canadian delegate. The reference to the use of "all means that modern science (physics, chemistry, etc.) makes available" finds confirmation, anyway, in Nikolay Rogdayev's summary in Russian.

[Amsterdam Congress, Morning Session of August 30, 1907]

Translated from "Congrès Anarchiste tenu à Amsterdam, Août 1907," p. 205–12

[*The discussion on syndicalism and the general strike continues during the Thursday August 29th evening session, after which, during the Friday August 30th morning session, four motions presented on the subject are put to vote. The first is the Cornelissen–Vohryzek–Malatesta motion.*]

1ˢᵗ CORNELISSEN–VOHRYZEK–MALATESTA MOTION[250]

The International Anarchist Congress considers unions to be both battle organizations in the class struggle for improvement of working conditions as well as unions of producers that can be of service to the transformation of capitalist society into an anarchist communist society.

Thus the Congress, while admitting the eventual necessity of creating special revolutionary syndicalist groups, recommends that comrades support general union organizations in which they have access to all workers of the same trade.

However the Congress considers it the anarchist's task to build the revolutionary element within these organizations and to propagate and support only those forms and demonstrations of "direct action" (strikes, boycotts, sabotage, etc.) that have in themselves a revolutionary character and tend toward the transformation of society.

The anarchists consider the syndicalist movement and the general strike as powerful revolutionary means, but not as substitutes for the revolution.

They furthermore recommend that comrades, in the event a general strike is proclaimed for the conquest of power, support the strike but invite them at the same time to use their own influence to push the unions to assert their economic demands.

The anarchists think that the destruction of capitalist and authoritarian society can only be achieved through armed insurrection and violent expropriation and that the use of the more or less general strike and the syndicalist movement must not make them forget the more direct means of fighting the military force of governments.

[*The motion, which in addition to the authors' signatures, bears the signatures of Jean Wilquet, Emma Goldman, René de Marmande, Nikolaj Rogdaev, and Ladislav Knotek, is approved with 33 votes for and 10 against. The other three motions, presented respectively by Friedeberg, by Dunois and by Siegfried Nacht and Monatte, are also approved by a large majority.[251] Discussion follows on the subject of "Antimilitarism as a strategy*

---

250   [Author's note] The first three paragraphs of this collective motion are by Cornelissen; the fifth by Vohryzek; the fourth and sixth by Malatesta.

251   In this regard, the writer of this report observes: "The reader will perhaps be amazed that, despite their evident contradictions, all four motions were accepted. There is indeed a breach of the parliamentary custom, but it is an intentional breach. It was not appropriate that the opinion of the majority

*of anarchism." Given the short amount of time available before the afternoon's antimil-
itarist congress, after a brief discussion, the following motion is simply put to vote. It is
a motion proposed by Malatesta and others, which expresses the anarchist position to
bring to the congress.]*[252]

*Anarchists, wanting the full liberation of humanity and complete freedom of the individ-
ual are, naturally, essentially, declared enemies of any kind of armed force in the hands
of the State: army, gendarmery, police, magistrature.*

*They compel their comrades—and in general all men who aspire to freedom, to fight
according to the circumstances and their own temperament, and with all means, from
individual revolt, to isolated or collective refusal of military service, to passive and active
disobedience and the military strike—for the radical destruction of the instruments of
domination.*

*They express the hope that all people involved will respond to any declaration of
war with insurrection.*

They declare that they think anarchists will provide the example.

This motion that bears the signatures of Malatesta, Marmande, Thonar,
Cornélissen, Ramus and Domela Nieuwenhuis, is approved without discussion.
. . .

---

suffocate or seemed to suffocate that of the minority. The majority therefore thought that it was necessary to vote, *for* or *against*, after each of the
motions was presented. Now, all four collected a majority of favorable votes.
Consequently all four were approved." We add that an example of a delegate
who approved several motions was Luigi Fabbri. In this regard, his daughter
Luce observes: "Monatte saw no other path to revolution than the union;
however, by Luigi Fabbri's suggestion, he accepted to remove from his motion
the sentence: 'the union suffices onto itself' and to introduce the following
parenthetical phrase: 'without losing sight of the fact that anarchist action is
not entirely contained within the sphere of trade organization.' Thanks to this
parenthetical phrase, the difference between the two motions could seem to
merely consist of the emphasis placed on one or the other of the two forms of
struggle, equally necessary" (*Luigi Fabbri: Storia d'un uomo libero* [Pisa, BFS,
1996], 78).

252 According to Karl Walter (*Freedom*, December 1907), before the motion on
antimilitarism was approved, Malatesta made a brief observation: "Malatesta
would like to point out the difference between Anarchists and some other
Anti-Militarists. Some of the latter take simply the financial or economic
viewpoint of the agitation; others would like to abolish armies but not the
police."

[Amsterdam Congress, Afternoon Session of August 31, 1907]

Translated from "Congrès Anarchiste tenu à Amsterdam, Août 1907," p. 220–23

[*The Friday, August 30th afternoon session was held jointly with the antimilitarist congress. During the last three sessions, that is, the August 30th evening session and the Saturday, August 31st morning and afternoon sessions, the remaining issues on the agenda are discussed.*]

Finally the last issue is addressed: *Esperanto.* Comrade CHAPELIER has contributed a voluminous report on this issue, but limits himself to asking for the adoption of the following resolution signed by him with Malatesta and Rogdaëff:[253]

The International Anarchist-Communist Congress of Amsterdam, considering:

1. that the multiplicity of languages represents an intellectual and moral barrier and therefore a hindrance to the propagation of revolutionary ideas;

2. that even during its debates, it has been observed that the difficulties and unavoidable inaccuracies of translation have made us lose at least three quarters of our time;

3. that the use of a common language would facilitate the exchange of communications of the LIBERTARIAN INTERNATIONAL;

4. that no modern language would meet the necessary conditions of neutrality, ease, and flexibility;

5. that among all artificial languages, Esperanto is the only one that is seriously used and seems destined for success;

Expresses the wish that all anarchists or at least the militants study Esperanto and that in the near future our international congresses can be held in the international language.

[*Since Chapelier's motion encounters opposition and there is not enough time for an in-depth discussion, upon Malatesta's suggestion the following motion is put to vote instead, and approved without difficulty.*]

The Congress, while acknowledging the usefulness of an international means of communication, declares itself incompetent to judge the proposed international language (Esperanto).

The Congress expresses the wish that comrades able to address this, shall study the matter of an international language.

Comrade Emma Goldman, president, then declares that this was the last item on the agenda and that the Congress has completed its works. And she invites the able doyen[254] Errico Malatesta to say a few words of farewell.

---

253 [Author's note] Text of *Le Communiste* (no. 4).

254 [Author's note] Although he was only fifty-three years old at the time of the Congress, Malatesta was nevertheless the doyen of congress participants!

MALATESTA rises and with a strong and penetrating voice delivers the following speech:

Comrades, our Congress is over. The bourgeois newspapers of all colors have announced to the world that this first international Congress would be held in chaos, confusion, and incoherence. Even some comrades predicted that logically it would only have served to throw a little more disharmony into our ranks.

Reality has proven all of these prophets wrong. Despite the insufficiency of material preparation, imputable only to our poverty, despite the difficulty there was in understanding and being understood among delegates of different origins and languages, this first Congress has admirably succeeded. It did not just absolutely destroy the perfidious hopes of all its enemies; I can say that it surpassed the most optimistic hopes of its supporters.

Far from provoking a division in the anarchist field, it opened the path that leads to fruitful union; it encouraged comrades who until now have been fighting in isolation, to join hands over borders so we may all walk together toward the anarchist future. Without a doubt, divergences of views have appeared among us; however they only affected secondary points. We all came to agreement in affirming the essential principles.

And could it be otherwise? Do we not all want, with equal fervor and all of our being, the liberation of humanity, the complete destruction of Capitalism and the State—the social Revolution?

Our first Congress shall bear its fruit, if all those who are here, once they return to their own countries, look less at the work completed than at that which remains to be done and if all set to work again on propaganda and organization more than ever with confidence and energy. To work, comrades!

. . .

Our Interviews: Enrico Malatesta [by Sorgue][255]

Translated from "Nos Interviews: Enrico Malatesta," *La Guerre Sociale* (Paris) 1, no. 42 (October 2–8, 1907)

A PROPAGANDIST OF DIRECT ACTION. —BEGINNINGS OF PROPAGANDA BY THE DEED IN ITALY. —MALATESTA ACTS. —BRIGANDS ARE THE HEROES. —THE OPINION OF THE AUTHOR OF "BETWEEN PEASANTS" ON SYNDICALISM.

[*As the summary shows, the article mostly consists of a portrait of Malatesta, which is followed by this interview, corresponding to the last point in the summary*]

At the anarchist congress in Amsterdam:

— *Hey! good morning, Malatesta.*

Smiling, my friend from London holds his hand out; and we chat:

— *Will your International do big things?*

— *I really hope so, Sorgue. In any case, this meeting, which has brought together comrades from every country, will go down in the history of our movement. It is very good that a current of sympathy and agreement could be created among anarchists from everywhere: this will surely make our international action more effective.*

Thinking of the informative and exciting, as well as friendly debate which took place on the question of the relations between Anarchy and Syndicalism, in which Monatte, with his original eloquence, defended the anarcho-syndicalist views and Malatesta defended, no less eloquently, the views of traditional anarchism, ending up by fairly making concessions to his young competitor, I ventured to ask this question, perhaps a little aggravating:

— *Does it seem to you that syndicalism is capable of directing the social and labor protest movement down an effectively revolutionary path?*

A moment of hesitation; then:

— *Without a doubt, syndicalism is a precious means to awaken and elevate the consciousness of the working class and prepare it for revolt. Nevertheless, do not confuse the means with the end.*

And raising his voice, which trembled with combativeness, Malatesta concluded:

— *The end? It is anarchism![256] And the union, the strike, the antimilitarist propaganda, the insurrection must always be considered as expressions of direct action aiming at anarchist ends.*

---

255   "Sorgue" is the pseudonym of the syndicalist militant Antoinette Durand de Gros, wife of journalist Auguste Cauvin.

256   It is more likely that Malatesta, as per his speech at the congress, referred to "anarchy" as the end.

Anarchists Facing Socialists and Syndicalists[257]

Translated from "Gli anarchici di fronte ai socialisti e ai sindacalisti," *Il Giornale d'Italia* (Rome) 7, no. 251 (September 9, 1907)

INTERVIEW WITH ERRICO MALATESTA AFTER THE AMSTERDAM CONGRESS.

Amsterdam, September.

The anarchist Congress that recently ended was undoubtedly ultra-revolutionary and violent in substance, but it was less bombastic and violent than other congresses in the form and in the language of the speakers and in the discussions.

The German congress participants were numerous, more than all others; then came the French, with a considerable delegation from the *Confédération générale du travail*; the Italians, the Belgians, the Bohemians, the English. Very few representatives (two or one at most) from Austria, the United States, the Argentine Republic, Poland, Bulgaria, Serbia, and Sweden. Rather characteristic and numerous was the Russian delegation, including several women. Also numerous, naturally because it was held in their homeland, were the Dutch delegates. Among others, a Chinese anarchist provided his excuses by letter, unable to participate due to illness. As with all congresses, even in this one the element of order par excellence was the German element; almost continuously doctor Lange from Berlin acted as president of the sessions.

Malatesta

To give the readers of a newspaper that fights against all subversive ideas and all violent propaganda—but wants to be familiar with all present-day expressions and follows them with modern and broad criteria—an approximate idea of the theoretical and practical outcome of the Congress, I interviewed the one who exercised the greatest influence there and was the oldest militant of anarchism among the congress participants, namely Errico Malatesta, the well-known revolutionary who was Bakunin's disciple and one of the first propagators of socialism in Italy.

He was the representative of Italy per the deliberation made during the national Congress of his party, held, as you may recall, in Rome last June. Another five Italians were with him, including a pair from Rome, but Malatesta was the most remarkable figure. His hair and beard are very black, yet starting to go gray; his black eyes, lively and deep, give him an air of energy and faith, and exert a strange suggestion upon those who listen to him, as also happened during the

---

257   The unsigned interview was performed by Luigi Fabbri, as he confirms in the Spanish version of his biography on Malatesta. At the time Fabbri lived off of journalism. In the interview, therefore, he temporarily steps out of the militant's shoes to wear those of a journalist.

debate at the recent Congress, which fulfilled his old dream, the rebirth of the revolutionary International.

Malatesta seemed annoyed when first approached for an interview. Then he told me why he did not like this type of journalistic activity; almost never, in interviews, has his thought been clearly expressed. Therefore in London he regularly turns down those who come to make him speak.

— This is of no use, though—he said to me;—ultimately, after Morral's attack in Spain, an editor from a conservative English newspaper came to me to find out what I thought on the matter. I replied that I would not reply. After having uselessly insisted, this gentleman ended by telling me: "Alright, no matter: I already have my nice interview in pocket, even without you!" Besides—Malatesta added smiling—the real interview must be done in such a way that the interviewee is not aware of it, and does not even know that he is dealing with a journalist, let alone an *interviewer*. If you interview me, letting me know about it first, and I need to dictate you my answers, I might as well write an article... in which I would say only that which suits me.

But I tenaciously insisted.

Anarchism in Decadence? A Desertion

And since another interview with Saverio Merlino—who proclaimed the decadence of anarchism and the uselessness of its congresses—has recently made the rounds of the newspapers,[258] I mentioned it to Malatesta to provoke him, and he replied to me:

— I read that interview. Merlino has an excellent past, as one of the most active and intelligent anarchist militants. But, despite and perhaps because of that past, which troubles him, he gave singular proof of a lack of understanding and even discretion. He has been far from us and outside of the anarchist movement for too long to be able to judge it with a precise knowledge of the facts. But we need not deal with him, and it would be too cruel to insist on this subject; it is apparent that Merlino in some way must excuse his desertion, and explain why he is no longer with us...

— Yes, but I am not talking about his change of direction, rather his opinion that anarchy is in decadence, and that the movement that takes its name has very little or no importance.

— This is quite natural! it is not strange that anarchy appears to be in decadence and makes little racket during periods of calm. Such is the fate of all parties of revolutionary action, which become important only during times of revolution.

---

258   The interview, signed by Cesare Sobrero, appeared in *La Stampa* of Turin on June 19, 1907, with the title "La fine dell'anarchismo?" (The end of anarchism?) and was then reprinted in various newspapers. For Merlino, socialism had already absorbed the essential part of the anarchist program. Therefore, he declared, "both the anarchist international Congresses as well as the partial Congresses, constitute nothing more than attempts to give life to a cadaver."

Since anarchism is an anti-legalitarian movement, which denies legality and does not concern itself with the law except to fight it, it must necessarily make a bad impression in times when it is compelled to operate more or less within legal limits. Consider that anarchism proposes the abolition, the complete elimination of the state and capitalism, and wants to get there without hesitation; now this, naturally, seems too much or too little to the public that runs behind immediate but illusory petty reforms. But this seeming weakness, which lasts until the open rebellion of a revolution becomes possible, is in practice its strength, because it prevents it from degenerating and preserves that character of radicalism and irreconcilability, which will allow it one day to prevent the revolution from being limited to a simple formal change and being exploited to the benefit of a new dominant class.

Anarchists and Socialists
— What relations do you have with socialists?
— Since I live far from Italy, I do not know enough to go into details. I could tell you about theoretical relationships, but I believe that would be useless, since there is a whole pamphlet literature on that subject that you could easily consult. I prefer to tell you our position in the movement, as revolutionaries. Now, we find ourselves somewhat in the same position (the comparison is worth what any comparison can be worth) as the Italian revolutionary patriots found themselves before 1859,[259] facing the legalitarians of that time, those who would have been satisfied with constitutional reforms of an administrative nature and who considered the unity of Italy to be a very far-off dream. Probably, if there had not been the intransigents, the Mazzinians, etc., Lombardy-Venetia would today be something like Hungary, a relatively autonomous State, but still dependent on Austria. Instead the intransigent patriots wanted to chase away the foreigner, before anything else; therefore, they could not collaborate with him in the administration of Italian matters. This made them powerless to participate in legal struggles for the mitigation of the Austrian regime and the development of the national forces.

But their intransigence saved the future; because of it, the feeling of independence was kept alive and in the end the foreigner was chased away.[260]

Likewise socialism, taken in the widest and original sense of the word (of which the anarchists are the extreme avant-garde), namely liberation of the

---

259 The year 1859 represented a turning point for the *Risorgimento*. In that year the second independence war took place, during which Parma, Modena, Tuscany, and Romagna transitioned to pro-Savoyard governments. At the end of the war, Lombardy was ceded to the Kingdom of Sardinia. The next year the Expedition of the Thousand took place, which led to the formation of the Kingdom of Italy in 1861.

260 Here, the editors of the *Giornale d'Italia* protect themselves with a note in the margin observing how "the memory of the struggle for unity in Italy is not appropriately cited to corroborate anarchist doctrine" and claim that it should lead to the opposite conclusion than the one drawn by Malatesta.

individual from any form of exploitation and authority, will be saved by these ir-reconcilable intransigent anarchists,—saved from the pitfalls of external enemies and from internal degeneration.

— Fine! but then what use is a congress like the one that ended today? Could you tell me what you have achieved?

— You too attended the sessions, so you can know yourself...

— The public sessions, yes; but then there were also the secret sessions...

At this point Malatesta stared at me, with his black eyes, and seemed to rec-ollect that he was speaking with a journalist. He smiled, and then, after a moment, answered me:

— Oh, secret, that is not the right word. Say private, instead. But this is a matter that does not concern you... In any case, what a congress can produce is known... I am not disappointed with it, certainly! but it would be more reason-able to consider it, not as an extraordinary act, from which extraordinary results must emerge, but as one among many expressions of the anarchist propaganda and agitation activity.

The Syndicalists

— I asked you before about your relations with the socialists. But now there is syndicalism, and it is making an uproar. Many insist, especially in Italy, that it is nothing more than disguised anarchism, some kind of method to make anarchy seep more easily through the working masses. Is there any truth to that?

— I do not really know if the Italian syndicalists have this intention. I be-lieve not. But in fact it is not true that anarchism is syndicalism, or vice versa. We said so at the Congress; syndicalism, for anarchists, is not a theory, but a method. It would be more precise to say that we are advocates of union struggles, but not of syndicalism.

— Look! like Ferri at the socialist Congress in Rome. He too said he was for the unions against syndicalism...

— Perhaps, but with an entirely different objective. Union organization that uses the general strike, *sabotage*, etc. as methods of struggle, is a very effective method of revolutionary struggle. And we accept it as a means, one of the many means of revolution, which however does not exclude the others, and much less can replace anarchism.

Unanimity

— I observed a strange thing in your Congress: the unanimity in your resolu-tions. How is unanimity possible in a congress of thinking people and, what's more, revolutionaries?

— Why do you want there to be divisions? If our Congress had been an academy of doctrinal and philosophical discussion, certainly unanimity would have been impossible, and there would have been as many currents as congress participants. But when it is not a question of philosophy, but of practical action to carry out and practical objectives to define, we are all in agreement, because we all want the same thing.

— What do you want, then?

— I told you earlier, and you can read it in all our newspapers, pamphlets and books: the abolition of the State and the sharing of the social wealth, through the expropriating revolution.

— I know, but this concerns the far future…

— Who told you that? it is not at all a far future, at least not by our desire. And if, besides, it will take time to get there, it certainly will not be because we want so.

The Amsterdam Congress

Translated from "Le Congrès d'Amsterdam," parts 1–3, *Les Temps Nouveaux* (Paris) 13, nos. 21–23 (September 21 and 28 and October 5, 1907)

I.

I am not going to provide a detailed report on the Congress, this has already been done by other newspapers; and moreover, in a little while the International Correspondence Office shall publish the text of the resolutions in a brochure, as it was mandated, while other comrades shall take charge of the publication of the most important speeches and reports.

Rather I shall try to give a concise idea of the outcome that seems to me to have been produced by the Congress, and I will analyze the main ideas emerging from the debates, as completely as the need to be brief will allow and as impartially as it is possible for a partisan.

First of all, I must say that the Congress exceeded the most optimistic hopes.

This Congress met under inauspicious circumstances. Many comrades, perhaps the majority, had watched its preparation with a hostile or indifferent eye: some considered it nothing more than a useless chitchat; others feared an attempt at centralization and appropriation. And even many of those who most care about an understanding between comrades and who believe most in the efficacy of coordinated efforts, remained perplexed, fearing that the Congress was only an occasion to sour spirits and increase dissent.

Despite all of this, the Congress succeeded very well. Many comrades, from every country and of different tendencies, came either in their own name or as delegates of established groups, met, discussed, and reached agreements.

A spirit of frankness, fraternity, and good will always prevailed among the congress participants: we saw and met each other, we examined differences and points of contact, and, without anyone sacrificing anything of his personal ideas, we always reached a fundamental agreement, which will allow us to fight alongside one another for the common cause.

The first issue presented to the congress participants was the approach to take as regards the antimilitarist Congress. The matter had no real importance—because, being anarchists, evidently we can only be antimilitarists in the most radical sense of the word—and it was merely about establishing how we would express our hatred of militarism and our firm decision to combat it and tear it down by all means possible. I therefore would not have spoken of it, had it not incidentally provoked a question that often causes misunderstandings among us, and on which it is good to clearly explain ourselves.

There were comrades who proposed to remove the issue of antimilitarism from our agenda and to meet on this issue at the antimilitarist Congress. Others countered that if the antimilitarist Congress only brought together anarchists, there was no reason to have a special congress on a point taken from the anarchist program; and if, to the contrary, the antimilitarist Congress was also attended by non-anarchists, as was indeed the case, it was more reasonable to formulate our opinion on the subject amongst ourselves, and then go to defend it at the antimilitarist Congress.

No agreement could be reached on this point and the issue was settled by a vote that gave a slight majority to the advocates of the second proposal.

This use of the vote displeased some comrades who believed that in the act of voting there was a violation of anarchist principles and it displeased them so much that some of those who had proposed to vote were so affected that the next day they wanted to apologize before the Congress for the "inconsistent" act, attributing it to the irritation caused by a long discussion that remained without a solution, precisely because it was not due to any substantial difference. But the majority of those who had voted refused to admit that the vote was an act contrary to anarchist principles, in this case; and this is what I would like to draw comrades' attention to.

It was observed that one must not confuse two essentially different things, even when it happens that they have the same name and appear in the same external forms. The vote that anarchists reject, that they must reject unless they contradict themselves, is the vote by which they renounce their own sovereignty, the vote that gives the majority the right to impose their will upon the minority, the vote that is used to make and justify the law.

But the vote used to record opinions certainly has nothing anti-anarchist about it, just as the vote is not anti-anarchist when it is only a practical and freely accepted means to resolve practical issues that do not allow for multiple solutions at the same time, and when the minority is not obliged to submit to the majority, if this does not suit or please them.

We voted on the conditions under which we would attend the anti-militarist Congress, because it was necessary to decide what we would do; but, naturally, if the minority had persisted in the idea of going to the antimilitarist Congress without prior discussion among anarchists, they would have been free to do so, under the sole condition that they could not force the majority to follow them—and this, it seems to me, is all that a minority can lay claim to in anarchy.

And the proof that all recognize the fairness of this viewpoint, at least in practice, is that afterward all the proposals made at the Congress were put to vote to record the opinion of those present; however, whatever the number of votes obtained, all proposals had a right to the same publicity, all were equally submitted to the comrades, so that they can take them into greater or lesser consideration, as they will please. While on practical issues (session times, appointment of the committee to keep order during discussions, etc.) we voted and followed the will of the majority, because no one wanted to renounce, for such issues, the advantage of discussing together, that is the Congress itself.

II.

And now we arrive at the issue that was or seemed the most important for the Congress to discuss, that of organization.

Comrades are familiar with the often bitter and malicious discussions and polemics that have afflicted us for many years on the questions of organization, individualism, and free initiative. Therefore we expected to see a bitter battle on this terrain, from which perhaps an irreparable scission would result.

Nothing of the sort. We discussed with intensity, but we reached a conclusion that may seem unexpected for many people, without however surprising those who—not lingering on questions of words, on the coarseness of language and on personal prejudices—study the psychological and social forces that produce the anarchist movement.

And the conclusion was (or at least seems to me that it was) that—except for the mystics of non-resistance who have no hold over the masses and whom the governments themselves call back alas!—to the harsh reality of the struggle; except for a few extravagant ones, who perhaps serve, as extravagant people often do, to open new ways of futuristic thought and action, but who do not count much among the forces currently acting; and except for certain individuals, bourgeois in fact and by aspiration, who call themselves anarchist to make themselves interesting to the ladies of their world—all of us, revolutionary anarchists, whether we call ourselves individualists or communists, organizationists or anti-organizationists, and whatever our theoretical ideas, all actually agree in practice; we all want the same thing and just about by the same means.

We are all irreconcilable enemies of the State, of Capitalism, and of Religion, we all seek to acquire the moral and material force necessary to tear down the governments, expropriate the capitalists, and make the social wealth available to all, so that everyone, pushed by social instinct and by the necessities of life, may organize, in full freedom, a society of peace and happiness for all.

Certainly, by applying to all anarchists the impression that I gleaned from the discussions in Amsterdam, I am only expressing my personal opinion. Unfortunately, very few comrades of the tendency called individualist or anti-organizationist were represented at the Congress, and I can only make assumptions on the attitude they would have had, should they have been there. However, if only the echo of Amsterdam served to calm polemics and push comrades to seek points of contact and possible collaboration, rather than exaggerate differences and linger on the errors and weaknesses of each, the Congress would already have been useful.

Among the comrades present at the Congress, agreement and a desire to collaborate seemed evident to me.

There were comrades (mainly Croiset from Amsterdam) who insisted on the rights of the individual, on free initiative and on the dangers of oppression of the individual by the collective; there were those (mainly Dunois) who insisted on the idea of solidarity, cooperation, and organization. But the differences only depended on each speaker's point of view, and I was unable to discover any fundamental dissent in anything that was said. And this had to be the impression of all congress participants, if we can judge from the favorable welcome received when I pointed out this general agreement.

The feud between individualists and *societarists*, I say, is only a feud of words. All those who think, anarchists or not, are individualists in the sense that they clearly know that the individual is the living reality, whose happiness is the only important thing; and all are *societarists* because they all know that society, with its fellow members, is the necessary condition for the development, the happiness, the very existence of the human individual. A distinction is in order, though. There is the individualism of he who is only concerned with himself, who wants the greatest development of his own person but remains indifferent to the suffering of others, or even benefits from it, and this is the individualism of kings,[261] capitalists, and oppressors of all kinds; and there is the individualism of those who, in order to be happy, need to know that others

---

261   The original text reads "soi" (self) instead of "roi" (king). We made this correction based on a subsequent errata corrige.

are too, those who want freedom, well-being, full development of *all* individuals, and this is the individualism of anarchists.

Likewise, there is the societarism of those who see in society a terrain to exploit, an organization made to place everyone's strength at the service of the interests and will of a few, and this is, once again, the societarism of the oppressors and the authoritarians; and there is the societarism of the anarchists who want to organize society in such a way that every individual finds in it not obstacles to his activity and expansion of his personality, but a means to be more free and powerful. On this point, I said, there cannot be and there is no disagreement among anarchists.

And if we look at it closely, even on the practical issue of organization, there is no disagreement, or at least no essential one. Here, too, there is a mix up that would not have lasted so long, if we had met more often and with more reconciling intentions than in the past.

The "anti-organizationists" have in mind the authoritarian flaws that contaminate almost all existing organizations, and in wanting to push away authoritarianism, they appear to push away the principle of organization, which is nothing but the adaptation of the means to the purpose one wishes to reach. And the "organizationists," becoming attached to words, imagine that the others want to live in isolation. In fact, one can only be "disorganized" when he does nothing, or only does the rare things for which the forces of an isolated individual are enough: when we want to do something, we seek the elements necessary to do it, and, whether this is called organization, or understanding, or nothing at all, we are forming an association, to which an extension and a duration shall be given as required by the pre-established purpose we have in sight.

Thus, we often see that "anti-organizationists" are better organized than many of those who always preach organization; as, conversely, we often see more authoritarian residues in groups proclaiming the "absolute" freedom of the individual than in others accused of having authoritarian tendencies, because they claim to support organization. Therefore, as I concluded in my speech, of which I am only providing the inspiring idea, let us drop the questions of words and look at the facts: if we find that we have something to do together, let us look for the means to be able to do it. The establishment of an anarchist international association was proposed. Let us establish it, if we think cooperation between all of us, anarchists of different countries, is possible and useful: it will live and develop if it succeeds in demonstrating its utility.

As for me, I believe it is a matter of urgency, for moral as well as material reasons, that we multiply relationships amongst ourselves and that we enable ourselves to be able to rapidly appeal to the solidarity of all of us every time the need arises, both to resist against the international reaction, as well as to do work of revolutionary initiative.

This was also the opinion of the Congress and the anarchist International was thus established.

In reality it is nothing but a moral link, an affirmation of the desire of solidarity and common struggle. But this is precisely what matters most.

As a material organ, a correspondence bureau was appointed to facilitate relations among members and establish archives of the anarchist movement, which will remain available to comrades. But all this, in my opinion, only has secondary importance.

What matters, I repeat, is the desire to fight together and the intention to maintain relations, so we do not have to search for each other when the moment to act arrives, with the risk that the moment will pass before we find each other.

III.

After finishing the discussion on organization with a resolution in which everyone wanted to clearly confirm that the anarchist International would be an association of groups and individuals in which "nobody can impose his will and diminish the initiative of others," we went on to discuss syndicalism and the general strike.

This discussion was certainly the most important of the Congress, and naturally so, since it concerns a matter of practical and immediate interest, which has the greatest significance for the future of the anarchist movement and its probable results, and since it was precisely on this matter that the only serious difference of opinion was demonstrated among congress participants, some giving the labor organization and the general strike an excessive importance and considering them almost the same thing as anarchism and revolution, the others insisting on the full idea of anarchism and wanting to consider syndicalism only a powerful but danger-ridden means to reach the achievement of the anarchist revolution.

The first trend was mainly represented by comrade Monatte, the French General Confederation of Labor, and a group that wanted to call itself the "youth," despite protests from the young people, much more numerous, of the opposing trend.

Monatte, in his remarkable report, spoke to us at length about the French syndicalist movement, its methods of struggle, and the material and moral results that it has already achieved, and ended by saying that syndicalism suffices onto itself as a means for accomplishing the social revolution and realizing anarchy.

I vigorously protested against this last statement. Syndicalism, I said, even if augmented with the adjective revolutionary, can only be a legal movement, a movement that fights against capitalism in the political and economic milieu that Capitalism and the State impose upon it. Therefore it does not have a way out, and cannot obtain anything permanent and general, other than ceasing to be syndicalism, and no longer striving toward the improvement of the conditions of wage-earners and the conquest of a few freedoms, but instead the expropriation of wealth and the radical destruction of the state organization.

I acknowledge all the utility, even the necessity, of active participation by anarchists in the labor movement, and I do not need to insist to be believed, for I was one of the first to deplore the anarchists' attitude of haughty isolation after the dissolution of the old International and to push comrades again down the path that Monatte, forgetting about history, calls new. But this is only useful under the condition that we remain first and foremost anarchist, and that we do not cease to consider all the rest from the point of view of anarchist action and propaganda. I am not asking that the unions adopt an anarchist program and be comprised of only anarchists:—In this case they would be useless, because they would be duplicates of anarchist groups, and would no longer have the quality that makes them dear to anarchists, that is to say, the quality of being today a field of propaganda and tomorrow a means of steering the masses in the street and having them take possession of the wealth and organize production for the collectivity. I want unions widely open to all workers who begin to feel the need to unite with their comrades to fight against the masters; but I also know all the dangers for the future presented by groups made with the purpose of defending particular interests in today's society, and I ask that anarchists in unions take upon themselves the mission of saving the future by fighting against the natural tendency of these groups to become closed corporations, in antagonism with other workers even more than with masters.

Perhaps the cause of the misunderstanding lies in the belief—mistaken, in my opinion, though generally accepted—that the interests of the workers are converging and that, consequently, it is enough for workers to set about defending their interests and seeking the improvement of their conditions, for them to be naturally led to defend the interests of the entire proletariat against the masters.

The truth is, in my opinion, very different. Workers endure, like everyone, the law of general antagonism that results from the regime of individual property; and this is why interest groups, always revolutionary at the start, as long as they are weak and need solidarity with others, become conservative and exclusive when they acquire strength, and with the strength, consciousness of their specific interests. The history of English and American trade unionism shows us the way by which the labor movement degenerates, when it is limited to the defense of current interests.

It is only in view of a complete transformation of society that the worker can feel solidarity with the worker and the oppressed with the oppressed; and it is the anarchists' role to keep the flame of the ideal ever burning and seek to direct as much as possible the entire movement toward the conquests of the future and revolution, even, if necessary, to the detriment of small advantages that some fractions of the working class can obtain today, and that are almost always obtained to the detriment of other workers and the consuming public.

But in order to be able to carry out this role of propulsive agents within the unions, it is necessary that anarchists abstain from holding positions, especially paid positions.

A permanent and salaried anarchist official of a union is lost as an anarchist. I am not saying that he cannot sometimes do good work; but it is good work that men with less advanced ideas would do in his place and better than him, while he must sacrifice his personal opinions to conquer and keep his employment, and often do things that have the only purpose of making up for his original sin of being anarchist.

The issue is clear. The union is not anarchist, and the official is appointed and paid by the union: if he acts like an anarchist, he puts himself in contrast with those who pay him and shortly loses his position or causes the union's dissolution; if, instead, he fulfills the mission for which he was appointed, according to the will of the majority, then good-bye anarchism.

I made similar observations concerning the method of action characteristic of syndicalism: the general strike. We must accept, I said, and propagate the idea of the general strike as a rather practical way to begin the revolution but without deluding ourselves that the general strike could replace the armed fight against the forces of the State.

It has often been claimed that, through the strike, the workers will be able to starve the bourgeois and get them to come to terms. I could not imagine a greater absurdity. The workers would already be long dead of hunger before the bourgeois, who have available all the accumulated products, would begin to seriously suffer.

The worker, who has nothing, no longer drawing his salary, must take possession of products by force: he will face police officers and soldiers and the bourgeois themselves, who want to stop him; and the issue will be quickly resolved with rifle shots, bombs, etc. Victory shall belong to he who can be the strongest. Let us therefore prepare ourselves for this necessary fight, instead of limiting ourselves to preaching the general strike as a kind of panacea that should resolve all difficulties. Besides, even as a way to start the revolution, the general strike can only be used in a rather relative way. Food services, including obviously the services for transporting foodstuffs, do not allow for prolonged interruption: therefore it is necessary to revolutionarily take possession of the means to ensure provisioning even before the strike itself has developed into an insurrection. Preparing for that cannot be the role of syndicalism: this can only provide the troops able to accomplish it.

On these issues thus expounded on by Monatte and by myself, a very interesting discussion began, although it was somewhat stifled by the lack of time and the tedious necessity of translation into several languages. We concluded by proposing several resolutions, but it does not seem to me that the differences of tendencies were well highlighted; it takes much insight to uncover them, and in fact the majority of congress participants did not uncover them at all and equally approved the different resolutions.

This did not prevent two very real tendencies from being expressed, although the difference exists more in the future development anticipated, than in the current intentions of the people.

I am convinced, in fact, that Monatte and the group of "youth" are as sincerely and profoundly anarchist and revolutionary as any "old beard." They would deplore with us the desertions to be feared among union officials, but they would attribute them to individual weaknesses. And here is where the error lies, for if it were only a question of mistakes imputable to individuals, the damage would not be great: the weak vanish quickly and the traitors are soon known and made powerless to cause harm. What makes the damage serious, though, is that it depends on the circumstances in which the union officials find themselves. I invite our anarchist syndicalist friends to reflect upon this, and to study the respective positions of the socialist who becomes a deputy and the anarchist who becomes a union official: perhaps the comparison will not be useless.

And with this the Congress was practically finished: there was no more strength, nor time. Fortunately the issues that we still had to discuss were not of great importance.

There was, it is true, antimilitarism; but among anarchists this could not give rise to debate. We therefore limited ourselves to affirming, in a resolution, our hatred of militarism, not only as an instrument of war among peoples, but also as a means of repression, bringing together in a single condemnation the army, the police, the judiciary and any other armed force in the hands of the State.

A resolution against alcoholism was proposed, but we went on with the agenda. Certainly nobody would have hesitated to applaud a resolution against the abuse of alcoholic beverages, although perhaps with the belief that it would be pointless; but the resolution proposed also condemned moderate use, considered more dangerous than abuse. That seemed to us as too strong; in any case, we think it is a topic that should instead be discussed by doctors…, assuming that they know something about it.

Finally, there was the matter of Esperanto, dear to comrade Chapelier. The Congress, after a necessarily brief and superficial discussion, recommended that comrades study the question of an international language, but refused to make a decision on the merits of Esperanto. And I, who am a convinced Esperantist, must agree that the Congress was right: they could not deliberate on something they did not know.

Allow me to finish with the words that were in the mouths of all congress participants, when the time came to disband: The Congress was held and was a great success; but a Congress is nothing, if it is not followed by the everyday work of all comrades.

Everyone to work.

Errico Malatesta.

Anarchism and Syndicalism

Freedom (London) 21, no. 223 (November 1907)

The question of the position to be taken in relation to the Labour movement is certainly one of the greatest importance to Anarchists.

In spite of lengthy discussions and of varied experiences, a complete accord has not yet been reached—perhaps because the question does not admit of a complete and permanent solution, owing to the different conditions and changing circumstances in which we carry on the struggle.

I believe, however, that our aim may suggest to us a criterion of conduct applicable to the different contingencies.

We desire the moral and material elevation of all men; we wish to achieve a revolution which will give to all liberty and well-being, and we are convinced that this cannot be done from above by force of law and decrees, but must be done by the conscious will and the direct action of those who desire it.

We need, then, more than any the conscious and voluntary co-operation of those who, suffering the most by the present social organisation, have the greatest interest in the Revolution.

It does not suffice for us—though it is certainly useful and necessary—to elaborate an ideal as perfect as possible, and to form groups for propaganda and for revolutionary action. We must convert as far as possible the mass of the workers, because without them we can neither overthrow the existing society nor reconstitute a new one. And since to rise from the submissive state in which the great majority of the proletarians now vegetate, to a conception of Anarchism and a desire for its realisation, is required an evolution which generally is not passed through under the sole influence of the propaganda; since the lessons derived from the facts of daily life are more efficacious than all doctrinaire preaching, it is for us to take an active part in the life of the masses, and to use all the means which circumstances permit to gradually awaken the spirit of revolt, and to show by these facts the path which leads to emancipation.

Amongst these means the Labour movement stands first, and we should be wrong to neglect it. In this movement we find numbers of workers who struggle for the amelioration of their conditions. They may be mistaken as to the aim they have in view and as to the means of attaining it, and in our view they generally are. But at least they no longer resign themselves to oppression nor regard it as just—they hope and they struggle. We can more easily arouse in them that feeling of solidarity towards their exploited fellow-workers and of hatred against exploitation which must lead to a definitive struggle for the abolition of all domination of man over man. We can induce them to claim more and more, and by means more and more energetic; and so we can train ourselves and others to the struggle, profiting by victories in order to exalt the power of union and of direct action, and bring forward greater claims, and profiting also by reverses in order to learn the necessity for more powerful means and for more radical solutions.

Again—and this is not its least advantage—the Labour movement can prepare those groups of technical workers who in the revolution will take upon themselves the organisation of production and exchange for the advantage of all, beyond and against all governmental power.

But with all these advantages the Labour movement has its drawbacks and its dangers, of which we ought to take account when it is a question of the position that we as Anarchists should take in it.

***

Constant experience in all countries shows that Labour movements, which always commence as movements of protest and revolt, and are animated at the beginning by a broad spirit of progress and human fraternity, tend very soon to degenerate; and in proportion as they acquire strength, they become egoistic, conservative, occupied exclusively with interests immediate and restricted, and develop within themselves a bureaucracy which, as in all such cases, has no other object than to strengthen and aggrandise itself.

It is this condition of things that has induced many comrades to withdraw from the Trade Union movement, and even to combat it as something reactionary and injurious. But the result has been that our influence diminished accordingly, and the field was left free to those who wished to exploit the movement for personal or party interests that had nothing in common with the cause of the workers' emancipation.

Very soon there were only organisations with a narrow spirit and fundamentally conservative, of which the English Trade Unions are a type; or else Syndicates which, under the influence of politicians, most often "Socialist," were only electoral machines for the elevation into power of particular individuals.

Happily, other comrades thought that the Labour movement always held in itself a sound principle, and that rather than abandon it to the politicians, it would be well to undertake the task of bringing them once more to the work of achieving their original aims, and of gaining from them all the advantages they offer to the Anarchist cause. And they have succeeded in creating, chiefly in France, a new movement which, under the name of "Revolutionary Syndicalism," seeks to organise the workers, independently of all bourgeois and political influence, to win their emancipation by the direct action of the wage-slaves against the masters.

That is a great step in advance; but we must not exaggerate its reach and imagine, as some comrades seem to do, that we shall realise Anarchism, as a matter of course, by the progressive development of Syndicalism.

Every institution has a tendency to extend its functions, to perpetuate itself, and to become an end in itself. It is not surprising, then, if those who have initiated the movement, and take the most prominent part therein, fall into the habit of regarding Syndicalism as the equivalent of Anarchism, or at least as the supreme means, that in itself replaces all other means, for its realisation. But that makes it the more necessary to avoid the danger and to define well our position.

Syndicalism, in spite of all the declarations of its most ardent supporters, contains in itself, by the very nature of its function, all the elements of degeneration which have corrupted Labour movements in the past. In effect, being a movement which proposes to defend the present interests of the workers, it must necessarily adapt itself to existing conditions, and take into consideration interests which come to the fore in society as it exists to-day.

Now, in so far as the interests of a section of the workers coincide with the interests of the whole class, Syndicalism is in itself a good school of solidarity; in so far as the interests of the workers of one country are the same as those of the workers in other countries, Syndicalism is a good means of furthering international brotherhood; in so far as the interests of the moment are not in contradiction with the interests of the future, Syndicalism is in itself a good preparation for the Revolution. But unfortunately this is not always so.

Harmony of interests, solidarity amongst all men, is the ideal to which we aspire, is the aim for which we struggle; but that is not the actual condition, no more between men of the same class than between those of different classes. The rule to-day is the antagonism and the interdependence of interests at the same time: the struggle of each against all and of all against each. And there can be no other condition in a society where, in consequence of the capitalist system of production—that is to say, production founded on monopoly of the means of production and organised internationally for the profit of individual employers—there are, as a rule, more hands than work to be done, and more mouths than bread to fill them.

It is impossible to isolate oneself, whether as an individual, as a class, or as a nation, since the condition of each one depends more or less directly on the general conditions of the whole of humanity; and it is impossible to live in a true state of peace, because it is necessary to defend oneself, often even to attack, or perish.

The interest of each one is to secure employment, and as a consequence one finds himself in antagonism—i.e., in competition—with the unemployed of one's country and the immigrants from other countries. Each one desires to keep or to secure the best place against workers in the same trade; it is the interest of each one to sell dear and buy cheap, and consequently as a producer he finds himself in conflict with all consumers, and again as consumer finds himself in conflict with all producers.

Union, agreement, the solidarity struggle against the exploiters,— these things can only obtain to-day in so far as the workers, animated by the conception of a superior ideal, learn to sacrifice exclusive and personal interests to the common interest of all, the interests of the moment to the interests of the future; and this ideal of a society of solidarity, of justice, of brotherhood, can only be realised by the destruction, done in defiance of all legality, of existing institutions.

To offer to the workers this ideal; to put the broader interests of the future before those narrower and immediate; to render the adaptation to present conditions impossible; to work always for the propaganda and for action that will lead to and will accomplish the Revolution—these are the objects we as Anarchists should strive for both in and out of the Unions.

Trade Unionism cannot do this, or can do but little of it; it has to reckon with present interests, and these interests are not always, alas! those of the Revolution. It must not too far exceed legal bounds, and it must at given moments treat with the masters and the authorities. It must concern itself with the interests of sections of the workers rather than the interests of the public, the interests of the Unions rather than the interests of the mass of the workers and the unemployed. If it does not do this, it has no specific reason for existence; it would then only include the Anarchists, or at most the Socialists, and would so lose its principal utility, which is to educate and habituate to the struggle the masses that lag behind.

Besides, since the Unions must remain open to all those who desire to win from the masters better conditions of life, whatever their opinions may be on the general constitution of society, they are naturally led to moderate their aspirations, first so that they should not frighten away those they wish to have with them, and next because, in proportion as numbers increase, those with ideas who have initiated the movement remain buried in a majority that is only occupied with the petty interests of the moment.

Thus one can see developing in all Unions, that have reached a certain position of influence, a tendency to assure, in accord with rather than against the masters, a privileged situation for themselves, and so create difficulties of entrance for new members, and for the admission of apprentices in the factories; a tendency to amass large funds that afterwards they are afraid of compromising; to seek the favour of public powers; to be absorbed, above all, in co-operation and mutual benefit schemes; and to become at last conservative elements in society.

After having stated this, it seems clear to me that the Syndicalist movement cannot replace the Anarchist movement, and that it can serve as a means of education and of revolutionary preparation only if it is acted on by the Anarchistic impulse, action, and criticism.

Anarchists, then, ought to abstain from identifying themselves with the Syndicalist movement, and to consider as an aim that which is but one of the means of propaganda and of action that they can utilise. They should remain in the Syndicates as elements giving an onward impulse, and strive to make of them as much as possible instruments of combat in view of the Social Revolution. They should work to develop in the Syndicates all that which can augment its educative influence and its combativeness,—the propaganda of ideas, the forcible strike, the spirit of proselytism, the distrust and hatred of the authorities and of the politicians, the practice of solidarity towards individuals and groups in conflict with the masters. They should combat all that which tends to render them egoistic, pacific, conservative,—professional pride and the narrow spirit of the corporate body, heavy contributions and the accumulation of invested capital, the service of benefits and of assurance, confidence in the good offices of the State, good relationship with masters, the appointment of bureaucratic officials, paid and permanent.

On these conditions the participation of Anarchists in the Labour movement will have good results, but only on these conditions.

These tactics will sometimes appear to be, and even may really be, hurtful to the immediate interests of some groups; but that does not matter when it is a question of the Anarchist cause,—that is to say, of the general and permanent interests of humanity. We certainly wish, while waiting for the Revolution, to wrest from Governments and from employers as much liberty and wellbeing as possible; but we would not compromise the future for some momentary advantages, which besides are often illusory or gained at the expense of other workers.

Let us beware of ourselves. The error of having abandoned the Labour movement has done an immense injury to Anarchism, but at least it leaves unaltered the distinctive character.

The error of confounding the Anarchist movement with Trade Unionism would be still more grave. That will happen to us which happened to the Social Democrats as soon as they went into the Parliamentary struggle. They gained in numerical force, but by becoming each day less Socialistic. We also would become more numerous, but we should cease to be Anarchist.

E. MALATESTA.

SECTION V
Capitalists, Thieves, and Spies

For a Miserable Police Tool

Translated from "Per un miserabile arnese di polizia," *Cronaca Sovversiva*
(Barre, Vermont) 5, no. 45 (November 9, 1907)

*After the statements of respect, solidarity, and sympathy received by comrade
Luigi Galleani—on the occasion of the salaried vituperations hurled at him
by the ineffable Edoardo Alessi, prompted and rewarded by the consular and
domestic police—from socialists Carlo Tresca of **La Plebe**, Giovanni De Sil-
vestro of **La Voce del Popolo**, Caffaro of **Il Lavoratore Italiano**, Nimini of
La Ragione Nuova, now it is the turn of Errico Malatesta who writes from
London.* [262]

Dearest Gigi,

The mail brings me certain dirty libels against you, which stink of
police from a thousand miles away.

You certainly do not need it and do not doubt it; but I like to take
advantage of this occasion to restate the expression of my friendship and
my solidarity.

> *With much affection*
> ERRICO MALATESTA.

[An editor's note follows, signed "U.," [263] *which emphasizes the value of the
letter reproduced for "those who know Errico Malatesta and his unparalleled
epistolary laziness."]*

---

262   According to what Luigi Galleani himself reports in the October 5, 1907, issue
       of *Cronaca Sovversiva*, his diatribe with socialist Edoardo Alessi began after
       a socialist demonstration in May 1906 in Boston, where a brawl broke out
       between socialists and anarchists, after which Alessi and others filed a report
       against an anarchist. This was followed by a protracted and bitter controversy
       between Alessi and Galleani on how the events unfolded. When Galleani was
       invited to speak at a demonstration commemorating September 20th, anni-
       versary of the breach of Porta Pia, Alessi printed an open letter directed at
       the demonstration's organizing committee in which he slandered Galleani and
       deplored the choice of him as speaker. This was followed by testimonies of
       solidarity with Galleani by various sources.

263   Initial of "Ursus," pseudonym of anarchist Antonio Cavalazzi.

[Private Conversation, London, February 1908]

Translated from a report by "Virgilio" to the Ministry of the Interior,
London, February 12, 1908[264]

Upon receiving the letter from Molinari and company, Malatesta turned pale
with fury. He glanced at just three lines and threw the letter on the ground, then
picked it up again making a visible effort to contain himself.[265]

They also wrote me other letters, he said, and it amazes me that they make
me such proposals.

Those from Protesta Umana who always fought against me and Fabbri
should not make me such proposals. I do not believe in the possibility of an
anarchist daily and I would not be nor am I in a position to direct a newspaper.
They write me calling upon my kindness... but I am not kind, I am rather mean:
moreover, a newspaper takes away all your time; not just that, but I have never got
on well with anyone. Having a newspaper I need to read all the articles: when I
had the weekly newspaper I threw away all the articles they sent me and I wasted
all my time writing the newspaper myself. So my activity was not sufficient for
everything and I was not able to read all the correspondence that they sent me.

A daily newspaper cannot remain anarchist because it becomes the organ of
too many interests: the director and the editors need to live off of it and therefore
they will be condemned to compromise, they cannot say everything that they
should say without getting the newspaper sequestered and causing it to die.

Moreover, among the anarchists I represent a party, a well defined tactic,
"Organization"; now because of my character and because of the idea I represent
I have friends and bitter enemies, especially in Italy, where furthermore I do not
know if I can go. But even if I could, they would chase me away after a fortnight.

I would go, but for a coup de main, to give a push to an insurrection.

Then the daily paper represents commercial and mercenary interests and

---

264 Typescript, Archivio Centrale dello Stato, Rome, Casellario Politico Centrale,
box 2949. With regard to the reliability of this report and the next, see remarks
in note 237.

265 According to another report by the same "Virgilio," the letter in question, dated
February 8th and signed by Luigi Molinari, Ettore Molinari, and others, said:

The authority wanted and wants to suppress the weekly La Protesta Umana
and we respond by transforming the weekly into a daily. We hope this effort
succeeds. In any case we absolutely want to try.

Perhaps abusing your kindness, we announced that you would be the
director, sure that you will give us your moral and intellectual help.

We do not know if you want to or can come back to Italy: in such a case
we are at your disposal. But if you absolutely cannot come, your assiduous
collaboration and the knowledge that you are with us are enough.

La Protesta Umana had been founded in Milan in October 1906 by
Ettore Molinari and Nella Giacomelli.

anarchist editors are not there to do it. There will be interested loafers, but not free and disinterested editors like Fabbri. But the Milanese are against Fabbri...

Malatesta got excited saying as much and I saw that the Milanese initiative is going to ruin the entire plot organized between him and Fabbri to destroy La Protesta and replace it with La Lega Libertaria.[266]

They know—he added—that I do not want to know about it. Then he started to think and said: those people are against organization and form a daily that is already an organization.

Malatesta hence is against the daily newspaper because he says it takes too much money to do it and adds that even if they succeed in finding the money, they will squander it: that is all. The newspaper will only last three or four months, the time strictly necessary to eat up the money. According to him it is better to publish a weekly that can stay close to the anarchist idea. He says that La Protesta Umana can do more than a daily, although even La Protesta did nothing but shout all the time that it was necessary to send the King to death without putting the words into practice.

Less words and more action—he said.

He also thinks that friction and tension among the anarchists will follow this daily paper.

[Private Conversation, London, May 1908]

Translated from a report by "Virgilio" to the Ministry of the Interior, London, May 21, 1908[267]

...

Malatesta told me: The mission you will be performing is semi-official, not entirely official, but you will say what I tell you and you will write me with the answer they will give you.[268] You will say what I told you other times about the daily paper. I did not go because the newspaper does not seem useful for me, because I do not want to be a wage earner, because in times of turmoil a newspaper is a bad action, rather than a good thing.

I am not annoyed with them, as they believe and as some wanted to believe, writing me some time ago and even recently. You will say that if I did not write

---

266   This is probably a reference to the weekly *L'Alleanza Libertaria,* the publication of which was decided during a conference held in Rome in June 1907.

267   Typescript, Archivio Centrale dello Stato, Rome, Casellario Politico Centrale, box 2949.

268   According to what "Virgilio" Bellelli stated, when he was about to leave for Italy, Malatesta wanted to entrust him with the task of relaying his answer to the *Protesta Umana* group concerning the offer to direct a daily paper.

them neither for nor against, it was to not hinder their work, even if I did not like it. It is true, I got annoyed, for various reasons: first, because they appointed me director without asking me; second, because, after my appointment, they went on to appoint editors and correspondents without bothering with me.

What then did they want from me?

That I was a puppet? Listen closely. After the persecution, they wrote "if the police come again to our office, we will shoot at them. Well, the police came back and they searched and the "protesters" did not shoot at them as was their precise duty.

After a solemn public statement, either you do what you said or you make a fool of yourself. They therefore made fools of themselves. Did they want me to go there and myself fire the shots that they did not have the courage to fire?

When you take on a fight like that you must be ready to be apprehended. I am ready; but are they?

I do not approve of that kind of statement without carrying it out. Therefore, I would have had to carry the burden of statements I do not approve of being said until someone is sure that he can honor them. Certain things are only done during uprisings or at the start of revolution, that is when someone is sure he has a crowd ready to act behind him.

You will say that I very well understand the anarchists who do not want organization, who keep to themselves and act by themselves, but I do not understand the Milan anarchists. They are organizationists and associationists and they are against my organization and against the congress.

If they want organization, ours is an organization: otherwise, may they call themselves anti-organizationists.

Besides, you will say that I do not like either of the two trends that now compete in Italy, nay, you will say that I am opposed to both.

I supported Fabbri, but he is getting too weak, he is going too far backward. These others want to go too far ahead, it is not clear what they want and they only do stupid and damaging chit-chat. They were against my organization, and perhaps they still are, nevertheless they call me to direct the newspaper. Was it me who had to renounce my ideas or them?

Besides, I do not have money and if they called me there they would have to pay me. Now I am not saying that living off of propaganda is a bad thing, but it is not a good thing either. The paid propagandist has a monopoly over lectures, so to speak: the others have the task of listening. It is the same as with priests: the flock and the shepherd.

Then I will tell you that newspaper propaganda is good for nothing at the right moment because it is necessary to make use of secret organizations, of groups: hence something else altogether than what they have done so far and are still doing.

So you will say that I am not going to Italy, nor will I go. I would go however, but secretly, to reorganize and make things happen.

. . .

Why Italians Are Anarchists

Reynolds's Newspaper (London), n. 3035 (October 11, 1908)[269]

HOW THE PEOPLE WERE GOADED INTO DISCONTENT.
BY ERRICO MALATESTA.

The public concern in Anarchism has been so much aroused by the assassination within the last few years of King Humbert, the King of Portugal, the Empress of Austria, President McKinley, and, later, the attempt on the life of the present King of Spain on his wedding day, and so many extravagances have been written about Anarchists, and especially Italian Anarchists, and so many lies and slanders have been circulated by the Press about their character generally, that it will not, perhaps, be without some interest to hear what an Anarchist has to say on the matter.

I am an avowed Anarchist, but it is not my intention here to defend or explain the gospel of Anarchism. I only intend to show the real cause of political violence in Italy, and try and put the blame on the shoulders of those to whom it rightly belongs. To understand the Italian episodes and the position of the Italian Anarchists, it is necessary to know something about the moral disposition and material condition of the Italian people.

The Condition of the People.

Amongst all the modern nations, Italy is very likely the country in which the greatest discord exists between the aspirations for the moral development of the people and their real economical and political condition. Italy is one of the poorest countries in the world; it has a great number of

---

269   The first draft of this article in all likelihood dates back to 1900–1, and more precisely the period between August 1900, in the aftermath of Bresci's attack, and September 1901, in the aftermath of Czolgosz's attack. Proof is provided by an article from London on Malatesta, signed by Curtis Brown, dated October 3rd and published simultaneously on October 13th, 1901, in several US dailies, including the *New York Press*, the *Buffalo Express*, and the *Times* of Richmond, Virginia. In the last part of the article, which discusses Malatesta's literary talent, the author writes: "Although Malatesta keeps profoundly secret whatever connection he may have with the violent side of Anarchy, he makes no mystery of his adherence to the philosophical side of it. He even wrote an article on it not long ago, in the hope of getting it printed in one of the most staid and dignified of the English magazines. The magazine, however, wasn't going in for that sort of thing, and the article never got into print. It was not rejected for lack of literary ability, however, as one may judge from this concluding paragraph of it, which I copied from the original manuscript." The paragraph reproduced thereafter corresponds, with minor differences, to the last two paragraphs in this article.

inhabitants who live in a perpetual state of semi-starvation. They cannot read or write; but, in spite of this fact, the Italian poor and the Italian illiterate are not the stupid and resigned creatures which we find in other countries professing higher educational facilities. Perhaps it is because of the influence of the historic past of Italy; perhaps because of the habit of emigration, which brings the Italians into contact with the world at large, and leaves them always a hope—an illusion maybe—of better days; perhaps because the Italians, as a rule, do not brutalize themselves with strong drink. But the fact is, the Italians never accept their position, and are always struggling for, or at least dreaming of, a condition of independence and wealth. Their religion has very little real power over them; they are no doubt often superstitious, and fond of the theatrical spectacles of Catholic worship; but they are at heart a nation of unbelievers. They feel and believe that the ecclesiastical authorities are always on the side of what, rightly or wrongly, they regard as their oppressors. Patriotism appeals to them but little, because their Mother Country has never been to them but a stepmother. The Italian, too, is a selfish man, who cares only for the material interests of himself and his own immediate family, or he is a humanitarian who considers himself a citizen of the world, and yet passionately fond of an ideal state of Society; but in one way or another he is a dreamer, a struggler, and, above all, a discontent. Before the constitution of the kingdom of Italy, when the nation was divided into several sections, oppressed by foreign and native tyrants, a great popular movement developed in favour of liberty and social reforms.

Liberty and Welfare.

The ostensible end of this movement was the unity of Italy with a Democratic Government, but in the mind of the people this had only to be the external form of a quite new Constitution. With other names, other theories, and by other ways what the people hoped and what the agitators of the time led them to hope was the same thing[270] the Socialists and Anarchists are preaching to-day—liberty and welfare secured for all—to which is to be added, for the more enlightened fraction, the destruction of the Popish power, and for a more fanatical one the idea of restoring the past greatness of Italy and her becoming again the civilizer of the world. Hundreds of noble men lost their lives on the scaffold, thousands died in prison or on the fields of battle, but triumph crowned the long martyrdom. The tyrants were subdued, the foreigner was repulsed, and the temporal power of the Popes destroyed. What a joy, what a display of enthusiasm, but what a terrible delusion!

---

270   In the original text, the segment from "what the people hoped" to here is enclosed in parentheses. We have removed the parentheses, as this is the only way to make sense of the sentence.

The Policy of Charity.

Before the national revolution the economic condition of the people was, of course, very bad, but compared with the present state it was one of extraordinary comfort and prosperity. Nearly one-third of the soil belonged to the Monastic Corporations; it was badly cultivated, but even then the people managed to live on the products of the soil.

There were many provident institutions, and charity was freely dispensed for the destitute, but this was because the aristocracy knew they were hated by the middle classes, so they devised these provident schemes in order to command the support and goodwill of the poor. On the whole, everyone had at least a piece of bread to eat.

The new *régime* inaugurated itself by imposing on the Italian people a legion of plunderers that, with the protection of the Government, became possessed of all the riches of the suppressed Corporations, and, in addition, looted in many ways the public institutions. And from then until now all the political machinery has been used for the enrichment of the few to the detriment of the many. The public works, the banks, the national defence—all have been an opportunity and a pretext for the politicians to plunder. All the financial, politic, all the Civil and penal legislation, has been inspired by the desire of robbing the masses and preventing the resistance of the robbed. The result has been the most horrible misery for the toilers, and a state very near to misery for the lower part of the middle classes.

Inhuman Conditions.

It was this awful condition of things that drove thousands of Italians from their native shores to England, the United States of America, and other places abroad. In those countries they have established themselves in business. Many of them have become prosperous as hotel-keepers or managers; others, less fortunate, have managed to eke out a wretched existence by wheeling piano organs about the streets or pursuing the unexciting occupations of ice-cream and chestnut vendors. In many London and American hotels scores of Italian waiters can be found, each struggling for a living, but at the same time scrupulously saving every surplus penny, in the hope that some day in the dim and possibly distant future they may be able once more to join their compatriots in the land of sunny Italy.

It would take too long to describe here the truly inhuman conditions of life of the greater part of Italy's population. Even the Conservative Press cannot conceal the fact. The physical degeneration through starvation and faulty hygienic accommodation, the *pellagra* and malaria-stricken peasant of Italy is becoming classic as a matter for discussion among the medical men of the world. The beastly lives which the miners of Sicily, the wheat and vine growers of Puglia, the workers in the rice fields of Northern and Central Italy, are obliged to endure is a common topic in contemporary literature.

It may suffice for the general reader to remember that the Italian Government has continually to lower the physical standard to be able to find the men they want for the army amongst a degenerating population.

He might remember, too, that the riots caused by hunger are a common feature of Italian life, and that the innumerable Italian emigrants, who bring everywhere their low standard of life—always ready to accept wages which the English, French, and American worker would despise—are the outcome of a government which the majority of the Italian people repudiate.

Widespread Discontent.

With the psychic dispositions and the material conditions I have pointed out, is it astonishing that an intense and a widespread discontent pervades all Italian life? But why has this discontent so strong a tendency to manifest itself by more or less violent attempts on life?

Italians have been accustomed by an uninterrupted experience to expect nothing from Governments except through force or fear of force.

The liberation of Italy (whatever may have been its results) was the outcome of riots, insurrection, manslaughter, and wars. The most prominent and most honoured men of the national movement were men of violence and apologists of violence. All our history, all our literature, all our art are an apotheosis of violence and violent men. And after the unification, after what they call the *[r]isorgimento* (the resurrection) of Italy, violence continued being the only remedy against the violence of what the people felt to be their oppressors. Reforms only came after the people had shown a disposition to be violent, and it is even alleged that the Governments of Italy were passing coercive laws in order to test the spirit of resistance of the people.

Everybody is acquainted with the terrible condition of the Sicilian peasantry, but the Government only thought of Sicily, and spoke of necessary reforms, after the disastrous riots of 1893.

The Theory of No Violence.

It is easy to say that violence is the outcome of Anarchist preaching and propaganda, and to think that Anarchic activity can be suppressed by throwing its advocates into prison. Whatever may be the soundness of Anarchist doctrines, I maintain that Anarchism is the theory of no violence, and if an Anarchist, in spite of his feelings and his principles, is driven to employ violence, it is only when no other means are left to him. In Italy there is no liberty of speech, no liberty of the Press, no liberty of combination or strike. They regard with amazement and envy the liberty and freedom rightly demanded, and in many cases properly enjoyed, by the working classes in England and America. It is true that the English and American workers may not be satisfied with their lot, and believe that the time has come for emphasizing their demands and breaking down the oppressions of capitalists and trust magnates, but the worker in the countries I have named is far ahead of men of their class in Italy. There the gaol and the bayonet is the only answer to his pleadings for better economic conditions.

Whose is the fault, then, if the oppressed strike at the oppressors with the only arms they have left? We Anarchists deplore and regret its many sickening consequences, but we cannot shut our eyes to the true cause of the struggle.

We only ask for liberty of propaganda and organization, expecting the triumph of our ideas not by a *coup de main*, not by the employment of force or violence, but by the free consent of the people. Let us have liberty; it will be the best way for all concerned.

Bibliography

Translated from "Bibliographie," *Bulletin de l'Internationale Anarchiste* (London) 1, no. 7 (November 1908)

[*The column contains a brief unsigned summary of the book* Influencia del Anarquismo, *by Rufino Asenjo del Rio, after which the following note appears in French.*]

As regards this book, comrade Malatesta asks us to include the following lines:

I read in Del Rio's *Influencia del Anarquismo* that I allegedly declared, at the 1887 London Congress, that "Anarchism is the successor of Marx." I wonder where this could have been found! I never said anything of the sort, for the good reason that I do not think it. Furthermore, in 1887 I was in Buenos Aires and I do not believe there was a Congress in London that year.[271]

---

271   The same erroneous date is also found elsewhere, for example in a portrait of Malatesta published in the Lisbon-based *A Sementeira* in June 1912, which also said that Malatesta was sentenced to prison in Florence afterward. Since the latter statement must refer to his 1884 sentence, which was actually issued by the court of Rome, the London congress in question is probably the one that took place in 1881.

[Speeches Given in London on December 6 and 7, 1908]

Translated from "Rapporto Mensile del Mese di Dicembre 1908,"
by police commissioner Frosali, London, January 22, 1909[272]

. . .

Sunday December 6 during the daytime E. Malatesta attempted to give a lecture at Clerkenwell at the location indicated above;[273] but the Policemen and detectives invited him to leave and, since Malatesta resisted, by dint of shoving they moved him away from that location and prevented him from giving the Lecture. Malatesta's comrades were Gualducci, Spizzuoco Alfonso called "Alfredo," and Gentili.

Private and public meetings and lectures.[274]

Sunday December 6, at the Club at 5 o'clock[275] there was a lecture on "Socialism and anarchy" by "Gualducci," who pointed out that active anarchist propaganda was necessary. Malatesta, who was present, declared that the "Groups and organizations are useless, because they are too heavily monitored and monitorable, and that it is necessary that the revolution erupts from the triumph of anarchist ideas." He added that it was necessary "to act individually at the critical moment, because a single courageous and determined individual is enough, to make a whole Country fall into mourning." The subscription to purchase the newspaper "L'Alleanza" followed.[276]

Monday December 7: In the Club location, lecture by the Spanish "Tárrida del Mármol" in debate with Malatesta: "Tárrida" upheld a materialist argument, saying that science necessarily leads to anarchy, while Malatesta upheld the opposite argument that "replacing the matter with God, one commits the same error as putting God in the place of matter,[277] and science does not lead to anarchy, but is a means for helping humanity."

. . .

---

272   Typescript, Archivio Centrale dello Stato, Rome, collection "Divisione affari generali e riservati, Archivio generale," series 1909, box 4, folder 240.

273   This was the intersection "at the corner of Saffron Hill and Eyre Street, near the Italian church," a place chosen by the Italian anarchists to hold outdoor Sunday lectures on a regular basis.

274   Note in text margin.

275   The time is corrected by pencil to "5:20" or "5:30." The club in question is the International Workingmen's Society, offices shared by groups of various nationalities and located at 83 Charlotte Street.

276   The reference is to *L'Alleanza Libertaria* of Rome (see note 266).

277   Thus expressed, the argument would merely be a banal tautology. Ostensibly, Malatesta had maintained that Tárrida's argument contained the same fatalistic fallacy as the theological arguments, with the only difference that he used "matter" in the place of "God." For a similar argument, see, for example, "Liberty and Fatalism: Determinism and Will," in the volume of these *Complete Works* covering years 1913–18.

[Speech Given in London on January 7, 1909]

Translated from "Rapporto Mensile del Mese di Gennaio 1909,"
by police commissioner Frosali, London, February 25, 1909[278]

. . .

Thursday 7—At the Club, lecture by La Rosa Michele on the subject: Cooperativism and anarchy—arguing that by personally benefitting the anarchists, the cooperative movement helps the movement. He was challenged by Malatesta who said "that cooperativism does not reduce exploitation, and therefore cannot benefit the progress of anar. ideas." Gualducci, Spizzuoco Alfonso, and Defendi Enrico also took the floor, refuting the argument put forth by La Rosa.

La Rosa replied, counter-refuting Malatesta's objections and since the debate had changed direction and discussion had begun on "What are anarchist ethics," La Rosa cited a few passages from "Anarchist Ethics" by "Krapotkine" without citing the author.

Malatesta answered refuting that interpretation of anarchist ethics, and then La Rosa made fun of Malatesta, who had taken the liberty to contest the greatest and strongest anarchist intellectual.

. . .

[Speech Given in London on February 2, 1909]

TRANSLATION FROM A REPORT BY "VIRGILIO" TO THE MINISTRY OF THE INTERIOR, LONDON, FEBRUARY 3, 1909[279]

The meeting took place at the club yesterday evening.

. . .

Before getting to the lecture there was talk of Azeff, the anarchist and regicidal police officer from Russia.[280] Malatesta said it was necessary to go slowly in

---

278   Typescript, Archivio Centrale dello Stato, Rome, collection "Divisione affari generali e riservati, Archivio generale," series 1909, box 4, folder 240.

279   Typescript, Archivio Centrale dello Stato, Rome, Casellario Politico Centrale, box 2949.

280   Yevno Azef had been a member of the Russian socialist revolutionary party since 1894 and taken a leading role in the "Combat Organization" linked to the party. He is believed to have organized the 1904 attack during which the Russian minister of the interior Vyacheslav Plehve was killed. In January

believing that Azeff was a spy because the spy accusation came from two police officers and he could still be innocent. What is to Azeff's detriment is that he too disappeared and such an escape could confirm the accusation.

Malatesta then added that also in Paris there was a spy involved in the attack against King Alfonso and Loubet.[281] Actually it was the spy who directed the conspirators, whom he was supposed to detain before they launched the bomb. He was the one who gave orders, but it so happened that, at the eleventh hour, one disappeared and went off on his own to fire the bomb. Thus the police officer was deceived.

After that, Malatesta started his lecture. Very few were present: Bellelli, the two Spizzuoco, Gentili, who is a painter at the "Monico," Gualducci, La Rosa, Ravaioli, Ceresoli with a colleague from his barber shop, and a fellow called Corso.

Malatesta started: Must we talk about the International? Well, to be clear, let us start from the beginning, a little far back. Before anything else it needs to be said that anarchists are divided into two categories: those who want organization and those who do not want it, although not all are individualists.

But organization is something we cannot do without, whatever objective we undertake, unless the forces of a single individual are enough to accomplish it, in which case it must be a matter of small tasks.

Even attacks, including the ones they say are performed by isolated individuals, are always the outcome of long preparation, of prior agreements and therefore of an organization.

It is understood that cases of sudden and unplanned actions, in which a man pushed to the extreme, on the spur of the moment takes out a weapon and kills, are unorganized or can be unorganized.

But except for these very rare and exceptional cases, there is always organization—the conspiracy, as Police Headquarters say. They say that Morral's act was an individual act, but nothing could be more false. He was already linked to Ferrer and others.[282]

At this point Ravaioli said: but Angiolillo's attack was individual, without preparation.

Malatesta answered: certainly not! Here in the streets of London they

---

1909 it publicly came to light, based on the testimony of a former director of the Russian police, that Azef had been an agent of the Okhrana, the Russian secret police, since the beginning. The Russian socialist revolutionary party had already anonymously received a similar disclosure from a police officer in 1905, but did not believe it. At the time when the news went public, Azef had fled his residence in Paris.

281   On May 31, 1905, exactly one year before Mateo Morral's attack in Madrid, a bomb was thrown in Paris, along rue Rohan, against the French president Émile Loubet and his guest Alfonso XIII, king of Spain, as they were coming back from the Opéra. The two heads of state were unharmed.

282   Mateo Morral was in contact with Francisco Ferrer from 1903 and since late 1905 had been the librarian of his Modern School.

performed a public collection to give Angiolillo the money necessary to go and kill Canovas! Everyone knew these things, except the police, and at least one hundred people were involved in organizing the deed.

Except for the few cases in which, for insignificant matters, one person suffices and therefore there is no need for others, organization is necessary. It is understood that for a deed that ten people can accomplish, it is not necessary to find one hundred, since in this case the more people connive, the easier it is for some spy to infiltrate.

But organization pervades the world: for example, if you want to make a newspaper, you cannot do it without understanding, agreement with other people, which after all is nothing but an organization.

If I want to make a newspaper I do not need anyone: I can do it by myself because I know how to write, I know in every corner of the world someone whom I can approach either to find collaborators or to have them help me with sales: but not everyone is in this situation. Indeed in my case I am privileged and if I wanted to make use of this privilege in which I find myself I could become the leader of the movement.

Ceresoli: given the way the wind is blowing among the anarchists, it would not be easy, nor convenient.

Malatesta (smiling) Oh easier than you believe: it would be enough for me to start endlessly preaching against organization, like the other privileged ones do.

In general, you may have noticed that those who fight against organization are indeed cultured people, more or less authentic journalists. Why? because they have seen some personal benefit in that. They have assembled an organization behind themselves and they have done so unintentionally or unconsciously. In any case they speak poorly of all other organizations to preserve their own, because it helps in consolidating their privilege.

Therefore either they deceive themselves or deceive others, because they make use of organization and deny it.

He who preaches non-organization is the enemy of anarchism, because he calls himself an anarchist while he fails to fulfill the principles of anarchy, one of which is to organize ourselves for a purpose.

Those are the ambitious ones who want to be leaders. If I were ambitious and I wanted to be at the head of something I would act like them and I am sure that in a minute many would take me up. But I would be deceiving them. I recall that when I came back from America, here in London I made a newspaper "La Associazione," the result of which was the Capolago congress. The newspaper was successful and I received letters and encouragement from everywhere. I also recall that once the internationalists of Pistoia asked me for news about the anarchists of Pescia. Why was this? Because the ones from Pistoia, due to a lack of organization, did not have relationships with comrades in Pescia, which is just a few miles away.

Therefore they turned to me hoping that I, as editor of the newspaper, would have more news about them. This meant that the newspaper was becoming a means of useful organization for all and that it helped connect individuals and energies of scattered anarchists who did not know one another. And by doing this, did the newspaper deprive them of any of their freedom? None, rather it increased it.

I do not deny that if I had been ambitious, I could have made use of my position of privilege, but I wanted to organize the congress. The congress took place: 80 comrades participated.

What happened after? It happened that I, who received thirty letters a day for the newspaper, no longer received more than two a week. It happened that the comrades who came to the congress, both on the way there and on the way back, had stopped in different places and had built relationships with comrades, they had spoken, made agreements, and no longer needed the newspaper. Instead of decreasing they had increased their freedom.

To organize means to develop organs appropriate for a function. In an organization of men, every man is an organ that serves the function of the whole. On this note, you may have noticed that local organizations last longer than centralized ones. This happens because local organizations are motivated to act and practice more often and on more matters, while centralized and more far-flung organizations get in motion only in certain cases and for general matters.

The State is an organization, but it relies upon Municipalities, Provinces and other bodies. If the State disappears it does not mean that the smaller organizations cannot remain.

(Here he spoke of tramways and Postal services, as organizations which one cannot avoid, because they have no equivalents. Then he continued)

This is why we are at the mercy of the bourgeois by not having organization. The worker goes to work without even knowing what his work is used for. You for example (addressing Ravaioli) are a cobbler. You keep making shoes and more shoes and you do not know if there are few or many on the market or which markets need them.

Those who organize all the labor and have all the workers for themselves like herds and instruments, are in this case the industrialists, who take it upon themselves to produce the merchandise, and the merchants, who take it upon themselves to distribute it where it is lacking. But it is always a matter of organization, monstrous, if you will—because it is an organization of privileged people based on the worker's slavery—but still organization.

If fifty of us join forces, we feel stronger than if we are alone.

Do you want—still addressing Ravaioli—proof of the power of organization? In this moment every day we hear rumors of war between Austria and Italy. The Italian comrades write me that Italy must not go to war. It is curious reasoning. The war (I am opening a parentheses) can be desired or not—I say it can be desired by anarchists because one can hope to start the revolution after the war—but saying that Italy must not go to war with Austria is absurd, for if Austria thinks they should bring war to Italy, they are not going to refrain from that because of your chatter: on the contrary, the more Italians balk at fighting, the more blows they will inflict upon us. Therefore if Austria organizes for the war, the Italians also need to organize to escape worse damage.

In one case we could preach peace: if our Austrian comrades, too, did the same in their country, with a firm intention, if war broke out, to take up weapons against the government of their country and to start the revolution. In such a case it would be good to prevent the war but to do so it is necessary to have the means: that is, to have a strong anarchist organization in both States to offset the organization of war. Organization, I say, can make miracles.

I remember.

During the Russian-Japanese war, Germany threatened to invade Poland. What did we do then? we said that if this happened, we would give the order to all workers in every Nation of Europe to go on a general strike and start the revolution. Germany got afraid of a revolt at home and did not move (As you see he attributes more to the anarchists than they did).

Another example. When Loris threw the bomb at the Sultan and they wanted to execute him, we promoted an agitation threatening to bomb the Sultan if he carried out the sentence. I do not know how much influence we were able to have, but it seems that after our threats the Sultan got afraid and the sentence was not carried out.[283]

La Rosa: But Loris was innocent, it was the Armenians who had thrown the bomb.

Malatesta: Whatever it may be, I am saying that we may have helped to save Loris, but we would not have been able to do so if there had been no watchword, no organization.

But there is more, he says, still addressing Ravaioli: you are a simple worker who works all day long, you cannot read very well and in the evening, when you manage to finish reading a single article from the only newspaper that you can procure, you are already tired. Since you always read that same newspaper, you cannot have a personal opinion, only that of the newspaper. You do not have one of your own, but you manage to get in touch with others, talk with them, discuss. Such relationships with comrades are already an organization. You then make your own opinion based on the comparisons you make between different opinions. Later you want to communicate with other anarchists, who are far away: you

---

283   In Constantinople on July 21, 1905, the Armenian Revolutionary Front made an unsuccessful attempt at the life of sultan Abdul Hamid II. Among those arrested was the Belgian citizen Charles Edouard Joris, who was sentenced to capital punishment. After a dispute between the Turkish and Belgian governments concerning who had jurisdiction over the case, the Turkish government finally decided to free Joris and let him leave the country.

already know how to explain your ideas a little to friends who are on their way to those regions. You task them with bringing your words to those who are far away, you organize a correspondence of ideas between you and them by means of another comrade. Thus from the simplest organized forms you go to the highest. Organization is therefore necessary and useful.

For example, if I want to communicate with comrades from around the world I do not need to use anyone, because I have made my own friends and acquaintances more or less everywhere. But you who are new, with little education, you do not know anyone, you need someone to introduce you if you go to a foreign country, you therefore need organization even for this simple matter.

What would you say if someone, whom we do not know, came here to preach revolution or suggest an attack? If we do not know him, he could be as anarchist as he wants, but we would take him for a spy. Therefore he needs to be known: he needs organization.

United we have more means, more force, more freedom than divided.

It was in view of these considerations that we came to the idea of the Amsterdam congress and the establishment of the new International.

It is called an International because it was made with the intent of federating comrades of all Nations and eventually replacing the existing powers with our organizations. We are still at the beginning and I do not know if we will succeed. So far we have made little progress, but we will see if we can do better. (At this point Gualducci laughs ironically) We met, we discussed and established the basis of an organization to counter the organization of the States. If we do not succeed it will be due to a lack of organization and not the opposite.

. . .

TRANSLATION FROM "RAPPORTO MENSILE DEL MESE DI FEBBRAIO 1909," BY POLICE COMMISSIONER FROSALI, LONDON, APRIL 9, 1909[284]

Tuesday 2—At the Club, meeting of the Italian Group. Present: Malatesta, Belelli, Gentili, La Rosa, Perazzini, Gualducci, Defendi Enrico, Barretta, Ravaglioli and Corso.

Malatesta, spoke on the subject of "The International." He explained the system of various anarchist organizations and spoke at length about individual acts, mentioning the name of the known "Mor[r]al," saying that he was prudent in renting a single room to commit the act, and that way he would have been able to escape more easily the police search.

---

284   Typescript, Archivio Centrale dello Stato, Rome, collection "Divisione affari generali e riservati, Archivio generale," series 1909, box 4, folder 240.

[Speech Given in London on February 9, 1909]

Translated from "Rapporto Mensile del Mese di Febbraio 1909,"
by police commissioner Frosali, London, April 9, 1909[285]

. . .

Tuesday 9—Meeting of the Italian Group at the Club. Malatesta gave a lecture on the subject: "The history of the anarchist movement in Italy."

He recapitulated the history of the Ancona movements,[286] and spoke of his trial and his incarceration, and concluded saying "that the revolution is near, and even the most indifferent, like those of Clerkenwell, are already convinced of it and are ready to shake off the 'yoke.'"

. . .

On the Agents Provocateurs

Translated from "A propos des Agents provocateurs,"
Les Temps Nouveaux (Paris) 14, no. 45 (March 6, 1909)

Some comrades, knowing that I am a member of the correspondence Office of the A.I.,[287] ask me for explanations of the Office's attitude as regards this "anarchist international group," which was considered suspicious and which appears to have later been placed above any suspicion by the revolver shots fired by one of its presumed members.[288]

I will provide such explanations, although, truthfully, it seems to me there should be no need, as this concerns an issue of simple common sense.

The anarchist International is a publicly established association, and its correspondence Office, which is known by all and has a public

---

285 Typescript, same archive reference.
286 The term "movements" is manually corrected to "riots."
287 Anarchist International.
288 The February 20, 1909, issue of *Les Temps Nouveaux* had published a statement signed by Alexander Schapiro on behalf of the Correspondence Office of the Anarchist International. In that statement, Schapiro denounced an "International Anarchist Group" for having sent a letter of support to the Anarchist International together with a manifesto about a dynamite attack that had taken place in Brussels and an "expropriation" of 3,000 francs, 25 of which were sent to the International for a subscription. The statement refused any association with this group, branding it as police provocation. The next issue of *Les Temps Nouveaux*, on February 27th, reported a firefight between a Russian linked to the group in question and the police, which would have thus disproven the suspicions expressed by the International's Correspondence Office.

address, simply serves to facilitate the exchange of news, proposals, etc. among members.

Therefore it is not a secret society: that is not its purpose, and although it does everything possible to only amass sincere people, it would not offer, due to its method of recruitment, the guarantees which a secret society should offer.

Those who currently make up the Office, or several among those people, can be very well convinced of the need for secret agreements to achieve victorious revolutionary action. But if they wanted to conspire, they would not do so as members of the Office, and they certainly would not begin by providing their names and addresses.

Now, when individuals whom we do not know, and who perhaps do not know us, write us, at an address known to all the police of the world, and tell us about things which, whether they be good or bad, should remain secret in the very interest of those who are writing them and for the purpose that they put forth, we put our defenses up and think of the usual police shenanigans. And all the more so if such individuals, keeping themselves anonymous, lightheartedly risk putting other comrades in a disagreeable situation.

Certainly these things are not always the work of the police, given that, unfortunately, there are many sincere and devoted men who act like silly children: but these are just idiots, destined, by definition, to become the unconscious victims of any agent provocateur who takes it upon himself to go along with them and pass himself off as a terrible revolutionary.

This is why I believe that the Office did well to avoid dealing with the group in question.

E. MALATESTA.

[Speech Given in London on May 16, 1909]

Translated from "Rapporto Mensile di Maggio 1909," by police commissioner Frosali, London, June 30, 1909[289]

. . .

Debate: Consalvi Malatesta.[290]

Sunday 16. There was a debate between Consalvi and Malatesta.

---

289 Manuscript, Archivio Centrale dello Stato, Rome, collection "Divisione affari generali e riservati, Archivio generale," series 1909, box 4, folder 240.

290 Note in text margin.

Consalvi maintained "that progress and science are contrary to the development of anarchist theories and ideas"; while Malatesta maintained the opposite. The two, after a long discussion, did not change opinions.

Anarchists and the Situation

Freedom (London) 23, no. 242 (June 1909)

The First of May having become a sort of annual review of the Labour forces, it is well on such an occasion for Anarchists to ask themselves what their action should be in view of the constantly changing position of the movement.

This year also the First of May has passed very quietly, without anything exciting (in a revolutionary sense) happening. And yet never before has the situation been so full of promise and encouragement as in this year.

It is especially France which, retaining the vantage conquered during the revolutions of the past century, gives a revolutionary character to the situation.

The workers show clearly that they have at length lost all confidence in Governmental parties, even when these call themselves Socialist. They begin to understand that for emancipation they can count only on themselves, on direct action against Capitalism and against the State. Labour resistance becomes daily more intense, solidarity develops, strikes follow each other with increasing energy and combativeness. Already for the politicians—so-called Labour or Socialist, who go forth to preach peace and arbitration, to promise beneficent laws, profiting by the occasion to climb into some place as Deputy or Municipal Councillor—already for such there is no longer room on the field of strikes. Now, if "Socialists" wish to be elected, they must seek the support of some section of the bourgeoisie.

Conscious workers act—and already we begin to see blazing factories and fleeing masters. These are the first scenes of the great Revolution which will put towns and countryside in flames and produce a radical transformation in every social relation.

The peasants also emerge from their passivity and begin to throw off that prejudice against town-workers which has for so long been a power for reaction.

Again, the State employees who until recently boasted of their position as public functionaries, and held themselves aloof from the industrial proletariat—these commence to understand their true interests and to test their capacity for paralysing the State by disorganising its services. The postmen's strike and the meeting in the Paris Hippodrome, where thousands of State employees fraternised with workmen in private industries in the name of the Social Revolution to be accomplished, marked a decisive step forward along the road to emancipation. And whatever may be the immediate result (still uncertain at the moment I am writing) of the second postmen's strike, it is indisputable henceforth that the revolt has penetrated amongst the employees of the State, and is bound to grow.[291]

On the other hand, the patriotic prejudice has been breached with success, and antimilitarism filtering through the ranks of the Army saps at the base a society which only maintains itself by the brutal strength of soldiers and police.

And as in France, so more or less everywhere the spirit of revolt grows; direct action takes the place of a blind confidence in the elected and the protection of the law.

The Revolution is advancing.

Such are the Anarchistic ideas which force themselves even upon those who resist them. Anarchists, by their position as vanguard and their high ideals, have ever been unable to be more than a numerically small minority; they have been decried, calumniated, and persecuted in every way—and yet the new outlook of the whole contemporaneous social movement is due to the infiltration of their ideas.

Revolutionary Trade Unionism (Syndicalism), which sums up the new tendencies, is certainly not Anarchism; but the spirit that animates it is Anarchist, and all that it has of good is Anarchist.

But this is matter of history. What is important at present is to see what should now be our actual conduct when rendering to the revolutionary cause the services we are prepared to render.

It is evident that the dominant class will not permit the revolutionary tide to submerge them without making every possible effort to arrest it.

The methods which the Governments and the bourgeoisie can employ in order to check the revolutionary movement may be summed up under four heads—(1) persecutions, to smother the movement in the germ; (2) war, to evade the storm by provoking an outbreak of the

---

291   After striking a first time in March 1909 and receiving promises from the government, French postal workers went on strike a second time in May 1909, in response to a series of punitive dismissals. At the demonstration that took place at the Paris hippodrome on May 14th, a resolution was adopted that called for solidarity from other categories of workers. A few days later the Confédération Générale du Travail promoted a general strike, which however remained largely ignored.

atavistic savageness which still manifests itself in race and national hatreds; (3) corruption, in order to turn the movement aside from its emancipatory aims; (4) ferocious repression, the bloodshed which drains the best forces of a people and postpones the struggle for another fifty years.

The ordinary persecutions of police and magistracy have failed; and although Governments, owing to the anti-freedom instinct which forms the basis of their nature, do not renounce these, it is evident that they now only serve to render the conflict more bitter and violent.

War has become a little too dangerous, and could well precipitate rather than prevent the Revolution. War will not take place. In any case, we should simply have to intensify our antipatriotic and antimilitarist propaganda to render war less probable and ever more dangerous to the Government which had recourse to it.

There remain, therefore, two principal dangers for us to guard against—corruption and repression.

Corruption has already completely succeeded with the Parliamentarian Socialists, in such wise that in every country where Socialism was somewhat of a real menace to the existing system there has arisen an aristocracy formed of Socialist Deputies or would-be Deputies, which has become one of the best forces at the disposition of the bourgeoisie to divert or strangle the popular movement.

The same course will be tried with Revolutionary Trade Unionism.

Revolutionary Trade Unionism is not safe from corruption and degeneration. Apart from the question of individuals, who are always subject to mistakes and weaknesses, Trade Unionism by its very nature is a movement which cannot remain stationary. It must advance, develop; and its development either will approach more and more to Anarchism and make the Revolution, or modify itself, assume a bureaucratic character, adapt itself to the claims of capitalism, and become a factor in social conservation. To endeavour to lead Trade Unionism in the latter direction is at present the effort of every intelligent Conservative.

Old-age pensions, arbitration, the official recognition of Trade Union delegates, collective contracts, profit-sharing, co-operative societies, the recognised right of Trade Unions to hold property and to appear in a law court, are some of the methods employed by the bourgeoisie to arrest revolutionary impulse, and to stifle the growing desire for full emancipation and liberty by the ephemeral and illusory concession of some immediate ameliorations, and especially by the formation of a self-satisfied bureaucracy which will absorb the most intelligent and active elements among the proletariat.

It is, in the first place, against this danger that we must direct all our forces. We must take a more and more active part in the Trade

Union movement, strenuously oppose the formation in its midst of a bureaucracy of paid and permanent officials, propagate our tactics, fight against every idea of conciliation and compromise with the enemy, as well as against every tendency towards the pride and selfishness of individual Trade Unions. We must especially prevent the "workers' secretaries" taking the place of Members of Parliament, and see that Direct Action does not in its turn become a lie like the so-called sovereignty of the people.

In this way we can enable Syndicalism to retain its revolutionary character and become an increasingly powerful instrument of emancipation.

But then we will be faced with a final crisis. Of itself, and driven by the alarmed bourgeoisie, the Government will wish to put an end to the movement. Repression will commence seriously, and the Army, not as yet sufficiently permeated with the antimilitarist propaganda to be inoffensive, will be called upon to play its murderous rôle.

Will the revolutionists be in a position to successfully face military repression? This is the question upon which all depends: according to which way it is answered, it will be triumphant revolution and the inauguration of a new civilisation, or rampant reaction for twenty years and more.

We must, then, prepare ourselves for a struggle in arms.

How is it to be done?

It cannot be done in Trade Unions, nor in public groups open more or less to everybody. Neither can it be discussed in the newspapers. And yet it must be done.

Let Anarchists, and all who foresee the coming Revolution and would have it triumphant, ponder over the matter.

*
**

The above, having been written for Englishmen, may strike some as fantastic. England has not reached this point yet; but she will reach it, and sooner than is expected.

To-day, even if it would, a civilised country cannot remain separated from other civilised countries; and the French and Continental movement will not be without influence on the proletariat of this side of the Channel. Besides, English workers have the solid qualities of perseverance, the spirit of organisation, and personal independence, which will soon enable them to regain the time lost, once they escape from the noxious influence of politicians.

E. MALATESTA.

[Speech Given in London on September 17, 1909]

Translated from "Relazione Mensile di Settembre 1909," by police commissioner
Frosali, London, October 19, 1909[292]

. . .

Great meeting at 107 Charlotte Street to protest against the Spanish Government[293]

Friday 17 there was a public meeting to support the known Ferrer, during which the following spoke among others: Tarrida, Malatesta, Rocker, and the French (an.) Sorgue[294]

. . .

Malatesta stated that he was against the pro-Ferrer movement, because Ferrer was not a revolutionary anarchist and in Barcelona was only involved in the "Modern School" and not the active movement;

That such agitation would divert the anarchist party, introducing too much sentimentalism into it,

That instead it was necessary to emancipate the Spanish class from religious superstition and the clergy's influence, and to also make use of all means to change the system of Government.

. . .

---

292   Manuscript, Archivio Centrale dello Stato, Rome, collection "Divisione affari generali e riservati, Archivio generale," series 1909, box 4, folder 240. We ignored some punctuation marks of dubious interpretation at the beginning or end of paragraphs.

293   Note in text margin.

294   Francisco Ferrer had been arrested on August 31, 1909, for his alleged involvement in the Tragic Week, the series of antimilitarist and anticlerical workers' riots that broke out in Barcelona and other Catalonian cities between July 26 and August 2, 1909, following the government's decision to summon reserve troops to send to Spanish holdings in Morocco.

COMMUNIST. ARB. BILD. VEREIN,

107, Charlotte Street, W.

A GREAT

PROTEST MEETING

against the atrocities of the Spanish Government

will take place at the above Hall

on FRIDAY, SEPTEMBER 17th, 1909, at 8.30 p.m.

The following speakers will address the meeting—

JOHN TURNER, L. WITHINGTON, E. MALATESTA,
F. TARRIDA DEL MARMOL, P. VALLINA, S. NACHT,
R. ROCKER and J. WILQUET.

The London Section of the Anarchist International.

Eine grosse

Protestversammlung

GEGEN DIE GREUELTATEN DER SPANISCHEN REGIERUNG

wird stattfinden im obigem Lokal am

Freitag den 17 September 1909, um 8.30 abends.

Folgende Redner stehen auf der Rednerliste :

J. TURNER, L. WITHINGTON, E. MALATESTA, F. TARRIDA DEL MARMOL
P. VALLINA, S. NACHT, R. ROCKER und J. WILQUET.

Die Londoner Sektion der Anarchistischen International.

UN GRAND MEETING de

PROTESTATION

Contre les atrocites du gouvernement espagnol

aura lieu à l'adresse ci-dessus, le

Vendredi, 17 Septembre 1909 à 8.30 du soir.

Les orateurs suivants prendront la parole :

J. TURNER, L. WITHINGTON, E. MALATESTA, F. TARRIDA DEL MARMOL,
P. VALLINA, S. NACHT, R. ROCKER et J. WILQUET.

La Section de Londres de l'Internationale Anarchiste.

Workers' Friend Printing, 163, Jubilee Street, E.

Source: Archivio Centrale dell Stato, Rome

[Speeches Given in London on October 2 and 30, 1909]

Translated from "Rapporto Mensile di Ottobre 1909,"
by police commissioner Frosali, London, November 22, 1909[295]

Pro Ferrer Lecture at 107 Charlotte Street[296]

I have the Honor of reporting the following:

October 2 (Saturday) at 107 Charlotte Street, pro Ferrer lecture. Malatesta, Tarrida, Rocker and others spoke.

Malatesta said that Ferrer's work was not suited to the times and especially to Catalonia, and it was instead necessary to begin a forceful movement.

...

Pro Ferrer Rally at 83 Charlotte Street[297]

Saturday 30—Pro Ferrer rally organized by the "Freedom Group,"[298] and by those Germans who still frequent the old Club.[299]

It took place at Clerkenwell E. C. in the location of the workers' institute. This was once a "Chartist" club, now it does not have a clearly political color. The following spoke: Kitz (En. an.) Turner (English an.) Leggatt (English an.) Malatesta Enrico and Tcherchesoff (Russian an.) Rocker (German an.) Kaplan (Jewish an.).

About 150 subversives participated, half English and half Italian, from the Italian neighborhood.

Malatesta, speaking in French, recalled Ferrer's will, where he let it be said that no pilgrimages should be made to his tomb nor any wreaths laid down. He said: The Ferrer Case has shown us that medieval forces are not dead yet, as the anarchists erroneously reckoned, but this should not mislead them, after this case, to forget the reaction's modern forces, namely capitalistic exploitation. The only ones who rightfully protest against Ferrer's killing are the anarchists; all other parties that joined the protest would be capable of doing what the Spanish government did, if the occasion presented itself. Protestants are not better than Catholics, freemasons are not better than freethinkers. The English Government is comprised of freethinkers, but it does in India worse than clericalism does in Spain. The worst Government is always the one you are under.

---

295 Typescript, Archivio Centrale dello Stato, Rome, collection "Divisione affari generali e riservati, Archivio generale," series 1909, box 4, folder 240.

296 Note in text margin.

297 Note in text margin. In the note shown, a manual correction inserts a period after "Ferrer" and crosses out what follows.

298 Francisco Ferrer had been sentenced to death by a military court on October 10, 1909, and executed on October 13th.

299 The reference is to the International Workingmen's Society (see note 275) which, due to financial difficulties, had been transformed into a restaurant, of which two rooms on the upper floor were still occasionally used for anarchist meetings.

He ended by wishing that anarchist ideas triumph as soon as possible.

. . .

[Speech Given in London on November 11, 1909]

Translated from "Rapporto Mensile di Novembre 1909,"
by police commissioner Frosali, London, December 18, 1909[300]

. . .

Commemoration of the Chicago Martyrs[301]

Thursday 11—At 166 Jubilee Street (anarchist Club), lecture to commemo-rate the Chicago martyrs.

The following spoke: Malatesta Enrico in French, Tcherkesoff (Russian an.) Rocker (German an.) Leggatt (English an.) Turner (English an.) Kaplan (Jewish).

Malatesta recalled the causes that led to the Chicago trial, which were entirely economic and prove that even in democratic or republican countries the bourgeoisie uses the same methods to defend itself that Monarchist Spain uses.

He then did a little critical history of the movement of labor unions in America.

About 250 subversives present, and few Italians.

. . .

[Speech Given in London on October 13, 1910]

Translated from "Conferenza per commemorare l'anniversario della fucilazione
di Francisco Ferrer," London, October 14, 1910, and "Commemorazione della
fucilazione di Francisco Ferrer. (13 Ottobre 1910)," London, October 17, 1910, both
by police commissioner Frosali[302]

---

300   Typescript, Archivio Centrale dello Stato, Rome, collection "Divisione affari generali e riservati, Archivio generale," series 1909, box 4, folder 240.

301   Note in text margin.

302   Typescript, Archivio Centrale dello Stato, Rome, collection "Divisione affari generali e riservati, Archivio generale," series 1909, box 7, folder 188. The sum-mary of the lecture was sent by police commissioner Frosali in two parts. The first in chronological order contains the summary of the entire lecture, while the second contains, according to what the author writes, a summary of the first part of Malatesta's speech, to supplement what was already noted in the first report. However, since it is not clear how the two parts of Malatesta's speech should be assembled, we preferred to keep them separate, reproducing them in the chronological order in which they were written.

On October 13, 1910, at 8 p.m. in the location of the "Communist Club" at 107 Charlotte Street, W. Soho, there was a meeting to commemorate the execution of Francisco Ferrer, upon its anniversary.[303]

The room contained about 250 subversives of all nationalities.

[*Some of the Italian anarchists in attendance are then listed and the speeches by Harry Boulter, Fernando Tárrida del Mármol, Guy Aldred, and Jack Tanner are summarized.*]

Later the Italian anarchist "Malatesta Enrico" took the floor, speaking in French. After noting the current "apprehension" in all countries—which very much resembles the frame of mind that preceded 1848, and in some cases is similar to that of 1830–1831—he expressed the conviction that we are on the brink of major events. There is a lesson, he said, to take from the "Ferrer" trial and it is that the clerical enemy, against which we have forgotten to fight in these recent years, is still ready to come to the fore. The fact that the advanced part of the liberal movement is against clericalism is a good symptom, but it results from the organized action of the workers.

That human nature no longer wants clerical ties is proven by the birth of the Portuguese Republic, which nevertheless, once the first passions have passed, shall fall into the hands of the careerist intermediaries, as the French Republic fell into the hands of Briand, the former propagator of the general strike (At this point shouts of down with "Briand" were heard).[304]

The answer from the workers was not long in coming, as the strike in France was not long in coming, which proves many things.

1) That there exists a large number of workers who, even being outside of organizations, are ready for the revolution.

2) That workers' organization should be secret, to be able to prepare for action.

3) That the general strike cannot be successful unless at the same time people take possession of the necessities for life, since the suspension of certain trades increases the price of essential goods, thus harming more the workers than the rich classes. Hence, given that starting the general strike can subject them to deployment and martial law, people will need to be logical and take immediate possession of that which is necessary for life.

---

303 On Ferrer, see notes 294 and 298.

304 In Portugal, the last Braganza sovereign, Manuel II, was deposed on October 5, 1910, by a revolution that proclaimed the republic; a series of anticlerical measures were launched by the provisional government. Aristide Briand, supporter of revolutionary syndicalism and the general strike, became a socialist deputy in France in 1902. Over the following years he moved towards the center. In March 1906 his role as minister of public education was disapproved by the socialist leader Jean Jaurès and considered a sort of betrayal in the party ranks. On July 24, 1909, Briand succeeded Georges Clemenceau as prime minister.

4) The Government exclusively resists by armed force, and consequently the fight must necessarily be conducted on an equality of terms; therefore all workers must be armed, if not with government weapons, at least with improvised tools, prepared according to the dictates of science.

...

First Part of Enrico Malatesta's Speech, at the Communist Club at 107 Charlotte Street. He began with recalling that on October 13, 1909, Francisco Ferrer was executed in the fortress of Montjuich by the Spanish Government, which is guided and manipulated by Catholic priests. He said that Ferrer was not the violent anarchist preacher of armed and regicidal revolt; he was a placid and intelligent professor who little by little killed all religious prejudices in the students entrusted to him, thus making their minds take the first step toward emancipation, giving them freedom of conscience. Killing Ferrer, the priests struck a man who struck another,[305] they killed a man who taught his students that the earth existed by natural law; that we are products of the earth. With science in hand, he killed the religious idea without hurting anyone, without producing further material damage than shrinking the purse of the Catholics. That is why this homicide is so monstrous as to rouse protests around the world.

The second part already sent follows

The Brains of the Anarchist Movement

The Evening News (London), no. 9108 (January 6, 1911)

The Creed of Errico Malatesta.

Errico Malatesta has been called the brains of the Anarchist movement by the police of his native Italy.

Abroad he has been sentenced to death three times and spent some years in prison for his Anarchism. His lodgings are the rooms over a wine-shop in Islington, and there an *Evening News* representative talked with him about the behaviour of Anarchists in England.

A correspondent had written to this journal asserting that the Houndsditch assassins[306] had forfeited their lives not alone to English justice but to their

---

305   This sentence is probably missing something, but it is not clear how it should be completed.

306   On the evening of December 16, 1910, a group of thieves of Latvian origin, later identified as anarchists, were surprised by the police while they were trying to break into a jewelry store on Houndsditch, an alley in the East End of London. The thieves reacted by shooting, killing three police officers. On January 3, 1911 some of the thieves who had managed to escape were located in a house in East End and surrounded by the police. Thus began the so-called

comrades in Russia, because it was an unwritten yet stern law of the Anarchists that the English should go unharmed in return for their hospitality to foreign refugees.

If they had fled to Russia, said the correspondent, their own brotherhood would have condemned them to death.

Errico Malatesta, when the interviewer asked him if this was true, stared with his big, shining brown eyes into vacancy and eluded an answer, shrugging his shoulders in a way that suggested that it might be so or not, but that he was not prepared to discuss the unwritten laws of the Russian secret societies.

The Mistake of Taking Life.

In a few minutes, however, the ice was broken and he began to speak volubly in a heavy foreign accent.

"It is deplorable, this taking of life," he said. "It is a mistake, foolish, useless, criminal.

"But what in the world has it to do with Anarchism? The men were not Anarchists, but burglars and murderers, and they should be called burglars and murderers.

"Crippen was an American and must have had either Republican or Democratic opinions.[307] But when he murdered his wife nobody turned round and said, 'This is a result of Republicanism,' or 'This is what comes of Democratic teaching.'

"His politics did not lead him to kill his wife. Anarchism does not include the robbery of safes and the shooting of policemen who frustrate it.

"Nor must you believe in the criminals who call themselves Anarchists to lift themselves to a higher place.

"The burglar who, when he is caught, poses in this land as a revolutionary politician, reminds me of the bandits abroad who proclaim themselves Anarchists to cloak the meanness of their crimes. If they are not captured and they make fortunes, they settle down to a respectable retirement and frequently become political reactionaries of the extremest kind.

As Plain Unvarnished Robbers.

"Or if the magistrates let them know that they will be given extra imprisonment for terming themselves Anarchists they very quickly drop Anarchism and take their chances as plain, unvarnished robbers!

"In England, if a man picks pockets, you sentence him for picking pockets.

"You do not ask him if he is a Free Trader or a Tariff Reformer or a vegetarian and then raise a cry about the evils of Free Trade or Tariff Reform or

---

"Siege of Sidney Street," at the end of which, after a prolonged firefight and the burning of the house, two thieves were left dead.

307   Hawley Crippen was a US citizen condemned to death and hanged in London on November 23, 1910, for having killed his wife, burying her remains in the cellar of the house they lived in.

vegetarianism. You do not propose to suppress or expel Tariff Reformers or Free Traders or vegetarians![308]

"These men were not Anarchists when they were burglars. The fact is that they were savages. They had probably taken part in some revolutionary politics in Russia, but revolutionary politics do not tell a man to go about breaking into jewellery safes.

"They were used to Russian law, which is not law at all, but simply judgment on the spot. In Russia men are hanged for carrying firearms. They would have been hanged or shot by the police for burglary.

The Carrier of Arms.

"Their kind habitually carry arms in Russia, knowing that the pistol is their only saviour from death if they are detected. They are ignorant men, made and kept barbarous by Russian police brutality, and it is not easy for them to realise when they come to England that their circumstances are entirely different.

"They are not converted from their lifelong savage psychology by the mere change of residence. I am not defending their murders, but I am asking the Englishman to try to apprehend this fact. A Russian who happens to be a savage is not at once impregnated with the English view of English law. He cannot immediately get the 'atmosphere.'

"The Russian atmosphere of oppression is just as incredible to the English. Could you understand the Government that treated a reply to the ideas of Tolstoy as a political outrage on the ground that it was an offence to circulate Tolstoy's teachings and you had to mention them in answering them?

The Last Refuge.

"England is the last refuge left for Anarchists. We deplore the confusion of burglary and murder with Anarchism, for if England is closed to us we have no other place to look to for justice.[309]

"No Anarchist would willingly see the English or the English police injured. We have no reason to injure them. We owe our liberty to them. And we do not for a moment take any responsibility for men who murder because they are taken in an attempt at theft.

"An English thief in the same plight would have said, 'I have not succeeded,' and philosophically taken his trial. These Russians were fools to shoot, the

---

308   At the time, the debate between Free Traders and Tariff Reformers was one of the most lively discussions among British political parties.

309   The theme of political asylum was extremely topical, given that in 1905 the Aliens Act, a law on immigration, had been approved, which restricted the entry of immigrants into Great Britain, while formally protecting the right to asylum. The law's approval was boosted by the fear aroused by the presence of foreign revolutionaries in the country.

English burglar would have told them; they thus converted an ordinary offence into a fatal one.

"But you should put that down to their own ignorance and stupidity and their natural Russian outlook on these matters. It has no more to do with Anarchism than with Liberalism or Conservatism."

[Statement Made to the Police on the Houndsditch Murders][310]

Untitled typescript, [London], no date[311]

ERRICO MALATESTA,
residing at 118 High Street, Islington.
STATES:—

I am an Engineer and carry on business at No 15 Duncan Terrace, City Road. My workshop is situated in the basement at that address. I have been making experiments in the brazing of metals by means of oxygen and coal gas.

On the 2nd December 1910 I went to Messrs Broadhurst Clarkson and Co, 65 Farringdon Road, and there obtained a 6ft[312] cylinder of oxygen gas, a fine adjustment valve, a spanner, which I paid cash for. I also ordered a pressure gauge with a 3 way adapter, which was to be ready for me the next day. I called for the articles the next day, got them and paid for them. I also bought two pairs of dark goggles. I found that the 6ft cylinder did not contain a sufficient quantity of gas for my experiments and on 12th December 1910 I called upon Broadhurst Clarkson and Co and they agreed to exchange the 6ft cylinder for a 40ft cylinder.[313]

---

310 Malatesta was interrogated by the police because subsequent inquiries into the Houndsditch murders had shown that the thieves had purchased from Malatesta the oxygen cylinder that they brought with them to open the jewelry store's safe. In an interview with *Il Secolo* on January 25, 1911, (see below) Malatesta says he was questioned the day after the events, which took place on the night between December 16th and 17th. That would imply that this document, which is undated, actually records statements made over several interrogations, since it also contains references to events that took place on December 20th, therefore after the first interrogation.

311 London Metropolitan Archives, London, collection "City of London Police, Cases," series "Houndsditch Murders," folder "Statements." The folder in question contains statements issued to the police during the course of the investigation into the Houndsditch murders.

312 One foot corresponds to 30.48 centimeters. Three feet equal one yard. The volume measurements expressed in feet, as in this case, are understood to be cubic feet.

313 The new cylinder was delivered the next day at Malatesta's workshop.

On Thursday 15th December 1910 some time in the afternoon a man who spoke bad French and who gave the name of L. Lambert and his address as 85 Dean Street, Soho, age 25 to 30, 5 feet 5 or 6, medium dark moustache, turned up at ends, dark hair and complexion, long face thin build, dress dark overcoat, black hard felt hat, I should know him again, called upon me and said that he had heard of me at the Au Petit Riche restaurant, 44 Old Compton Street, Soho (I do some work at the Restaurant) as an engineer who might be able to do something for him. I asked him what he wanted done and he said that he was going to give a lantern show for which he would want a cylinder of oxygen. I told him that I had a 40 foot cylinder which I could sell him. It was arranged that I should supply him with the 40 ft cylinder, a pressure gauge, a valve and about 15 or 20 yards of rubber tubing for which he was to pay £5 and he paid me £1 on account. He asked me to get the cylinder and other things ready by the following afternoon when he would send a man for them and pay the balance. The pressure gauge, valve and cylinder which I supplied to him were those I obtained from Broadhurst Clarkson and Co, the rubber tubing I bought at a shop in Tottenham Court Road close to Hanway Street.[314]

The following afternoon a young English lad about 18, 5 feet 2 or 3, dark hair, cut close, dressed in dark clothe[s] wearing neckerchief and cloth cap, appearance of a coster called and said that he had been sent by Mr Lambert for the cylinder and other things. He paid me the balance £4, and I gave him the articles which he placed on a costers barrow and took away. I did not ask him where he was going to take them to. I have not seen Mr Lambert since the day he ordered the articles.

About 12 months ago I met a man whose name and address I do not know, at the Anarchist Club in Jubilee Street, who was introduced to me as a "comrade." He was I understand a Russian Political refugee and an engineer. During the past 12 months he has used my workshop to do any little job he has had. Sometimes he would come two or three times a week. I last saw him on Friday afternoon at my workshop.[315] He is about 21 or 22, 5 ft 8 or 9, dark hair and small dark moustache, medium build dark complexion, dress dark jacket suit, black hard felt hat, but sometimes wears a dark cloth cap.

The rubber tubing, gauge, valve and cylinder No 1780 now shown me are the articles I sold to the man L. Lambert. I have never seen the cutter and flexible

---

314 The person known as Lambert was Fritz Svaars, one of the two men who would then die in the Siege of Sidney Street. On December 15th Malatesta wrote to Broadhurst Clarkson & Co. (see the volume of the *Complete Works* containing his correspondence) asking to come collect the cylinder to fill it, which was done the next day. According to the testimony of the errand boy, the cylinder was delivered full between 1:30pm and 1:45pm. Malatesta then went to the company on the morning of the 17th, to ask if a certain repair commissioned by him had been made.

315 The man in question was George Gardstein, another of the protagonists of the Houndsditch events on December 16th. Gardstein died a few hours after the firefight with police, due to his injuries. The Friday afternoon Malatesta refers to is that of December 16th.

tubing now shown to me, and it has the appearance of having been made up from several parts.

On Tuesday December 20th 1910, in company with Detective John Landy of the City of London Police, I went to the Mortuary attached to the London Hospital, Whitechapel Road. E., where I saw the face of a dead man whose body was lying on a slab. I recognised it as the face of the man, previously referred to who during the past 12 months I have allowed to use my workshop. I do not know his name. He was introduced to me as a "comrade." I do not recollect who it was who introduced me to him. I knew him as "the Russian." He spoke a little French and English.

Purchase of Oxygen by C. Malatesta [by William Newell, Police Inspector]

[London], January 9, 1911[316]

With reference to the subject named in margin, I beg to report having interviewed Mr. C. Malatesta,[317] Engineer, 15 Duncan Terrace, and 112, High Street, Islington, who informed me that about the beginning of December last, he purchased 40 feet of oxygen gas for experimental purposes and at the same time hired a cylinder no. 4571,[318] from Brim's British Oxygen Gas Company Ltd., Elverton Street, Westminster. He gave his name as M. Julie, 13 Wilmington Square, E.C., and his reason for so doing was that he was of opinion that the above named Company and Broadshaw[319] Clarkson & Co., 63 Farringdon Road, E.C., were one and the same firm and he would be able to obtain the gas at a cheaper rate.

About ten days later Mr. Malatesta conveyed the empty cylinder by taxi-cab from his workshop at 15 Duncan Terrace to Messrs. Brim & Co., and gave the driver something excess of his legal fare.[320]

. . .

---

316   London Metropolitan Archives, London, collection "City of London Police, Cases," series "Houndsditch Murders," folder "Statements." We used the subject indicated in the text margin as the document title.

317   The incorrect initial for the first name probably comes from an incorrect reading of Malatesta's signature. In fact, in a copy of Malatesta's December 15th letter to Broadhurst Clarkson & Co., the signature is transcribed as "C. Malatesta."

318   The document shows "45V1" as the cylinder number, but other sources show the number was 4571.

319   This is a misspelling for "Broadhurst."

320   The report by Inspector Newell continues and confirms, on the basis of cross-checks, both of Malatesta's visits to the Brim company, which took place respectively on December 5th and 16th. In sum, on December 16th Malatesta got rid of both 40-foot cylinders he had, selling one to the so-called Lambert and returning the other to the Brim company in exchange for the deposit previously paid.

The Anarchist Malatesta Explains his Relationship with the Russians to Our Correspondent

Translated from "L'anarchico Malatesta spiega al nostro corrispondente i suoi rapporti coi russi," *Il Secolo* (Milan), January 25, 1911

(Our phonogram)

London, 24 night.

This evening I had the opportunity to converse at length with the Italian anarchist Enrico Malatesta, who, as I phoned you, was indirectly involved in the mysterious Houndsditch drama. Malatesta told me: "About a year ago I met a young Russian who claimed to be a political refugee and said he was interested in works of mechanics. He was a very intelligent man and when he found out that I had a small mechanic's workshop he asked me if I could let him come there to carry out work on an invention that he was preparing. I had no difficulty in consenting, all the more because my other occupations kept me far from the workshop from morning to evening. Thus the Russian, whose name I do not remember and whom I never even asked who he really was, arrived at the workshop when I had already left in the morning and usually left before I returned in the evening, so that, given also my occasional absence, I rarely saw him.

— And why did you never ask him about his personal information?

— Because, Malatesta responded, this is what we are used to do. In the first place they are very reluctant to give their name, in the second place it happens that when these refugees leave London to repatriate they are almost inescapably arrested at the border and hanged after rather quick proceedings. You will understand that no one wants to be suspected, even if he is above suspicion, of knowing the personal information of these refugees and having denounced them in due time to the Russian police. Am I making myself clear?

— Of course! I said, but now could you tell what is the story with the machine and the oxygen tube you sold to the Houndsditch crooks?

— The matter is very simple and I already explained it to the police, who seem to have accepted my version. In early December I wanted to experiment to see if soldering metals with a blowtorch, or what we call heat welding, was easier and more economic with the new machine or with the old system. So, I bought one of those hoses and did a few tests. However I found that this new procedure consumed too much oxygen and that the metal soldering was too commercially expensive. So, I said one day in my workshop, in the presence of the young Russian, that I would like to sell the device. A few days later a gentleman introduced himself to me. He spoke French properly, but must not have been of French nationality. He was well dressed and told me he had been referred to me by a friend. This gentleman, who said his name was Lambert, wanted a device for magic lantern projections, capable of producing a very bright light, as he could not arrange for electric light. I offered the oxygen cylinder, which I would sell him for 15 pounds sterling.[321] He accepted and gave a down payment of one sterling. While I took it upon myself to fill up the oxygen cylinder again, he made the necessary arrangements to send someone to fetch the device the next day; in fact, the day after a boy came to fetch the device and paid the balance, collecting the relative receipt. When the police found the device they noticed that it bore the make and address of the manufacturing company. Two hours later they found out that it had been sold to me and I, interrogated in turn, gave all the necessary explanations in an interview with the inspector that lasted a couple of hours.[322] Two days later I was invited to visit the police again and I was brought to the mortuary of *London Hospital* where the cadaver of the man assumed to be Gardstein and discovered in a room of the house on Good Street lay.[323] Immediately I recognized the cadaver as my Russian. It was only then that I understood that this person, knowing of my intention to get rid of the oxygen cylinder, had sent someone to buy it on his behalf. This was certainly a dirty trick, because it put me in serious difficulties. Fortunately I had made the purchase and performed the sale in broad daylight and my good faith was evident even in the eyes of the police, who were convinced that my workshop could not have been used to produce the other instruments which the wrongdoers were equipped with, because it was too small and lacked the technical means necessary.

Here is the exact version of the matter, in Malatesta's own words. But it is certain that this incident will be revisited with the continuation of the judicial investigation, and that Malatesta shall again be interrogated.

---

321 The amount of 15 sterling is probably a typo, since in the statement made to the police, Malatesta said he had sold the cylinder for 5 sterling.

322 In contrast with Malatesta's testimony here, in late December the London newspapers that followed the investigation of the Houndsditch affair, for example the *Evening News* of the 29th and the *Westminster Gazette* of the 30th, still spoke of the oxygen cylinder as an unresolved mystery, with the police still looking for the identity of the man who had acquired it from the Islington sellers.

323 The exact address is 59 Grove Street. This is the house of Fritz Svaars, where Gardstein, wounded, was brought and where the police found his dead body.

Capitalists and Thieves

The Syndicalist (London) 1, no. 5 (June 1912)

Originally published as "Capitalistes et voleurs," *Les Temps Nouveaux* (Paris) 16, no. 23 (February 18, 1911)[324]

[REGARDING THE TRAGEDIES IN HOUNDSDITCH AND SIDNEY STREET

In an alley of the City, there is an attempted robbery at a jewelry store, and the thieves, surprised by the police, flee by making their way out with revolver shots. Later, two of the thieves, found in a house in the East End, defend themselves again with revolver shots, and die in the battle.

Fundamentally, nothing extraordinary in today's society, except for the exceptional vigor with which the thieves defended themselves.

But] these thieves were Russians, perhaps Russian refugees, and maybe they also went to an Anarchist club on days of public meetings, when they were open to everybody. And naturally the capitalist Press avails itself to declare war upon the Anarchists. If one were to believe the bourgeois papers one would think that anarchy, that dream of justice and love amongst men, is nothing but theft and assassination; and with these lies and calumnies they certainly succeed in turning away from us many people who would be with us if they only knew what we want.

Thus it will not be useless to state once more the position of Anarchists respecting the theory and practice of theft.

One of the fundamental points of Anarchism is the abolition of the monopoly of the land, raw material, and the instruments of production, and thereby the abolition of the exploitation of other people's labour by those who hold the means of production. Any appropriation of other people's labour, everything that serves to enable a man to live without giving to society his quota of production is, from the Anarchist and Socialist point of view, a theft.

The landlords, the capitalists have stolen from the people, by violence or by fraud, the land and all the means of production, and in consequence of this initial theft, they are enabled, day by day, to take away from the workers the products of labour. But they were happy thieves, for they became strong; they made laws in order that they might justify their situation, and they have organized a whole system of repression to defend themselves against the claims of the workers as well as against

---

324   The English version is abridged. We have integrated it with an original translation of the missing parts, enclosed in square brackets. According to Rudolf Rocker, the first version that appeared was actually the Yiddish version published by *Der Arbayter Fraynd* in London on January 27, 1911, which we were unable to locate. However, this version was undoubtedly a translation of Malatesta's manuscript, which likely was written in French.

those who would like to replace them by doing as they did themselves. And to-day their theft is called property, commerce, industry, &c., the name of "thief" being reserved, in common language, for those who would like to follow the example of the capitalists, but, because they arrived too late and in adverse circumstances, cannot do it without putting themselves in conflict with the law.

However, the difference of names currently used does not suffice to hide the moral and social character of the two situations. The capitalist is a thief who has succeeded either by his merits or by those of his ancestors; the thief is an aspiring capitalist who is but waiting to succeed to become a capitalist, in fact, and live without working on the product of his theft, that is to say, on other people's labour.

As enemies of the capitalists, we cannot sympathise for the thief who aspires at becoming a capitalist, and being in favour of their expropriation by the people for the profit of all, we cannot, as Anarchists, have anything in common with an operation whose object is to get some wealth to pass from the hands of one owner into those of another.

[I am speaking, of course, of the professional thief, the one who does not wish to work and seeks the means for being able to live like a parasite from other people's labour. A man whom society denies the means to work, and who steals rather than starve to death and watch his children perish of starvation is something very different. In this case theft (if it can be called that) is a rebellion against social injustice, and may become the most sacred of rights and even the most imperious of duties. But the capitalist press avoids mentioning these cases, because it would have to put on trial the social order that it has the mission of defending.

Certainly, the professional thief, too, is in large part a victim of the social environment. The example that comes from on high, the education received, the repulsive conditions under which he is often obliged to work, readily explain why men, who are morally no better than their contemporaries, when faced with a choice between being exploited or being exploiters, choose to be exploiters and seek by any means available to them to become just that. But these extenuating circumstances might as readily apply to capitalists, and therefore the substantial sameness of the two professions is just better demonstrated.]

Thus Anarchist ideas cannot drive people to become thieves any more than to become capitalists. On the contrary, by giving to the discontented an ideal of superior life, and a hope of collective emancipation, they turn away, as far as possible in the present midst, from all those legal or illegal doings which are but an adaptation to the capitalist system and tend towards perpetuating it.

Notwithstanding all this, the social midst being so strong and personal temperaments so different, there might possibly be amongst the

Anarchists a few who go in for thieving as there are some who go in for commerce or industry; but in that case both are acting, not because of their Anarchist ideas, but in spite of these.

E. MALATESTA.

[Testimony Given during the Committal Proceedings for the Houndsditch Murders, London, March 7, 1911][325]

VETERAN ANARCHIST IN COURT
Daily Express (London), no. 3404 (March 8, 1911)

...

The most interesting witness of the day was Mr. Enrico Malatesta, the veteran Anarchist, from whom the oxygen cylinder found at Exchange-buildings was purchased. His evidence showed that for the past twelve months Gardstein, the man who died at 59, Grove-street, had been a constant visitor at his workshop in Duncan-terrace, Islington, and had worked there on his own account.

"I did not know his name," said Mr. Malatesta, "I called him 'the Russian.' I was introduced to him at the Anarchist club in Jubilee-street as a 'comrade.' We do not like to ask the names of Russian refugees, for there are plenty of police spies about, and the refugees often return to Russia. We prefer not to know too much."

...

HOUNDSDITCH MURDERS
Daily Mail (London), no. 4653 (March 8, 1911)

...

Enrico Malatesta, of Duncan-terrace, Islington, giving evidence, said he sold the cylinder found in Exchange-buildings to a Frenchman giving the name of Lambert on December 15. A lad fetched it next day.[326]

---

325 In the British legal system, committal proceedings comprised the first phase of a trial, that is, the preliminary hearings to decide on an indictment. Consequently, Malatesta twice provided testimony during the trial on the Houndsditch affairs, one during the committal proceedings, which lasted from December 1910 to March 1911, and one during the actual trial.

326 A more detailed account of this part of Malatesta's statement can be found in

Malatesta recognised the photograph of Gardstein as that of a man who used to work in his workshop during the past year. "I was introduced to him," said the witness, "in the Anarchist Club in Jubilee-street as a 'comrade.'"

Mr. Bodkin:[327] Did you know his name?—We don't like to ask the name of Russian refugees.

Who are "we"?—Anarchists. The refugees very often go back to Russia, and there are plenty of police spies. One prefers not to know too much. I used to call him "the Russian."

What did he do in your workshop?—He had an invention to develop. I have seen him doing a small piece of turning, filing, or forging.

Wheels?—Not exactly. Once I saw him making a kind of pump. At other times he had small pieces of mechanism.

. . .

[Testimony Given during the Trial for the Houndsditch Murders, May 2, 1911]

"TRIAL OF DUBOF, ZURKA . . ." *OLD BAILEY PROCEEDINGS ONLINE*, REFERENCE NUMBER T19110425-75[328]

. . .

ENRICO MALATESTA, engineer, 112, High Street, Islington. I have a workshop at 15, Duncan Terrace, where I keep various kinds of tools and a furnace. This photograph (Exhibit 3) is of a man who worked there. I did not know his name; I know now that he was Gardstein; I called him "The Russian," as he came from Russia. I first saw him about fifteen months ago; I met him in a club in Jubilee Street; it was a working men's club—an Anarchist club. He asked me if I could give him the use of my tools because he had an invention to develop. He used to turn and file

---

the *Jarrow Express* of March 10th: "Among the witnesses was Enrico Malatesta, who described himself as an engineer, living at High-street, Islington, with a workshop in Duncan-terrace. He stated that in December he was trying to braze steel and iron in connection with making a cycle, and bought among other things a cylinder of oxygen. On December 15th a Frenchman, giving the name of Lambert, called at his workshop. Lambert, who was a stranger, bought the cylinder and other apparatus for £5, paying £1 down. An English-looking lad called on December 16th (the day of the shooting), paid the remaining £4, and took the thing away. The witness now identified the cylinder, gauge and other articles found in Exchange-buildings."

327 Archibald Bodkin was the trial prosecutor.
328 Consulted February 25, 2014.

pieces of metal, but I did not see him often as I was not working in the workshop much then. I did not pay him anything nor he me. He could only speak a few words of English or French, so we talked very little. I used to leave the key with my landlord to give him. Some time before December 16 I had the idea of brazing metals by means of oxygen. I may have had a few words with Gardstein about it. For the purpose of my experiments I bought a cylinder of oxygen, a pressure gauge, a spanner, an adaptor, and a pair of goggles from Messrs. Broadhurst. I bought at first a 6 ft. cylinder and afterwards a 40 ft. cylinder. On December 14 a man came and asked me where he could buy a cylinder of oxygen as he had a dynamite shock to make.[329] I agreed to sell him all the things I had bought for £5. I wrote to Broadhurst's, asking them to fetch the 40 ft. cylinder and fill it with oxygen, which they did. This man paid me £1 and the man who fetched (about 4 p.m. on December 16) the things paid me the balance, £4. I think Gardstein was there on the morning of that day. I have since identified the things that I sold.

. . .

What Is to Be Done?

Translated from "Che fare?" *L'Alleanza Libertaria* (Rome),
no. 133 (September 21, 1911)

Having been far away for so long, and unable to take an active part in the fight in Italy over the last few years, I loathe saying words that would seem liable to throw cold water on passions, even if they are poorly grounded, and to put obstacles in the way of keen people's initiatives, even if they seem ill-timed to me.

For this reason, as on previous occasions, I hesitated to give my opinion on the planned Congress. But many friends insist that I provide it, and I make up my mind to do so, though I know that, under the current circumstances, I am more susceptible than others to poorly judge the situation. As conscious anarchists, comrades will be able to exercise their critical minds and take my words for whatever they are worth.

A National Congress of anarchists in Italy seems highly inappropriate to me, at this moment.

I have no objection to Congresses or Conventions, which in fact I wish were more frequent, so that comrades can meet, mesh, understand each other, and mutually encourage to take action. But years of experience teach me that when Congresses are not well prepared, or do not respond to a deeply-felt need, they turn out useless or worse.

---

329   According to Malatesta's earlier testimonies, the man known as Lambert visited on December 15th and his reason for purchasing the cylinder was to make magic lantern projections.

In this case, what sort of Congress is this supposed to be?

Do you want a Congress to discuss the divergences in principle and strategy that exist in our camp? Perhaps that would be, now, the most useful of all, as preparation for more concrete work. But then it would be necessary to open wide the doors to all those who call themselves anarchists, insisting that representatives of the most opposite tendencies come. This is not the intention of the Congress initiators, though; moreover, given the personal issues that currently intertwine with the issues of ideas, it would be very difficult to hold a calm and productive discussion.

Do you want a Congress to resolve the hundred personal issues that obstruct the work of propaganda? A Congress, and especially a Congress of anarchists, poorly lends itself to acting as an investigating judge and jury! And then it would be again necessary to invite everyone, accused and accusers; and it would result in each being judge and judged, and the decisions, taken by a numerical majority, would depend on the prevalent opinion in the location where the Congress is held, on the economic conditions that would allow one or the other party to participate in greater numbers, on the eloquence and skill of this or that person, and on a thousand other chance circumstances, but never on the intrinsic substance of the issues. And the decisions of the majority, which in reality would offer no guarantee of truth and justice, would be scornfully pushed away by the succumbing minority or minorities, and the net result would be new personal issues and the embitterment of the old ones.

But no: the initiators and the participants want a Congress that is not about "chit-chat," a hard-working Congress, which begins serious and sustainable work of organization and revolutionary preparation. Wonderful! But for that, it would be necessary to bring together people who know they have the same objectives and want to reach them with equal or converging means; people whose sincerity one can fully trust. And I do not believe this is possible today, with the many existing misunderstandings about the comrades' ideas and intentions, with the hundred personal issues that tear us apart, and in the presence of an enemy who watches vigilantly.

So, what is to be done?

In my opinion, if there must be a Congress, it should happen not at the beginning, but at the conclusion of strenuous work to clarify ideas and build agreement between people.

For anarchists, the situation now would be more favorable than ever. The socialists, who theoretically had to renounce almost all "scientific" postulates, have in practice descended... down to the monarchy. The syndicalist misunderstanding (I am referring to syndicalism and indeed not the union movement, which is an entirely different thing) is debunked or nearly so. The laboring masses, a little due to the infiltration of our ideas and more due to the natural unfolding of events, are drawing increasingly closer to our methods.

We, the anarchists, taken as a group, are the only ones who, after forty years of fighting, have remained loyal to their flag; the only ones who have not compromised with the enemy and have not allowed themselves to be corrupted either by easy successes and the desire for positions, or by material interests. And we could attract to us the sincere socialists who are disgusted by the betrayal of their leaders, and the syndicalists who scorn politicking and do not want to see the labor movement used as a springboard for a new crowd of arrivistes and traitors. We could re-energize the working class movement, and give it a clearer vision of the objective to reach and the means by which it can be reached.

We presently cannot, though. Our influence remains disproportionately inferior to the greatness of our program and this is because of that confusion of ideas and those personal divisions that I deplored above.

The readers should not believe that I am for concord at all costs. I believe instead that artificial concord, not founded on real harmony of ideas and feelings, is a lie that cannot and must not last.

I would not want anyone, in a tribute to concord, to sacrifice even the least part of their ideas; I believe that all tendencies have the right to develop and that the appearance of new ideas and attitudes is a sign of life and progress in a movement such as ours. However, "new" ideas should be truly new and new attitudes should not boil down to new words. And this is not always the case.

For example, I have often read writings that attempt to discredit my ideas, but which merely repeat, using different terminology, what I myself have argued and argue. Likewise, I have often seen ideas being attributed to comrades who scorn them, for the easy pleasure of refuting them afterwards. And this, let us be clear, is true for the so-called individualists against the so-called organizationists, as well as for the latter against the former.

As regards personal issues, I would not want, in a tribute to concord, our movement to be made a refuge for all scoundrels inclined to cover themselves with the flag of a party. If there are serious personal issues, they need to be resolved, in one way or another; but it should be truly base behavior that is addressed, and not gossip, animosities, and petty individual grudges.

We need to keep ourselves in check: to discipline our combative spirit and our desire to contradict; to discuss questions of ideas without the preconception of wanting to find enemies in everyone, so as to triumph over everyone, and mind the intimate meaning more than the verbal form of things that are said; to discuss personal issues, as much as possible between us, without acrimony, with the spirit of truth and justice.

Then we will probably find that we are actually more in agreement than it seems. And in any case each person would know with whom he truly agrees, and to what extent, and what they could do together.

And then, of course, the vexed question of organization would also be resolved. Each person would unite with those he agrees with and believes he can usefully work with, operating in the ways he believes to best fit the anarchist spirit and his practical purpose, without fighting other groups but rather looking at them with sympathy and keeping ready to cooperate with them whenever it seems useful.

Errico Malatesta.

[Speech Given in London on October 20, 1911]

LONDON MOVEMENT. ERRICO MALATESTA AND THE TRIPOLI WAR [BY E. B.]

Translated from "Movimento londinese. Errico Malatesta e la guerra di Tripoli," *Germinal* (Ancona) 1, no. 11 (November 5, 1911)[330]

The other night Errico Malatesta gave a lecture cum debate on the Italian-Turkish war at the German Communist Club on Charlotte Street No. 107.[331]

In his introduction, which seemed a little masterpiece, the speaker said he was not an enemy of homelands as aggregates,[332] but as districts at the service of governments or classes, representing special political, military, and financial interests in conflict with other interests of other homelands.

---

330   As regards this summary, the spy "Virgilio"—that is, the author of the summary itself, Ennio Bellelli—wrote in a report dated October 30th: "Malatesta . . . tasked a friend with summarizing his speech, a summary that was sent to Il Libertario. He himself saw the article and approved it . . . The summary was also sent to Germinal of Ancona." The *Germinal* version and the *Libertario* version, published on November 9th with the same date and signature, correspond in substance but differ on several points of the narrative. We have reproduced the *Germinal* version because it was the first to be published, but we have complemented it with footnotes containing the most salient points on which the *Libertario* version differs.

331   The *Libertario* version adds that "the suspicious local authorities had, a few days prior, prevented [the lecture] from taking place at another location already rented on Greek Street."

332   Rather than "aggregates," the *Libertario* version reads "topographic spaces inhabited by specific nuclei of population."

Just as parochialisms are no longer possible in a homeland, so homelands and their borders must be excluded from internationalism.

Italy was never greater than when, persecuted and oppressed, she saw her children shed their blood and eagerly sacrifice themselves to free the people. Then, Garibaldi in faraway America and in Europe, Nullo in maimed Poland, and a thousand others elsewhere, held high the name of Italy.[333]

But how the Italy of today has degenerated from the Italy of Nullo and Garibaldi! Forgetful of her past, her heroes and the long martyrdom, she invades a land not her own to make it her dominion.

To attack Tripoli and a people who have no weapons and cannot defend themselves is certainly not glorious action. I hope the invading Italians get a good thrash and get soundly defeated. You will see, they will be so idiotic to let themselves be defeated, and they will have deserved it.[334]

The speaker notes with sorrow that now the popular masses are for the war.

In the discussion part, to the observations made by some Italians and non-Italians, he responded demonstrating that industry and hard work form the wealth of nations, and not conquests. England owes its great prosperity not to violence but to the steam engine that was invented here and to the more advanced wool-processing technique.

The Mediterranean sea will always be Italy's, if Italy can offer more abundant, better, and cheaper merchandise to other people, whether the Germans or some other people rule in Tripoli.[335]

In any case I would be delighted, he says, should Italian soldiers be pushed back and thrown into the sea by the Turks defending their territory, and I hope that the Arabs use all individual and collective means to avenge themselves against the invaders.

He replies to a French comrade on individual action and propaganda, saying that he too would prefer collective action over individual action, but sometimes personal acts, such as those by Bresci and Angiolillo, count more than collective acts.[336] He assesses an act, be it individual or collective, by the usefulness of its effect.

---

333   Francesco Nullo, a former soldier of Garibaldi, died in 1863 fighting for independence in Poland. In the *Libertario* version the references to Nullo are replaced with references to Nino Bixio, who never fought in Poland, though.

334   In the *Libertario* version, only the first sentence of this paragraph is printed, slightly modified. The next short paragraph is also absent in *Il Libertario*.

335   In *Il Libertario* this paragraph reads: "The Mediterranean sea will always be Italy's, if Italy can offer greater quantities and greater quality of merchandise at better prices than the other competitors, and can dominate all the markets of the Aegean and the Ionian, whether the Germans, the French or the Turks rule in Tripoli." Moreover, the next paragraph is replaced by the following: "In fact, you can see that the Italians are unable to win against American competition despite the protective duties on grain."

336   The references to Bresci and Angiolillo are missing in *Il Libertario*, as well as the last sentence in the paragraph.

He is certainly not against oral or written propaganda, but notes that the last English strike, for example, had a greater effect among the English workers than twenty years of anarchist journalism and lectures.

He observes that, unfortunately, there are few anarchists and they are not yet capable of stopping wars such as the Tripoli war in Italy, or the Moroccan war in France.

He does not deny that in France there were protests against the Moroccan expedition, just as in this rally people are protesting against the Tripoli one; but in vain. He repeats that he nevertheless hopes to see the Italians resoundingly thrashed.

Italy raises its voice with Turkey because Turkey is weak and has no ships; but it avoided reacting against Austria, like France, which bullies Morocco, humiliated itself before Germany, because it is afraid of it.

So, overbearing with the weak and cowardly with the strong.

Before going to Tripoli, Italy should think about draining the Pontine marshes, and reclaiming the Ager Romanus and other uncultivated lands.

What benefit will the Italian workers derive from the occupation of Tripoli?

The land there is barren and infertile and the Italians have neither capital nor initiatives to put to use there. It will therefore be the English, the French and the Jews of the International Israelite Bank who will create industries there to intensify exploitation of Italian labor.

It is therefore better that our workers continue going to America where at least the wages are higher, because the American worker is accustomed to living like a man and being respected; while the Arab is accustomed to living off of nothing and our workers could not withstand the competition.[337] *(Applause)*

London October 28, 1911.

TRANSLATION FROM "CONFERENZA DI ENRICO MALATESTA SULLA GUERRA ITALO-TURCA," ENCLOSURE NO. 1 TO A REPORT BY POLICE COMMISSIONER FROSALI TO THE MINISTRY OF THE INTERIOR, LONDON, OCTOBER 28, 1911[338]

Spizzuoco Giovanni takes the chair.

Malatesta starts off saying: my enemies accuse me of being anti-patriotic, but tonight I want to speak as a patriot. If the action of one's own country coordinates with the high purposes of humanity he accepts patriotism. He understands how one can be proud of belonging to a country that twice gave civilization to

---

337 This last paragraph is missing in the *Il Libertario* version.
338 Typescript, Archivio Centrale dello Stato, Rome, Casellario Politico Centrale, box 2950. We have taken account of corrections made by hand to the document.

the world. Even during its time of shame, when Italy was under the foreign yoke, it offered warriors to other Nations. The fields of Greece, of the South American Republics, of Poland, of France, are sprinkled with the bones of ardent Italian patriots, of lovers of freedom. He understands the pride of a nationality that comes from Garibaldi, Mazzini, and Pisacane. He understands this, although he sees how these feelings somewhat resemble those of impoverished petty aristocrats who now, in idleness, boast about the glory of their fathers. We could more rightfully be proud if we also contributed to a greater homeland.

However, he is ashamed of the national heritage that comes from Crispi and Giolitti, of the Italy that opposes Turkey because it has no navy and is weary but obeys to the impositions of Germany, Austria, England.

Where is this Italy, now so strong against a people who were trying to regenerate themselves (see the Young Turks),[339] when it comes to defending our compatriots enslaved in Brazil, after having been tricked, under working conditions that are slavery; why does it not go to Trento and Trieste; why does it not take Italian Malta, where the residents are oppressed by England. Why? Because it is craven and afraid. But if the Italy of today is unworthy of Mazzini, it is also unworthy of Macchiavelli; for this war is not only harmful to the proletariat but does not help the bourgeoisie either; that Italian bourgeoisie that is so stupid that it does not even know how to exploit. Why instead of going to the Tripoli sands, does it not cultivate Italy? The bread that yields eight times the seed in Italy, yields 18 in England, 20 in America, and 22 times in Belgium and France. The Apulian aqueduct has been under construction for 25 years: how many years will pass before major works are performed in Tripoli? Water is still transported by boats from Venice to Apulia. Even now when Vesuvius erupts, the common people bring sacred images to stop the flow of the lava. And they are going to Tripoli to bring civilization.

If Tripoli were useful from a commercial perspective the capitalists would have gone there first, or the English, the French, the Germans. The Italian bourgeoisie will suffer increased taxes, as will the people; they will make money on the war, or rather someone, very few, will make money, but the money will come from Pantaloon's pockets.[340] The military supplier and a few officials will make money. What do you hope to sell to these poor Arabs? The total population is only 1,500,000. As our friend Rossi says, over there you can dress a kid with a handkerchief, a woman with a tablecloth, and a man as tall as he with a bedsheet. Conquer Tripoli, while Germany and England economically conquer all of Italy. You know who really conquers Turkey? The United States of America that sends

---

339 The Young Turks were a political party intended to bring reforms and oppose the dominance of European powers in Turkey. In 1908 they led a military revolt after which, the next year, sultan Abdul Hamid II was deposed.

340 Pantaloon is a traditional comedy character. The proverbial phrase "paga Pantalone" (Pantaloon pays) means that it is always the common people that end up paying for the mistakes of those in power.

iron, merchandise, machines over there, pushing and chasing away even England from the market. Do you not understand that the world has changed? You still have views from the Middle Ages, when the conquests of land coincided with economic exploitation. Now the fight is on the economic terrain and you are falling behind, by spending money on unproductive wars.

Instead of giving a third civilization to the world, Italy has become "the European policeman." Who was asked for policemen when "Crete," longing to reunite with Greece, needed to be chased back into slavery? Italy!

Why do you not use the magnificent natural forces of the Apennines? Because the Italian bourgeoisie that leads you, is too stupid.

I know a latifundium owner who has land, which took me three days to ride through on horseback. Did he cultivate it? Not a chance. Having invested his small profit in Belgian railway stock, he lives in idleness and his farmers are constrained to emigrate and get themselves exploited in America.

Certainly the Turkish government was bad. In fact it was the only one worse than the Italian government; nevertheless it treated the Arabs as brothers.

You will see how the whites, that is Europe, will treat them. Watch how the French mistreat the Arabs in Morocco and even within Algeria. Watch how they are treated even in Egypt.

I do not hope that the Turks win, although this could be a healthy lesson, but I hope that the Arabs rise up and throw both the Turks and the Italians into the sea. Perhaps it is not probable, you tell me, perhaps no; nevertheless remember that Italy managed to get beaten by the Ethiopians, a people slightly superior, today, to the Arabs, as poorly armed as them, and lacking the Arabs' glorious traditions.

Remember that the Arabs were very close to winning at the time of Arabi Pasha's insurrection.[341] You will conquer Tripoli: you will have a new edition of the Banca Romana,[342] and the foreigners, France, Germany, England, will enter it commercially, and you will not be able to close the doors of Tripoli to them using duties, otherwise they will respond by closing those few outlets that you have abroad.

Remember: the Italy of today is vainglorious, craven, feeble, full of fear: there was enthusiasm also at the time of the Ethiopian war; lectures are worth little, but facts are worth a lot: the news came out that ours were getting a drubbing at Adua and behold even in Naples where the enthusiasm was highest the women threw themselves under the trains to stop soldiers from leaving: the enthusiasm disappeared and the war finished. Why? Because it was not fought for freedom but to oppress. Let us educate ourselves and when we are educated and strong we will never go again to oppress, but we will find wealth in our country.

---

341   The insurrection took place in Egypt in 1882, to liberate the country from French and British influence. Malatesta and other anarchists went there to take an active part in the events.

342   See note 63 above on the Banca Romana scandal.

It is not true that colonial conquests bring wealth. Switzerland has no colonies and it is certainly richer than Italy. Do you believe that France is rich because it has Madagascar, Africa, Morocco? No, it is rich due to the industry of its inhabitants, because it cultivates its land, because the French worker does not work for cheap, which the Italian worker does, nor would he accept the conditions that you accept working in a kitchen. It is rich because *it has had two revolutions and soon it will have a third.*

Do you believe that England is rich because it has India??? Perhaps the class of officials benefits from it, but not the people: it is rich because it had steam and railways, 50 years before the other nations, because it has coal, because its capitalists exploit first their natural wealth.

And even if that were true it would come down to this: Look at that lad who got rich massacring and robbing; let me go and do a little massacring and robbing too. No, this is the ethics of the decadent Roman state, it is not mine, it should not be that of the Italian people. After 20 years of socialist propaganda, it is sad to have to be here tonight to repeat such sad things: nevertheless it is necessary to admit it today: the Italian people, unworthy of itself, is drunk on presumed glory. Presumed glory, since it is indeed one of the arguments used by the warmonger socialist Defelice, who accepts this war because it will not cost us a single man.[343] Thus glory itself disappears and only madness and monkey business, pure and simple, remain.

In response to proposals made by English comrades to give lectures with the help of English radicals, Malatesta objected. Given the conditions of the current Italian mentality and the lack of a free press, the sellout press would not fail to say: they would have liked to take Tripoli.

It is distressful but there is nothing else to do but *hope that actions speak instead of words.*

In response to a Frenchman who asked him if he meant individual acts, Malatesta responded:

"I am not a supporter of individual acts unless they are done with judgment, and at the appropriate time: collective acts are more effective, except those of Angiolillo and Bresci, which were both judicious and timely."

---

343   Giuseppe De Felice Giuffrida had been one of the main organizers of the workers' Fasci in Sicily in 1893. He progressively moved on to reformist positions and supported the Libyan venture, in which he saw an opportunity for commercial development in Sicily on the so-called "fourth shore." The other three shores of Italy were the Tyrrhenian, Adriatic, and Ionian.

The Twenty-Fifth Anniversary of "Freedom"

Freedom (London) 25, no. 271 (November 1911)

On Saturday, October 28th, a number of comrades assembled at tea and conversazione in the Food Reform Restaurant, Furnival Street, Holborn, to celebrate the twenty-fifth anniversary of the publication of FREEDOM.

. . .

E. Malatesta urged the *Freedom* Group to persevere unflinchingly in their work. There was great necessity for it, as was proved by the possibility of such piratical adventures as that of the Italian Government in Tripoli and by other Governments who sent their soldiers to butcher people wholesale.

. . .

[Speech Given in London on December 9, 1911]

Translated from a report by police commissioner Frosali to the Ministry of the Interior, London, December 16, 1911[344]

Subject: Lectures by Enrico Malatesta in the "London Social Studies Group" location—
    . . . I have the Honor of announcing to this Honorable Ministry that the known "Malatesta" Enrico is now an assiduous regular at the location on Meard Street, No. 6, where he gives propaganda lectures every Saturday in the afternoon hours.
    The first lecture was given this past Saturday the 2nd on the subject "Anarchy."
    He repeated the same arguments he has expounded on in many other lectures of the kind, and the ideas he advocates in his writings.
    This past Saturday the 9th another lecture by Malatesta, in the same location, in the French language. About 50 anarchists were observed, mostly French.
    The topic "Syndicalism." Malatesta criticized Syndicalism, "which has all the defects of a closed caste organization, and does not tend toward general progress. It is in other words, crystallized worker egoism, devoid of that broad-mindedness that anarchism brings, demanding the well-being of all, including enemies."
    On this point there was discussion: Malatesta maintained "that material well-being must be extended—under the anarchist system—even to those who

---

344   Typescript, Archivio Centrale dello Stato, Rome, Casellario Politico Centrale, box 2950. We have silently normalized the use of quotation marks, when it was irregular or incoherent in the original text.

do not think as we do"—The syndicalists present said:"food must be taken away from the bourgeois, who do not work"—And Malatesta responded: "and then you are replicating present society!"

...

For a Prisoner of the State

Translated from "Pour un prisonnier d'état," *La Guerre Sociale* (Paris) 5, no. 52 (December 27, 1911—January 2, 1912)

LITERATURE, THE PRESS, THE LEGAL PROFESSION, PARLIAMENT AND THE WORKING CLASS UNITE TO HONOR GUSTAVE HERVÉ AND DEMAND HIS LIBERATION.[345]

...

Enrico Malatesta

My dear comrade Almereyda,[346]

All issues of ideas aside, it is with true pleasure that I welcome the occasion you are offering me to express all of my admiration for Gustave Hervé's selflessness and courage.

Although I cannot accept neither Hervé's jacobin and statist ideal, nor his uncertain and vacillating tactic,[347] I consider him always as a precious force for the revolution that is to come.

Fraternally yours.

Errico Malatesta

...

---

345   The article consists of over four pages of individual statements of solidarity with Gustave Hervé, from figures in the world of politics, syndicalism, and culture. Hervé had risen to fame in 1901, publishing an article in the socialist press that evoked the image of the French flag planted in a dung heap. He then established a movement called "herveism" after him, which promoted antimilitarism and socialism by means of military insurrection and the general strike in the event of war. In 1906 he founded the weekly *La Guerre Sociale*, which sought to unite socialists, syndicalists, and anarchists around his antimilitarist program. Hervé was imprisoned in March 1910, after being sentenced to four years for press crimes.

346   Miguel Almereyda was the editor of *La Guerre Sociale*, replacing Hervé.

347   The French text uses "vaillant" (courageous), but the context suggests that this is a typo for "vacillant." Beginning with his incarceration in 1910, Hervé had begun revising his position, expressing doubts on the project to unite all of France's revolutionary forces into a single party, softening his previous anti-parliamentarism and introducing the slogan of "revolutionary militarism."

A Hopeful Start

The Syndicalist (London) 1, no. 1 (January 1912)

ENTHUSIASTIC SYNDICALIST LEAGUERS OPEN THE CAMPAIGN OF 1912, WITH A
HAPPY COMBINATION OF FROLIC AND ZEAL.

NEW Year's Eve was celebrated by the Industrial Syndicalist Education League
by a "Feu de Joie" in the big hall of Anderton's Hotel on Fleet Street. The brightly
illuminated room was filled with an assemblage of comrades famous in the annals
of England's working class struggle; and the occasion furnished an enthusiasm
that will last far into the coming months.

...

After another contribution of song and story from the "group on entertainment,"
reinforced this time by Bro. Tom Mann himself, Comrade Malatesta of Italy congratulated the League on its libertarian ideals, and Bro. John Turner of the Shop
Assistants' Union declared that Syndicalism was giving to progressives a much
needed opportunity to translate their theories into action.

...

War and Anarchists

Translated from "La guerra e gli anarchici," *La Guerra Tripolina* (London),
single issue (April 1912)[348]

There is no nefarious deed, no wicked passion that interested parties do
not seek to excuse, justify, and even glorify with noble reasons. This is at
heart a source of comfort, for it shows that certain loftier ideals devised
by humanity over the course of its evolution have already seeped into
the universal consciousness, and survive and prevail even in times of the
greatest aberration. Yet it is no less necessary that the deception be exposed, and the sordid interests and atavistic brutality lurking under the
cloak of noble sentiments be denounced.

Thus, in order to justify and persuade the people to accept the war
of robbery that the Italian government meant to perpetrate against the
populations of Libya, it was not enough to mendaciously proclaim that

---

348   *La Guerra Tripolina,* which had the generic subtitle of "Publication by an
Anarchist Group," was published by Malatesta's group to express their point
of view on the Italo-Turkish war and militarism. The newspaper opened with a
statement saying it had received and registered "with pleasure" the support of
the Italian Revolutionary Group of Paris. Collaborators included Felice Vezzani
and Silvio Corio. According to informers at the Italian consulate in London,
5000 copies of the publication were printed and distributed free of charge.

the undertaking would be simple and that the Italian proletariat would reap great economic benefits from it. It would truly be excessive if a man, other than a complete brute, were to be incited to commit a murder by merely telling him that the intended victim is defenseless and has lots of money and that there is no risk of being discovered and punished! So, other loftier motives had to be advanced and the naïve persuaded that this was a rare case in which one might become rich while performing a generous and magnanimous act. And they brought out the need to develop "the energies of the race" and show the world what "our folk" are worth, the right and duty to propagate civilization and, above all, the love of the country and the glory of Italy.

We shall not concern ourselves here with the alleged material benefits, first of all, because, in our view, these could never justify aggression, and then because at this point few people believe any longer in such benefits, unless we are talking about the profits of a small number of monopolists and military suppliers. But it is worth our while to examine the moral arguments that have been deployed to justify the war.

Italy, they say, is not given her due place in this world. Italians are oblivious of their potential energies; they need to be shaken out of their lethargy. Life is energy, strength and action and struggle, and we want to live!

All well and good. But since we are men and not brute beasts and the life we want to live is a human life, there must be qualifications for the energy to be expended. Is it the energy of the predatory beast to which we aspire? Or that of the braggart, the bandit, the cop, the executioner? Or—and perhaps this is the example that best fits this case—that of the cowardly thug who, having got a sound thrashing in town, heads home and demonstrates his courage… by beating his wife?

The energy of civilized people, the force that genuinely brings an intensity to life is not the sort expressed in inter-human struggles, bullying the weak, oppressing the defeated. But it is the sort deployed in the struggle against the adverse forces of nature, in tasks of useful toil, in the demanding research of science, in helping to spur forward those who lag behind, in lifting up the fallen, in securing ever greater powers and well-being for all human beings.

Yes, certainly, Italians are lacking in energy. Cowardly and idle, the bourgeoisie is not even able to exploit available workers and forces them to leave and be exploited abroad; and the workers let themselves be driven from their homeland in search of a crust of bread, and now they are being sent to Libya to murder and be murdered for the profit of a few greedy speculators, to win new territory for those who prevent them from enjoying the land of Italy. It is not war, though, that will give them energy and the will to progress, any more than turning to a life of theft and prostitution energizes those who cannot and will not work.

To work and to claim the fruit of their labor, that is what the Italians need, like any other people.

*
**

We, the warmongers say, are bringing civilization to the barbarians.

Let us take a look at that.

Civilization means wealth, science, freedom, brotherhood, justice; it means material, moral, and intellectual advancement: it means the abandonment and condemnation of brutish struggle, and the advancement of solidarity and conscious and voluntary cooperation.

Above all, civilizing involves inspiring sentiments of freedom and human dignity, raising the value of life, encouraging activity and initiative, respecting individuals and the natural or voluntary associations into which men may enter.

Is this what the soldiers of Italy, at the service of the Banco di Roma, are going to do in Africa?

Despite Verbicaro[349] and the Camorra, despite illiteracy, despite the uncultivated and malaria-infested land and the thousands of municipalities without water, without streets, without sewers, Italy is still more civilized than Libya. She has skilled and strong workers; she has doctors, engineers, agronomists, artists; she has great traditions, an intelligent and kind people who, when not suffocated by poverty and tyranny, have always proved themselves capable of the most exacting and noblest tasks. She could climb quickly to the highest rungs of human civilization and become a mighty factor for progress and justice in the world.

Instead, deceived and intoxicated by those who oppress and exploit her and prevent her from developing her qualities and her wealth, she sends soldiers and priests to Africa, she brings carnage and robbery, and in the vile endeavor to reduce a foreign population to slavery, she makes a brute and a slave of herself.

May people mend their ways soon!

*
**

And now we come to the main subject: patriotism.

---

349   When the Calabrian town of Verbicaro was hit by a cholera epidemic in 1911, a violent revolt broke out against the local authorities, who were considered responsible for the epidemic. The episode caused a sensation and was interpreted as a manifestation of barbaric primitivism. Giovanni Giolitti's government addressed the revolt more as an issue of law and order than of public health. An intense campaign of repression ensued, and the town was militarily occupied by the army for the next three years.

Patriotic sentiment undeniably has a great allure in every country and serves the people's exploiters admirably well by overshadowing class antagonisms and, in the name of an idealized solidarity of race and nation, draws the oppressed to serve, against themselves, the interests of their oppressors. And this is all the more successful in a country like Italy which has for so long been oppressed by the foreigner and was released from that only yesterday after fierce and glorious struggles.

But what does patriotism actually consist of?

Love of birthplace—or rather, greater love for the place where we were raised, where we received our mothers' caresses, where we played as children with other children, and as youth won our first kiss from a beloved girl—preference for the language we understand best and, therefore, more intimate dealings with those who speak it: these are natural and beneficial phenomena. They are beneficial because, while they quicken the beating heart and create firmer ties of solidarity within human groups and nurture the originality of types, they do no harm to anyone and rather than hinder, they favor general progress. And if those aforementioned preferences do not blind us to the merits of others and to our own shortcomings, if they do not make us contemptuous of a broader culture and broader relations, if they do not inspire a laughable vanity and arrogance that makes us believe we are better than another just because we were born in the shadow of a certain bell-tower or within certain borders, then they can turn out to be an essential element in the future development of humanity. Since, once distances have been nearly abolished by advances in machinery, political obstacles cleared away by freedom, and economic obstacles banished by general comfort, those preferences remain the best guarantee against the rapid influx of huge masses of immigrants into those areas best favored by nature or best prepared by the labors of past generations; something that would pose a serious threat to the peaceful progress of civilization.

But these are not the only feelings upon which so-called patriotism feeds.

In antiquity, man's oppression of his fellow man was accomplished mainly by means of warfare and conquest. It was the victorious foreigner who seized the land, forced the natives to work it for him, and was, if not the only master, certainly the harshest and most despised. And while this state of affairs has all but disappeared from the nations of the European race, where the master is now, in most cases, a fellow countryman of his victims, it still remains the prevalent characteristic in Europeans' relationships with peoples of other races. Thus the fight against the oppressor has had, and still has, the character of a fight against the foreigner.

Unfortunately, but understandably, hatred of the foreigner as oppressor turned into hatred of the foreigner as foreigner, and turned gentle love of homeland into that feeling of antipathy and rivalry toward other peoples, which usually goes by the name of patriotism, and which the domestic oppressors in various countries exploit to their advantage. Civilization's mission is to dispel this nefarious misunderstanding, and bring all people together as brothers in the fight for the common good.

We are internationalists, meaning that, just as the tiny homeland that revolved around a tent or a bell-tower and was at war with neighboring tribes or towns has been superseded by the larger regional and national homeland, so we extend our homeland to the whole world, feel ourselves to be brothers of all human beings, and seek well-being, freedom, and autonomy for every individual and group. Just as, back in the days when Christianity was believed and heartfelt, Christians regarded the whole Christendom as their homeland and the foreigner that needed converting or destroying was the pagan, so we regard all of the oppressed and all who struggle for human emancipation as our brothers. And all oppressors, all whose prosperity is built upon the woes of others, are our enemies no matter where they were born or the language they speak.

We abhor war, which is always fratricidal and damaging, and we want a liberating social revolution; we deplore strife between peoples and we champion the fight against the ruling classes. But if, by some misfortune, a clash were to erupt between one people and another, we stand with the people who are defending their independence. When Austrian soldiery were running about the plains of Lombardy and Franz Joseph's gallows were going up in the town squares of Italy, the Italians' revolt against the Austrian tyrant was noble and holy. Now that today's Italy invades another country and Victor Emmanuel's infamous gallows are being erected and put to work in the marketplace in Tripoli, it is the Arabs' revolt against the Italian tyrant that is noble and holy.

For the sake of Italy's honor, we hope that the Italian people, having come to its senses, will be able to force a withdrawal from Africa upon its government: if not, we hope that the Arabs may succeed in driving it out.

And with such thoughts, it is us, the "anti-patriots," who will have salvaged whatever part of Italy's honor can be salvaged in the face of history, in the face of humanity. We shall be the ones to show that in Italy there is still a gleam of the sentiments that moved Mazzini and Garibaldi and the glorious scores of Italians whose bones are strewn across every battlefield in Europe and the Americas where a holy battle was fought, and who endeared the name of Italy to all men, in all countries, whose hearts thrilled to the cause of freedom, independence, and justice.

ERRICO MALATESTA.

LONDRA, APRILE, 1912.

LA GUERRA TRIPOLINA.

Pubblicazione di un Gruppo Anarchico.

Riceviamo e registriamo con piacere l'adesione del Gruppo Rivoluzionario Italiano di Parigi.

LA GUERRA E GLI ANARCHICI.

Non v'è azione nefanda, non passione malvagia che non si cerchi dagl'interessati di scusare, giustificare ed anche glorificare con nobili motivi. Questo è in fondo una cosa consolante, poichè dimostra che certi ideali superiori elaborati dal l'umanità nel corso della sua evoluzione sono entrati oramai nella coscienza universale e sopravvivono e s'impongono anche nei momenti di maggiore aberrazione; ma non è perciò meno necessario di svelare l'inganno e denunziare gl'interessi sordidi e le brutalità ataviche che si ascondono sotto il manto di nobili sentimenti.

Così, a giustificare e far accettare dal popolo la guerra di rapina che il governo d'Italia intendeva perpetrare contro le popolazioni della Libia non pastava bastare l'annuncio bugiardo della facilità dell'impresa e dei grandi vantaggi economici che ne sarebbero venuti al proletariato italiano. Sarebbe veramente troppo il voler indurre un uomo, che non fosse un bruto completo, a commettere un assassinio dicendogli solo che l'assassinato è inerme ed ha molti quattrini e che non v'è pericolo di essere scoperto e punito: bisognava dunque addurre ragioni più elevate e persuadere gl'ingenui che si era di fronte ad un caso raro in cui era possibile arricchirsi facendo un'azione generosa e magnanima. E tirarono fuori la necessità di sviluppare "le energie della razza," e mostrare al mondo il valore di "nostra gente," il diritto ed il dovere di propagare la civiltà, e soprattutto l'amor di patria e la gloria d'Italia.

Non ci occuperemo qui dei pretesi vantaggi materiali, primo perchè per noi essi non giustificherebbero l'aggressione e poi perchè oramai a questi vantaggi pochi ci credono più, a meno che non si tratti dei profitti di un piccolo numero di accaparratori e di fornitori militari. Ma esamineremo, chè ne vale la pena, le ragioni morali con cui si è voluto giustificare la guerra.

L'Italia, si è detto, non occupa nel mondo il posto che le compete. Gl'Italiani non hanno coscienza delle loro energie potenziali: bisogna scuoterli ed uscire dal letargo. La vita è energia, è forza, è azione, è lotta, e noi vogliamo vivere!

Sta benissimo. Ma poichè siamo uomini e non bestie brute e la vita che vogliam vivere è vita umana, bisognerà pure che l'energia da spiegare abbia delle qualificazioni. È' forse l'energia della bestia da preda quella a cui si aspira? O quella del bravaccio, del brigante, dello sbirro, del boja? O quella—e forse questo è il paragone che meglio si attaglia al caso—del bruto vigliacco che, avendone toccato in piazza, torna a casa a dar prova di bravura...bastonando la moglie?

L'energia della gente civile, la forza che produce davvero intensità di vita non è quella che si spiega nelle lotte inter-umane, colla prepotenza contro i deboli, coll'oppressione dei vinti. Ma è quella che si esercita nella lotta contro le forze avverse della natura, nei compiti del lavoro fecondo, nelle ardue ricerche della scienza, nell'ajutare a progredire quei che restano indietro, nel sollevare i caduti, nel conquistare per tutti gli esseri umani sempre maggiore potenza e maggiore benessere.

Sì, certo; gl'italiani mancano di energia. La borghesia, pavida ed inerte, non sa nemmeno sfruttare i lavoratori che si offrono e li costringe ad andare a farsi sfruttare all'estero; ed i lavoratori si lasciano cacciar via dal loro paese in cerca di un tozzo di pane, ed ora si fanno mandare in Libia ad ammazzare e farsi ammazzare pel beneficio di pochi ingordi speculatori, per conquistare nuove terre a coloro che impediscon loro di godere delle terre d'Italia. Ma non è la guerra che darà loro energia e vo ontà di progredire, come non dà energia a chi non sa e non vuol lavorare il mettersi a vivere di furto e di prostituzione.

Lavorare e pretendere il frutto del loro lavoro, ecco ciò che bisogna agr'Italiani, come a tutti g.i altri popoli.

Noi, dicono i guerrajuoli, apportiamo la civiltà ai barbari.

Vediamo un po'.

Civiltà significa ricchezza, scienza, libertà, fratellanza, giustizia; significa sviluppo materiale, morale ed intellettuale; significa l'abbandono e la condanna delle lotte brutali, ed il progredire della solidarietà e della cooperazione cosciente e volontaria.

Civilizzare importa anzitutto ispirare il sentimento della libertà e della dignità umana, elevare il valore della vita, spronare all'attività ed allo iniziativa, rispettare gl'individui e gli aggruppamenti naturali o volontarii che gli uomini fanno.

È' questo che vanno a fare in Africa i soldati d'Italia al servizio del Banco di Roma?

Malgrado Verbicaro e la Camorra, malgrado l'analfabetismo, malgrado le terre incolte o malariche e le migliaja di comuni senza acqua, senza strade, senza fogne, l'Italia è pur sempre più civile della Libia. Essa ha operai abili e coscienti; essa ha medici, ingegneri, agronomi, artisti; essa ha grandi tradizioni, ha tutto un popolo intelligente e gentile che, quando non è stato soffocato dalla miseria e dalla tirannia, ha mostrato sempre capace delle opere più ardue e più nobili. Essa potrebbe ascendere rapidamente alle più alte vette della civiltà umana e divenire nel mondo un possente fattore di progresso e di giustizia.

E invece, ingannata ed ubbriacata da coloro stessi che l'opprimono e la sfruttano e le impediscono di sviluppo le sue qualità e le sue ricchezze, essa manda in Africa soldati a predi, essa porta strage e rapina, e nel tentativo infame di ridurre in schiavitù un popolo straniero, essa s'imbrutisce e si fa schiava essa stessa.

Venga presto l'ora del ravvedimento!

E veniamo all'argomento magno; il patriottismo.

Il sentimento patriottico ha incontestabilmente un fascino grande in tutti i paesi e serve ammirevolmente agli sfruttatori del popolo per far perder di vista gli antagonismi di classe e, in nome di una solidarietà ideale di razza e di nazione, trascinare gli oppressi a servire, contro i loro stessi, gl'interessi degli oppressori. Ciò perchè riesce tanto più facilmente in un paese come l'Italia che è stato lungamente oppresso dallo straniero e ne è liberato solo ieri dopo lotte cruenti e gloriose.

Ma in che consiste propriamente il patriottismo?

L'amore del loco natio, o piuttosto il maggiore amore per il luogo dove siamo stati allevati, dove abbiamo ricevute le carezze materne, dove bambini giocammo coi bambini, e giovanetti conquistammo il primo bacio di una fanciulla amata, la preferenza per la lingua che comprendiamo meglio e quindi le più intime relazioni con coloro che la parlano, sono fatti naturali e benefici. Benefici, perchè, mentre risaldano il cuore di quei vivi palpiti e stringono gli solidi vincoli di solidarietà nei varii gruppi umani e favoriscono l'originalità dei varii fipi, non fanno male ad alcuno e non contrastano, anzi favoriscono, il progresso generale. E se le dette preferenze non rendono ciechi ai meriti altrui ed ai proprii difetti, se non vi fanno apprezzatori di una più vasta cultura e di più vaste relazioni, se non ispirano una vanità e boria ridicole che fa credere che si val meg lo di un a tro perchè si è nati all' ombra di un certo campani e o in certi dati confini, allora esse possono riuscire elemento necessario nell'evoluzione futura dell' umanità. Poichè,

abolite quasi le distanze dai progressi della meccanica, abolite dalla libertà gli ostacoli politici, aboliti dall'agiatezza generale gli ostacoli economici, esse restano la garenzia migliore contro il rapido accorrere di masse enormi di emigranti verso i siti più favoriti dalla natura o meglio preparati del lavoro delle generazioni passate; cosa che crescerebbe un grave pericolo per il pacifico progredire della civiltà.

Ma non è solo da questi sentimenti che è alimentato il cosiddetto patriottismo.

Nell'antichità l'oppressione dell'uomo sull'uomo si compieva principalmente a mezzo della guerra e della conquista. Era lo straniero vincitore che s'impadroniva delle terre, che costringeva gl'indigeni a lavorare per lui, ed era, se solo l'unico, certo il più duro ed esecrato padrone. E questo stato di cose, se è quasi sparito nelle nazioni di razza europea, dove il padrone è ora il più delle volte un compatriota delle sue vittime, resta ancora il carattere prevalente nei rapporti degli europei coi popoli di altra razza. Quindi la lotta contro l'oppressore ha avuto ed ha spesso ancora il carattere di lotta contro lo straniero.

Disgraziatamente, ma comprensibilmente, l'odio dello straniero in quanto oppressore divenne odio dello straniero in quanto straniero, e trasformò il dolce amor di patria in quel sentimento di antipatia e di rivalità verso gli altri popoli, che si suol chiamare patriottismo, e che gli oppressori indigeni dei varii paesi sfruttano a loro vantaggio.

È compito della civiltà e di dissipare questo equivoco nefasto, ed affratellare i popoli tutti nella lotta per il bene comune.

Noi siamo internazionalisti, vale a dire che, come dalla patria minuscola, che si raccoglieva intorno ad una tenda o ad un campanile e viveva in guerra colle tribù o coi comuni circostanti si è passato alla più grande patria regionale e nazionale, così noi estendiamo la patria al mondo tutto, ci sentiamo fratelli di tutti gli esseri umani e vogliamo benessere, libertà, autonomia per tutti gl'individui e tutte le collettività. Come per i cristiani, all'epoca in cui il Cristianesimo era creduto e sentito, la patria era la Cristianità tutta quanta e lo straniero da convertire o da distruggere era il pagano, così per noi son fratelli tutti gli oppressi, tutti coloro che lottano per l'emancipazione umana e nemici tutti gli oppressori, tutti coloro che il proprio bene fondano sul male altrui, dovunque essi sien nati e qualunque sia la lingua che parlano.

Noi aborriamo la guerra, fratricida sempre e dannosa, e vogliamo la rivoluzione sociale liberatrice; noi deprechiamo le lotte fra popoli ed invochiamo la lotta contro le classi dominanti. Ma noi disgraziatamente un conflitto avviene fra popolo e popolo, noi siamo con quel popolo che difende la sua indipendenza.

Quando le soldatesche austriache scorazzavano le campagne lombarde e le forche di Francesco Giuseppe si ergevano sulle piazze d'Italia, nobile e santa era la rivolta dagl'italiani contro il tiranno austriaco. Oggi che l'Italia va ad invadere un altro paese e sulla piazza del mercato di Tripoli si erge e strangola la forca infame di Vittorio Emanuele, nobile e santa è la rivolta degli arabi contro il tiranno italiano.

Per l'onore d'Italia, noi speriamo nel il popolo italiano rinsavito, sappia imporre al governo il ritiro dall'Africa; e se no, speriamo che gli arabi riescano a cacciarnelo.

E così pensando, siamo ancora noi "gli anti-patrioti" che avremo salvato in faccia alla storia, l'onore dell'umanità, anzi ciò che è di salvabile dell'onore d'Italia. Sarem noi che avrem mostrato che non è completamente spento in Italia il sentimento che animò e Mazzini e Garibaldi e tutta quella schiera gloriosa d'italiani che coprì delle sue ossa tutti i campi di battaglia di Europa e di America dove si combattè una santa battaglia, e fece caro il nome d'Italia a quanti, in tutti i paesi, ebbero un palpito per la causa della libertà, dell'independenza, della giustizia.

ERRICO MALATESTA.

The Rome Attack

Translated from "L'attentato di Roma," *La Guerra Tripolina* (London),
single issue (April 1912)

A young Roman bricklayer made an attempt at the life of the King of Italy.[350]

This episode should seem ordinary in a country that raises statues and releases hymns praising Monti and Tognetti, Felice Orsini, Agesilao Milano, Guglielmo Oberdan.[351] But such is not the case. Now, it is no longer a matter of historical events that, in the end, served to open the path to power for today's dominators. Instead, now the matter is the bursting of an exacerbated proletarian soul, an act that sounds a warning and a threat to the banqueters at the Italic feast, even if it was ill-advised and ineffective. And naturally the bourgeoisie, disturbed in its peaceful enjoyment of usurped power and wealth, unanimously rises to curse him, and, as usual, drags along with it that part of the unconscious people who always shout hosannas to the strongest and rage against the fallen.

We do not know Antonio Dalba and the specific reasons that caused him to act. But it is easy to understand the factors that produce similar events.

This time we will not speak of the general and permanent causes of collective and individual revolt: the poverty of workers, the exploitation and humiliation to which they are subjected. We will instead linger on recent and immediate causes, which can be summarized in the Tripoli war, the propaganda and suggestion of violence that this war has brought about, the struggles and the poverty that this war is producing.

For the dubious interests of a handful of capitalists, priests, and politicos, for the ambitions of the military castes, for the vainglory of the king, Italy has been dragged into a hideous war, the scarce national wealth has been squandered—even though it was so necessary for the country's development—the glorious traditions of struggles for independence have been trampled, and desolation, bloodshed, gallows have been brought to a harmless population, which was believed to be incapable of defending itself. And in order to be able to do this, the people were intoxicated with sophistry and lies, so much as to make Italy seem to be a country of bloodthirsty barbarians and thieves.

Every freedom is suppressed; and the oppression intended to be imposed upon the Arabs naturally falls back upon the Italians. From the bullets of soldiers to the brutality of police officers, to the judges'

---

350   On March 14, 1912, in Rome, Antonio D'Alba fired two revolver shots against the carriage carrying Victor Emmanuel III and the queen to the Pantheon for a mass in memory of Humbert I. The royals were unharmed.

351   On these historical figures see "Malatesta Boasts," on p. 17 of the current volume.

ferocious sentences, to the thrashings by nationalists, when there are a hundred against one... everything emits violence and arrogance.

Faced with so much reaction, so much resurgence of the old barbaric soul, most men of progress, overwhelmed and aching, wait for the inevitable hour of repentance which will allow them to regain the terrain lost and to go further. But others do not have this wisdom or this patience, and since the masses are idle and every civil protest is smothered, they resolve to act alone and raise their avenging hand.

Whose fault is it?

Is the action right, though, is it useful?

Lacking the freedom to say everything we think, we prefer to keep silent.[352]

Still, even after all the reservations imposed upon us by conviction or prudence, we cannot help but show—in this moment, in which murder for theft is raised to the rank of civic virtue under the mantle of love for country—our respect, our admiration for Dalba, for Masetti,[353] for all those who, with no concern for personal safety, sacrifice themselves for a cause that they believe is right.

ERRICO MALATESTA.

Errico Malatesta: To the Italian Colony of London [For a Personal Fact][354]

The Anarchist (Glasgow) 1, no. 8 (June 12, 1912)

Translated from "Errico Malatesta alla colonia italiana di Londra (Per un fatto personale)," London, April 22, 1912[355]

I learn that as a sequel to my propaganda against the war, Signor ENNIO BELLELLI[356] continues to insinuate, and to some persons definitely affirmed, that I have sold myself to Turkey, that I am a Turkish spy.

This thing is indeed to[o] ridiculous, and too clear are the motives of this insane slander, and I should not take any notice of it if it had not come from Bellelli, and did not afford me the opportunity to go to the

---

352   According to a March 23, 1912, report from the London consulate to the Ministry of the Interior, after receiving news of the attack, Malatesta allegedly exclaimed: "too bad he missed."

353   At dawn on October 30, 1911, in the courtyard of a barracks in Bologna, the soldier Augusto Masetti, member of a regiment leaving for the war in Libya, fired a rifle shot that injured his superior.

354   The square brackets are in the original text.

355   Published as a printed leaflet.

356   See note 170 above on Bellelli.

bottom of a question that for many years torments me and everybody else, or almost all those who know Bellelli.

Bellelli calls himself (or used to) an Anarchist, but most persons consider him an obtuse and mysterious type of man, and many look upon him as a[n] Italian Police Spy. They say that although he has a large family he lives well and expensively without any evident means of existence, and that the trade in books he says he carries on is a lie that can easily be shown up. Some have asked him for explanations but Bellelli has answered angrily that he is not bound to explain his business to anyone.

I interested myself in this question but could not arrive at anything positive, and therefore did not think it my duty to break off the relations I had with Bellelli. Some friends have blamed me for this, but I knew that if I had acted otherwise, I should have been obliged to prove the charge, and proofs I had not. And I knew also that when charges of this kind are made, and cannot be proved by evidence, the results are dissensions and conflicts that do more damage than a spy can do... especially if the spy has already been tacitly put in Coventry.

Then came the Italian expedition to Tripoli, and Bellelli, after some hesitation, declared himself a partisan of the war with all its worst consequence of annexation, massacre of the Arabs, and the scaffold.

Such opinion which in another mind might be honest, cannot be so in Bellelli, who used to call himself an Anarchist.

For what interest did he sustain a cause which is opposed to all the ideas and sentiments which constitute Anarchism? Or if he is a sincere partisan of the war, for what interest did he feign to be an Anarchist?

At last there was a sure reason to break off the relations, and I broke them. But I made no charge because I was always lacking evidence, and then because I did not want to supply him with the means of evading the question by saying that he was accused because he was a 'Patriot.'

But behold Bellelli now accused me. Well, I offer my life to the examination of the Public. Bellelli cannot any more allege an offence against his dignity by refusing to submit to an examination of his life. I pledge to submit myself to any enquiry which anybody may wish to make into my affairs. I pledge myself to demonstrate how I earn every cent I can dispose of, from whence comes every slice of bread I eat: let Bellelli do the same.

If I don't prove to the satisfaction of all my friends and enemies the clear and honest origin of my means of existence, I authorise the public to treat me as a Turkish Spy. If Bellelli does not do the same he must allow that it has been proved that he is an Italian Spy.

If Bellelli is an honest man, he will accept this challenge, and should be grateful to me for offering the way to clear himself with dignity from the atmosphere of suspicion and mistrust which surround[s] him.

Therefore, if he feels quiet in his conscience, let him convoke a public meeting to debate on myself and him. Or if he does not wish to put himself to this inconvenience, let him inform me that he is disposed to present himself to the public to accuse me, or to defend himself, and I will convoke the meeting.

ERRICO MALATESTA,
92 High Street, Islington, N.

London, 22nd April, 1912.

[Speech Given in London on May 8, 1912]

Translated from a report by police commissioner Frosali to the Ministry of the Interior, London, May 22, 1912[357]

Subject: Lecture by Enrico Malatesta on the topic of "Individualism" at 99 Charlotte Street—Higher Education Group —

I have the Honor of reporting to this Superior Ministry that on this past 8th the known Enrico Malatesta gave a lecture at the above-mentioned location, in the presence of the "Italian Anarchist Group"—

The selected subject: "Individualism"—

Malatesta expounded on the usual and old theories and concluded by singing the praises of Bonnot, the French bandit, and declaring that he would have done better to organize a large armed band to be able to effectively act against the bourgeoisie.[358]

He ended by saying that the anarchist ideal could not completely triumph until the working masses take possession, by violence, of the belongings of the hated bourgeoisie.

He was applauded, and praise was also given to the martyr comrade "Bonnot"—

---

357   Typescript, Biblioteca Franco Serantini, Pisa, collection "Errico Malatesta," folder "Consolato d'Italia Londra, 11." We have taken account of corrections made by hand to the document.

358   Jules Bonnot was an illegalist French anarchist, member of a band named after him which committed several robberies using state-of-the-art technologies, such as automobiles and repeating rifles, still unavailable to the police. Bonnot died on April 28, 1912, in a firefight with the police. Malatesta's alleged praise of Bonnot should be accepted with much caution, especially in light of the later article "The Red Bandits," published in the volume of these *Complete Works* covering the years 1913–18, in which he expresses an entirely different position on the subject.

Errico Malatesta Convicted

Translated from "Errico Malatesta condannato," *Il Libertario* (La Spezia) 10, no. 450 (May 23, 1912)[359]

. . .

92, High Str. Islington

London N. 14 May '912

Dear comrades,

I am enclosing a leaflet that I published last month, and which clearly explains what the matter is.[360]

Since Bellelli will probably have to leave London and go practice his trade elsewhere, it is advisable to warn all comrades, publishing (at least in summary) my manifesto, and reporting the outcome of the dispute.

Bellelli denied having said that I am a Turkish spy, but he refused to show that he is not an Italian spy and to explain how he earns his bread. He did not want anything to do with public meetings or juries of honor, and instead filed a lawsuit.

Therefore I consider the dispute as resolved, and thus may the entire Italian colony here consider it so.

Bellelli could not have found a better way to convert suspicions into certainty!

The criminal trial remains, but this has no moral importance, all the more because the judgment shall not address the issue, but whether I had or did not have the right, according to English law, to publish the incriminating paper.

Affectionate regards

E. MALATESTA

. . .

359　Ennio Bellelli responded with a lawsuit for defamation to Malatesta's manifesto published above. This article, published after the trial, provides a summary of it, containing Malatesta's letter reprinted here. The letter had been sent after Bellelli's lawsuit but before the trial. The same letter was published in *L'Avvenire Anarchico* of Pisa on May 24th. See the following documents for more information on the trial and its outcome.

360　The reference is to the manifesto to the Italian colony in London.

[Defamation Trial Deposition, London, May 20, 1912]

CENTRAL CRIMINAL COURT SESSIONS PAPER: MINUTES OF EVIDENCE, VOL. 157, PART 932, P. 211–13[361]

. . .

ENRICO MALATESTA (prisoner, on oath). I am an electrical engineer, carrying on business as E. Malatesta and Co., 13, Windmill Street, Tottenham Court Road. I am an Italian subject. I have been in England for the last 12 years. I go up and down from Italy to England. I am not a professed Anarchist, but I believe in liberty and justice for everybody.[362] It is 12 years ago since I came to settle in England. When I came to England the last time I had four years' deportation to the island where I was. The police have a right to deport. I was obliged for four years to live on one of those small islands in the Mediterranean. I escaped and went from Malta to England. I first met prosecutor in London 10 years ago. He was an Anarchist and went to Anarchist meetings. He was a frequent visitor to these meetings. One of its tenets is hatred of war between nations. Belili posed as a bookseller. I published this circular. As far as I know Belili is certainly not carrying on a legitimate business as a bookseller. I have said that I believed him to be a spy and he has said that I have sold myself to the police. Bellili has told me nothing. When he says he is not an Anarchist it is a lie. He did not turn me out of his house. His wife insulted me and I went out. He then tried to put himself on good terms with me, but I refused. Belili has never called me a Turkish spy, but has said so to other people. He has no business at all. He lives in three small rooms with his wife and six children. I have been there many times, because I used to give his children arithmetic lessons. One of the rooms is used as a kitchen. He has only a few books for private use. I have never seen a new book to be sold. Twelve years ago he used to sell some books. I purchased a few from him. I have ordered books from him, but could not get them. Ten years ago I saw him supply books; not the last five or six years. He has only private books in his house—some 100—what anybody would have. Bellili and I have had a controversy over the Turco-Italian war. He was a partisan of the war. It became a little violent, because he called himself an Anarchist, being in favour of the war. I was sure he was not an Anarchist. He never told me he was in the pay of Turkey. In my opinion this document has a very great interest in London for political refugees. Bellili attended a conference of Anarchists and posed as an Anarchist.

Cross-examined. When I published the circular I said that many people

---

361 Printed, The National Archives, London.
362 Compare this passage to the report below from *The Daily Herald*, in which Malatesta instead professes he is an anarchist, and the related note 366.

might think Bellili was an Italian police spy. When I say that he is not doing an honest trade as a bookseller I mean to imply that he is getting his money as an Italian police spy. When I say he is a liar, I mean it. When I said I could show how I get every 6d. of my income I meant I was getting my living honestly. I challenged Bellili to do the same. I have been sentenced in Italy, but always for political offences—never to 30 years' imprisonment or anything of the kind. I did not go to Bellili's house on purpose to say that I disagreed with the Italians over the war. I did not say I was against all the Italians—I am an Italian myself. Bellili said at the Italian Colony that I wished all the Italians would get killed—or something of the kind—to influence the Italian Colony; but he has failed. Mrs. Bellili told me that she had a brother, who was a lieutenant in the Italian Army. I used no violent language, but Bellili was not ashamed to put his wife in the question. I do not like to quarrel with ladies. I did not say that everybody who murdered an Italian was a friend of mine, or that they should be crucified. I was a frequent visitor at Bellili's house until his wife insulted me and then I went away. Afterwards I met Bellili at a shop kept by a friend of mine. I have seen Bellili on several occasions, but have had no conversation with him. It was in April I issued the circular and had it printed. It was printed in Paris. I had about 500 copies distributed.

Re-examined. I never said that Bellili was an Italian spy until I proved that he was.[363]

...

---

363 *La Gogna*, a single-issue published in July 1912 to definitively unmask Bellelli, reports the following excerpt from the hearing:

> The Plaintiff's Counsel having asked if he had ever said Bellelli was an Italian spy, he answers:
>
> "No. Now I could, but I did not say so before because I could not prove it. Now I have the proof."
>
> P. C.—*You told us that in your opinion Mr. Bellelli did not make an honest living as a bookseller?*
>
> Malatesta—*I am certain of that.*
>
> P. C.—*Do you mean that the money he possessed, he had earned by being a spy?*
>
> Malatesta—*Yes.*

Malatesta awaiting trial.
Source: Fédération Internationale des Centres d'Études et de Documentation Libertaires (FICEDL)

ITALIANS AT LAW

The Daily Herald (London), May 21, 1912[364]

THE FAMOUS MALATESTA TO BE DEPORTED.

...

The accused gave evidence on his own behalf. He said he was an electrical engineer, of Windmill-street, Tottenham Court-road, living in High-street, Islington. He was an Anarchist. He had been in England since 1880. Formerly he had four years' administrative deportation (under a now extinct law), and he had to live on a small island in the Mediterranean; but he escaped.

Vulgar Idea of Anarchism.

When Mr. Bellelli came to England ten years ago he was an Anarchist. Bellelli had no stock, but he had several hundred books for his personal use.

"When you wrote your circular before the case," asked counsel of Malatesta, "have you ever said that Bellelli was an Italian police spy?"—No.

In reply to the Common Serjeant, he said that the Italian colony in London numbered 6,000 and the Anarchists numbered 100.

Mr. Macdonald:[365] Is there any truth in the vulgar idea that an Anarchist is a man who throws bombs?—No. We believe in liberty and justice.[366]

---

364   Summaries of the trial appeared in several English and Italian newspapers. Here we are providing the summary that best sums up the details which appeared in the press and were not contained in the official minutes.

365   John McDonald was Malatesta's defense attorney.

366   The same exchange is reported, using the same words, in the *Daily Express's* summary on the same day. Furthermore, the *Daily Express* as well as the *Star* attributed to Malatesta the statement that he was an anarchist. The crucial distinction on which the issue hinged is not so much between anarchists and non-anarchists, as between those who committed attacks, which corresponded to the prevalent view of an anarchist, and those who did not. This is clearly shown from the debate at the appeal hearing on June 10, 1912, largely focused on the definition of anarchist, according to the *Daily Express's* summary of the next day, which bore the telling headline: "Malatesta Fails in His Appeal. Counsel's Definition of an Anarchist." His counsel stated that Malatesta was an anarchist, explaining: "As I understand it, an Anarchist is a man who objects to the social state as it exists. He disagrees with control of the State by a group of individuals who create a monopoly and do not create an equal opportunity for all." The counsel continued, explaining that for anarchists "the organisation could be such that the producers and consumers could be, and should be, brought together without the intervention of the third party, which is called the social state." And he concluded: "Malatesta does not profess to be an Anarchist in the sense that he throws bombs." Similarly, during the parliamentary debate on the Malatesta case, Ramsay Macdonald recalled that "Malatesta was once shot at by the very school of Anarchists with which he is now being mixed up."

The accused said that Bellelli had attended meetings as an Anarchist, and when counsel pointed out that Bellelli had denied that he was an Anarchist he answered "He's a liar."

Asked if it were possible for Bellelli to live on the profits of his shop, the witness said: "He has no business."[367]

. . .

TRANSLATION FROM A REPORT BY POLICE COMMISSIONER FROSALI TO THE MINISTRY OF THE INTERIOR, LONDON, MAY 22, 1912[368]

Subject: Dispute: Belelli Enrico[369] and Malatesta Enrico—Sentencing of Malatesta Enrico, for libel[370] —

. . .

Malatesta's Questioning
I am an electrician with a workshop on Wind Mill Street, Tottenham Court Road, and I live on High Street, Islington. I am an anarchist. I came to England, the first time, in 1880. I have lived in England for 12 years. Before settling in England I was sentenced in Italy to 4 years of forced residence (under the purview of a law that no longer exists) and I was forced to live on a small island in the Mediterranean; but I succeeded in escaping.

When Belelli came to England, 10 years ago, he said he was an anarchist. Belelli has no workshop, nor book storage, but he has many volumes for his personal use.

To the question of his Attorney (McDonald) whether before writing the circular note for which he is accused, he had said that Belelli was a spy of the Italian police, Malatesta responds: "No" –

To a question by the Judge, Malatesta responded:

Of the six thousand Italians living in London, 100 are anarchists—

---

367 It is not clear if the "witness" refers here to Malatesta, previously called the "accused," or to one of the witnesses later questioned.

  The trial ended with Malatesta being sentenced to three months of imprisonment. Moreover, his deportation was recommended, based on the 1905 Aliens Act. An intense protest campaign in support of Malatesta followed, culminating on June 9th with a large demonstration at Trafalgar Square. The first degree sentence was confirmed during the appeal hearing on June 10, 1912. The deportation order was instead revoked on June 17th by the Home Secretary.

368 Typescript, Biblioteca Franco Serantini, Pisa, collection "Errico Malatesta," folder "Consolato d'Italia Londra, 10." We have taken account of corrections made by hand to the document.

369 Bellelli's first name was "Ennio."

370 The report by police commissioner Frosali contains a summary of the entire hearing, but does not provide the source. In another report he specifies he did not personally attend the trial. His summary of Malatesta's questioning substantially follows that of the *Daily Herald*.

To the question of his attorney (McDonald) whether the common idea that prevails among the majority is true, namely that an anarchist is a man who throws bombs, Malatesta responds: "No, we believe in freedom and in justice."

Malatesta concludes with saying, that he is not guilty of libel, that Belelli attended all anarchist meetings, and when Attorney McDonald remarked to him that Belelli denied being an anarchist, Malatesta responds: "He's a liar"—

Having been asked whether Belelli could have lived on the profit from book sales, Malatesta answers: "He does nothing."

. . .

Malatesta. Reception by Revolutionists after Release

The Daily Herald (London), no. 92 (July 30, 1912)

A GRINDING SYSTEM.

Malatesta is free! He was released late yesterday afternoon from Wormwood Scrubs Prison, and proceeded at once to the home of his friend, G. Defendi, in Soho, where he presided over an Anarchist meeting of welcome, and received congratulations from friends till late in the evening.

His release came as a surprise even to his comrades, for his three months' sentence, even with the fortnight's reduction for good conduct, did not officially terminate till this morning. The reason for this clemency is, of course, not far to seek. Malatesta was asked by a warder yesterday morning whether or not he expected to be met by friends at the prison gates. He did expect, he admitted, that a few comrades would be there to greet him: as a matter of fact, a demonstration had been arranged. So with that subtlety peculiar to Scotland yard it was decreed that he should be released in secret yesterday afternoon. As in the case of Tom Mann, the authorities were anxious to prevent any manifestation of public opinion against official acts of oppression.

A Room Full of Revolution.

Very few rooms in London have held so many veteran revolutionists at one time as the little back parlour in Arthur-street, where Errico Malatesta held his court last evening.

The DAILY HERALD representative was practically the only man in the room who could not speak at least three Latin tongues. Here were half a score of the "most dangerous men in Europe." Portet, the heir of the martyr Ferrer, himself on the eve of another departure for Spain; Tarrida del Marmol, whom Spain watches more vigilantly than any other of her exiles, Tcherkesoff, by title a royal prince, by choice one of Russia's most noted anarchists; Marina, Malavasi, Marquez, Rossi, Corio.

An Impression of English Prisons.

"Ah," said Malatesta, patting one small black head with a naive preoccupation which betrayed a congenial habit, "it is good to get out if only for this. I am also glad of the opportunity to thank the DAILY HERALD for your vigorous stand in my defence: and your readers, too, for their generous response to the appeals of our Defence Committee.

"And soon I am going to write you a special article, which will tell you better than I can express it now what I think of your prison system. Only give me a little time to think it over; I am a little tired now.

"But I will tell you this: I'd much rather go to prison in any country in Latin Europe than here. In Italy, for instance, where, as you know, I have had a pretty fair experience as a political prisoner, I could see my friends, I could read. I had an amount of freedom altogether which seems to be quite unknown here. Our warders, too, are not mere machines; they associate with you; sometimes they even do favours for you. But here, ugh! it is one monotonous, grinding system, which treats you all as dogs.

"In Italy, too, I should have had a fairer trial. If a judge in Italy had spoken to an advocate, as the judge who tried me addressed my lawyer, he would have torn off his gown and left the court. But you may be sure, I shall tell the DAILY HERALD readers more of this later on.[371]

"Now I return again to my peaceful life, a little electrical engineering, a little inventing, if I can find the knack again—and a little agitation, perhaps, too. But I shall stay in England; that is settled. As to Bellelli, my accuser, I should prefer to dismiss him with silence. I have been to prison for a few weeks, but I am afraid the incident will make him uncomfortable—if conscience counts for anything—for the rest of his life."

[Conversation with Luis Tulio Bonafoux]

Translated from Luis Tulio Bonafoux, "Malatesta," *Bandera Proletaria*
(Buenos Aires) 6, no. 331 (September 24, 1927)[372]

. . .

— My health is good. My friends said I was sick… thinking they were doing me good.

---

371   Actually, no articles by Malatesta appeared in the *Daily Herald* over the next few months.

372   This excerpt is part of a long portrait of Malatesta by his journalist friend Bonafoux. The conversation took place a few days after Malatesta's release from prison, in Defendi's shop. We have not been able to locate the original edition of the article, though we know that it appeared before the end of 1912, since a Portuguese version, published by *A Lanterna* (S. Paulo) of January 25, 1913, without citing any source, bears the date "London, 1912."

— How did they treat you in the English prison?

Malatesta raised his shoulders, as if perplexed:

— Oh!... Neither good nor bad... You know, "all prisons are the same"....

And he added, with a genuinely philosophical intonation:

— After all, it was an opportunity for me to get to know an English prison... perhaps the only one I had never known. Strange things happen here. The day before I was to leave, the chaplain came to me and said unctuously: "Mr. Malatesta, will your friends come to wait for you tomorrow at the prison gate?" "Perhaps" I answered. "Would you be glad" the chaplain replied "to leave today?"... I left one day earlier, although my sentence had already been commuted for good behavior.

. . .

[Speech Given in London on August 18, 1912]

Translated from a report by police commissioner Frosali to the Ministry of the Interior, London, August 20, 1912[373]

Subject: Malatesta Enrico—Anarchist —

. . .

On the evening of this past 18th he gave a lecture at the location of the Social Studies Circle of London at 99, Charlotte Street, on the subject of "conception of the revolution."

Deafening applause broke out as soon as the lecturer appeared in the hall.

Malatesta gave a brief report on his own news, and on the dispute with Belelli, and then got into the subject.

He said among other things ... "that only workers care about starting a revolution, and that the objective can also be achieved by parliamentary action."[374]

He said "that he was in support of violence, and therefore of throwing dynamite and bombs, but judiciously."

He explained "that judiciously means "depending on the need;" for example he would not blow up the ports because merchandise must be unloaded in the city, so as not to starve the "people," but the banks should be blown up to destroy the documents contained therein."

. . .

---

373 Typescript, Biblioteca Franco Serantini, Pisa, collection "Errico Malatesta," folder "Consolato d'Italia Londra, 23." We have taken account of corrections made by hand to the document and silently normalized the use of quotation marks, where it was irregular or incoherent in the original text.

374 It is unnecessary to emphasize how untrustworthy this source is, in attributing such a statement to Malatesta.

[Speech Given in London on September 8, 1912]

Translated from a report by police commissioner Frosali to the
Ministry of the Interior, London, September 10, 1912[375]

Subject: "Ferrer" Evening School—at 99, Charlotte Street—W.

Following up on my note with the same number from this past 4th
I have the Honor of reporting that on the evening of this past 8th the
inauguration of the above-mentioned School took place.[376]

Twenty-five youth of both sexes participated, and a few subversives of different nationalities.

The known Malatesta Enrico, expressed wishes for the smooth operation of
the school and violently attacked the Church and Spanish Court.

Regarding the school, he pronounced himself in favor of secular education.

There was nothing else remarkable to be reported.

[Speech Given in London on September 15, 1912]

Translated from a report by police commissioner Frosali to the
Ministry of the Interior, London, September 17, 1912[377]

Subject: Malatesta Enrico—Anarchist —

I have the Honor of reporting to this Superior Ministry that on this
past 15th at 9pm the known Malatesta Enrico, at the corner of "Grove"
Hammersmith W. spoke to a large audience, comprised mostly of English
workers, on the theme "Anarchy."

---

375 Typescript, Archivio Centrale dello Stato, Rome, collection "Divisione
affari generali e riservati, Archivio generale," series 1912, box 36, folder 32
(cat. I4).

376 The Francisco Ferrer school had been founded on November 23, 1910, and
later closed due to a lack of resources. In two previous notes with the same
number, dated August 31 and September 4, 1912, police commissioner Frosali
relayed the news of the school's reopening and sent an entry ticket for the
September 8th inaugural evening. The ticket announced that Malatesta would
give a brief speech on the subject "Ferrer and the Modern School movement."
The ticket also shows that the school's name was "Ferrer Sunday School," in
juxtaposition with Sunday catechism schools.

377 Typescript, Biblioteca Franco Serantini, Pisa, collection "Errico Malatesta,"
folder "Consolato d'Italia Londra, 28." We have taken account of corrections
made by hand to the document.

He explained to the crowd that anarchy aspires to making poverty disappear, abolishing the police, universal equality, and well-being.

He was warmly applauded.

[Speech Given in London on September 22, 1912]

A RALLY IN LONDON FOR ETTOR AND GIOVANNITTI
Translated from "Un comizio a Londra pro Ettor e Giovannitti," *Avanti!* (Rome) 16, no. 265 (September 23, 1912)

They telegraph us from London, the night of the 22nd:

In the afternoon a protest rally was held in Trafalgar Square to support Ettor and Giovannitti.[378]

Many thousands of people attended, feverishly applauding Enrico Malatesta, who was the main speaker at the rally.

He told the story of the Lawrence strike and showed how capitalism in the United States of America, the sole party responsible for the massacre, is using a number of cavils to hold Ettor and Giovannitti—two strong labor organizers, two claimants of the rights of the exploited—responsible for a crime committed by police officers. so as to get rid of them and continue undisturbed the work of exploitation.

He mentioned all the rallies that have been held or that are being held in Italy to support Ettor and Giovannitti and said that not only in Italy and in England, but throughout the world, the proletariat should rise up against the abomination that is being attempted in the American republic.

---

378   In January 1912 textile workers of Lawrence, Massachusetts, mostly women and immigrants, went on strike in response to a wage cut. The strike organizers included Joseph Ettor and Arturo Giovannitti, Italian-language members of the direct action union Industrial Workers of the World. On January 28th, a worker, Anna Lo Pizzo, was killed during clashes between strikers and police. Ettor and Giovannitti were deemed responsible for the event and arrested. On April 17th, a third worker, Joseph Caruso, was arrested under the accusation of being the actual killer of Anna Lo Pizzo. Meanwhile, in March 1912, the Lawrence strike had ended victoriously. The trial began on September 30, 1912.

SCAPEGOATS IN GAOL

The Daily Herald (London), no. 139 (September 23, 1912)

AMERICAN CONSTABLE GOES FREE. VICTIMS RELEASE DEMANDED.

There was a striking scene in Trafalgar-square, yesterday afternoon, when the demonstration to demand the release of Joseph J. Ettor, Arturo Giovannitti and William D. Haywood was held.[379]

The circumstances under which the three were arrested in America, upon an amazing charge, have been related in the HERALD.

The textile workers of New England, U.S.A., were on strike.[380] The trio were prominent—as they had long been in the several movements for the promotion of better conditions amongst the workers.

During a riot the bullet of a policeman's revolver found a billet in the body of a woman, named Annie Lopizzo, and instead of the officer being the subject of proceedings the authorities actually arrested Ettor and Giovannitti as accessories before the fact.

This was in January, 1912. Recently Haywood was imprisoned on a similar charge, and the three have been in gaol since their apprehension.

International Character of the Meeting.

In English, Italian, French and German the international character of yesterday's demand was emphasised. One of the greatest favourites with the intensely sympathetic crowd was the veteran Malatesta, who has himself known what life behind prison bars is like, and who gratefully exclaimed to his English comrades by way of preface to his impassioned oration in Italian, "It is to you I owe my liberty. Had it not been for the protest of the public the police would have gained their point and sent me away from England."

The rugged features of the Italian revolutionary glowed with animation as he caught the answering fire in the eyes of hundreds of his compatriots, the while he reminded them of how Ettor and Giovannitti were of the same blood as they and told of the bitter struggles of the class war in Italy.

Some measure of the enthusiasm displayed may be taken from the dramatic response to the appeal of the chairman, Mr. W. F. Watson (A.S.E.)[381] for contributions to the defence fund.

379　"Big" Bill Haywood was one of the leading figures of the Industrial Workers of the World, who took over from Ettor and Giovannitti in organizing the Lawrence strike and other strikes it inspired, in the textile industries of other cities. Haywood and others were accused of conspiracy in relation to the Lawrence strike, but the accusation was dropped in January 1913. The *Daily Herald* article, however, seems to associate Haywood with Ettor and Giovannitti's trial, though he was not involved with it.

380　The term "New England" refers to the Northeastern region of the United States that encompasses six states, including Massachusetts.

381　The Amalgamated Society of Engineers (ASE) was a British union.

"The police will not permit us to collect," he said, "but we can't stop you throwing anything on the plinth." The hint was taken, and for several minutes the air was thick with the shower of coins which rained upon the speakers. It was literally a case of embarrassment of riches, and so successful was the move that there was an encore performance later in the afternoon.

. . .

POLICE PROHIBIT A COLLECTION.

A resolution demanding the release of Ettor, Giovannitti and Haywood, the three New England trade-union leaders who have been arrested on a charge of moral complicity in the murder of a girl killed during a strike riot, was passed at an international protest meeting held in Trafalgar-square yesterday. (1) Malatesta, the political refugee, speaking. He addressed the meeting in Italian. (2) Picking up coins thrown on the plinth. The police would not allow a collection to be made.

Source: *Daily Mirror* (London), September 23, 1912

TRANSLATION OF A REPORT BY POLICE COMMISSIONER FROSALI TO THE MINISTRY OF THE INTERIOR, FLORENCE, SEPTEMBER 27, 1912[382]

Subject: Meeting in Trafalgar Square in defense of: Giovannitti Arturo and Ettor Giuseppe[383]

Following up on my previous correspondence[384] I have the honor of reporting to this Superior Ministry that on this past 22nd in Trafalgar Square (London) there was a pro-Giovannitti and Ettor meeting.

Among the many speakers (see enclosure No. 1)[385] the known Enrico Malatesta took the floor, in the Italian language. He repeated the story of the Lawrence strike, already well-known: "The Italians are drawn to America[386] by the temptation of high wages, but once they get there they find no assistance, neither from representatives of the Italian government, nor from a permanent Italian labor organization.

"They must accept wages that, although high for Italy, are low for the United States.

"When someone is poor, what do the presumed freedoms of press, speech, association matter?

"As a matter of fact Ettor and Giovannitti are in prison only for having spoken. We are pleased that Italians were at the head of the movement during the famous strike. In doing so they demonstrated that they are no longer the Chinese of Europe. The two prisoners must be saved. The uprising must be pushed to its extremes, even boycotting American products.

"He is all the more delighted that the leaders of the movement were Italian, thus offering a strong antithesis to the Italy that goes to assassinate helpless Arabs."

When he spoke of the Arabs he got animated, and the audience applauded warmly.

"He ended with thanking (speaking in English) those who worked for him during his last imprisonment."

. . .

---

382   Manuscript, Archivio Centrale dello Stato, Rome, collection "Divisione affari generali e riservati, Archivio generale," series 1912, box 36, folder 35 (cat. K1A). In reproducing the summary we kept the author's quotation marks, even when they enclosed speech reported indirectly.

383   Note in text margin.

384   Frosali had notified the ministry of the rally in a letter dated September 20th.

385   This is a flyer that announced the demonstration, with Malatesta listed among the speakers.

386   The phrase "drawn to America" corresponds to the Italian "sfruttati in America," which literally translates as "exploited in America." Our departure from a literal translation is strongly suggested by the context.

Grande Corteo
e Comìzio

in difesa di Ettor, Giovannitti,
Caruso minacciati della pena di
morte in America a cagione della
loro attivita' in favore della
causa dei Lavoratori.

AVRÀ LUOGO

Domenica 6 Ottobre.

Il corteo partira da Soho Squ., W.
alle 3 p.m. precise, si rechera a
Clerkenwell Green, ove avra luogo
il Comizio.

Sono invitati tutti gli uomini
di cuore.

Source: Archivio Centrale dello Stato, Rome

[Speech Given in London on October 6, 1912]

Translated from a report by police commissioner Frosali to the
Ministry of the Interior, Montecatini, October 12, 1912[387]

Subject: Unrest to support Ettor Giuseppe and Giovannitti Arturo. [388]

Following up on my note from this past September 27th No A[389] I have
the honor to report to this Superior Ministry that on this past 6th there was a
meeting in London in the Clerkenwell Green location (Italian neighborhood) to
support Ettor Giuseppe and Giovannitti Arturo.

The first to take the floor was the known "Paravich Noel" . . .

Then the floor was taken by the known "Malatesta Enrico," who, after deploring that the Italians had not responded to the invitation to attend the Rally
in large numbers, found a way to heavily criticize the war in Tripolitania and the
Royal family of Italy.

. . .

[Speech Given in London on October 21, 1912]

INTERNATIONAL LIFE. ENGLAND.
HERVÉ MALATESTA DEBATE. [BY J. BARRISON]

Translated from "Vita Internazionale. Inghilterra. Contradditorio Hervé Malatesta,"
L'Internazionale (Parma), November 2, 1912

Organized by Guy Bowman at Shoreditch Town Hall, in London, there was a
meeting with Hervé, on the subject signified by this motto "*War against war.*"
At the opening of the meeting, presided over by comrade Tom Mann, the audience was very large. First Josiah Wedgwood (member of Parliament) spoke, then
Hervé took the floor. He gave his lecture in three parts, each in turn translated
by Bowman.

Many Frenchmen were present and when the "gènèral" came to speak of

---

387   Manuscript, Archivio Centrale dello Stato, Rome, collection "Divisione affari
        generali e riservati, Archivio generale," series 1912, box 36, folder 35 (cat.
        K1A).
388   Note in text margin.
389   See the previous document.

methods used—exact repeat of the latest articles in G. S.[390]—he was frequently interrupted.[391] These methods, in fact, are very different from the old insurrectional strategy... mandatory arbitration and other trifles of the same value! to then arrive at the realization of the "socialist Ideal," the Federation of the United States of Europe, on the model of the American states; this made a large number of French listeners jump in surprise. After the translation George Lansbury, socialist deputy, gave a speech warmly applauded by the English, and Malatesta then took the floor for the debate. With bitter and harsh words he showed his astonishment over Hervé's speech "worthy of a democratic bourgeois," he noted the dangerous errors and expressed his sorrow in seeing that Hervé, whom he had considered as having revolutionary merit, after he "corrected his aim" walks the same line as the parliamentary parties, spreading errors and narcotics. Malatesta spoke in French and was translated by Bowman.

...

TRANSLATION FROM AN UPDATE TO MALATESTA'S BIOGRAPHICAL CARD SENT BY POLICE COMMISSIONER FROSALI TO THE MINISTRY OF THE INTERIOR, LONDON, DECEMBER 17, 1912[392]

...

October 21, 1912:

Antimilitarist meeting at Shoreditch Town Hall with the participation of Hervé. Malatesta Enrico although not listed among the speakers, interrupted many times Gustave Hervé, and then definitively took the floor in French, which the anarchist Bowman translated bit by bit into English.

Malatesta began with saying that he once thought highly of Hervé as an active force for the revolution. Now no longer because he makes propaganda for the vote. He negated many statements of fact enumerated by Hervé, for example that the United States of America can be taken as a model for the future United States of Europe; that the secular school which now exists in France was the work and product of the socialist party while he says it was the work of the popular agitation caused by the Dreyfus affair.

He said that military war is of secondary importance as compared to social war, which keeps going every day. He said he is against mandatory arbitration, advocated by Hervé, in international matters, since it confirms the existence of

---

390   "G. S." stands for "*Guerre Sociale*."
391   When Hervé came out of prison in 1912, his change of strategy developed in the meanwhile roused harsh criticism from the revolutionary ranks, sometimes expressed in open protest.
392   Typescript, Archivio Centrale dello Stato, Rome, Casellario Politico Centrale, box 2950.

laws and governments. The only method of fighting the war is to prepare the armed insurrection of workers; in this way the frightened Governments they will not dare enter the war and we will move closer, through social revolution, to the united society of the future.

By accepting and trusting politicos, the people prepare their own deception and create their own traitors.

...

[Speech Given in London on October 24, 1912][393]

THE CASE OF GUSTAVE HERVÉ [BY M.N.][394]
Freedom (London) 16, no. 283 (November 1912)

Considerable surprise and ill-feeling were created by the news that Hervé, the editor of the Paris *Guerre Sociale*, hitherto believed to be an uncompromising antipatriot, antimilitarist, and insurrectionist, was, since his recent release from prison, working on much more moderate lines, apparently renouncing his former opinions and methods. When he proposed to state his standpoint and to give his reasons to an immense Paris audience at the Salle Wagram (September 25), some denied him a hearing, and a great row ensued. He has now lectured in London (Shoreditch Town Hall), and also spent an evening at the Communist Club, Charlotte Street, explaining more intimately the reasons for his new attitude. The latter meeting really became a debate between Hervé and comrade Malatesta, both stating their case repeatedly at full length and fighting it out to the bitter end.

[Hervé's point of view is presented first. He expressed regret for having used strong language in the past, such as his dictum that "the national flag belonged to the dungheap." His "anti-patriotism" meant opposition to the feudal and bourgeois tradition, not to the revolutionary tradition. He had always belonged to the Socialist Party, which meant to achieve its aims by the vote, if possible, or by revolutionary action, if necessary. He had formerly depreciated the vote, but now he had ceased to believe in the absolute inefficiency of the vote to bring about reforms. No revolution could be victorious without

---

393   There is a discrepancy, concerning the date of the debate in question, between the two accounts we are publishing, which is October 24th according to *Freedom*, and October 25th according to the account by the Italian police. We trusted *Freedom*'s account, which is dated October 30th, both because it was written a few days after the event and because, in all likelihood, the writer was a direct witness.

394   The summary's author is probably Max Nettlau.

or against the army. He therefore opposed propaganda for generalized desertion. Revolutionists ought instead to serve in the army and become efficient, to prove themselves on the day when the army would be used against the people. Abstaining from making propaganda against the vote meant for him acquiring a new, immense audience among the peasants of certain regions, who would never have understood the utility of not voting for socialists against the bourgeois candidates, at the same time that they saw the necessity of revolutionary action.]

Malatesta opposed him in several long speeches brimming with recollections of his own revolutionary career, past and present. His main point was the absolute incompatibility of propaganda for the vote *and* the preparation of revolutionary action at the same time. Those who believe in the vote will always wait to see its effects, and never resort to revolutionary action. Again, co-operation with other parties, Socialists and Republicans, has been tried over and over again in Italy and Spain, and always failed, the bourgeois deserting the common cause. Malatesta was strongly influenced by the case of Andrea Costa, once the pride of the Italian Internationalists (who all exclusively prepared insurrectionary movements, and whose plain language was well understood even by the peasants and soldiers, without special diplomatic moves for their use). Costa's conversion to Parliamentarism at the end of the "seventies" did much harm to the Italian movement. Malatesta had also witnessed, about 1880, in Paris, the beginnings of French Parliamentarian Socialism, when its initiators apparently only accepted it as a means of propaganda and protest, whilst long since, like Costa, they were completely absorbed by it (*vide* the Labour Party). All this, said Malatesta, augured very badly for Hervé's evolution, of which Hervé himself saw only the beginning, whilst the example of so many others is there to show where such efforts to compromise and to conciliate things which cannot be conciliated usually lead.

Blanqui and Mazzini both adopted revolutionary means exclusively; they did not think of resorting to Parliamentarism at the same time. Desertion is no general remedy, of course. If all Italian, all French, all Spanish revolutionists deserted, in ten years they would all be outside their own country, powerless exiles. But special military propaganda in Hervé's case is useless; the Army will always be the enemy; and Portugal and Turkey were not examples which would interest Anarchists and the workers.[395] Hervé's niceties about the flag of Valmy as different from that of Wagram were historic trifles;[396] what matters is the flag

---

395 The army's insubordination had played an important role in both the 1908 Turkish revolution and the 1910 Portuguese revolution.

396 Valmy and Wagram were, respectively, the scene of two battles: in 1792 the former marked the first major victory of the French army in the wars that followed the French Revolution; in 1809 the latter was one of the most important Napoleonic victories. In an attempt to defend himself from the reactions triggered by his image of the French flag planted in a dung heap, Hervé had made a distinction between the Valmy flag, symbol of the republic, and the Wagram flag, symbol of militarism and wars of conquest.

of the present Army which shoots down strikers and serves for colonial conquests—this flag under all conditions belonged to a worse place even than the dungheap.[397]

. . .

TRANSLATION FROM AN UPDATE TO MALATESTA'S BIOGRAPHICAL CARD SENT BY POLICE COMMISSIONER FROSALI TO THE MINISTRY OF THE INTERIOR, LONDON, DECEMBER 17, 1912[398]

. . .

October 25, 1912:[399]

Debate between Malatesta and Gustave Hervé at 107—Charlotte Street—Communist Club —

Malatesta Enrico responded to Gustave Hervé that it is not possible to be at the same time reformist and revolutionary, to be socialist, who accepts the vote, and at the same time prepare for the armed revolution.

Hervé will have to decide, otherwise he will share the same fate as Costa, who started by being a protest candidate and died the president of the Chamber of Deputies.

He then discredited Socialism, as usual, and wished that Hervé would remain loyal to his concept of the armed insurrection.

. . .

---

397   In his biography of Malatesta, Max Nettlau writes retrospectively, concerning Hervé's abandonment of insurrectionism: "I believed, in truth, that he was well within his rights, given his past, to adopt more moderate forms of procedure. In the assembly held on Charlotte Street, Malatesta had an infinitely superior acumen. He understood that the Hervé of the past had disappeared and mercilessly proceeded to demolish the man who stood before him. From the beginning, he predicted his traitorous future." Hervé became an interventionist in 1914 and then an admirer of Mussolini.

398   This is the same document referenced in note 392 above.

399   See note 393 above on the event date.

[Speech Given in London on November 13, 1912]

Translated from an update to Malatesta's biographical card sent by police commissioner Frosali to the Ministry of the Interior, London, December 17, 1912[400]

. . .

November 13, 1912:

Meeting for the Chicago martyrs at St. Andrews Hall on Newman Street Oxford Street W.

Malatesta Enrico expressed the usual ideas from the previous years, and went on a tirade against the Tripoli war (I am enclosing the manifesto)—[401]

Malatesta and the English anarchist P. E. Tanner proposed, and the assembly approved, a protest agenda, for the immediate liberation of the known Maria Rygier from the Italian prisons.[402] It was decided to send a copy of the agenda to S. E. the ambassador of Italy in London. And so it was done —

On Peter Kropotkin's 70th Birthday

Translated from "Dans le 70ᵉ Anniversaire de Pierre Kropotkine," *Les Temps Nouveaux* (Paris) 18, no. 33 (December 14, 1912)

Naturally, I wholeheartedly share in the tribute being made to Kropotkin on the occasion of his seventieth birthday.[403] Nevertheless, I have many doubts on its appropriateness and good taste.

Expressions of this kind always seem a little like goodbyes being made to someone who is retiring. Now, I think—and I am certain that this is the opinion of all those who know him closely—that Kropotkin, despite his age, considered advanced, is still so full of life and enthusiasm, is still so young that we can hope that the phase during which we shall take stock of the immense services he will have provided to the cause of human emancipation is still very far away. He could still provide many other services before his glorious career is over.

---

400   This is the same document referenced in note 392 above.
401   Besides the commemoration of the Chicago martyrs, the leaflet announcing the demonstration listed among its goals the request to free for Ettor, Giovannitti, Haywood, and Caruso. The trial for Ettor, Giovannitti, and Caruso ended on November 23rd with an acquittal.
402   Italian anarchist Maria Rygier had been arrested the year before for an article praising Augusto Masetti's act (see note 353) and was later sentenced to three years in prison, sparking an intense protest campaign also in the anarchist press outside of Italy.
403   Kropotkin's birthday was December 9th.

I was asked to summarize Kropotkin's thought. I believe it is better to recommend that everyone read his books and urge others to read them. His thought, which in many ways is blended with the collective thought developed within the old International and the anarchist movements in different countries, was so clearly expressed by him in his propaganda pamphlets that there is really no need to interpret it. In any case, I truly lack the courage to put a hand on his luminous explanations.

I prefer, on this occasion, which is above all else a celebration among friends, to speak of Kropotkin as a man.

Kropotkin's great charm is that within him the scholar, the writer, the propagandist, the friend, the private man, are all fused together in a harmonious unit that constitutes the most fully *human* person that I have ever met in my life.

He loves mankind. All that he thinks and does is a result of this goodness, of this great love for mankind, for all men, which appears to be the essential quality of his being.

All his life is a work of love, whether he studies physical geography and natural sciences, whether he examines the life of human societies, whether he joins revolutionary uprisings and the bitter fights against tyrants and exploiters; the motive that makes him act is always that ardent desire to render men more free, more powerful, more happy.[404]

If the eminent abilities bestowed upon him by nature and the privileged conditions in which he found himself have placed him above the mass of his more humble and more unfortunate brothers, this has not caused him to become presumptuous. Unlike many little "great men" he has not gone about despising the masses, he did not close himself up in the ivory tower of the "misunderstood." To the contrary, he used his superior abilities as fine-tuned weapons to fight the battle of human progress, and has always thought that greater abilities grant greater duties. So much that he has always been tormented by a type of remorse due to the fact that he was able to develop himself and arrive at his high moral and intellectual level, while enormous throngs of workers rot in poverty and in ignorance; and it is with a certain delight of atonement that he has consecrated his life to fighting against the injustice of which fate has made him the involuntary beneficiary. And this, not as a consequence of any

---

404   Concerning this portrait of Kropotkin, Malatesta would recall in the 1931
       article "Peter Kropotkin. Recollections and Criticisms by One of His Old
       Friends" (published in the volume of these *Complete Works* covering the years
       1924–32) that Kropotkin "felt offended because in an article written on the
       occasion of his seventieth birthday, I had said that kindness was the first of
       his qualities." In light of Malatesta's subsequent critique of Kropotkin, one
       can retrospectively argue that, in emphasizing love as the main source of
       Kropotkin's anarchism, Malatesta implicitly reiterated his own voluntarist
       vision, in contrast with the scientism attributed to Kropotkin.

metaphysical idea of Duty and of Justice, but simply due to the necessary influence of the strength, of the wealth of his moral nature.

A systematic intellect, he framed anarchist understanding within a philosophic structure that can be accepted or not. But, theory aside, he is an anarchist—communist anarchist—because he wants men to be happy, and he is convinced that the good of all can only be achieved through the freedom of each and every one and cooperation, the conscious and voluntary solidarity of all.

This is why I love him; it is for this that he is loved not only by all those who profess anarchist ideas, but all men of heart who dream of a better humanity.

Errico MALATESTA.

[Speech Given in London on December 14, 1912]

Translated from a report by police commissioner Frosali to the Ministry of the Interior, London, December 19, 1912[405]

Subject: Malatesta Enrico, and Kropotkine Peter —

I have the honor of reporting that on this past 14th (Saturday) in a cafe on Camomille Street E. C., several international anarchists held a tea in honor of the known anarchist Kropotkin.

The invitations were personal, and rather few of them were distributed.

Malatesta spoke in French and, alluding to Kropotkin, said "that all must recognize how great the work of this Russian was, and still is. He has brought to anarchy all of his vast and deep knowledge, the importance and the charm of an aristocratic name, and his great enthusiasm and good heart.

"He wished that Kropotkin would live for many more years."

Malatesta on the occasion of Kropotkin's birthday (he turned 78 years old this past November 9th)[406] went to see him in Brighton, and spent a few days there.

---

405   Typescript, Archivio Centrale dello Stato, Rome, Casellario Politico Centrale, box 2950.

406   As previously mentioned, Kropotkin was actually born on December 9th and had turned 70 years old.

On Insurrection

Translated from "A propos d'Insurrection," *Le Mouvement Anarchiste* (Paris),
no. 6–7 (January–February 1913)

Lately there has been a lot of talk about responding to a possible declaration of war with the insurrection.

Very well. Even if we do not really have the strength at this moment to rise up, it is always useful to prepare our minds for the idea of revolt against the government's impositions.

But there is no need to get accustomed to considering war as a necessary condition, or even a useful condition, for a popular insurrection.

First, war, whether it has begun or is simply expected, is the worst situation imaginable for a triumphant insurrection. Nationalist passions and prejudices, racial aversions, if not hatred—unfortunately still very much alive deep in the souls of the people—are awakened and overexcited by the propaganda from the mainstream press and by all the methods of lying the governments and the ruling classes possess. Domestic political and economic issues lose significance, and class antagonisms are forgotten in the name of a presumed national solidarity, from which the dominators alone benefit. And the governments can take the liberty of using preventive and repressive measures, whether legal or arbitrary, that public opinion would not allow during ordinary times.

This is so well sensed by the very people who make a specialty out of preaching insurrection in the event of war, that they mainly rely on the hope of defeat. But even then conditions would be highly unfavorable, because the insurrection would run the risk of being initiated more to get revenge and prevent capitulation, than to change the political and economic organization of society from top to bottom; because the insurrection would have to be started in the presence of a victorious foreign army, which would not fail to help the remains of the national army in its work of repression; and because that part of the population that under other circumstances would be favorable, or at least passive, would be against us, as they would see the insurrection as a sort of betrayal before the "enemy."

If war could be a good occasion for rebelling and attempting social transformation with a probability of success, then the revolutionaries, far from seeking to prevent it, should do everything in their power to see it break out. Since that is not the case, we are against the war; which does not prevent us, should it break out, from doing everything in order to benefit from it, despite the unfavorable circumstances, in the interest of social revolution.

What if war does not break out, anyway, as it is indeed very likely?

We cannot say, as Hervé said at Shoreditch Hall[407] (perhaps for pedagogical considerations in view of the audience before which he spoke): "may the capitalists leave us in peace, may they sort out their disputes before the Court of the Hague, or otherwise we shall start the insurrection," as if it was not clear that the capitalists, in peace or in war, always end up settling things at the expense of the workers.

As for us, we do not threaten insurrection only to prevent war; we want insurrection because we believe it to be the indispensable means to do away with poverty and oppression, to tear down the economic and political power of the bourgeoise, to destroy the State, to perform expropriation and make available to all the means of production and life, and thus open the way to the establishment of a social order based on freedom and well-being of each and every one.

It is therefore more interesting to preach, and especially prepare, the insurrection in the event of economic crises (strikes, high cost of living, etc.) or in the case of political events (police brutality, fights between bourgeois parties, etc.), or even, if one wishes, over everything and nothing, that is, any time one feels the strength to undertake it with a probability of success.

As long as the current society continues, there is always a reason to rebel. The essential is to acquire the strength to do so, to gear up so we are able to take advantage of favorable circumstances or to provoke them.

For an insurrection to take place and triumph, it is necessary that the spirit of revolt is developed within the masses, that there is a sufficient minority that conceives and desires a better order of things, believes in its possibility and is convinced that it cannot be obtained through legal and peaceful means.

This should be the purpose of propaganda, worker agitation, and resistance carried out every day and by every possible means against masters and governments. But there also needs to be material and technical preparation, so that we are in a condition to oppose an adequate resistance to the means of ferocious repression that the governments possess and do not hesitate to use. And this is what should preoccupy the revolutionaries and especially the anarchists, who regard force as the only way to overthrow a system that is based on force and uses force to sustain and defend itself. And they must think about this in advance, starting today, because such things cannot be improvised at the moment in which they are needed.

---

407   Regarding this lecture, see the speech given in London on October 21, 1912 on p. 350 of the current volume.

Otherwise, just as we would not be able now (it is useless to delude ourselves) to effectively oppose war if the governments decided to declare it, because we have not prepared in time, so we would be powerless to benefit from any other occasion that shall present itself.

E. MALATESTA.

[Speeches Given in London on February 8 and 15, 1913]

Translated from an update to Malatesta's biographical card sent by police commissioner Frosali to the Ministry of the Interior, London, March 28, 1913[408]

London—February 8, 1913: Debate at 9 Manette Street—Soho—W—between Martin (French Socialist) and Malatesta Enrico (Italian Anarchist)
Martin states he was an anarchist and although he recognizes the beauty of anarchist ideas, he deems them impractical.

He says that in 40 years of propaganda anarchists have done nothing but mistreat each other, while the socialists have, through propaganda and action, obtained that which is commonly called "social legislation" in almost all modern States.

Malatesta Enrico responds and says: "I do not at all doubt Martin's honesty, but it is a strange coincidence that all those who abandoned anarchist ideas, from COSTA to BROUSSE in Paris, precede their renunciation with a fervent hymn to the beauty of the aforementioned ideas.

"I understand abandoning something ugly, unjust, but I do not understand abandoning something only because it is very beautiful, very right.

"He personally never praises enemies, he disparages them. If he found the ideas of Socialism to be beautiful and right, he would not praise those ideas platonically and then follow others, but he would follow those.

"He expounds on the fundamental concepts of anarchy and then says... 'socialists obtained improvements thanks to the pressure of incessant anarchist critique.[']

"He performs a thorough critique of socialist systems and accuses party members of having risen to power promising the workers equality, freedom, abolition of wage labor, and having remained in power settling for... perhaps a visit to the Quirinal, or a post in the Ministry.[409]

---

408   Typescript, Archivio Centrale dello Stato, Rome, Casellario Politico Centrale, box 2950. In reproducing the summary we respected the author's practice of enclosing even indirect speech in quotation marks.

409   The Quirinal is one of the historical hills in the heart of Rome. It is the site of the Quirinal Palace, which was at the time the king's residence.

"It is a collective betrayal at the expense of sacred and generous ideas, for which hundreds of people suffer death, prison, and exile."

Given the late hour, the debate is postponed until Saturday February 15th.

London—February 15, 1913: Debate at 9 Manette Street—Soho. W. between Martin (French Socialist) and Malatesta Enrico (Italian Anarchist).

Malatesta opens the debate: He says that anarchist ideas are, at heart, ideas of human solidarity, turned into a system.

"He demonstrates this premise.

"He says that good and bad people are found in any religion.

"... whatever their God, they all die; a dagger, a few centimeters of iron, a little bit of lead, a bomb, kill the orthodox Tsar, as well as the protestant president of the United States, as well as the Catholic King of Italy...

"... a single immutable law rules the world, and this is human solidarity...

"He adds 'that everyone must benefit from shared work, without distinctions, and there are only two ways to obtain this, full and complete freedom, with its inevitable evils, and force.[']

"He says that bread cannot and should not be denied even to those who do not work, and that everyone has the right to work in the fields and in the workshops..."

He expounds on this concept with citations and examples.

"... anarchists only ask that this be accepted into practice: that all those who break the great natural law of solidarity be chased away.

"If you do not want to make a revolution in the anarchists' way, make it the way you like.

"For example, it is a clear and established fact that wheat is necessary to make bread, and bread is necessary for our lives: someone monopolizes wheat through speculation, or taxes its entry: chase away those who monopolize or tax, I don't care how you do it, with a kick or with a bomb: it only matters to me that they go. Perhaps just scaring them off will be enough. But do it yourself, do not send another to do your duty: a deputy.

"Your work must be, even now, remunerated without deductions, therefore do not miss the chance to ask for increases, improvements, keeping the destruction of this system in sight; but do it yourself: do not hope that others do it for you—Do not ask by means of envoys if you do not want to be betrayed.

"This is the difference between socialism and anarchism.

"If you want a day in the sunshine go outside yourself, do not appoint a representative to go get such and such quantity of oxygen.

"Freedom is like oxygen, it is a personal thing."

The meeting applauded uproariously, and Martin could only say a few words, continually interrupted by Malatesta and the participants, subversives of various nationalities.

London March 8, 1913: At 9 Manette Street—Soho—W.
Debate between Malatesta Enrico (Italian anarchist) and Tarrida del Marmol (Spanish anarchist)
The subject: Metaphysics versus natural Sciences –

[Speech Given in London on May 7, 1913]

Translated from a report by police commissioner Frosali to the Ministry of the Interior, London, May 9, 1913[410]

Subject: Malatesta Enrico and the anarchist newspaper La Volontà[411]

Following my note dated April 16, 1913, No. 131,[412] I have the honor to report that on the evening of this past 7th the Italian anarchist group met at 9 Manette Street, to discuss the program of the new newspaper, which should be published this coming June, and that will be published in Ancona.

Malatesta presided over the session, and the discussion was animated.

He said: for 50 years anarchists have made no progress for the following reasons:

1) The legalitarian propaganda of socialists.

2) The intransigence of anarchists in abstaining from joining socialist labor unions.

3) The individual acts of some anarchists, which are deplorable and condemnable.

Therefore the new newspaper should intensify revolutionary propaganda within the socialist unions; a tactic that should be accepted by those who will be drawn to the newspaper.

It will address anarchist organization and reorganize the ranks, disciplining them to prevent the legalitarian socialists from having free rein and precluding violence in the event of a strike.

It will actively take care to prepare the labor union to forcibly ask for class improvements and not allow for inertia, as in the past, in the event of an uprising,

---

410   Manuscript, Archivio Centrale dello Stato, Rome, Casellario Politico Centrale, box 2950.

411   Note in text margin.

412   In that note, which actually bore the date of April 17th, Frosali reported that "the known anarchist LUIGI FABBRI will soon go to ANCONA, to take the nominal management of the newspaper 'LA VOLONTÀ' which will actually be directed by the anarchist Malatesta Enrico."

acting vehemently instead, certainly not with the hope of achieving anarchist ideals, but with the firm resolution to tear down the current government. Even if the current government is replaced by a form of republican government, a step forward toward progress will have been taken.

The newspaper should absolutely deny party solidarity with those criminals who seek to justify their criminal acts, calling themselves anarchists.

Malatesta will direct the newspaper from London.[413]

---

413   The first issue of *Volontà* would come out on June 8, 1913.

SECTION VI
Press Clippings

Bresci's Antecedents:
Crime Predicted in New York

Daily Express (London), no. 85 (July 31, 1900)

New York, Monday[414]

. . .

Corroboration of the plot comes from Signor Melateria, a former Italian Deputy, now a resident of Paterson.

He said to-day that he was aware of a plot being afoot to kill the King, but he denied that he knew Bresci.[415]

. . .

Malatesta Does Not Know Bresci

Translated from "Malatesta no conoce á Bresci," La Época (Madrid) 52, no. 18016 (August 6, 1900)

The London correspondent of a New York newspaper held an *interview* with the anarchist Malatesta, who has taken refuge in London for a few weeks.

Malatesta states that, during his stay in New York, he never heard Bresci's name nor that of his comrade Lazzi,[416] as both are completely unknown to him.

News about Malatesta

Translated from "Notizie di Malatesta," Il Mattino (Naples), August 26–27, 1900

They telegraph us from Paris, 25:—The freelance journalist Frey, correspondent of *La Patrie* from London, sends his newspaper the following information on the anarchist Malatesta.

---

414 July 30th.

415 Other newspapers from the same day report the same statement with an abundance of other details. For example, the Madrid-based newspapers *La Época* and *Heraldo di Madrid*, the latter as correspondence from Paris, put in Malatesta's mouth, citing his name without mangling it, the story of Carbone Sperandio, an individual who committed suicide a few days prior, leaving behind a letter that revealed he was the man originally designated by conspirators to kill King Humbert.

416 The name, which is not clearly legible in the digital copy consulted, could also be "Luzzi." In any case, in the news related to Bresci, there is no other trace of either of the two versions of the name, nor any other similar name.

He lives near a grocer named Defendi. His room is nearly bare of furniture: it contains a table, two chairs, two bicycles, and a few tools. Malatesta does not always work, wanting to rest, to have—he says—his share of paradise. Squat, stocky, very strong, his forehead is furrowed, his eyes ardent, the expression assertive. He says he is a disciple of Bakunin, speaks many languages, writes articles, and gives anarchist lectures.[417]

Statements by Malatesta

Translated from "Declaraciones de Malatesta," *El Defensor de Córdoba* (Spain) 3, no. 636 (September 17, 1901)

The famous anarchist Enrico Malatesta stated, to a journalist who had asked for his opinion, that the American Government does not have the right to be outraged over Czolgosz's deed, because it itself assassinates Filipinos and Cubans, "and he who lives by the sword dies by the sword."

Washington at a Glance
[by Charles P. Stewart]

Schenectady Gazette (Schenectady, New York), December 18, 1939

[*The article is about Otto Kuusinen, the new president of Finland. In relation to Kuusinen's anarchist past, the author makes a digression on anarchists.*]

In pre-war times there was a colony of them in London, England being the only country on earth where they were tolerated. As a London resident then, I knew a lot of 'em. One was the celebrated Italian anarchist, Malatesta.[418]

---

417   We included this short piece as a proxy for a long interview that was never published, because of Spanish censorship. The *Patrie* article mentioned appeared on August 26th with the title "Chez l'anarchiste Malatesta." This in turn mirrored, without citing it as a source, the long article "Los anarquistas en Londres" (*Heraldo de Madrid,* August 22nd), whose author, Luis Bonafoux, had met his friend Malatesta at Varlaam Cherkezov's house. In Bonafoux's article, he provides a vivid portrait of Malatesta, but as regards the conversation they had, he limits himself to explaining: "I cannot transcribe what he told me; partly because he refers to things known by those who carefully follow the anarchist movement in Europe and America, and partly because it is impossible to adapt it to the rules of our press and the canes of our rulers."

418   Among other anarchists he met in London, the author mentions Pedro Vallina and Francisco Ferrer. Vallina had moved to the English capital in May 1906 (see note 208) and Ferrer had visited it in spring 1909, a few months before the arrest that led to his death sentence and execution.

...

I, being rather liberal, was pretty well liked by 'em.

"But how," I asked Signor Malatesta one day, "are you going to maintain any kind of an economic system with no government?"

"Oh," said he. "I suppose some sort of communistic arrangement will have to be provided for something co-operative."

...

Chronology

1900

APRIL 13	Malatesta returns to London from America.
JULY 29	Gaetano Bresci kills king Humbert I in Monza.
SEPTEMBER	Malatesta and his group publish the single issue of *Cause ed Effetti*.
SEPTEMBER 2	Malatesta is invited by the *Cosmopolitans* club to give a lecture on "Anarchism and crime."
SEPTEMBER 9	Continuation of the debate hosted by the *Cosmopolitans* club.

1901

JANUARY 5	Malatesta speaks at a libertarian celebration in support of *L'Internazionale* at Athenæum Hall.
JANUARY 12	Publication of the periodical *L'Internazionale* begins.
MARCH 14	Malatesta speaks at another event in support of *L'Internazionale* at Athenæum Hall.
JUNE 8	Malatesta speaks at a rally at Athenæum Hall to support the victims of Spanish oppression.
JUNE 18	Malatesta and others meet French trade unionists who are visiting London.
SEPTEMBER 6	Leon Czolgosz shoots US president McKinley, who dies eight days later.
OCTOBER 6	Malatesta participates in a lecture by Harry Kelly about McKinley.

1902

MARCH 8	Malatesta gives a lecture on "The duty of anarchists in the present era."
MARCH 18	Publication of the periodical *Lo Sciopero Generale* begins.
MARCH 23	Malatesta speaks at a rally in Trafalgar Square promoting solidarity with Spanish workers.
OCTOBER 4	Publication begins of the periodical *La Rivoluzione Sociale*, edited by Malatesta.
DECEMBER 27	Malatesta speaks at a celebration to support *La Rivoluzione Sociale* held at Athenæum Hall.

1903

MARCH 18	Malatesta speaks at an event commemorating the Paris Commune at Athenæum Hall.

August–September	Malatesta plans a pamphlet on the action of anarchists in Labor Chambers.

1904
Unknown date	Debate with socialist Nicola Barbato.

1905
January 27	Malatesta speaks at a rally against tsarist repression at Wonderland Hall.
February 25	Malatesta speaks at the inauguration of the Popular University.
February 26	Malatesta participates in a lecture about Russia by Cherkezov at the Popular University.
March–April	Malatesta teaches classes at the Popular University.
Sept. 20 and 27	Malatesta gives two lectures at the anarchist circle on Hampstead Road.
October 22	Malatesta participates in a lecture by socialist Torquato Barsanti.
November 16	Malatesta gives a lecture "On the origins of the world" at Wonderland Hall.
December 2	Malatesta speaks about Russia at the anarchist circle on Hampstead Road.
December 3	Malatesta gives a lecture on "The resistance society movement in France, Italy, and England."

1906
May 1	Malatesta goes to Paris, where he collaborates on the single issue *Verso L'Emancipazione*.
July 13	Malatesta gives a lecture on anarchist attacks at a club on Charlotte Street.
December	Luigi Fabbri visits Malatesta.

1907
Summer	Malatesta meets Spanish writer Pio Baroja in London.
August 21	Malatesta gives a lecture on "The labor movement from an anarchist perspective" at the Bath House.
August 25–31	International anarchist congress of Amsterdam.

1908

FEBRUARY	Malatesta is offered the position of director as part of the proposal to transform Milan's *La Protesta Umana* into a daily paper.
DECEMBER 6	Malatesta participates in a lecture by Pietro Gualducci on "Socialism and anarchy."
DECEMBER 7	Debate on science and materialism with Fernando Tárrida del Marmol.

1909

JANUARY 7	Malatesta participates in a lecture by Michele La Rosa on "Cooperativism and anarchy."
FEBRUARY 2 AND 9	Malatesta speaks at the Italian anarchist group about the International and the history of the anarchist movement in Italy.
MAY 16	Debate with Alfredo Consalvi.
SEPTEMBER 17	Malatesta speaks at a public meeting in support of Ferrer at a club on Charlotte Street.
OCTOBER 2	Malatesta speaks at a lecture in support of Ferrer at a club on Charlotte Street.
OCTOBER 30	Malatesta speaks at a rally in reaction to Ferrer's execution, which took place on October 13.
NOVEMBER 11	Malatesta speaks at an event commemorating the Chicago martyrs at a club on Jubilee Street.

1910

OCTOBER 13	Malatesta speaks at an event commemorating Ferrer at a club on Charlotte Street.
DECEMBER	Malatesta is interrogated by police after the Houndsditch murders of December 16–17.

1911

MARCH 7	Malatesta is interrogated during the committal proceedings for the Houndsditch murders.
MAY 2	Malatesta testifies at the trial for the Houndsditch murders.
LATE MAY	Malatesta becomes seriously ill with bronchial pneumonia.
SEPTEMBER	Malatesta expresses his intention to resume an active role in the movement in Italy.
OCTOBER 20	Malatesta gives a lecture on the Italian-Turkish war at a club on Charlotte Street.

OCTOBER 28	Malatesta participates in a celebration for the 25th anniversary of *Freedom*.
DECEMBER	Malatesta gives a Saturday afternoon lecture at a location on Meard Street.
DECEMBER 31	Malatesta participates in the New Year's celebration held by the *Syndicalist League*.

1912

APRIL	Malatesta and his group publish the single issue *La Guerra Tripolina*.
APRIL 22	Malatesta publishes a manifesto against the spy Ennio Bellelli, who files a complaint.
MAY 8	Malatesta gives a lecture on the theme "Individualism" at a location on Charlotte Street.
MAY 20	Malatesta is convicted for libel and sentenced to three months in prison, with a recommendation for expulsion.
JUNE 9	A demonstration at Trafalgar Square tops off the intense press campaign protesting Malatesta's sentence.
JUNE 17	The expulsion order is revoked.
JULY 29	Malatesta leaves prison.
AUGUST 18	Malatesta gives a lecture on the subject "Ideas of the revolution" at a location on Charlotte Street.
SEPTEMBER 8	Malatesta speaks at the Ferrer Sunday school on "Ferrer and the Modern School movement."
SEPTEMBER 15	Malatesta speaks outdoors on the subject "Anarchy."
SEPTEMBER 22	Malatesta speaks at a rally in support of Ettor and Giovannitti at Trafalgar Square.
OCTOBER 6	Malatesta speaks at a rally in support of Ettor and Giovannitti at Clerkenwell Green, in the Italian neighborhood.
OCTOBER 21	Malatesta participates in Gustave Hervé's lecture at Shoreditch Town Hall.
OCTOBER 24	Debate with Hervé at the Communist Club on Charlotte Street.
NOVEMBER 13	Malatesta speaks during an event commemorating the Chicago Martyrs at St. Andrews Hall.
DECEMBER 14	Malatesta speaks at a birthday celebration for Kropotkin at a cafe on Camomille Street.

1913

FEBRUARY–MARCH   Malatesta participates in a series of debates at a location on Manette Street.

MAY 7   Malatesta discusses the plan for the future newspaper *Volontà* during a meeting of the Italian anarchist group.

Index of Publications

Index